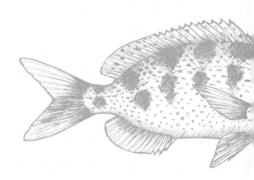

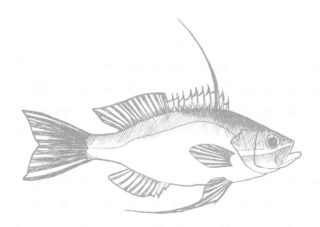

TEXAS SEAFOOD

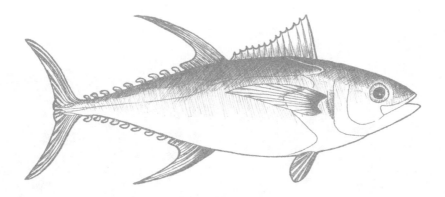

TEXAS SEAFOOD

A COOKBOOK AND COMPREHENSIVE GUIDE

PJ STOOPS AND BENCHALAK SRIMART STOOPS

UNIVERSITY OF TEXAS PRESS
AUSTIN

Support for this book comes from an endowment for environmental studies made possible by generous contributions from Richard C. Bartlett, Susan Aspinall Block, and the National Endowment for the Humanities.

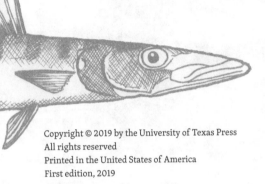

Requests for permission to reproduce material
from this work should be sent to:
 Permissions
 University of Texas Press
 P.O. Box 7819
 Austin, TX 78713-7819
 utpress.utexas.edu/rp-form

♾ The paper used in this book meets the minimum requirements of ANSI/NISO Z39.48-1992 (R1997) (Permanence of Paper).

Library of Congress Cataloging-in-Publication Data

Names: Stoops, PJ, author. | Stoops, Benchalak Srimart, author.
Title: Texas seafood : a cookbook and comprehensive guide / PJ Stoops, Benchalak Srimart Stoops.
Description: First edition. | Austin : University of Texas Press, 2019. | Includes bibliographical references and index.
Identifiers: LCCN 2018054754
 ISBN 978-1-4773-1803-4 (cloth : alk. paper)
 ISBN 978-1-4773-1921-5 (library ebook)
 ISBN 978-1-4773-1922-2 (non-library ebook)
Subjects: LCSH: Cooking (Seafood) | Seafood—Texas.
Classification: LCC TX747 .S683 2019 | DDC 641.6/9209764—dc23
LC record available at https://lccn.loc.gov/2018054754

doi:10.7560/318034

TO JJ AND BB

Everything good in our lives emanates from you.

TO MOM AND DAD (GAIL AND STEVE)

Without you both, without your love, support, and encouragement, none
of the good stuff would ever have happened. We love you both. We only
hope that we can do for our children what you have done for us.

ขอมอบให้ยายเหรียญกับแม่ จากการที่เติบโตในครอบครัวชาวนาไม่ได้ร่ำรวย ต้องทำงาน
ช่วยงานตั้งแต่เด็ก เรียนรู้การปลูกผัก ทำนา ทำสวน หาปลาในช่วงฤดูฝนปลาในนาและ
คลองก็จะเยอะ ยายกับแม่ก็สอนวิธีขอดเกล็ดปลา วิธีแหล่ปลา
การทำอาหารและเก็บรักษาปลา

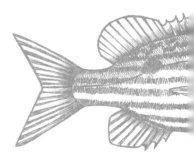

CONTENTS

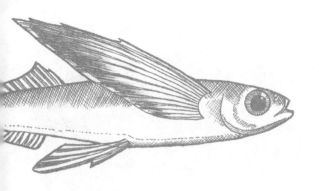

INTRODUCTION

Of all the peoples who have lived on the Texas Gulf coast, none appreciated and relied on our natural bounty more than those who were here before the arrival of Europeans. We do not even know what this people called themselves; we know them only as the Karankawa, which is the corrupted form of the possibly pejorative exonym bestowed on them by other indigenous peoples. They were not a monolithic people, but rather several related tribes, all of whom shared common cultural and linguistic ties going back millennia and rooted in coastal subsistence. They were among the first peoples with whom Álvar Núñez Cabeza de Vaca came into contact when he and his crew were shipwrecked near what is now Galveston Island. (Although we recommend reading Cabeza de Vaca's firsthand account of his travels, we caution that the book contains little in the way of good evidence for anything aside from the fact that Cabeza de Vaca was indeed lost and wandering for a few years. He treats most of the Native peoples he meets with scorn and generally gives only cursory and derogatory descriptions of their customs and habits.)

The *Karankawa* fared no better against European brutality and disease than any other indigenous people. By the late eighteenth century, they had mostly retreated to less hospitable areas in what is today southern Texas and northern Mexico. In 1858, the last of the Karankawa were apparently slaughtered by Texas Rangers on Padre Island, thus passing from the pages of history, another people lost in the slow, centuries-long American genocide. We have traces of their language, though these represent at best fragments of corrupted vocabulary from one dialect. These traces were obtained only in 1891 (more than thirty years after the last of the Karankawa had died), by a linguist working with an old woman named Alice William Oliver, who had apparently grown up near one of the last surviving bands. Of course, there is absolutely no way to test the accuracy of any of this information.

The Karankawa stayed on barrier islands and near bays during the fall and winter months, harvesting and consuming incredible amounts of oysters, rangias, and other shellfish. They also fished extensively, though how far out and what fish they targeted remain subjects of debate. In the large midden mounds that pepper the Texas coast, archaeologists have found bones from all the usual inshore species, as well as sharks and even tuna and other species found farther offshore today.

The Karankawa used and understood the northwestern Gulf Coast region like no one before or since. During the spring and summer (which are, not coincidentally, the seasons of coastal mosquitoes and hurricanes), they would retire inland, sometimes to what is now known as the Piney Woods, sometimes to the edge of the Texas Hill Country. Here they would harvest and subsist on all manner of wild plants and game. When the weather cooled to a sufficient degree, the Karankawa would return to the coastal grounds.

The world of the Karankawa is one we cannot accurately imagine. However, we need hardly reach so far back in time to see a glimpse of a much different coast. The taming and reshaping of the Texas coast happened almost within living memory— the Texas and Louisiana section of the Intracoastal Waterway was started in 1925; it was the last leg of a canal that would connect Boston to Brownsville. Today, factories and tourist infrastructure dominate the landscape from Beaumont to Brownsville; drilling platforms dot the horizon; the Intracoastal Waterway, which forever altered and disrupted the very flow of water, meanders parallel to the coast.

The eminent (and controversial) fisheries scientist Daniel Pauly first popularized the concept of "shifting baselines of perception," which boils down to the observation that the waters in which we all fish (meaning basically all coastal and inland parts of the world) are fragments of what they were even a generation ago, and the waters of our parents' generations are shadows of what they were a generation before that, and so on. Consequently, each generation views the waters they inherit as "normal" and "natural," thus disguising the extent of loss and degradation.

Fifty years ago, Red Snapper were bigger on average than they are today, and they could be caught off the Texas City dike, along with groupers. While this seems impossible to today's fishers, we have talked to old-timers who insist it is true. The bays fifty years ago teemed with life to a degree rarely seen today. Going back fifty years before that, the situation is more extreme. The Texas coast we have all grown up with is not the Texas coast of our parents; which in turn is not the same as the Texas coast of their parents. Today, most Texans see the Texas coast and Gulf waters as a fun place to visit and a place to maybe catch a few fish. Most seem to have lost an appreciation for what we have right here.

THE GULF AND US

For our part, we are both new to the Gulf. Twelve years ago, the Gulf of Mexico was just a place PJ had been to a few times; for Benchalak (who goes by the nickname Apple, which we'll use throughout the book), it was just a place on a map, a place halfway around the planet. In the intervening years, we learned a lot, read too much about fish, talked about Texas seafood to anyone who would listen, spent lots of time waiting on boats, sold a lot of fish, ate every bit we couldn't sell, worried when the boats didn't go out, worried when they didn't catch what we needed, pleaded with chefs to buy strange things we knew were good, made a tiny bit of money but lost a hell of a lot more.

We had no particular reason to get involved in the fish trade—neither of us had any family in the fishing trades in the Gulf or anywhere else, and aside from PJ's experience in restaurants and Apple's experience in eating everything, we had no particular knowledge of the business. As a further obstacle, we knew nothing of Gulf seafood. Once, before PJ started dealing fish, he found himself in the retail store of a dock in Freeport, Texas. In a brown tote, covered with wet oyster sacks, was a mass of live crabs. He couldn't believe his luck! Those crabs looked very similar to those used in Thailand for, among other things, Phat Pong Gali Bpu. PJ had found curry crabs! It was a couple of weeks before he read enough to realize that they were *Callinectes sapidus*—common Blue Crabs—one of the most traditional of Gulf seafoods and one of the most valuable. We had much learning to do.

So, we started meeting boats, buying from the docks, and going directly to our chef customers in Austin (and later Houston). These chefs—Chris Shepherd, Hugo Ortega, Bryan Caswell, and Justin Yu, among many others—would support our work for the next several years, first on our own (under the company name Stoops and Son); then at Louisiana Foods under that Gulf icon Jim Gossen; then again when we went back out on our own one more time (this time as Stoops and Family). Originally, we went after the "bycatch" (fish and other marine animals caught incidentally while targeting other species) and exotic species because those were the only fish we could make something on without dealing in large volumes. After all, our operation consisted only of PJ, some Igloos, and the pickup (which had replaced the original Honda Odyssey), so 300 lbs. of Almaco Jacks meant we would make at least a little money that day; 300 lbs. of Red Snapper meant that we would barely break even. After a few years, bycatch had become our calling card.

Through our years of relying on wild fish to pay the bills, we fell in love with our corner of the Gulf. Our memories of our children's younger days are inextricably linked with being at the beach, fishing, finding shellfish, and, most of all, eating fish, all kinds of fish. Though they have lost some of the knack, both of our kids (especially our oldest, JJ) could at one point name more local fish than most of our customers. Even now, a family day means, whenever possible, a day at the beach. Both of our kids know their way around fish, and crabs, and anything else edible that swims or crawls. Our youngest, BB, is a dispassionate, ethical, and efficient cleaner of any sort of sea animal, though she might be even better at assisting in the killing and cleaning of chickens. Seafood is how we celebrate anything and everything.

A BYCATCH INTERLUDE

At this point, we might as well broach the subject of bycatch, for it forms the heart of this book. Most of the species described in these pages are "bycatch," which is an umbrella term for all incidental catch of nontargeted species. In conservation and seafood sustainability circles, the term seems to be reserved for large photogenic species like turtles, marine mammals, sharks, and iconic fish. For our purposes, we use the term more inclusively to include all species, big and small, regardless of their ability to inspire human emotions.

Most fisheries contend with bycatch issues to some extent, though any method using dragged nets is about the most indiscriminate, followed by any gear that is very large (longlines stretching tens of miles or massive seine net operations). To illustrate the point—according to the National Marine Fishery Service, on average, shrimp accounts for 16 percent of the weight dragged up by Gulf shrimp trawl nets. The other 84 percent is made up of more than seventy species of fish and invertebrates. Almost all of this bycatch is discarded overboard.

Why do we eat and, through this book, promote the eating of bycatch and alternative species? Is it just for the sake of something new? Is it just to test the boundaries? For us, the answer is simple. Resources are finite, but if fished and managed rationally, the Gulf can provide us and future generations with large and dependable supplies of highly nutritious protein.

Rational management and rational fishing mean elimination of waste from bycatch and high-grading (keeping only the most desirable sizes of targeted species and discarding the rest). It means operating highly regulated and completely transparent multispecies fisheries. It means catching a little of many species, rather than thousands of tons of one species. It means allowing small catches of some species and larger quotas of those fish that are most resilient to fishing pressure (for more information on quotas, see fisheries.noaa.gov). It means science-based ecosystem management, as opposed to management on a species-by-species basis. It means promoting and mandating responsible methods of harvest. It also means rational use of the animals landed.

All such management and stewardship mean nothing, however, if no one wants to eat the fish. Most easily harvested fish can be eaten, and most of those edible species can withstand some fishing pressure (provided, of course, that the management is in place and effective). The trick is to get regulatory agencies on board, the fishers catching, and the public buying all at the same time. Some progress has been made, but much work remains.

Everything should be kept. Everything should be landed. Finding outlets for the various species is more or less challenging, depending on the fishery and method of harvest. For hook-and-line fisheries (almost all finfish), the bycatch species caught tend to be relatively easy to market. Difficulties exist for those animals with odd skin or odd bone structure or odd meat color, but nothing substantial. Close to 100 percent of this bycatch is directly edible.

Trawl bycatch (specifically shrimp in the Gulf) is a different matter and one that requires a suite of complicated solutions. Given that more than sixty-five species make up White Shrimp bycatch, and probably twice that number make up offshore shrimp bycatch, finding markets and outlets is quite a task. Most White Shrimp (inshore) bycatch is directly edible, and the majority of offshore bycatch is as well. Oily fish, white fish, flatfish, crustaceans, shellfish, gastropods, cephalopods, jelly-fish—all of these are found in abundance in Gulf shrimp nets.

For those species for which no markets may be found, uses still exist. Icelandic regulations, for example, require trawlers to retain the whole catch. Bycatch that is not directly edible by humans is bought by the government at guaranteed prices (low, but rational) for use in fish meal and fish oil production. We are aware of arguments against such government involvement, but those arguments generally don't make sense to us. Government exists for exactly this kind of situation—rational use of common resources. The water, the coastline, the fish—they belong to all of us after all.

To achieve anything like this approach would be a decades-long project, and management agencies do not generally like these kinds of ideas, as regulations and enforcement become increasingly complicated. But it can all be accomplished. (Parts of this section were adapted from a post entitled "Why Bycatch?" from PJ's long-defunct blog *Professor Fish Heads*.)

A WORD ON WILD FISH AND FARMED FISH

This book is devoted to the natural bounty of the Texas Gulf Coast region, and our goal with it is to convince more people to seek out—and protect—the treasures we have at our doorstep. To be clear, though, we are not advocating a diet based solely on wild-caught seafood.

We humans don't eat very much wild food at all. A wild chicken is small, skinny, and exceedingly tough. A wild tomato is pea-sized. Wild corn doesn't even exist. We don't eat wild chickens, or wild tomatoes, or wild corn. We are not only content with domesticated versions of these foodstuffs (and hundreds of others), we rely on them, we demand them. Human civilization would collapse without the crops and animals we have spent sometimes thousands of years creating.

Somehow, though, opponents of aquaculture (cultivating aquatic species for food) often seem to forget the importance of farming in human history. All of the arguments used against aquaculture could be made—and with just as much validity—against terrestrial farming as well. Never has a farm existed anywhere in the history of humans that did not, in some sense, degrade the already existing environment. But it would be silly to suggest that agriculture should just stop entirely. The same principle applies with aquaculture.

Any modern preoccupations with eating exclusively wild fish are dangerous vestiges from long ago, when the world was larger and there were fewer humans running around on its surface. Two billion humans, largely without access to modern transportation and refrigeration, could drive many species to extinction, and bring others closer to the brink. Seven and a half billion humans (and counting), able to transport perishable fish across the planet and store seafood for a year or more frozen, have a much more substantial effect.

Fish (like carp, tilapia, mullet), crustaceans, and shellfish have been cultivated to some degree for thousands of years, usually in low-intensity subsistence settings. Industrial aquaculture is a product of the twentieth century. Farmed shrimp didn't exist until the 1930s; farmed salmon, not until the 1960s. The majority of species farmed today do not have long histories of cultivation, and the best aquaculture is yet to come. Every year the industry makes incredible advances in species selection, stock health and welfare, feed, and mitigating environmental consequences.

In other words, eat wild fish, enjoy and savor wild seafood, but don't eat *just* wild fish. Give farmed fish the respect it deserves.

THE SCOPE OF THIS BOOK

Most of the animals we describe we've seen on the docks, or on commercial boats, or on our own expeditions. We've caught more than a few of them, and we've eaten so many of others—like the Triggerfish and Almaco Jack—that they might never again grace our table. We've sold (or tried to sell) a lot of these species to chefs in Texas. A very few species, like the Opah and Florida Horse Conch, we have not yet seen from our local waters. But everything in this book may be found, under the right conditions, in Texas waters or in adjoining federal waters.

We only describe edible (or potentially edible) fish and animals, and we are far from exhaustive in doing that. We only partially describe some groups, like the sharks, and only give the briefest of sketches of the panoply of marine eels in the Gulf. In all, we describe less than 15 percent of the finfish in the Gulf and a tiny percentage of the native invertebrates. We did more than scratch the surface, but not by much.

The Gulf of Mexico, in terms of fish, is cosmopolitan, meaning we have very few species that are only found here. Fewer than 100 of the more than 1,400 species of finfish in the Gulf are endemic; the rest also occur in seas and oceans elsewhere. The strength of Gulf fisheries is its variety of species also present in more distant waters. Admittedly, most of those 1,400 species are of little interest to humans in terms of food. A surprising number, though, are not only edible but make for viable and sometimes quite large fisheries elsewhere.

Of the fish species described in this book, probably every single one is fished somewhere, and the majority are available in the United States. This means that one may actually purchase a great number of the species described herein (from other waters, not ours). In a city like Houston, with its own highly cosmopolitan population, we easily find at large markets many dozens of species of fish, crustaceans, and mollusks. So even without a local harvest source, you may still prepare most of these recipes.

When one can eat fish seven nights a week (and when sometimes one has too much fish in one's truck so must eat fish seven days a week), one tends to find lots of ways to eat fish. Similarly, when one has literally hundreds of pounds of unsellable fish in one's truck, one tends to get creative in preserving as much as possible. In this book, we include some of the techniques and recipes that have served us well. We also have some recipes from old customers, fellow fish lovers, chef friends, and some people who just know and love fish.

Whether you are looking to identify a strange creature or figure out how to cook it, we hope we provide at least some guidance.

We want our fellow Texans to think more about our Gulf and everything in it good to eat. We want everyone everywhere to think about their own local waters, and maybe think about them a little differently.

NOMENCLATURE

Throughout the book, we use the fish names most common in Texas. Capitalized names are used for specific fish; lowercase names refer to general types or classes of fish.

Should you decide to do further research on any of these species, we highly recommend that you use the scientific name in your search. Common names, while helpful enough in informal contexts, are useless in terms of accurate information and education, due to their informal and inconsistent usage.

THE GULF AND FISHING

THE GULF OF MEXICO, GENERALLY SPEAKING

The Gulf of Mexico is better described as a sea, enclosed on the west and south by Mexico, on the north and east by the United States, and on the southeast by Cuba. The main current in and out of the Gulf is called the Gulf Loop Current, which enters the Gulf as the Yucatán Current, between Mexico and Cuba. From there, the main branch heads north and west, until it reaches halfway to Louisiana, where it loops back toward Florida; a smaller branch veers west immediately from the main current at around the Yucatán Peninsula. This smaller branch roughly follows the Mexico, Texas, and western Louisiana coasts (though it is a considerable distance offshore) in a clockwise direction, before rejoining the main branch right around where it makes its turn east and south, heading out of the Gulf. A small counter-clockwise current, originating in the waters from the mouth of the Mississippi, runs from the east and close to the shore from Texas down to Mexico. This all means that a great deal of water (and wildlife) travels from the Caribbean and southern Gulf to northwestern waters, while there is very little exchange of water (and thus flora and fauna) from the eastern Gulf to the west. This is why some Florida and eastern Gulf species (like the Red Grouper and Alabama Shad) simply do not exist here.

Although the northern reaches of the Gulf can see some chilly winter weather, as a whole it is a tropical sea, a fact that informs everything from seagrasses to finfish species. We do have some species—mackerels, tunas, herrings—that are completely at home in colder waters, but most Gulf species prefer or require sunnier climes than those on offer in, for example, New England.

The Texas part of the Gulf is characterized by its very gradual slope from the shoreline to the edge of the continental shelf, and then the continued gradual slope down to the abyssal plain. The Texas Gulf just does not get very deep very quickly. The continental shelf is sandy and muddy, with rocks and reefs few and far between, though such bottom is more common on the long continental slope.

COMMERCIAL FISHING

Commercial fishing in the US federal waters of the Gulf of Mexico (beyond nine miles from shore) is regulated by the National Marine Fisheries Service (NMFS) branch of the National Oceanic and Atmospheric Administration (NOAA). Federal fisheries include Red Snapper, all groupers, most tilefish, highly migratory species (e.g., fish like tunas and Swordfish), and shrimp (at least those caught in federal waters). The Texas Parks and Wildlife Department (TPWD) has its own regulations regarding commercial fisheries in state waters. The Texas Department of State Health Services (TDSHS) regulates molluscan shellfish.

The following are but brief sketches of commercial fishing methods in the Gulf. A fuller exposition is not necessary here, and, more importantly, our experience was always in the peddling, not the catching, of fish. We do not feel adequate to provide anything more than a cursory description. While all of these methods are used throughout the world, we only describe them in the context of the northwestern Gulf.

BANDIT RIG

A bandit rig is the mainstay commercial offshore hook-and-line method used in the northwestern Gulf. Red Snapper, Vermilion Snapper, and shallow-water groupers are the species targeted with this gear. The rig itself is electric or hydraulic and is mounted to the boat itself. The motor is attached to a large spool, maybe a foot across, on which is coiled hundreds of feet of very stout monofilament line. The line plays out from the spool through the end eye on a flexible arm about three feet long. At the end of the line comes the tackle, which consists of ten to thirty short drop lines, each armed with a large circle hook. The whole thing terminates in a heavy window weight, weighing several pounds. The hooks are baited (with squid or mackerel), then the line is dropped all the way to the bottom. Some boats fish right at the bottom, and some fish a few feet off the bottom, depending on the situation at hand and the species being targeted. Bycatch is limited to juveniles of the targeted species, as well as mixed species appropriate to the environment.

LONGLINE

In longline fishing, a single very stout monofilament line, from one to more than thirty miles long, is laid down horizontally in a straight line by a boat, which then comes back either immediately or hours later, and reels the line in. Baited hooks on drop lines are attached every few feet to the main line. Depending on the length of the main horizontal line, hundreds to several thousand hooks may be in the water at one time. The main line is either weighted to sink to the bottom (bottom long-line) or attached to buoys to stay higher up in the water column (floating or pelagic longline). In the northwestern Gulf, both types of longlines are used—pelagic for Yellowfin Tuna and Swordfish; and bottom for Yellowedge Grouper, Golden Tilefish, and other deepwater groupers. Bycatch can be more extensive in both fisheries but is still relatively limited. Fewer discarded fish survive when thrown back in the water.

TROLLING

In the trolling technique, at least two, and up to several, lines are played out behind the boat. The lines, which run through outriggers on either side of the boat, might terminate in artificial lures, spoons, or dead baits, all cunningly rigged to look like bait fish. The rigs, combined with the action resulting from being dragged behind a boat, goad targeted fish into biting. A variation of this method called greenstick fishing uses a single very tall and flexible rod. Yellowfin Tuna, Swordfish, King Mackerel, Wahoo, and other fast pelagic predators are targeted in this way. The very little bycatch that occurs with this method is limited to juveniles of the targeted species and, very rarely, protected species. Because the fish are caught almost individually and at the surface, they usually survive their return to the water.

HANDLINES

Handlining is an ancient fishing technique still used the world over. The gear consists of nothing more than a length of thick monofilament line (or thin rope) a few dozens of feet long; a few feet of thinner monofilament, which is tied to one end of the primary line; one or two short drop lines armed with circle hooks; and a two- or three-pound weight fastened at the very end. The hooks are baited, and the line is cast to rest at the wanted depth. When a fish bites, the rope is pulled in by hand. This method involves no mechanized or specialized equipment. Vermilion Snappers and Greater Amberjacks are sometimes targeted this way, though very few commercial boats use handlines anymore. Bycatch is limited, and unwanted species returned to the water stand a good chance of survival.

ROD AND REEL

Rod-and-reel fishing is exactly what it seems. While very few commercial boats use rod and reel, a few here and there sometimes do. Of course, the rods and reels and tackle are heavier than recreational equipment. This method is mostly limited to pelagic fish like Wahoo, Yellowfin Tuna, and Swordfish. As in handlining, bycatch is limited, and unwanted fish are easily released.

TROTLINES

Essentially, trotlining is inshore or freshwater longlining. There is no real difference. In Texas, this is the only method used to commercially fish Black Drum and freshwater fish like catfish. Because most fish don't bite on such baits and gears, bycatch is not much of an issue.

GIGS

Gigs are only used in bay fishing, and mostly for flounder. The gig is essentially a spear with one to three prongs (usually one). One or more fishers, in a small commercial bay boat at night, search for flounder on the bay floor with the aid of spotlights. The flounder fishery in Texas is tiny. No bycatch at all occurs with this method.

PURSE SEINES

In the Gulf, purse-seining is used only for the harvest of Gulf Menhaden, the single largest fishery here. After spotting a school of fish (these days with the aid of planes), two boats start laying a large net in a wide circle around the school. When the circle is complete, the boats draw up the bottom of the net, creating a pouch. The net is slowly drawn closed, and then the entire school is dragged into the boats.

TRAWLS

In the US federal waters of the Gulf, only shrimp may be targeted with trawls—no finfish are targeted with trawls at all in our waters. A trawl is essentially a net, its mouth held open, dragged behind a boat. Some animals are targeted with mid-water trawls, meaning the gear is designed to keep the nets at a certain place in the water column. Most trawlers, though, drag directly on the seafloor. The thick beams that keep the net open, as well as the tickler chains that stir up the ground in front of the net, can really do some damage to bay and sea bottoms. While this type of fishing is devastating to areas with high concentrations of corals, shellfish, and vegetation, it is much less destructive in waters with sandy and muddy bottoms (which are exactly the kinds of bottoms we have in the northwestern Gulf).

Of course, without some modifications, trawling is completely indiscriminate in terms of what is caught—if an animal is in front of the net, it is caught. These days, shrimpers across the Gulf are required to have working BRDs (bycatch reduction devices) and TEDs (turtle-excluding devices) on every tow. There is still a large amount of small finfish and invertebrate bycatch, which makes up 25-85 percent of the raw catch. Various state laws allow shrimpers to sell at least some portion of their bycatch (except protected species). It's a gray area, and not one most shrimpers wish to get involved in, so almost all of the bycatch goes overboard. Fish and sea life caught by trawling are usually too injured to survive once returned to the water.

TRAPS

In Texas and most of the Gulf, traps are used for crabs and crabs only (both the Blue and the Stone). Rectangular traps, made of wire, are set in bays, then retrieved some hours later. The waters are always shallow, and the crabs are always alive when they come out of the water. If the crab is too small or is a berried female, it may be returned to the water with an excellent chance of survival. Bycatch is minimal, and all unwanted animals thus caught (be they undersize crabs or toadfish or Oyster Drills) are easily returned to the water unharmed.

DREDGES

Dredges are basically like the scoop on an earthmover. The dredge is dropped to the oyster reef (which is usually at least a dozen and a half feet down), then the boat drags the dredge for a bit, scraping up a layer of the oyster reef. When the dredge is brought up, the empty shells are tossed back. No bycatch is really caught, except Oyster Drills and sometimes Slipper Shells. The environmental impact can be somewhat mitigated through the redistribution of shucked shell waste back into the bays, thus restoring the hard substrate of the reefs. Even with such mitigation, dredges are inordinately destructive.

MISCELLANEOUS NET METHODS

The miscellaneous group of methods includes butterfly nets, dip nets, strike nets, gill nets, and seines. Aside from the menhaden purse seine, these net-fishing methods are commercially prohibited in Texas waters as well as in federal waters in the northwestern Gulf.

RECREATIONAL FISHING

Neither one of us knows how to fly-fish, and we generally don't use many lures to fish. We also don't specifically target Redfish or Speckled Trout. We are not, in other words, sport fishers. We fish (or forage) to get things to eat, not to cross animals off a list as if they were items at the grocery store. We don't really understand the attraction in hunting for fish with absolutely no intention of eating any of them. We don't understand throwing back perfectly good table fish while waiting for a trophy fish. Others may disagree, but we concentrate on filling a cooler rather than filling a slot.

Always fish legally. This means having a license and following the regulations. In state waters (which in Texas means nine miles out) and federal waters (two hundred miles out), make sure you are up to date on gear restrictions as well as catch, size, bag, and possession limits. There are not nearly enough game wardens to patrol all of the waters of Texas, so chances are you will mostly be operating under the honor system whenever you go fishing. Do the right thing. If you cannot keep or do not want a fish, return it to the water in the best manner possible to ensure its survival. This is not only the law but the right way to fish.

We don't have much to add to the already abundant literature regarding the catching of fish. We have learned as we went along, and we suggest you do the same. Find an all-purpose knot, learn it well, and use the hell out of it. Learn how to change rigs with the tides and weather. Find a fishing spot that harbors lots of different fish, not just one species. Keep your eyes open for new things to catch, and broaden your own spectrum of edibility.

Keep whatever you can, take it home, find out how to cook it, and give it a try. You will be surprised by how much you like some fish you might have dismissed before as junk, trash, or inedible. Do not throw a fish back because of its reputation or appearance.

KILLING YOUR CATCH

Never toss a freshly caught and still very much alive fish into a cooler and leave it to slowly die. To do so is not only needlessly cruel but detrimental to the quality of the meat of the fish. The situation is exactly analogous to land animals in slaughterhouses. A quick death (and appropriate bleeding) make for better meat.

You will not only need to quickly dispatch and bleed the catch but also to rapidly cool it. Before you even put a line in the water, prepare your cooler (the cooler should have a drain with a screw cap). Remove everything but the ice, and make sure the drain cap is on tightly. Don't leave the ice in a bag, but pour it in loose. You will want the smallest cooler possible, that is, big enough to hold what you hope to catch, but small enough to not need a lot of ice and water. You should be able to fill the cooler about a quarter of the way with the ice. Next, get some clean seawater (from the beach, not a backwater), and fill the cooler slightly under halfway. Salted fresh water can substitute for the seawater. But do *not* use just fresh water for saltwater fish (by the same token, do not use salt water for freshwater fish).

You will need a place to work on the fish—this can be the beach or the ground, or a piece of wood brought for the occasion. You are now ready to catch some fish.

After you have caught an acceptable fish, disentangle it from the rig and line, then kill it immediately. We describe three ways to get the killing done.

HEAVY BLUNT OBJECT   Place the fish belly down on the beach or work surface and place your weak hand firmly over the dorsal and pectoral fins, fixing them and the fish in place. Strike the fish soundly on the back of the head with a mallet, right between and slightly behind the eyes. If you hit the fish hard enough, every muscle will briefly tense, then the fish will become totally limp—it will never feel anything ever again. If you didn't hit it right, it will flop around wildly in pain. Do the animal a kindness and always strike slightly harder than you think necessary; strike it twice if you're not sure. Then, with your knife, cut the bottom half of the gills away from where they attach at the body. Continue cutting down until you get through the bottom of the gills—this will sever major blood vessels and allow the animal to bleed out. Place it in the cooler and let it bleed and chill down.

TOP OF THE HEAD This method should only be used for fish you will be filleting. Place the fish on its side, belly away from you. Find where the top of the gill plate meets the head, which will be right where the head meets the body. Holding a knife at almost a 90° angle from the work surface, place the tip at the junction where the tops of the gills run into the head. Plunge the knife in until it pierces the fish completely, then bring down the blade in a single chopping motion (like a paper cutter). You will cut through the backbone, the main blood vessels, and the top of the head. Basically, you are detaching the top of the head (but *only* the top). As before, you know you did it right when the fish's muscles flair, then all slowly relax into limpness. Just before the caudal fin, cut through the tail enough to go through backbone (and that blood vessel), but no farther, as you will want to keep the tail on. Place the fish in the cooler to bleed out and chill down. Remember that the head and tail should not be removed in this process. Leaving the fish intact not only makes it easier to process later, but Texas fishing regulations require it.

IKE JIME The ike jime method most closely mirrors that used for the commercial slaughter of land animals. It is also the most difficult to master, for you will need to locate and then spike the brain in order to dispatch the fish. Of all of these methods, however, it produces the best result. You will need, in addition to a knife and a work surface, a spike. This spike need only be about five or six inches long, not including the handle. It will need to be a sharp spike. We suggest an awl or punch. You will also need a length of wire at least as long as the fish. You can use steel leader material, or a guitar string, or anything in between. The wire just needs to be stout enough to work down the spinal shaft of a fish, and thin enough to do so easily. Place the fish belly down, facing you. Grasp it firmly with your weak hand, then take the awl or punch or spike and drive it into the fish's head, between and slightly behind the eyes. The spike should go into the head at about a 45° angle relative to the snout. Once the spike pierces the head, you will know it has reached the brain when you get to what feels like hollow space. Work the spike around in a circular motion to destroy the brain entirely. Remove the spike, then notch the tail as described in the last method. Insert the wire into the hole in the head and feel around until you find the spinal shaft. Work the wire all through the fish until the end comes out of the notch in the tail. Run the wire up and down the shaft, destroying every bit of spinal cord. Next, open the gill plate and find the backbone. Holding the knife at a 90° angle from the fish, put the point on the backbone, then whack the butt of the knife with your hand or a mallet, cutting completely through the backbone (and that blood vessel). Place the fish in the cooler to bleed and cool.

We never gut our fish until we get home. The moment a fish is gutted, all those blood-rich areas are exposed to oxygen and moisture, which makes them a playground for bacteria.

RECREATIONAL SHELLFISHING

Recreational shellfish harvesting is perfectly legal, provided one follows the simple Texas Parks and Wildlife regulations pertaining to the harvesting of bivalve shellfish and other invertebrates.

First, recreational harvests of bivalves are only allowed from November through April. Recreational harvesting of bivalves is also limited to areas so designated by the Texas Department of State Health Services, which is the governing shellfish authority in Texas. Their website always has maps of open waters, but do not trust those, as they are not always updated. Call the toll-free automated line instead. It takes three minutes. Harvest only in open waters, and know you are harvesting legally and safely.

Snails are a bit of a gray area in terms of seasons, but not in terms of species. The recreational fishing guide lists any applicable limits. Read all the regulations, for the relevant bits are usually hidden among the chaff. Oysters, clams, and other bivalves have daily limits as well. Also listed is a prohibition on the taking of certain species in certain southern Texas waters during certain months. We cannot recommend highly enough recreational shellfishing. It is our favorite thing to do.

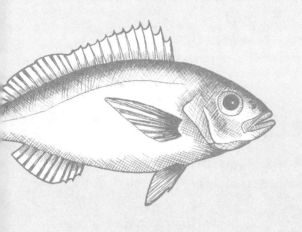

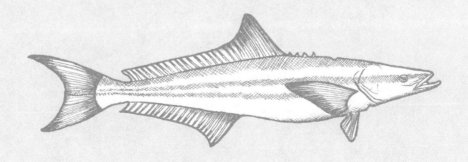

FISH

Roughly speaking, there are three kinds of fish:
the cartilaginous fish (Chondrichthyes), the jawless fish (Agnatha), and
the bony fish (Osteichthyes). Cartilaginous fish are sharks, rays, and
chimaeras; jawless fish are things like hagfish and lampreys (which we
do not cover in this book); and bony fish are every other fish in the sea. It
is probably not necessary to add that bony fish are the largest living class
of fish, and indeed the largest living class of vertebrates, with tens of
thousands of species.

The bony fish share several traits, few of which are meaningful to
lay people like ourselves. The most important characteristic is the bony
skeleton. In some fish, like certain species of puffer, this skeleton has
degraded into just a few rounded bones; in others, like the herrings,
bones seem to sprout fully formed from every millimeter of flesh. Some
massive fish have soft bones (Swordfish), and some have bones hard
enough to crack knife blades (Black Drum).

Sharks and rays, covered later in this book, have soft sinewy bodies
buttressed with delicate cartilage skeletons. The biggest shark is easily
dismembered with even a small, poorly honed knife; that same knife will
slice right through the smaller sharks and rays. We don't cover chimaeras
in this book, as they live deeper than Gulf commercial boats ever fish.

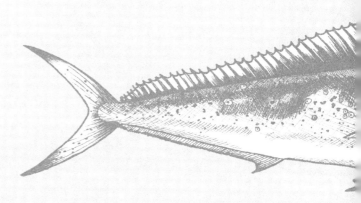

CHAPTER 2

INSHORE MIXED BAG

If you fish the way we fish, you will more than likely encounter a lot of the fish in this section. The majority swim in bays big and small, as well the waters right off the beach; a few prefer slightly deeper water. The Bluefish and tripletails range farther offshore also and are included here because this was the most appropriate (though not ideal) chapter in which to include them.

Basically, every fish in this category may be caught while fishing from dry land. A boat might increase the number of fish you catch, but we do not own a boat, and we always manage to come home with at least a couple of dinners. One might also catch other fish from dry land, most notably the sharks and rays, which are described later in the book.

Of the fish in this chapter, the snook is the most coveted in the eyes of sport fishers, followed by the tripletail; the flounders and Sheepshead are the most respectable catches for the table. We've caught neither snook nor tripletail ourselves, and while we love flounder, we do not usually seek it out. We're happy to end up with any of these fish—or dozens of others—at the end of our line. While we enjoy fishing, we do it mostly to fill our bellies.

A fair number of the species in this chapter end up as bycatch in the White Shrimp trawl fishery. Sadly, they are considered trash (which, we hope to demonstrate, they are certainly not), so are almost always thrown overboard (resulting in a massive waste of resources).

We do not describe the Striped Bass (*Morone saxatilis*), as it does not really occur in Texas salt waters.

SHEEPSHEAD

Archosargus probatocephalus

COMMON NAMES: Convict Fish, Sheepshead Bream, Bay Snapper (erroneous—this is *not* a snapper)

HABITAT: Inshore waters—bays, passes, inlets, jetties, and estuaries—are the preferred habitat of the Sheepshead. While it may sometimes venture other places, by and large the Sheepshead stays around structures, piers, and rocky places, for that is where it is best adapted to feed.

RANGE/DISTRIBUTION: The Sheepshead is found from at least New York through all waters of the Gulf to the western Caribbean and northern Atlantic coast of South America, with large populations occurring throughout the northwestern Gulf.

DESCRIPTION: The Sheepshead is so called because of its teeth, which do indeed resemble a sheep's, though the Sheepshead uses its teeth not for cutting grass but to crush things in shells. It's called a Convict Fish because of the vertical silver-white stripes that alternate with the dark gray brown of the body. Aside from those traits, the Sheepshead looks like most porgies, with a small head and oval body. The face is the same dark gray brown, as are all the fins. Eyes are silver.

EATING: As mentioned above, it eats mostly things in shells—barnacles, clams, shrimp, mussels, oysters. Unsurprisingly, this diet

makes the flesh of the Sheepshead succulent, sweet, slightly fatty, and rich. While most fishers know the delights of Sheepshead, it is not a common market fish in most of Texas (as opposed to Louisiana, where it has long enjoyed a good reputation). Fillet- ing a Sheepshead isn't the most enjoyable fish-related job—the scales are large and firmly embedded, the fillets are thin, and the awkward ribs lower the meat yield consider- ably. That said, boneless fillets of Sheepshead are certainly worth the effort expended, so don't shrink from the task.

AVAILABILITY: Sheepshead is easily available in New Orleans and throughout southern Louisiana but woefully difficult to find in Texas markets. Even seafood companies don't always carry it. Luckily for us all, Sheepshead is easy to catch. All you need is some shallow coastal waters with rocks or piers or jetties, and a light fishing pole, a bottom or floater rig, and some cut shrimp or squid. Catch your limit and consider yourself lucky.

PINFISH AND PIN BREAM
Diplodus holbrookii and *Archosargus rhomboidalis*

COMMON NAMES: Pinfish: Spottail Bream; Pin Bream: Western Atlantic Sea Bream

HABITAT: Both species are associated with seagrasses, vegetation, mangroves, and to a lesser extent, rocks and structures. Both are found everywhere in bays and shallow waters; smaller numbers swim in offshore waters down to a hundred feet or a bit more.

RANGE/DISTRIBUTION: Both species are found predominantly in the Gulf of Mexico, with smaller populations occurring outside the Gulf in contiguous waters.

DESCRIPTION: These fish are never very big, neither ever reaching more than two pounds. They are both silver to copper, with painfully sharp dorsal fin spines. The Pinfish has a few faint brown vertical stripes and a large black spot on the tail. The Pin Bream's stripes are horizontal and gold, and its spot is more faded and situated right at the shoulder.

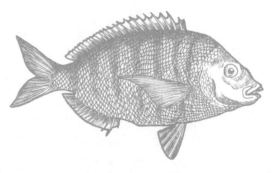

EATING: Lots of species of porgies, in many genera, swim the seas. We've found that the whole family is easily divided into two broad categories, based not on taxonomy but rather on ease of processing. In other words, just because we *can* fillet a fish, does that mean

we *should* fillet that fish? Concerning some porgies, the answer is yes; concerning others, we should be more circumspect.

Regarding the Pinfish and the Pin Bream, there is simply no question. The fish are small, the fillets are thin, and there is no belly meat. If you fillet a few of these, then look at the amount of flesh, you might find yourself cursing these fish. Better to cook them whole, especially fried. They will acquit themselves admirably.

AVAILABILITY: Little to no commercial availability of either species exists, nor are there consistent fisheries locally or really anywhere in the Gulf. They are considered dregs even by bycatch standards, so they are rarely available at the restaurant level either. Go catch your own. Fish as you would for Piggy Perch (see that entry for more information).

GULF FLOUNDER AND SOUTHERN FLOUNDER

Paralichthys albigutta and *Paralichthys lethostigma*

HABITAT: These flounders occur year-round in bays, passes, and inlets; during the fall spawn (and smaller spring spawn), they are mostly caught in passes leading to open water. They spend most of their time half-buried in the seafloor, waiting to ambush unwary prey.

RANGE/DISTRIBUTION: The Gulf Flounder occurs throughout the Gulf and Caribbean up to the Carolinas; the Southern Flounder is limited to the northern Gulf and Atlantic coast up to the Carolinas.

DESCRIPTION: Both species look like typical left-hand flatfish, and we cover both species together, as they are almost indistinguishable in regard to catching or buying or eating. The head (and mouth) are small. The

eye side (which is the side that faces up, of course) is brown, or several shades of brown; some fish sport dots or patterns. The bottom side of the fish is usually completely white. A small legal fish will weigh a bit more than a pound, while a "fish story" flounder (colloquially called a "doormat") might weigh close to ten pounds or even more.

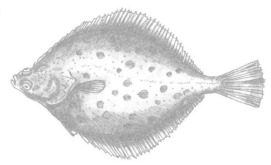

A third species, the Broad Flounder (*Paralichthys squamilentus*) is slightly smaller, but otherwise looks like the other two (though with a rounder body and lighter skin). It generally stays offshore, only occasionally wandering into shallower waters. The Winter Flounder (*Pseudopleuronectes americanus*) occurs all along the US Atlantic coast and almost into the Gulf of Mexico, but not really into Texas.

EATING: We've not yet met the fish-eating soul who doesn't enjoy flounder. The fish has only small and convenient bones, and produces fine long, thin white fillets, perfect for a wide range of techniques and recipes. The cooked flesh flakes into tiny pieces, and one would have to look far for a better raw fish. Flounder is also unequivocally the best fish for stuffing, whether the fish is boned before or not.

AVAILABILITY: Flounder is widely and easily available in grocery stores, though it just about never comes from Texas fisheries. The most consistent year-round fisheries are in the Carolinas and in Mexican Gulf waters. Some flounder comes from Louisiana, but large catches are limited to fall and spring spawn runs.

The lack of commercially available Texas flounder is an intentional consequence of fisheries regulations. Flounder populations have been and still are suffering long-term declines, mostly as a result of environmental degradation. The flounder, it turns out, is quite a sensitive fish. In an effort to address and halt this decline, fisheries officials have curtailed commercial fisheries more every year. Current catch limits make it almost impossible for all but the smallest commercial operators to keep fishing. We should note, of course, that recreational fisheries have been similarly restricted, but the vastly larger population of recreational fishers has hampered management goals.

Recreationally, flounder is generally fished with a rod and reel or a gig.

GAFFTOP CATFISH AND HARDHEAD CATFISH

Bagre marinus and *Ariopsis felis*

HABITAT: These two catfish inhabit shallow waters everywhere, including brackish and muddy waters.

RANGE/DISTRIBUTION: While both species are found on the lower US Atlantic coast and the northern Atlantic coast of Brazil, they are far more common in the Gulf of Mexico and the Caribbean Sea.

DESCRIPTION: The Food and Drug Administration (FDA) decreed years ago that the only species of catfish that could be marketed as catfish were those species native to the fresh waters of the United States, that is, the Channel Catfish (*Ictalurus punctatus*) and the Blue Catfish (*Ictalurus furcatus*). Thus, per

FDA regulations, the *only* legally accepted market name of the Gafftop Catfish is either Gafftopsail Fish or Gafftopsail Whiskered Fish, and the only acceptable name for the Hardhead Catfish is Whiskered Fish. (These names are relevant only in regard to the FDA. See accessdata.fda.gov/scripts/fdcc/?set=sea-foodlist.) Nomenclature nonsense notwithstanding, both of these species are indeed true catfish (the family is large and diverse).

That they are catfish goes far toward describing the fish themselves. Both species lack scales, both have thick bony heads, and barbels sprout from the snout of both as well. The barbels themselves are slightly less impressive than those of freshwater species. Both of these fish have V-shaped tails, which is distinguishing relative to other catfish species (which generally have broom-shaped tails). Both fish are bluish gray to tan on top; both have white bellies. Gafftops have a couple of elongated dorsal fins that are connected to each other with a thin webbing. This feature apparently reminded someone somewhere some time ago of something nautical, from whence came the name Gafftop.

The Hardhead's name is more straightforward. Its head is indeed hard, though that in and of itself does not distinguish it from any other catfish. What makes the Hardhead's head notable is the size, or rather the length, of it. On a smaller Hardhead Catfish, the head may take up almost a third of the length of the animal. Even in the older fish, the head remains pretty stout.

Gafftops are the largest of the two species, though neither species attains the prodigious size of their landlocked freshwater cousins. Even a big Gafftop generally won't weigh even ten pounds, while a large Hardhead is usually less than five pounds.

We should also mention that on both species, the first dorsal fin and pectoral fins are hard and bony and terminate in nasty barbed spines. More on those spines below.

EATING: If you like wild catfish (and if you don't, perhaps we need to have a talk), then you will like this fish (provided you pay attention to the information below about location). Gafftops fillet just like any catfish, but we have always found that cutting catfish into steaks made for a much more cookable product. Hardheads are most easily dealt with by simply chopping the heads off. Both of these fish are great whole on the grill or in the oven. Obviously, one cannot go wrong with frying these fish.

The only people who seem to enjoy these fish are those who go fishing because they want to eat fish. We include ourselves in this group. On the other hand, those who fish for sport first, and with nary a thought toward dinner, disdain the Gafftop and despise and insult the Hardhead. We recommend these fish knowing we will change few minds. The world is divided into those who eat catfish and those who do not.

AVAILABILITY: The population of both species far exceeds any demand. All you have to do to get as many of these fish as you could possibly ever eat . . . is go catch them. They are not targeted and very rarely marketed. Gafftops are quite fun to catch; Hardheads are just dinner.

One should always pay attention to where one fishes, but one should take a little extra caution with these fish. These two species are notorious for accumulating industrial toxins in their flesh, and current state law prohibits consumption of these species if the fish were caught within certain relatively closed bay waters. Closed waters are listed in the TPWD recreational fishing guide. Also, these are opportunistic fish that eat everything—they will taste like where they live and what they eat. If you catch them in a small enclosed

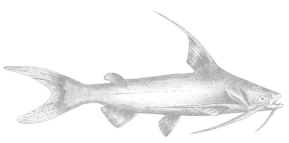

bay with little water exchange, you will take home fish that taste vaguely of bog. Happily, beach fishing along open waters eliminates these potential problems. Just use a standard bottom or drop line rig, with a stout weight at the end, on a surf rod. As usual, we believe several hooks prove most effective (and as always, use circle hooks). Bait the hooks with just about any dead bait (live bait in this situation veers dangerously toward casting-pearls-before-swine territory). Cast, set the line, place the rod in the holder, and relax on the beach. Even if nothing else is biting, you'll at least catch a Hardhead or two.

If you should catch either of these fish, you should probably remember those spines we mentioned earlier. The spines stick hard and deep; the barbs make sure to leave a ragged (and easily infected) hole in your hand (or leg, or wherever the spines make contact). You may avoid the barbs by simply grabbing and holding the fish the right way. First, keep the fish on the ground. Letting it flop around in the air is not only cruel to the animal but also a great way to get a barb in a really bad place. Second, remain calm—if you are calm, the fish will not flop as much (of course, that advice applies to every fish in this book, but especially, if we may be a touch subjective, to marine catfish). Third, slowly take hold of the fish head. Use your weaker hand, and approach from the tail of the fish. Get your fingers between the barbs and the fish's body, then lace your fingers around the barbs, which will pretty much put you in control of where the fish (and consequently the spines) go. From this vantage point, you may safely unhook and pick up the fish.

STRIPED MULLET

Mugil cephalus

HABITAT: The Striped Mullet lives in shallow coastal waters, including bays, inlets, passes, beaches, canals, bayous, marshes, and muddy holes. In other words, everywhere. During their spawn (in the late fall and early winter), Striped Mullets leave their protected coastal haunts and head to open sea.

RANGE/DISTRIBUTION: This species is found all around the world in warm temperate to tropical waters.

DESCRIPTION: First off, we have several species of mullet scattered throughout the Gulf, and more species exist elsewhere. We only describe this species (also called the Gray, Flathead, and Flathead Gray) simply because it is the largest and most abundant. Also, what works for one mullet will work for the rest.

The Striped Mullet has to be one of nature's most unassuming fish. It doesn't look like much: stubby fins on a skinny cigar body; a flat, bony head; large doe eyes; and a round mouth devoid of teeth. It doesn't swim very quickly, nor is it a great predator—it is, in fact, a vegetarian. It doesn't get very big, with a large adult seldom ever reaching five pounds. It has a white belly, green to brown, gray, or copper back, and horizontal black stripes running from head to tail.

EATING: People the world over love eating mullet. Even in the eastern Gulf, it is a targeted food fish and a local favorite. It seems, though, that the mullet-eating world ends at the mouth of the Mississippi

River—everyone to the east eats it, whereas few to the west ever do.

It is delicious—an excellent frying fish and a great fish to cook whole (the abdominal cavity is quite large and easy to stuff). Filleting is simple, but don't even try to get any meaningful belly meat, for the belly itself is basically just a piece of skin with a little flap of muscle.

While the meat itself does taste very nice, it is the eggs of the mullet that actually have more of an established reputation in gastronomic history. For thousands of years, the eggs (encased in two connected membranes

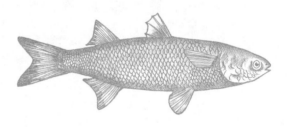

called lobes) have been salted, then pressed and dried into a delicacy known in modern English as bottarga. The finished product, thinly sliced to serve, is neither too salty nor too fishy, but rather a perfect marriage of the two. Bottarga is still produced in large quantities throughout the Mediterranean world; all the names by which it is known throughout this area derive from an Arabic root, which itself derives from an older Greek root, which is derived from far more ancient Egyptian or Phoenician roots.

The price for quality product may run into the hundreds of dollars per pound, which has resulted in predictably bad situations. In Texas, the fishery was not regulated for many years, and PJ recalls hearing stories from old-timers about guys walking around with tens of thousands of dollars' worth of mullet roe. Eventually the regulatory agencies got around to changing the fishery, and today basically no mullet roe is harvested commercially in Texas waters (during the spawn times, possession of fish longer than twelve inches is prohibited; because breeders tend to be bigger than that, the fishery has effectively been regulated out of existence). Unfortunately, the same regulations apply to recreational fishers as well, so you'll probably not be getting ahold of a lot of fresh Texas mullet roe. If you should get lucky, though, we highly recommend making some bottarga. It is a forgiving process, as long as you maintain a degree of vigilance.

Finally, we must not neglect the mullet's other guts and innards. The milt is almost as large as the roe and is delicious fried. The rest of the innards are suspiciously similar to those of a chicken, except mullet offal tastes cleaner than chicken offal. Livers are nice and light without getting chalky, intestines are easily cleaned and fried, and the gizzard is everything a gizzard should be. Yes, mullets actually have gizzards that look only slightly different from poultry gizzards, and which are used for the same purposes. All in all, it is one of the handiest, Swiss-Army-knife fish we have.

We feel we should add a bit of a caveat here: mullet tastes like the waters in which it lives. Brown, still waters mean muddy mullet. Areas with lots of continuous water movement always produce clean, tasty fish. If you should cut into your mullet and discover gray to very light brown meat, remember two things: the fish was caught in still waters, and you shouldn't eat it.

AVAILABILITY: Because mullets are fished elsewhere in good numbers, finding them is simple if you live in a city large enough to have grocery stores and markets that cater to immigrant communities. Most Asian markets carry mullet. If you do find mullet in

a store in Texas, the fish is *always* from other waters (usually the eastern or southern Gulf if not much farther away). You will rarely find an egg-bearing mullet for sale.

RIBBONFISH

Trichiurus lepturus

COMMON NAMES: Largehead Hairtail (proper common name), Saberfish, Cutlass-fish, Beltfish, Swordfish

HABITAT: The Ribbonfish prefers bays, inlets, passes, and deeper coastal waters.

RANGE/DISTRIBUTION: The species is found in temperate and tropical oceans and seas throughout the world, with the largest populations in the western Pacific.

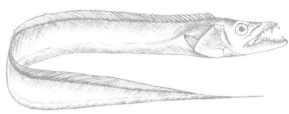

DESCRIPTION: The Ribbonfish, perhaps not surprisingly, is an exceedingly narrow fish, rarely more than an inch wide (and usually less). The snout is bony and pointed and filled with long, large dagger teeth (despite this, Ribbonfish have almost no jaw strength, instead using their teeth to impale prey). Most of the length of the animal is muscle and bones, with all organs close to the head. The Ribbonfish does not have a tail—the body just tapers off to a mere ribbon of fin material (as thin and delicate as a sewing thread). Very large specimens can be up to four feet long, though even then they only weigh a pound or two.

EATING: The Ribbonfish is an absolutely and unequivocally delicious fish, and one that any fish eater would enjoy. It has the flake of wild catfish, the unctuousness of conger eel, the cooked color of halibut, and the taste of grouper. Most people unfamiliar with Ribbonfish are at first skeptical (and understandably so); the first taste is always a revelation.

The fillets are very long and always quite thin. Like most fish, the Ribbonfish has no pin bones or guts past the anal vent. While in most fish, that length of uninterrupted fillet is short, in a Ribbonfish, that stretch of fillet makes up most of the animal. The skin is extremely thin, meaning it is almost unnoticeable after cooking. Because of the lack of small bones, it is one of the best fish to "chunk" or cut into cross-section steaks (like the old-fashioned salmon cut).

Ribbonfish may also be steamed, sautéed, roasted, fried, and grilled with great success.

AVAILABILITY: Ribbonfish is available in most large Asian markets in any larger city, though, alas, always frozen (or refreshed) and rarely from the Gulf of Mexico or indeed any American fishery. Almost all of the US supply comes from the western Pacific Ocean, where Ribbonfish are not only targeted but indeed compose one of the largest wild-capture fisheries in the world. Unfortunately, the quality of these fish is what one would expect—subpar and not worth the money (though sometimes you might find ike jime Ribbonfish, which is altogether worth buying).

Unfortunately, no commercial fishers target Ribbonfish in Gulf waters. Or rather, no commercial fishers in the Gulf target Ribbonfish intended for human consumption, but a small bait fishery exists (mainly as bycatch from shrimp trawlers, destined for sport fishers and grouper longliners). Ribbonfish caught for bait are generally small and poorly handled; most humans prefer eating larger Ribbonfish, after the animal has put on decent fillets.

Most recreational fishers consider the Ribbonfish to be a nuisance and waste of bait, but there is a small and devoted recreational fishery in Texas, composed mostly (if not all) of middle-aged men who immigrated decades ago from Vietnam. While techniques differ, the most impressive uses the following equipment: a cane pole (no reel, of course) with an eye fixed at the tip, about seventy-five yards of 10-pound-test monofilament, one small hook, and a small piece of shrimp. No weights or other rigging are used. The hook is tied to one end of the line, the shrimp is affixed, the line is passed through the eye of the pole, and the remainder of the line is loosely coiled around the fisher's open hand. The line is cast, and then slowly wound back on the hand with a rolling movement. The strike of the fish is often imperceptible to an onlooker, for the pace of the hand never changes (also, Ribbonfish do not fight very hard once hooked). Using this technique, men fishing from land are able—when tides, turbidity, and wind cooperate—to cast an unweighted bit of cut shrimp more than fifty yards and haul in dozens of Ribbonfish, one after the other, pausing only to rebait. It is truly one of the more remarkable displays of pure fishing that one can find on our Gulf coast. Alas, the technique is more easily described than mastered.

BLUEFISH

Pomatomus saltatrix

HABITAT: Though usually considered a coastal fish, Bluefish is a rather peripatetic species, found from fast-moving waters on the beach to far offshore, down to several hundred feet.

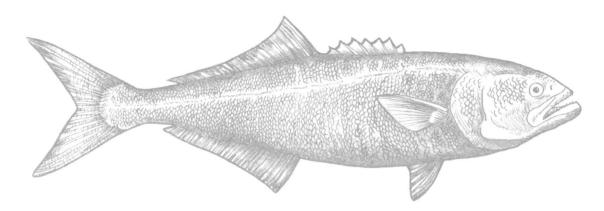

RANGE/DISTRIBUTION: It ranges everywhere in the Atlantic and Indian Oceans and all associated waters; it is also present in the waters of Southeast Asia, Australia, and New Zealand, but is absent from most of the rest of the Pacific Ocean.

DESCRIPTION: The Bluefish isn't blue like the sky. It isn't even always very blue. But it's always at least kind of blue and it always has a white belly (most of the time it's greenish blue gray on the back and sides; very large fish tend to a more uniform gray blue, but we don't really have large Bluefish here). Though the lips are large (relative to other fish of similar size and build), the head is not of any unusual size. The body is somewhat streamlined, built more for endurance than speed; fins all around are small and rounded. Scales are thin and more or less deciduous. The Bluefish is a pelagic predator but loiters in areas for extended periods during migrations.

Regarding size, Bluefish caught in or adjacent to Texas waters are on average much smaller and younger—rarely weighing more than three pounds—than those caught in or near Florida waters, and Florida Bluefish tend to be smaller than those caught farther up the east coast (which can easily weigh ten pounds or more).

EATING: Bluefish are targeted both commercially and recreationally on the east coast (where a common name is "snapper," in reference, apparently, to its ferocious bite). The commercial value of the fish, even in local markets there, is pretty low, as it spoils quickly, the meat is slightly gray, and it tends to fishiness. Aficionados love the strong taste, though most fish eaters are far less enthusiastic.

Perhaps not surprisingly, we have always enjoyed the larger east coast variety, but the few hundred pounds we have seen over the years from local boats targeting Vermilion Snapper were fish of a different color (and taste, size, and quality). The first time we brought one home was a revelation. We were expecting gray, strong-tasting fillets; those we got were pretty opaque white and tasted as clean as a jack, with a touch of snapper. We figured the differences in appearance and texture had to do more with age than anything else. We were only partly right, if a grizzled old commercial fisherman was to be believed. This fisherman, who had been fishing commercially in the Gulf for more than three decades at that point, explained to us that young Bluefish use the Gulf as an estuary. While they migrate through the shallow waters of the Gulf, they consume large amounts of squid and other invertebrates. As they grow older, they travel to Florida and up the east coast, where they start eating large amounts of menhaden and oily fish. The difference in taste is due as much to diet as to age. While we can't vouch for the accuracy of this proposed life history, it certainly makes sense.

In our opinion, Texas Bluefish certainly ranks among the most edible of Gulf fish, though it is also one of its most underappreciated species. At our house, we rarely fillet Bluefish, but instead wrap it in fatty pork products and smoke it for a couple of hours. That's pretty much the only way we cook Bluefish, and we suspect that no better way exists. On the other hand, were our Bluefish slaughtered and handled in the correct way, they would make impeccable sushi.

AVAILABILITY: Sometimes Vermilion Snapper boats bring in a few Bluefish, but unfortunately there is no commercial coastal fishery in the Gulf. The only Bluefish likely available in Texas are those fished on the east coast and shipped here. We have already noted the substantial differences in the east coast fish. Added to that is the fact that Bluefish does not travel well and has a limited shelf life even in the best of situations, which means you will more than likely be disappointed. However, if you persist in your quest, know that Bluefish may be had at larger seafood markets and departments in any larger city. We advise against such a course of action, unless you are able to inspect the fish personally.

We have never had much luck targeting Bluefish in Texas, and the few we've caught have always been surprises landed while fishing off the beach or in passes. If you do catch one (or many), we cannot recommend enough spiking the brain, as Bluefish benefits more than most from this treatment.

COMMON SNOOK
Centropomus undecimalis

HABITAT: This species lives in shallow waters over all types of bottoms. The Common Snook is a lurking predator, migrating daily and seasonally.

RANGE/DISTRIBUTION: It occurs in the Gulf of Mexico, Caribbean Sea, and down to Brazil, but is most common in the middle of that range. Snooks are relatively sparse in our part of the Gulf. In Texas, they were traditionally rarer in the northern part of the state; in our gradually warming times, though, snooks are becoming more and more common throughout the state.

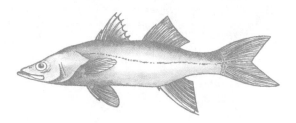

DESCRIPTION: The head is distinguished by the snout, which scoops down somewhat toward the mouth, resulting in almost a duckbill shape. The mouth is wide and large with a pronounced underbite, and the lower lip has a slight hook right at the very tip. Its body is long, not very tall, and moderately thick. Scales are large and metallic silver, giving the Snook an armored appearance. The entire lateral line is marked with a stark black stripe. The forked caudal fin has rounded edges and is tan yellow, as are the rest of the fins.

EATING: The Snook is easy to scale, clean, and fillet. Bones present no unusual problems, and the shape of the fish is nothing new. The meat is pink when raw, and fillets look just like any other large white fish fillet.

Snook is delicious but not very memorable. Those times we've eaten it we walked away from the table happy, but we cannot at this writing recall exactly what it tasted like—white fish for sure, with a tender flake.

AVAILABILITY: Commercial harvest of Common Snooks in Texas is prohibited. Imports are common, however, especially from Central America. You can try to catch your own, but fishing is a hit-or-miss proposition.

GULF TOADFISH
Opsanus beta

HABITAT: Gulf Toadfish prefer grassy bays, jetties, and anywhere they can find a crevice or nook in which to hide, and they stay close to their burrows.

RANGE/DISTRIBUTION: This species is limited to the Gulf of Mexico and southern Florida waters.

DESCRIPTION: Gulf Toadfish is a small fish, rarely even reaching a pound. The head is about twice as wide as the body, and the mouth inside that head is large and fearsome as well (though its small size diminishes its threat). The body tapers quickly to a small tail, and fins are small all around. In general shape, a toadfish kind of looks like a less extreme Monkfish. Toadfish are always some shade of brown, with patterns, splotches, and mottling all over the body and fins. Given that they like to hide in rocky crevices, such a camouflaging color pattern isn't very surprising. Contrary to myth and attestations from fishers, Gulf Toadfish do *not* have any venomous spines. They just look like they do.

EATING: It is absolutely delightful as a whole fried fish; filleting is easy, but it takes more

than a few toadfish to make any weight. The fish has no scales and is easy to gut.

AVAILABILITY: No fishery exists, and these are never for sale anywhere to anyone. It is simply not a fish of volume interest here or elsewhere. Commercial crabbers often find Gulf Toadfish in their traps, but the fish are always returned to the water.

If you want to eat Gulf Toadfish, then you'll have to catch your own. Fortunately, this is rather easy to do. Just spend all night in the dark, fishing with a small pole on the jetties. You can't see much, the wind is generally a pain, and if you're not careful, you'll lose every rig you cast to the rocks, but you'll come back with at least a few toadfish. Use a lightly weighted line and cut bait; cast

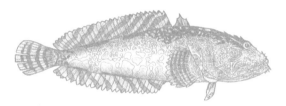

right beyond the rock line, then slowly jig the line back, always trying to keep the hook a few inches above the rocks themselves. The toadfish, nestled in the jetties, cannot resist the possibility of such an easy meal.

ATLANTIC MIDSHIPMAN
Porichthys plectrodon

HABITAT: Atlantic Midshipmen live close to the seafloor, especially in sandy and muddy places (i.e., most of Texas's offshore waters).

RANGE/DISTRIBUTION: It can be found from Argentina to the Caribbean Sea and the Gulf of Mexico.

DESCRIPTION: If this were a big fish, it would look like a sea monster, a dragon. But it's only six or seven inches long at most, so it looks more like a bizarre species of salamander or newt. It has a large, flat armored head with a huge mouth; large upturned eyes, mounted almost on top of the head; and a body that tapers into a tiny caudal fin. Dorsal and anal fins are delicate and continuous for the length of the body.

Like its cousin the Gulf Toadfish, the Atlantic Midshipman has no scales. Its underside is dark yellow to gold, while the back and body are brown to copper to platinum. Sometimes the color is solid, but sometimes the background is a paler shade covered with irregular spots.

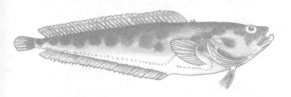

EATING: For years we just tossed this fish into the soup pot. Then we did a little more digging and found out it was related to the Gulf Toadfish, a fish we had already grown to love. We learned our lesson and have since then simply gutted the little guys and fried them one by one. The meat slides off the bone. It's not a common fish, but grab it if you can.

AVAILABILITY: Commercially, the Atlantic Midshipman is only ever bycatch from White Shrimp boats, which means it's not sold or marketed at all. You might catch a few as part of the mixed catch from a cast net, but midshipmen are more at home slightly farther offshore, too deep for a cast, even if you have a boat. Of course, if you have a boat, recall that recreational shrimp trawling is legal.

LADYFISH

Elops saurus

HABITAT: The Ladyfish lives along beaches, in passes and larger bays, usually, but not always, in deeper bays and fast-moving waters.

RANGE/DISTRIBUTION: It occurs along the US Atlantic coast, through the Gulf and Caribbean, and down to Brazil, but is most common in the Gulf.

DESCRIPTION: The Ladyfish is long, slender, and coated with silver scales. Its snout and caudal fins are tinged with gold, but the rest of the fish is white and silver. It looks something like an elongated herring, to which it is closely related. Most Ladyfish weigh less than a pound; some can get significantly larger.

EATING: Though Ladyfish itself is slightly fatty and quite flavorful, the work involved in getting any usable meat sadly discourages most people. The flesh turns mushy quickly, no matter how the fish is killed and handled (and we've tried everything). Even an

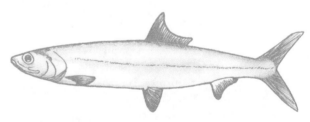

hour after it dies, it's difficult to get a clean fillet. The best—and maybe only—option is to scrape the meat free from the backbone and skin and use it for fish balls, purees, and similar preparations. However, scraping the meat is only part of the job. Ladyfish are bony (though not nearly as bony as their true herring cousins), so the meat must be passed through a drum sieve or food mill before you use it for anything. From whole fish to boneless meat, the process takes ten minutes. It's very easy to do.

AVAILABILITY: There is no targeted or bycatch fishery for Ladyfish. You will need to catch your own, which should be an easy and pleasant task. Ladyfish strike all kinds of bait and rigs, to the point that they can be a real nuisance to fishers who do not appreciate the treat. Ladyfish swim very close to shore, so fishing from beach, pass, and inlet is effective. Unless you are familiar with seasonal and daily migration patterns, don't count on catching a lot at a time (for the record, we ourselves are not familiar with the particulars of Ladyfish lives). This is one of those fish that seems to bite when nothing else will. So next time you're fishing at the beach and only the Ladyfish are biting, take home a cooler full, clean them the right way, enjoy eating them, then reflect on a successful trip.

ATLANTIC TRIPLETAIL

Lobotes surinamensis

HABITAT: This species lives on or near the surface of the water in deeper inshore waters, as well as offshore. Tripletails are lazy loners.

RANGE/DISTRIBUTION: It can be found worldwide in tropical, semitropical, and temperate waters.

DESCRIPTION: The Atlantic Tripletail doesn't really have three tails. It has one. The other two tails are really just overly large dorsal and anal fins. The fish is almost as tall as it is long, and it's thin as well. The head is tiny, the mouth insignificant. Its color runs from bronze to silver to gray to olive to black to brown and so on. Sometimes the coloration is monochromatic, but usually it is a jumble of mottled colors.

EATING: Atlantic Tripletail has an impeccable reputation as a food fish. It is quite good, but not good enough to leave a lasting impression. The fillets are wide, thin, and lacking in complicated bones. It tastes like a white fish. This is another fish we suspect enjoys more repute than it necessarily deserves. Never underestimate an odd-looking fish with white, rather insipid meat. Filleting is a snap, especially as the gut cavity is very large and there's no real meat to speak of on the belly.

AVAILABILITY: Because tripletails are solitary fish with odd habits (like floating on the surface of the water like a piece of jetsam, a behavior known as "basking"), they are hard

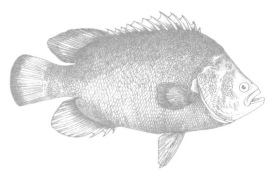

to target. Certainly, they are not targeted anywhere in Texas waters. The few Atlantic Tripletails that make it to market come from gillnet fisheries in one of several Central American countries.

INSHORE LIZARDFISH

Synodus foetens

HABITAT: This fish inhabits all kinds of inshore waters, particularly over muddy and sandy bottoms.

RANGE/DISTRIBUTION: It ranges from the US mid-Atlantic to Brazil, including the Gulf of Mexico and the Caribbean Sea.

DESCRIPTION: Sometimes common names can be misleading. Characteristics, traits, and colors can be exaggerated in order to come up with a name. That is not the case with the Inshore Lizardfish. It looks more like a legless skink with gills than a fish—even the scales are distinctly lizard-like. We have two species of lizardfish here—the

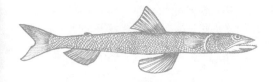

Inshore and the Offshore. The Offshore is small, whereas the Inshore is large, or larger, at any rate—both are less than a pound, but sometimes come close to it. We have only seen two or three Offshore Lizardfish, probably because they are usually too small to get caught by commercial finfish methods.

EATING: We would characterize this fish as good but not spectacular to eat. Inshore Lizardfish are not particularly bony, but they are more than a little dry, so stay away from the grill or oven. They fry up nicely, though, and Apple uses the picked meat for *laap*. (Every single species covered in this book can be used for *laap*, a recipe for which may be found on page 236. When in doubt, make *laap*.)

AVAILABILITY: There are no commercial landings or fisheries for this species that we know of, and lizardfish are never marketed. Our regular inshore fishing techniques have worked more than once for lizardfish. Basically, everything you would do for searobins, you would do for lizardfish, except

you would want to fish muddier, rather than sandier, bottoms.

HOUNDFISH AND ATLANTIC NEEDLEFISH

Tylosurus crocodilus and *Strongylura marina*

HABITAT: These species prefer very shallow coastal waters (no deeper than a few dozen feet). They are more common in places with running clear water rather than in back-bay muddy waters.

RANGE/DISTRIBUTION: Both species occur from around the Carolinas to Brazil and everywhere in between. The Houndfish has a more global distribution, occurring also in parts of the Indian Ocean and Southeast Asian waters.

DESCRIPTION: They are both shaped like darts with terrible mouths. The Atlantic Needlefish snout looks like the beak of an

extinct dinosaur ancestor of birds—long, exceedingly thin, and filled with tiny needle teeth. The Houndfish mouth looks more like that of an alligator.

Beyond their heads, they are both very long fish, perfectly round and elongated. Dorsal and anal fins don't even start until more than one-third down the length of the body. The dorsal, anal, and caudal fins, and the caudal finlets of the Houndfish, vaguely resemble those of a tuna. The Atlantic Needlefish's fins are rounded and less prominent. Needlefish can grow to more than three feet long and weigh over five pounds. The Houndfish is larger, reaching five feet and thirteen pounds or more.

EATING: Both are excellent to eat. The skin is edible enough, but not memorable. Fillets are easy to cut from whole fish, and bones are few and easy.

The meat is not steaky but certainly more firm than white fish. Basically, it has enough texture to be toothy but not chewy. The boneless meat takes well to most cooking methods. The absolute best way to cook them is on the grill.

AVAILABILITY: Though they are fished throughout most of their range, neither species is fished commercially in the American Gulf. Also, they are rarely taken as bycatch from any fishery. If you want to fish your own, use a wire leader and a shiny lure (sometimes live shrimp works well also). Some recreational fishers gig these fish, especially the Houndfish.

In a few other places, needlefish garner a little more respect as a targeted species. One of those is Owariki, an island in the Solomon Islands chain. There, a few traditional fishers still use unbaited spooled spider silk attached to small kites; no hooks are used

at all. To a needlefish, the silk resembles an insect, and the kite keeps the line flitting at the surface of the water. The needlefish strikes the line, gets snared in the silk, and is quickly reeled in by the fisher, who is in a small canoe nearby. The BBC produced a video a few years ago documenting the practice; we recommend you take the time to look it up online.

SEAROBINS (BIGHEAD, LEOPARD, BLACKWING, AND BIGEYE)

Prionotus tribulus, Prionotus scitulus, Prionotus rubio, and *Prionotus longispinosus*

HABITAT: Searobins prefer grassy, sandy, muddy, and rocky bottoms in shallow coastal waters down to a few dozen feet. They are very common in shallow bays.

RANGE/DISTRIBUTION: All of these species are limited to the Gulf of Mexico, the Caribbean Sea, and surrounding waters. Other closely related species are found throughout the world.

DESCRIPTION: We describe all four of our local species together because their main differences have to do with size more than anything else. All taste equally good, and all are almost equally as likely to be caught (the Bighead leads the pack in catches, mainly due to its size). All look almost the same, with minor variations in coloring and markings.

Searobins have large, boxy, spiked, and armored heads, which are roughly triangular in shape. Past the head, the body tapers quickly and dramatically to a small tail. Most of the fins are small, but the pectoral fins are gigantic and rounded, almost half as long as the body itself. One might expect, with fins that large, that the searobin could glide through the air like a flying fish. But the searobin is a heavy, thick-boned, bottom-dwelling fish that uses those large pectoral fins instead to walk across the bay floor, foraging for clams, snails, shrimp, and anything else it can find.

EATING: Searobins are an outstanding fish for the table. While the searobin has only started to gain a reputation as a food fish in Texas in recent years, it (or one of its close cousins) has been highly regarded elsewhere for a long time indeed. PJ first saw searobins while he was working in southern France, where searobins are a traditional, almost essential ingredient in Bouillabaisse. Throughout the Mediterranean, eastern Atlantic and western Pacific regions, people eat searobins; meanwhile, most Texans are unaware of this jewel in our waters. The raw meat is pale and translucent; when cooked, it is snow white, with a taste and texture that almost reminds one of crab.

Fillets are easy to extract and are pretty much boneless. However, because most of the body length is made up of the head, filleting always seems like a terrible waste. It's better to cook the whole fish—the tail meat is still easy to get at, and the head hides quite a bit of meat as well.

AVAILABILITY: Searobins are not generally available at the retail level. Seafood companies sell some searobins, just about all of which are from Pacific waters (New Zealand to Japan). Sometimes searobins appear out of east coast fisheries, though catches are small and sporadic.

So, while more expensive restaurants do have some access to this fish (albeit at a very high price), don't expect to find it at the market. As with a great many species in this book, either order it online or catch your own; we, of course, recommend the latter course of action. Use a Carolina rig or a drop line with a weight at the end of the line. Fish in sandier, rather than muddier, bays. A boat is a fine idea but not necessary for this fish—fishing from land generally works well enough, as long as you're prepared to possibly get a little wet. We find shallower bays are more productive, if only because they allow for wading to secluded spots. Fish toward evening and all night long. You might find yourself pleasantly surprised at how many you catch.

LITTLE FLATFISH (BAY WHIFF AND OFFSHORE TONGUEFISH)

Citharichthys spilopterus and *Symphurus civitatium*

HABITAT: These two fish species occur in bays and coastal offshore waters, usually in less than sixty feet of water.

RANGE/DISTRIBUTION: They occur in the Gulf of Mexico and Caribbean Sea.

DESCRIPTION: The Bay Whiff looks like a tiny flounder; the Offshore Tonguefish looks like a tiny tapered tongue with two tiny eyes right on the tip. Only the former is illustrated, due to its similarity to sole. Neither of these species grows much bigger than an adult's hand.

EATING: We've seen only a very few of these fish big enough to fillet. For the rest—into the soup pot! Flatfish provide good body to a fish soup—they break down and almost dissolve into the broth. If you should end up with a few pounds of these, you may count on, if nothing else, a superior *soupe de poisson* for dinner.

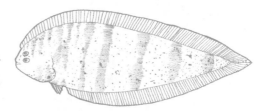

They may also be dried completely and then deep-fried, in which case the entire animal is edible.

AVAILABILITY: Nowhere will you see these fish for sale. If you make friends with a shrimper, then you can get all your gullet can handle. Barring that, learn how to throw a cast net, and get a small boat that travels well in bays and nearshore waters.

GULF BUTTERFISH AND HARVESTFISH

Peprilus burti and *Peprilus paru*

HABITAT: These closely related species live in different parts of the same seas. The Harvestfish lives in shallow waters, from close to beaches to a few miles out, while the Gulf Butterfish, for its part, usually sticks to deeper waters, where it is encountered as deep as six hundred feet or more. Both are pelagic fish, migrating horizontally and vertically on a regular, even daily, basis.

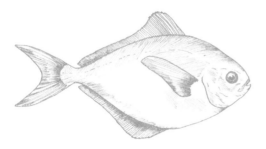

RANGE/DISTRIBUTION: The Gulf Butterfish is limited to Gulf waters, with some stragglers on the lower US Atlantic coast. The Harvestfish ranges from New England through the Gulf and the Caribbean, and down the South American Atlantic coast.

DESCRIPTION: Both of these species are small, always weighing less than half a pound and sometimes only a few ounces. Both are metallic silver, with no visible scales. The Gulf Butterfish has a larger head—being almost twice as big as that of the Harvestfish—and more rounded; its eyes are almost twice as large as well. In shape, both are about the same—oval, almost circular. Bodies are quite narrow. Both species have small mouths.

EATING: These are both excellent pan fish. In fact, they are among the best. Because they are so thin, they cook in no time and are always crisp, never oily. The meat resembles pomfret (both species are in the pomfret family, Bramidae, after all): slightly fatty but with no oily taste.

AVAILABILITY: These fish are bycatch from White and Brown Shrimp boats but are never targeted by boats in the northwestern Gulf of Mexico. The Harvestfish enjoys a good reputation on the US Atlantic coast and is commercially targeted throughout that part of its range (as is another species closely related to the Gulf Butterfish, which goes by the simple name Butterfish [*Peprilus triacanthus*]). These east coast species are occasionally available from upscale fishmongers and seafood companies.

Catching your own might prove difficult unless you have recreational access to a boat. Either make friends with a shrimper, or, more conveniently, ask your fishmonger to get some for you from the east coast.

SOUTHERN STARGAZER

Astroscopus y-graecum

HABITAT: Shallow coastal waters over mixed bottoms is the preferred habitat for this species. Stargazers like to bury themselves and ambush their prey, so they prefer sandy, silty areas. Beaches are prime real estate for Southern Stargazers.

RANGE/DISTRIBUTION: They range from the Caribbean and Gulf waters up to the Carolinas at least.

DESCRIPTION: The head, viewed from above, is circular. Eyes are placed on top of the head, the better with which to spy unwary prey. The mouth is located on the top of the head also, right at the edge. After the ungainly head, the body tapers to a broom tail. Pectoral fins are large and fan-shaped. The top of the body is tan to brown and speckled with a thousand white dots—perfect camouflage coloring. All fins are brown to black, with light stripes.

The Southern Stargazer produces an electrical shock as a defense mechanism, a fact that we recommend bearing in mind if you chance upon one in the wild. Watch out for the dorsal spines as well, which are reputedly venomous (having never been poked by one, we don't know).

EATING: Cook this wonderful fish as you would a toadfish. Or as you would any small, odd-shaped fish: fry it or steam it whole.

AVAILABILITY: At least in American waters, these are never commercially fished and are not regular bycatch from any commercial fishery. If you are fishing and happen to catch one, do keep it. However, if you want to avoid receiving a nasty shock, keep the following information in mind:

- Do not touch the fish while it is alive.
- Do not attempt to get the hook out. Cut the line.
- Immediately put the fish in ice or ice water (you should be doing this with all of your catch anyway).
- After the fish is dead, it no longer produces a shock.

CHAPTER 3

CROAKERS (SCIAENIDAE) AND GRUNTS (HAEMULIDAE)

In the croaker family, one will find some of the more popular coastal game fish—Redfish and Speckled Trout (and, to a lesser extent, Black Drum). The rest of the family is more or less disregarded by too many recreational fishers, the possible exception being the Atlantic Croaker, whose fall spawn was once eagerly anticipated by throngs of devotees. (These days, the spawn is less spectacular, and the devotees are fewer and fewer in number. Whether from overfishing [in the form of bycatch from shrimp fisheries], environmental degradation, excessive competition from rival species, or climate change, croaker numbers in the northwestern Gulf have dwindled in the last few decades.)

Grunts on the whole are slightly flashier than the croakers, even though most of them in our part of the Gulf tend to browns, grays, silvers, and pale yellows. They taste at least as good as the croakers, if not better.

The families are described together for the sake of convenience and superficiality. Most are inshore fish, and most are small panfish. All species in both families make a lot of noise when hauled out of the water: the croakers croak by manipulating their swim bladders; the grunts grunt by grinding their teeth. Species of croakers and grunts live all over the world, mostly in warm to tropical waters.

All of these fish are fun to catch, provided the proper-sized gear is used. We use little rods with 12-pound-test line, circle hooks, and egg weights for most of these fish, though much more substantial equipment is needed for Redfish and Black Drum (and different rigging as well). The smaller members of these families love to eat squid and one another. We prefer to use squid as bait because it is tough and stays on the hook, meaning we usually get at least two fish from each piece of bait.

REDFISH

Sciaenops ocellatus

COMMON NAMES: Red Drum, Channel Drum, Channel Bass (erroneous)

HABITAT: Redfish can be found in bays, inlets, passes, surf, estuaries, and jetties—basically anywhere in coastal Texas waters. Sometimes they also live in open Gulf waters, as far as thirty miles from shore.

RANGE/DISTRIBUTION: Redfish occur all down the US Atlantic coast from New England to around Florida and into the northern Gulf of Mexico. Redfish like warmer (but not quite tropical) waters, so populations are most concentrated in areas from Florida through Texas.

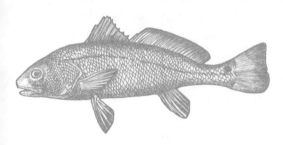

DESCRIPTION: The Redfish is not red at all. The closest it comes is an occasional deep orange, and even that is limited to its caudal fin. The rest of the body is goldish, and the belly is completely white. One or a few black dots decorate the lower back and tail, but there's not a lick or a dash of red. We suspect the name was intended in a relative sense, that is, the Redfish (a drum) is only red relative to the Black Drum. In that context, the name makes sense. Or at least it makes sense until you see a Black Drum, which itself is not really black at all.

The Redfish can reach an impressive size, up to sixty pounds or more and more than four feet in length, though most recreational catches are between one and twenty-five pounds. It shares several of the traits common to the grunt/croaker family: a downward-facing mouth along with a pronounced overbite, barbels under the chin, a barrel chest, thick embedded scales, and drab coloration.

EATING: At the risk of eliciting accusations of contrariness, we've never loved to eat Redfish. We certainly don't mind doing so, for it is a nice enough eating fish (especially when it is just over the legal limit, for the smaller the Redfish, the better the flavor and texture). But we've never understood the excitement or the enchantment. Then again, we've never fished just for sport, and we suspect sport fishing for Redfish and eating Redfish are intertwined endeavors.

All this being said, when one catches a Redfish (or, more likely, when one buys a Redfish), one may certainly prepare it in several satisfying ways. It's a meaty fish even at twenty-two inches; closer to the upper legal limit it starts to become steaky. Most any cooking technique may be applied to the Redfish, though we don't suggest eating it raw (for reasons of taste rather than safety). If the fish is farmed, don't fry it, for it is too fatty.

AVAILABILITY: In Texas, commercial harvest of Redfish is illegal, in any and all situations. Commercial boats can neither retain nor sell Redfish. In fact, wild Redfish, no matter the origin, may not be bought or sold at all. For example, if a Texas seafood company buys wild Redfish from Mississippi (where a small commercial harvest is legal), then sells that Redfish to a restaurant in Texas, both the seafood company and the restaurant have broken the law. (Using samples of meat, Texas Parks and Wildlife Department [TPWD] can distinguish wild from farmed meat, making it more difficult to circumvent the law.) The reason for the commercial prohibition is part of a larger story, best told elsewhere. Suffice it to say, you are not eating wild Redfish in any restaurant in Texas, and you are not buying wild Redfish in any store in Texas. Redfish is farmed in the southern part of the state (in ponds rather than pens) and is widely available across the state in grocery stores and in restaurants.

Redfish is also farmed around the globe, though product quality and production standards—with a few very notable exceptions—are usually less than stellar.

BLACK DRUM

Pogonias cromis

COMMON NAMES: Drum, Puppy Drum (for fish under three pounds)

HABITAT: This fish inhabits soft bottoms in shallow coastal waters—everywhere and anywhere.

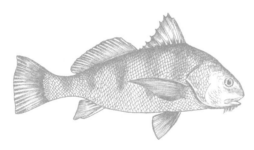

RANGE/DISTRIBUTION: Similar to the Redfish—US east coast populations are smaller, increasing in abundance farther south down the coast. Black Drum is plentiful around Florida and along the Gulf coast through Texas, as well as in some parts of the Caribbean and along the southern South American Atlantic coast.

DESCRIPTION: We previously noted that the Redfish isn't really red at all. The Black Drum, for its part, isn't really black. Young fish (called pups) are more or less silver with thick dark vertical stripes from head to tail (the fins are dark gray at this age). As the fish gets older and bigger, it is more gray silver than anything else, and the stripes will have faded or even disappeared entirely. Fins will also have faded. A fish larger than fifteen pounds is basically gray to very light copper, fins and all. Gray Drum might have been a more appropriate name.

The Black Drum's barbels cover the chin entirely, and the mouth is large (though still downward facing, the standard drum model). A pup's head looks too large for the delicate body behind it, though the fish does manage to grow into it somewhat (it remains slightly tapered throughout its life). A mature Black Drum resembles the largest bull Redfish. Dorsal fin spines are large, plentiful, and sharp—a fact to bear in mind when handling this fish.

This is the biggest species of drum in the Gulf, with mature fish sometimes weighing more than one hundred pounds (commercial catches are usually between three and twenty pounds; recreationally, two to over fifty pounds). Not surprisingly, the Black Drum can live for decades.

EATING: We adore this fish and are not alone, for the Black Drum has a solid history as a food fish in the Gulf Coast area, a history that runs from pre-Columbian indigenous inhabitants through today. Pups take well to steaming, roasting, or grilling; larger fish (up to about nine pounds) produce fantastic lean white fillets (though yield is admittedly poor, around 20 percent), and the meat from the biggest commercially available fish is almost like chicken.

We suggest never buying a drum larger than twenty pounds; if you should catch one that big or bigger, we urge you to let the fish go. Drums are an ideal host for a certain type of parasitic worm, which, while completely harmless to humans, is nonetheless off-putting and unappetizing. Even smaller drums may have worms, but those will be confined to its tail and belly, leaving the fillets unaffected. By the time it grows to twenty pounds or more, a parasitized drum will be riddled everywhere with those worms, so it's best to put it back in the water to make babies.

The scales are large and deeply embedded in the skin, so scaling is difficult (and dangerous, considering the force necessary to dislodge the scales, the tail-to-head direction in which one scales, and the large dorsal spines running in exactly the opposite direction). The ribs are thick and bend at an odd angle from the backbone, and the belly is quite thin, so don't expect to get much there. It isn't so much that the Black Drum is difficult to fillet, it's just different.

More positively, the Black Drum yields more than just meat. Recall that the head is quite large. A fish weighing around ten pounds has a head weighing around two pounds or more (including collars, assuming the fish was headed properly). A head this size is easily split and grilled or used in soup or roasted and can provide a decent amount of meat.

But there's more. The roe, milt, liver, and swim bladders are excellent as well. Few fish can boast such a distinction. While no one markets these delights directly, most drum are sold in the round (meaning they have not been gutted), so all you have to do is ask your fishmonger or the person at the seafood counter at a market that sells drum. Without a doubt, you will be stared at and won't be believed. Nonetheless, stand fast. You'll probably have to buy all the guts and sort them yourself.

The liver looks like any liver. The swim bladder is a thick-walled sac attached to the backbone. (See page 198 for a fuller discussion on swim bladders and their place on the table.) The roe looks like two orange sacs of fish eggs attached at one end (each sac is a lobe). The opaque white milt is divided into two lobes as well. If you want milt or roe, get a fish sometime between February and May, which is the spawning time for Black Drum.

AVAILABILITY: You can find Black Drum at seafood markets and supermarkets in any larger city in Texas and pretty much anywhere along the coast. Given the yield and market demand, it is always on the cheaper side. The majority of this Drum is from Texas fisheries, with the rest coming from Louisiana. Commercial Drum fishers in Texas use trotlines in bays (mostly in the southerly part of the state). The boats are smaller, with catches measured usually in hundreds rather than thousands of pounds. While more research needs to happen, the Texas and Louisiana fisheries appear to be in good shape and sustainable. In other words, this is a fish we all should eat more regularly. While current demand for the fish is always consistent, it's not nearly as high as we think it should be.

ATLANTIC CROAKER, SPOT, AND SILVER PERCH

Micropogonias undulatus, Leiostomus xanthurus, and Bairdiella chrysoura

HABITAT: All three of these fish live in shallow coastal waters, and all prefer mud and sand bottoms.

RANGE/DISTRIBUTION: The species can be found along the lower US Atlantic coast and in the northern Gulf of Mexico. These appear to be more temperate species, for they are limited to less tropical Gulf waters and absent from more southerly areas.

DESCRIPTION: The Atlantic Croaker is a typical sciaenid, with a big head and a heavy forebody tapering to a modest tail. It is not a big fish—we've never seen a five-pound Atlantic Croaker, and most have been a pound or less. The body is tan to pale gold, with faint angled vertical stripes running down the body. Fins are brown to pale gold.

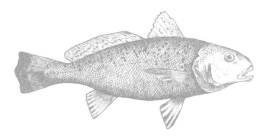

The Spot has a more compressed body and a fuzzy dark spot above the pectoral fin (hence the name). Its eyes give it a tired, harried, worried look. Aside from that (and its slightly larger head), it looks like an Atlantic Croaker, stripes and all, but it's smaller, rarely reaching even a pound. The Silver Perch is almost identical to the Spot, though it lacks the spot.

EATING: All three species are fine table fare, with the Atlantic Croaker having the best reputation of the three. You'll not find a Spot or Silver Perch worth filleting, so fry them whole. The biggest Atlantic Croakers—more than about a pound—produce fine fillets. Smaller fish are better served whole.

If you happen to go fishing at an inlet or pass, and you happen to go during the right moment of the fall, you will catch big, fat Atlantic Croakers, loaded with roe and milt, on their way to the open sea to spawn. These are the finest of the Atlantic Croakers; few

fish are better table fare (and the roe and milts are delicious).

AVAILABILITY: Larger Asian markets carry some kind of croaker (those fish being very popular in East Asia). These fish are usually not Atlantic Croaker, but are imported from outside the Gulf, most often from southern or Southeast Asian waters. Not a great deal of local croaker makes its way to restaurants, much less grocery stores. As for the Spot, it might as well not even exist. Asian markets sell small frozen imported cousins, but never the Spot itself.

We typically catch these species using our "small fish" gear. We never catch a lot of any of them, but they always make a nice contribution to dinner.

SPECKLED, SAND, AND SILVER SEATROUTS

Cynoscion nebulosus, Cynoscion arenarius, and *Cynoscion nothus*

COMMON NAMES: Speckled Trout, Speck, Trout; Speckled Seatrout: Spotted Weakfish

HABITAT: All three species inhabit shallow inshore waters, most commonly bays and seagrass meadows (Speckled) and beaches and outlets (Sand and Silver). None of these fish travel to deeper waters.

RANGE/DISTRIBUTION: The Speckled Seatrout has the most northerly range of the three species—it's found from the US mid-Atlantic coast to everywhere in the Gulf of Mexico. The Silver doesn't range quite as far north but is everywhere in the Gulf and possibly in the Caribbean and farther south. The Sand Seatrout is one of the few endemic Gulf species.

DESCRIPTION: Though they are all members of the Sciaenidae family, these three fish look nothing like other croakers or drums. They

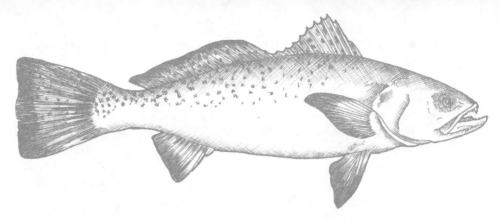

do indeed look more like trout than anything, but this is nothing but a coincidence
of evolution. Their snouts are pointed, and
their mouths are toothy, with pronounced
dagger-shaped incisors (especially the
Speckled).

Cynoscion, the "seatrout" genus in the
Sciaenidae family, includes a couple of
dozen species, all of which are found either
along the southern California and northern
Mexican Pacific coasts (to and through the
Sea of Cortez) or in the Gulf and American
mid-Atlantic waters. The genus is limited
to these areas, and no other members exist
worldwide.

Sciaenids in general have thick, tough
scales and stout bodies, whereas these three
species have thin, deciduous scales on delicate bodies. All three are metallic silver, with
light brown to tan fins. The Speckled has a
few or many black dots running down the
back, all above the lateral line.

The Silver is the smallest of the three
seatrouts, never reaching even a pound.
The Sand is slightly larger, but still under
a pound. The Speckled is by far the largest,
sometimes weighing as much as ten pounds
or more (though the average catch is closer
to three pounds).

EATING: Here again the seatrouts distinguish themselves from other members of
their family. The rich, soft flesh neither
resembles nor tastes like that of any other
sciaenid, or indeed any other fish. It is neither too fatty nor too lean, with the delicate
texture of a brook trout. Only the Speckled is
large enough to fillet. The Sand and Silver we
grill whole.

AVAILABILITY: On occasion, some little
coastal seafood market or other might have
some Silver or Sand Seatrouts for sale. In
general, however, you will have to catch your
own; all you need to do is fish off the beach,
using the standard "little fish" rig. You'll
catch more than just these two species of
course.

As for the Speckled Seatrout, there is
no commercial fishery in Texas, having
been outlawed at the same time as that for
Redfish. However, if it is legally harvested
elsewhere, it may be brought into Texas and
sold, provided every shipment of said fish is
accompanied by a special invoice designat-
ing provenance. The main source for wild
Speckled Seatrout is Mexico (other Gulf
states have commercial fisheries, but catches
are limited and harvests are generally sold
in-state).

Larger grocery stores and seafood markets in Texas sometimes carry Speckled
Seatrout, as do seafood companies. Half the
time these fish are not Speckled Seatrout at
all, but rather Weakfish (*Cynoscion regalis*),
a closely related (and commercially fished)

species, which is restricted to waters of the American Atlantic coast. The only difference between the Weakfish and the Speckled Seatrout is the dots along the back. The latter has them, the former does not. In all other respects, including taste, they are identical.

NORTHERN KINGFISH, SOUTHERN KINGFISH, AND GULF KINGFISH

Menticirrhus saxatilis, Menticirrhus americanus, and Menticirrhus littoralis

COMMON NAME: Whiting (used as a general name for all three species, and also the name we typically use)

HABITAT: These three fish can be found along beaches and in inlets, passes, and larger bays, usually in shallow, swift-moving waters. They are some of our favorite fish for beach trips.

RANGE/DISTRIBUTION: All three species range up and down the Atlantic coast: northern parts of South America and southern part of North America, and everywhere in the Gulf of Mexico.

DESCRIPTION: First, a word on nomenclature. A majority of fishers in Texas waters refer to these fish as whiting. But others call them kingfish. We call them whiting, which is indicative of nothing. Both common names, though, create some confusion. Look up "whiting" online, and the first search results are not our whitings but the Atlantic Whiting, an entirely unrelated fish (being a member of the cod family); likewise, search "kingfish," and the first results will be either the King Mackerel (described on page 62) or the Yellowtail Jack (a member of the jack family [Carangidae] not present in the Gulf).

One species is larger and silver; the other is smaller, striped, and silver; the last is smaller, striped, and brownish-copperish. We admit we've never been able to recall which is which, but we have always happily eaten all three.

Whiting looks like a scale model of a Redfish (to which it is, of course, very closely related). A large blunt head tapers to a thin tail, the snout is rounded and boasts a few barbels, and the mouth is oriented downward (for whitings feed near the bottom, something to keep in mind when fishing). Its scales are rather small. The largest of the three species might weigh a pound or so, while the smallest is usually half that. They are among the more commonly encountered inshore saltwater fish.

EATING: Whiting tastes better than the best puppy Redfish. The meat is very pale, the

flake delicate, the taste sweet and mild. Not being riddled with too many bones, they make easy eating as well. We always consider the day well spent when we go home from the beach with a cooler full of whiting, which makes the low esteem in which they are commonly held all the more disappointing. To too many fishers, a whiting on the hook means a waste of bait.

AVAILABILITY: You might occasionally find whiting at larger Asian markets, but don't bet on it. The few remaining fish markets in the few remaining coastal towns sometimes sell it, but don't bet on that either. Your best shot, as with a great many critters in this book, is to go fish it yourself.

Get a surf rod and a length of PVC pipe to serve as a seat for the rod. Attach to the end of the line two to three drop lines, each drop line terminating in a small circle hook (always use small circle hooks). At the end of the line, tie a five- to eight-ounce pyramid or spider weight (depending on wind and tides). The best bait is slivers of squid, threaded on the hooks.

When conditions are right, cast the line into the second or third "gut" (a gut is the valley between submerged sandbars running parallel right off the beach), plant the rod in the PVC, take the slack out of the line, and watch the birds (or play in the waves) for a few minutes, checking the pole occasionally. It might twitch and fidget a bit. As twitches become shudders, take up the rod and start reeling—no need to set hooks or go for speed; steady and smooth is the way. The majority of efforts yield at least one whiting. Sometimes you'll catch catfish, or rays, or Piggy Perch, or Ladyfish; don't throw these (or any others except those legally prohibited) back, though. They can all play a part in dinner.

BLACK MARGATE

Anisotremus surinamensis

HABITAT: The Black Margate occurs in nearshore and shallow coastal waters. It overwhelmingly prefers rocks and reef to sand and grass, so any Texas populations are concentrated farther south in the state.

RANGE/DISTRIBUTION: It is endemic to the Gulf of Mexico and Caribbean Sea, though more common in warmer areas of those waters.

DESCRIPTION: The Black Margate, like most members of the grunt family, bears an

eternally surprised expression on its face. The eyes are large and pale yellow, and the mouth is downturned. While all of the Black Margate's fins are black, the body itself is gray, save for a swathe of washed-out black across the front belly up to the pectoral fins.

The Black Margate is probably the largest grunt in coastal Texas waters, though we admit the bar for that accomplishment

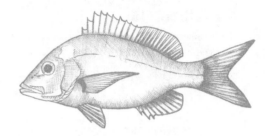

is rather low. Though they can reach ten pounds or more, most weigh half that or less.

EATING: This is a superb eating fish. We recommend cooking smaller Black Margates (less than two pounds) whole; always fillet larger fish.

AVAILABILITY: Even in southern Texas waters, where they are a common enough recreational catch, Black Margate populations can be spotty. We rarely ever see them in northern Texas waters.

There is no commercial fishery in Texas; we assume that Black Margates are commercially targeted in waters where they are more plentiful.

PIGFISH AND BLUESTRIPED GRUNT

Orthopristis chrysoptera and *Haemulon sciurus*

COMMON NAME: Pigfish: Piggy Perch (This is the colloquial name in Texas, and the name by which we always call this fish. The plural of this common name is "piggies.")

HABITAT: These two species can be found in bays, canals, marshes, beaches, and any other body of shallow salt water. Piggy Perch is exceedingly common in shallow bays; the Bluestriped Grunt prefers rockier places (which means, in our waters, jetties).

RANGE/DISTRIBUTION: The Piggy Perch is found up and down the east coast and

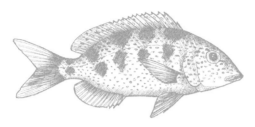

throughout the Caribbean and Gulf of Mexico; the Bluestriped Grunt is limited to the Gulf, the Caribbean, and the northern Atlantic coast of South America and is not as common in our waters.

DESCRIPTION: If you have ever fished off a bay pier with small gear, you have probably caught this fish. Piggies are small—very large ones might weigh a pound, but most are only a few ounces. Strictly speaking, the Piggy Perch is a grunt and not a perch at all; nonetheless, it looks just like a freshwater perch. The most striking feature is probably coloration: Piggies have turquoise blue to green mottling on their faces and backs, tan to white bellies, and yellow-orange stripes (made up of tiny dots) running from snout to tail. The tail is roughly the same color as the stripes.

On the other hand, if you've ever fished from jetties, using that same gear, you've probably caught a Bluestriped Grunt. It looks suspiciously similar to the Piggy Perch, except that it is yellow, with bold blue stripes running from snout to tail.

EATING: Grunts in the northwestern Gulf do not get the respect they deserve. Most people consider grunts in general to be at worst annoyances and at best bait, which is a shame, because both the Piggy Perch and the Bluestriped Grunt are fine indeed. They are small fish, so fillets are not really a practical option. However, they contain a decent amount of meat, the bones are predictable and easy to handle, and the whole fish is easy to cook.

AVAILABILITY: Over the years, this has become one of our family's favorite fish, and no trip to the beach is complete until we've caught a few. We fry them fresh; we half-dry and fry them; we completely dry them; we ferment them.

Unfortunately, the only way to get ahold of them is to catch them yourself. No commercial fisheries exist. Both species are bycatch on shrimp boats, but fish caught that way never make it to market. Both are also caught by bait boats and may be purchased live at better bait shops along the coast. Unfortunately, fish caught for bait are far too small for the table.

Catching them is a simple matter. Use cut squid on a small circle hook on a small pole. Weigh the line so you're fishing on the bottom; or use a cork to keep the bait near the top of the water column; or use neither weight nor cork, but simply a baited hook. Cast in shallow water and start catching. With a little patience (and luck), you'll go home with a dozen fish or more.

TOMTATE

Haemulon aurolineatum

COMMON NAMES: Orangemouth, Redmouth Grunt, Mother-in-Law

HABITAT: These fish prefer sandy, grassy, and rock and reef bottoms in waters a few dozen feet deep to more than a hundred feet deep.

RANGE/DISTRIBUTION: They occur down the US Atlantic coast, around the Florida peninsula, throughout the Gulf of Mexico, and down to Brazil. They are most abundant in the Gulf and off the southern coast of Florida.

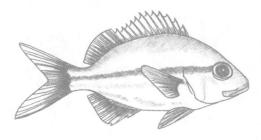

DESCRIPTION: Grunts are small, and the Tomtate is no exception. Most are less than half a pound, and a giant is still less than two. It has the typical grunt shape—pointed snout, skinny body, stout dorsal fin spines. The body is tan or beige, with fins slightly darker shades of the same colors; as the fish gets older, its color darkens considerably. A yellow or bronze stripe runs horizontally from the tip of the top lip all down the body and terminates in a large dark blurred splotch on the caudal peduncle. Eyes are copper colored. Certainly, the defining trait is the color of the inside of the mouth, which is sometimes cherry red, sometimes orange, usually a combination of both colors (though always so bright as to appear artificial).

EATING: We have quite a bit of experience cooking and eating the Tomtate, mostly because no one ever really wanted to buy too many. Apple usually scaled and cleaned it, scored the whole fish, and fried it (usually after marinating it in soy sauce, garlic, and salt); sometimes we would dry them outside; the biggest we would grill.

AVAILABILITY: Tomtate is never targeted here in the northwestern Gulf, but sometimes Vermilion Snapper boats unload a few pounds. (One name for this fish, Mother-in-Law, which, as far as we know, is limited to the northwestern Gulf, apparently derives from the low to nonexistent market value of the fish, its ubiquity, and the hassle involved with catching lots of them. To paraphrase an old crusty captain, "They always show up, you never want them around, they make a lot of noise, and they're not worth anything." We mention this merely as a humorous aside; we both love our mothers-in-law.) They are rarely to never available at the retail level and are just as uncommon in restaurants.

Recreational fishing is problematic as well, due to the depths at which the Tomtate lives. Happily, other grunts and small sciaenids work quite well in its place, and they are easier to catch.

CHAPTER 4
JACKS (CARANGIDAE)

Along with the drums, snappers, groupers, and mackerels, the jacks are one of the most prominent families of fish in the Gulf of Mexico, boasting more than two dozen species, most of which are found in our part of the Gulf; of those, more than a dozen are covered here. Curiously, of the commonly fished Gulf jacks, the Banded Rudderfish (*Seriola zonata*) and the Pilotfish (*Naucrates ductor*) seem to be completely absent from at least those parts of the northwestern Gulf in which commercial boats fish.

Members of the Carangidae family swim in all of the temperate and tropical seas and oceans of the world. Some stay close to rocks, reefs, and underwater structures; others are pelagic; others occur in both of these habitats. Most species share a common bullet shape, built for speed and chase. A few species, like the famous Florida Pompano, are more sickle shaped; some, like the moonfish and lookdowns, take the sickle shape to an extreme. With a very few exceptions, jacks are blue-water fish, meaning they are found in deeper, usually offshore waters.

All are predatory fish, and all are, with almost no exceptions, easily edible (most are excellent). Most species included here are fished commercially somewhere, if not in the Gulf itself.

AFRICAN POMPANO
Alectis ciliaris

HABITAT: This fish lives in blue water, generally on or near areas with structures or rocks.

RANGE/DISTRIBUTION: It is found in all of the world's tropical waters.

DESCRIPTION: This fish is unmistakably a jack, albeit one with a slightly flattened look. It has large lips; larger eyes; and a tall, narrow body terminating in the distinctive jack tail. A large specimen might weigh well over twenty pounds and be the better part of two feet tall, but no more than three or four inches thick. The skin is an almost reflective metallic silver, with no visible scales (after the fish dies, the tiny scales slough off, leaving a pale gray body). The tips of the dorsal and anal fins trail off into fine filaments that can stretch for several feet behind the fish.

Usually these tips are broken off throughout the life of the animal, but one sometimes sees spectacularly long fin tips, especially on smaller fish.

EATING: The curious shape of this species means that the fillets are very thin and wide (reminiscent of a John Dory fillet, though the two species are not related at all). The flesh is pale white, translucent to almost opaque. The African Pompano's diet relies on crustaceans

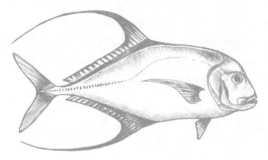

and shellfish, so its meat is fatty and almost unctuous. It is an excellent fish to grill or roast and an even better fish to eat raw, right off the bone.

AVAILABILITY: In the past, this species was typically bycatch from boats targeting Vermilion Snapper. But with fewer boats targeting Vermilions these days, fewer African Pompanos are being landed. If you have access to a boat, then you might be in luck, but rarely does one find thick schools of these fish. Very occasionally, seafood markets offer this fish.

ALMACO JACK, GREATER AMBERJACK, AND LESSER AMBERJACK

Seriola rivoliana, Seriola dumerili, and *Seriola fasciata*

COMMON NAMES: Almaco Jack: Bar Jack (colloquial), Kanpachi (Japanese)

HABITAT: All three species are at home in blue waters, rarely ever wandering far inshore. They are somewhat pelagic but not really migratory, and they are typically found around structures, rocks, and reefs.

RANGE/DISTRIBUTION: All three species live around the world in tropical and near-tropical waters. Even though the Almaco Jack is common in the Gulf of Mexico, other parts of the world have much larger populations (and more established fisheries). If you have eaten Kanpachi in a Japanese restaurant, then you have eaten this fish (and it was almost certainly farmed in the central or western Pacific). The Greater Amberjack is found basically everywhere the Almaco is found and is more well known to Gulf Coast residents. The Lesser Amberjack isn't as common in the western Gulf as it is in the eastern Gulf and in mid-Atlantic waters.

DESCRIPTION: A mature Greater Amberjack and a small Almaco Jack look like cousins. A mature Almaco and a young Greater Amberjack look like each other. The Lesser Amberjack looks like a young, emaciated Greater Amberjack with big eyes. All of which is to say that identification takes some practice.

All three have the typical hydrodynamic jack shape. All have similar coloration: shades of browns and yellows, light at the belly fading to dark brown on the back. The Greater Amberjack usually has a pronounced yellow stripe running from its snout through the eye to its back (the other two species usually have faded stripes). All three have heavy heads. The main differences between the Lesser and the Greater are the large eyes, slightly brighter coloring, and skinnier body of the former.

The Almaco Jack tends to look more condensed and ovoid than the Greater Amberjack, which looks longer and more stretched out. Beyond that, the Almaco has a distinctly taller dorsal fin than both the Greater and Lesser Amberjacks (hence one of its common names, Longfin Amberjack). Also, the Almaco has, on average, more gill rakers than the Greater Amberjack, but fewer than the Lesser Amberjack (gill rakers are the white bony spikes coming off the back of the gills; they are much easier to see than to describe!).

Commercially caught Greater Amberjacks usually weigh between twenty-five and seventy-five pounds; those caught recreationally tend to be bigger—up to one hundred pounds. Almaco Jacks are caught at all sizes. Fish weighing two pounds are as common as those weighing twenty. Sometimes Almacos can get very big—we've seen a couple of Almacos that pushed one hundred pounds. Neither of these fish is worth eating once they pass about seventy pounds.

Lesser Amberjacks are smaller fish, usually weighing less than fifteen pounds.

EATING: All jacks taste good, and these three are no exceptions—wherever these fish swim, they are hunted by humans. The meat of all three species ranges from pink to beige in color (the younger the fish, the pinker the flesh; by the time they are older, they have well-developed dark meat (see page 195 for more on dark meat).

They are all great steak fish, and may be grilled, roasted, baked, braised, or fried. Almacos and amberjacks are, like all jacks, a little fatty—but only a little.

Because of their size and shape, Almaco Jacks make the best fish on which to practice your filleting technique. The yield is very good, and the bones are easy to navigate.

Amberjacks and huge Almaco Jacks can get worms, which, like those common to Black Drum and Swordfish, are no threat to humans at all. Almost always, any worms are in the tail or belly, are easily visible, and easy to cut around.

AVAILABILITY: Greater Amberjack is the most common of these three species, though it is generally found as a restaurant, rather than a retail, fish. Sometimes one may find Almaco, though rarely does one find it for sale in grocery stores under that name.

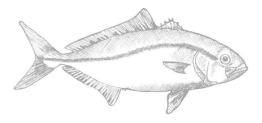

Almost universally, Almaco is marketed as Kanpachi, which is the Japanese name for the species. Almaco is farmed in Japan, as well as in Mexico and Hawai'i (the farmed fish is marketed under the intentionally corrupted name Kampachi). We eagerly await the day when the Gulf of Mexico boasts its own offshore Almaco Jack farms.

BIGEYE SCAD, REDTAIL SCAD, AND ROUND SCAD

Selar crumenophthalmus, Decapterus tabl, and *Decapterus punctatus*

COMMON NAMES: Jack Mackerel and Aji (Japanese) are used generally for all scad species.

HABITAT: These species occur from a few to many dozens of feet below the surface of offshore waters. They are schooling fish that usually congregate near reefs.

RANGE/DISTRIBUTION: Like most jacks, these species (or their close relatives) swim in all the warmer seas and oceans of the world.

DESCRIPTION: The fact that these fish are sometimes called "mackerel jacks" or "jack mackerels" should be an indication of their size and appearance—though the comparison falters when one views the fish head on, for the scads are thin where the mackerels are round. Most scads weigh a few ounces (quite a bit less than a pound, anyway, for most species); all are shiny, with minor differences in coloration and patterns. Our most common species is the Bigeye, the eyes of which are indeed appreciably larger than

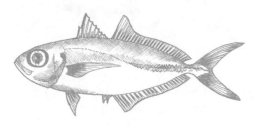

those of other species. However, we have not found a correlation between eye size and edibility—we have found all Gulf scads equally appetizing.

EATING: If you've spent any time in any decent Japanese restaurant, you will know this fish, for scads are well appreciated in Japanese cuisine; in fact, they are pretty highly esteemed throughout most of their native range—the one glaring exception being the United States. Scads are fatty but not overly so. They are rich, but only just enough. Cooking them is easy, and the process of dismembering the fish afterward is even easier (assuming you have cooked it whole). Like all jacks, scads are quite easy to fillet, even the smaller specimens. Fillets are best grilled, roasted, or sautéed in some olive oil with a lot of garlic. All in all, scads are one of our best fish.

AVAILABILITY: Most of the larger Asian markets will carry scads of some type, though rarely if ever from our waters. Though they swim everywhere in the blue waters of the Gulf, we have, with exactly one exception, only ever seen them from boats owned, captained, and crewed by Vietnamese and Vietnamese-American fishers. On those boats, scads were common. They were also never for sale, but rather were divided among the crew as part of their personal take.

ATLANTIC BUMPER

Chloroscombrus chrysurus

HABITAT: The Atlantic Bumper occurs from larger bays to blue water and everywhere in between. It is a migratory schooling fish.

RANGE/DISTRIBUTION: Warm temperate waters on both sides of the Atlantic are the preferred environment of this fish. A closely related species, *Chloroscombrus orqueta*, Pacific Bumper, swims in the Pacific. Further research might conclude that this is really one species.

DESCRIPTION: Its hemispherically bulging belly aside, the Atlantic Bumper looks like any other jack. In fact, it looks like an amalgam of several other members of its family. No visible scales are present, and the body is a uniform chrome. The only other splashes of color are the pale gold on the fins and the black dot on the caudal peduncle. While the Atlantic Bumper can apparently reach

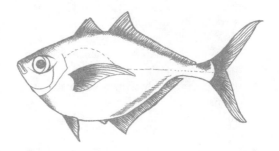

considerable size (more than twelve inches long), the vast majority in Texas are much smaller. We suspect, given that the Gulf of Mexico functions as an estuary for a large number of migratory species, that our part of the Gulf (or maybe the entire thing) is an estuary for this species as well, which would explain the paucity of large Atlantic Bumpers in our waters.

EATING: We assume larger Atlantic Bumpers would fillet quite handily and would yield good to excellent fillets. However, we've only ever had smaller specimens—from two to eight inches. The tiniest of these we gut, marinate, and dehydrate completely (to be fried later for snacks); the larger ones we steam or fry whole.

AVAILABILITY: There are no commercial fisheries whatsoever for this fish in Texas. Perhaps elsewhere the situation is different.

If you want to eat this fish, make friends with a shrimper or learn to use a cast net.

BLACK JACK

Caranx lugubris

HABITAT: One of the deeper-ranging Gulf jacks, Black Jacks cover some distance in their travels, but they stick to waters near the bottom.

RANGE/DISTRIBUTION: As with all jacks, the Black Jack occurs in pretty much all warm waters of the world. Populations here are smaller than in the western Pacific, where there are extensive fisheries.

DESCRIPTION: The Black Jack is mostly a stout body with a little head stuck at one end. The thick-scaled skin (darker gray than black) covers a tall and narrow body, which tapers to a narrow tail that ends in a standard V shape. Bony triangular studs—called caudal scutes—extend like a ridge along each

fillet side of the tail. Scutes are a common feature on lots of pelagic fish, including tunas, but jacks have the boniest.

EATING: We've often speculated that scarcity affects taste. We're still not sure if this is true. But whenever we have speculated on such things, the Black Jack has invariably come up. Is it inherently good, or is its tastiness tied to its frustrating unpredictability at the docks? The debate continues.

That said, we reckon the Black Jack does rank highly in terms of edibility. The flesh compares favorably to almost any other jack, being pale and only slightly fatty. It holds up well to grilling of course, and most any other kind of preparation.

AVAILABILITY: Forget about it, unless you catch it yourself. Maybe a couple dozen or so a year were landed by Texas commercial boats a few years ago. Rarely, grouper long-liners or snapper boats might catch one or two, but months can pass at the dock with no sightings at all.

BLUE RUNNER AND CREVALLE JACK

Caranx crysos and *Caranx hippos*

COMMON NAMES: Blue Runner: Hardtail; Crevalle Jack: Jack, Jackfish

HABITAT: Both species are pelagic. Crevalle Jacks are caught less than a mile offshore during the summer, whereas Blue Runners are typically found many more miles out, closer to blue water.

RANGE/DISTRIBUTION: These two species occur in nearshore temperate waters of both the eastern and western Atlantic, throughout most of the West African coast, along the eastern coast of North America through to northern South America, and eastward to at least the western Mediterranean and contiguous seas.

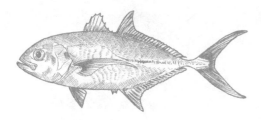

DESCRIPTION: We describe these two fish together not because of their physical appearances (which are not notable beyond the fact that they are both obviously jacks), but rather because of the esteem in which they are held by so many fishers, chefs, and eaters of fish. More on that below.

The Blue Runner looks like a rounded-off bullet with a V-shaped tail (the tail sports the hard scutes common to these kinds of fish). The skin runs from blue to black to tan to bronze to gray—always terminating in a white belly. It's a smaller jack, usually weighing less than two pounds and always less than five. All of the fins are small.

The Crevalle Jack more resembles the Black Jack than any other fish. It has a small head; a tall and narrow, though muscular, body; prominent caudal scutes; and thick skin and scales. Its color ranges from tan to gray to green gray to blue gray, terminating in a whitish belly. Most of the fins are a cornmeal color, but a splash of brilliant lemon

yellow starts at the bottom of the tail and covers the entire anal fin (a yellow so bright as to appear painted). Crevalles range in size from a few pounds to more than thirty.

EATING: The Blue Runner has a much better table reputation than the Crevalle (which has almost none)—indeed, for years there was a small secondary commercial fishery in the northwestern Gulf. Still the market for it is quite small, limited mostly to immigrant communities for whom Blue Runner is a common food fish (the fact is, it, along with closely related species, is a common market fish throughout most of its range, with one of the exceptions being here in the United States). The Blue Runner is an excellent fish and deserves more attention than it receives.

The Crevalle has a reputation for inedibility. The old joke is this recipe: "Take a chunk of Crevalle and season it with a lot of salt, pepper, Tabasco, lemon juice, chili powder, and garlic. Get a frying pan screaming hot, then sear the fish. Continue cooking the fish until it is very well done, mostly black on the outside. Remove the pan from the heat. Take out the piece of fish and throw it away. Eat the pan."

In reality, both fish are more than suitable for the table. They are great for smoking, and both are great on a grill (if you make sure that a bright sauce is served alongside, as both tend a little toward insipidness). When grilling (or baking or roasting) pieces of these fish, we advise wrapping them in bacon or something similar. Though they are slightly fatty, they will dry quickly during cooking.

We have always enjoyed the dark meat of both the Crevalle and the Blue Runner marinated and grilled. These fish, being fast pelagic swimmers, have abundant streaks of dark meat (see page 195 for a further discussion of cuts of fish and dark meat).

AVAILABILITY: Crevalle is rarely sold anywhere. Blue Runner is sold at all larger supermarkets catering to immigrant communities, though it is almost always imported from other waters rather than being locally sourced (the imported product being cheaper). PJ was told many times by lots of fishermen that Blue Runners were absolutely abundant enough to target as a major fishery. Boats could be filled trip after trip, and still the populations wouldn't suffer. Alas, there has never been wide, sustained local interest in this fish, resulting in a very low ex-vessel price. Abundance means little if the price of the fish is too low to make a living.

FLORIDA POMPANO AND PERMIT

Trachinotus carolinus and *Trachinotus falcatus*

HABITAT: These two species occur in clear, fast-moving inshore and nearshore waters, especially in areas with high currents and tidal action.

RANGE/DISTRIBUTION: The two fish have a similar range—roughly from the Carolinas, throughout the Gulf of Mexico and the Caribbean, and down the Atlantic coast to Brazil. Florida Pompanos are more common in the northern Gulf, with Permits taking over the farther south one progresses.

DESCRIPTION: Neither of these fish attains any great size, with the Florida Pompano being on average the smaller fish (up to a pound or two, compared to the Permit, which may be twice that size or more). Both fish are spade shaped, with blunt, stout snouts as the tip of the spade and pronounced V-shaped tails as the spade's handle. Their bodies are at least as tall as they are long.

The Florida Pompano is silver to gray to green gray to blue gray to blue on top and white in the middle, with a stark yellow band extending from the lower jaw to the anal and caudal fins. The dorsal and anal fins are pronounced and sickle shaped but not very long.

The Permit is grayish silver, with black edging along the anal and dorsal fins, both of which are longer and more graceful than the Pompano's.

EATING: Both of these fish are easy favorites across all parts of the Gulf of Mexico. The meat is fatty enough to remain moist through overcooking but lean enough to be fried.

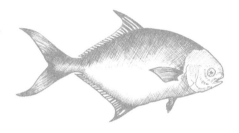

AVAILABILITY: Substantial Florida Pompano fisheries exist in Mexico and other Central American countries; Florida has a smaller but still quite large fishery as well. Generally speaking, Florida fish will be a touch smaller, a little bluer, a little more yellow. Imported fish will generally be gray on top, with not a hint of blue, and the yellow on the belly will also be faded.

Both the Permit and the Florida Pompano are rather unusual in that they freeze beautifully. Even fillets frozen in a home freezer thaw out and cook nicely (and taste decent). This is good news for the recreational fisherman, but it does mean that frozen Florida Pompanos are very often passed off as fresh by unscrupulous vendors. In such a case, only the eyes can tell the tale. The eyes of a formerly frozen Florida Pompano will look dead, their pupils calcified into little white marbles; the eyes of a fresh dead Florida Pompano will stare at you accusingly.

LOOKDOWN AND ATLANTIC MOONFISH

Selene vomer and *Selene setapinnis*

HABITAT: These two species live in shallow coastal waters. They are seldom to never found at depths greater than a few hundred feet.

RANGE/DISTRIBUTION: The Lookdown and Atlantic Moonfish occur from the upper American east coast all the way to at least Brazil, with their heaviest populations congregating around Florida, in the Gulf of Mexico, and in the Caribbean.

DESCRIPTION: If Victorian novels had been written by fish, then these two species would have been guaranteed a lifetime of work in the film adaptations—the Atlantic Moonfish as the disapproving, gossiping elderly aunt, widow of a military man who died fighting the Prussians; the Lookdown as the venal and puritanical country vicar, born with a hereditary title and his nose in the air.

Beyond that, both of these fish are exceedingly, impossibly thin. Centimeters are almost too large a unit of measurement for the younger fish, and even adults will rarely to never come close to being an inch thick. The abdominal cavities of both are large to accommodate all the organs (which themselves are almost flat—one wonders what a gluttonous Atlantic Moonfish looks like). They are so thin as to defy belief, almost as if they are the products not of nature but of a cartoonist's imagination.

More prosaically, they are both roughly circular in shape. While the two species are distinguishable, they are close cousins, and both look like a silver dollar after surviving a tussle with a locomotive. The heads are small and contained in a small area. The rest of the bodies are chrome silver, with no visible scales. Caudal fins in both species are small.

The Lookdown has more pronounced dorsal and anal fins, which jut out at forty-five-degree angles from the body and trail back most of the length of the fish; those of the Atlantic Moonfish are quite small by comparison. Neither species attains any great size—Lookdowns rarely get bigger than a pound or so; Atlantic Moonfish grow slightly larger and may sometimes weigh up to five pounds.

EATING: There's not a lot of meat to be had except on the largest specimens, but what meat there is tastes quite nice. The only feasi-

ble thing to do with all but the largest is cook them whole. On the rare occasion that you come across one of these fish large enough to fillet, by all means do so.

If you are lucky enough to see a shrimp boat unloading its bycatch, and you see juveniles of these species among the catch, try to sweet-talk the captain into selling you a few. Small Atlantic Moonfish and Lookdowns can be marinated, dried a little, and fried into chips. They are delicious this way and small enough that even gutting isn't necessary. Everything just turns crispy and delicious.

AVAILABILITY: You'll catch one if you fish long enough at jetties or piers. You might catch a bigger one if you are lucky enough to be offshore in the waters near reefs. Aside from that, these fish are pretty hard to find from any commercial boats, seafood companies, or grocery stores.

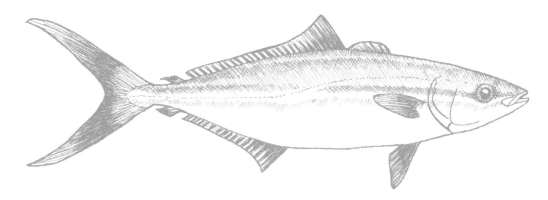

RAINBOW RUNNER

Elagatis bipinnulata

HABITAT: The Rainbow Runner is a highly pelagic blue-water fish.

RANGE/DISTRIBUTION: It lives throughout the world in temperate and tropical oceans and seas.

DESCRIPTION: A sleeker carangid, the Rainbow Runner is torpedo shaped, with a tail ending in a sharp fork. The top of the body is gray or dark blue, ending in a narrow horizontal band of dull gold spanning the length of the fish, which is interrupted by a bright blue band along the body, which is then followed by another band of bright blue, and finally, by a band of bright yellow. The underside is completely white, and the tail is dull gold. The pattern of bands may be different on some fish, but there is no mistaking this fish for another. They range in size from a pound to more than ten, though the most common landed size is between three and six pounds.

EATING: This fish is as delicious as it is frustrating. The Rainbow Runner is a famously inconsistent fish. Sometimes the meat is as firm as that of an amberjack; other times it falls apart like the meat of a Ladyfish. Sometimes, the flesh is beige; sometimes pink; sometimes as red as Bigeye Tuna; very rarely a dark haunting magenta—as magenta as a swatch of paint in a hardware store.

Provided the meat is firm enough, the Rainbow Runner makes superlative eating. Most jacks are a bit fatty, but only the Rainbow Runner (among wild, not farmed jacks) leaves one's hand glistening with fat. Even on smaller fish, bellies usually show signs of marbling. They are wonderful on the grill or roasted, but this is not a fish for frying or poaching. The Rainbow Runner is also a great fish to eat raw.

AVAILABILITY: Due to both its pelagic nature and preference for blue water, the Rainbow Runner is seldom caught by either commercial or recreational fishers. Those with whom we have spoken universally declared this fish among the smartest—if a couple are caught, the rest generally stop biting. Even if a fisher catches a decent load, the fish does not do well with any mishandling at all. Some fish, like snappers, are forgiving; Rainbow Runners are not. Slight fluctuations in temperature or ice coverage, rough handling, improper storage positions—all of these can and do destroy Rainbow Runners.

This is not a fish to look for, but it is definitely a fish to grab if the opportunity arises. If you should catch your own, slaughter it using the ike jime method, which does wonders for this fish especially.

CHAPTER 5
GREAT AND SMALL PELAGIC FISH

Tunas and Mackerels (Scombridae) and Herrings (Clupeidae)

The Scombridae and Clupeidae are two families rather easy to describe. All are more or less elliptically shaped, coming to points at the snout and caudal peduncle (the bit at the end of the body, right before the tail). All are fast-swimming pelagic fish. All have stronger-tasting fatty to oily flesh.

Most of us are familiar with at least several of the species in this family. Yellowfin Tuna has been a staple at middle- to high-end restaurants for years (though often called Ahi because the exotic commands a premium price); Bluefin Tunas abound at every Japanese restaurant that can pay the price; and all of the cans of tuna on the shelves of supermarkets across the country contain Albacore, Yellowfin, or (less commonly) Skipjack.

Other species, though, are either not generally as familiar along the western Gulf coast or are considered at best bait and at worst a nuisance. We happen to think that these lesser-known and lesser-appreciated species are among the best eating fish around. We eat any of these whenever we can, and the kids are always happy to see them gracing the table.

As for the herrings, anchovies, and sardines, one either loves them or can't stand even the smell of them. We eat sardines and anchovies regularly and think that everyone should as well; we eat rather less herring, though this fact should not reflect on herring. (PJ admits he finds digging through herring bones to be a bit tiresome. Apple, having grown up catching and eating little bony fish, just shakes her head, laughs, and helps herself to PJ's share.)

We do not describe in this chapter the Tarpon—it is a protected species and may only be fished recreationally and only catch-and-release at that (which means, in our opinion, that no one should be trying to catch them at all). Besides that, Tarpon, the world's largest herring, has none of the taste of its smaller cousins but more of the bones (at least according to Alan Davidson, to whom we always defer when we've reached the limit of our fish-eating knowledge). We also do not cover the two Gulf shads, the Alabama Shad (*Alosa alabamae*) and the Skipjack Herring (*Alosa chrysochloris*), nor the Bonefish (*Albula vulpes*). While they may occasionally swim into our part of the Gulf, they are rare indeed.

YELLOWFIN, BIGEYE, AND ATLANTIC BLUEFIN TUNAS

Thunnus albacares, Thunnus obesus, and *Thunnus thynnus*

HABITAT: All three of these tunas are highly pelagic blue-water species.

RANGE/DISTRIBUTION: Both the Yellowfin and the Bigeye are worldwide species, swimming in most of the temperate and tropical seas and oceans of the world (neither is as common in Mediterranean waters).

There are four species of Bluefin Tuna: the Atlantic (our local species), the Pacific (*Thunnus orientalis*), the Southern (*Thunnus maccoyii*), and the Longtail (*Thunnus tonggol*). These four species together range over a larger area than either the Yellowfin or the Bigeye. The Atlantic species is found broadly in all temperate and tropical parts of the Atlantic Ocean, the Gulf of Mexico, and the Caribbean and Mediterranean Seas.

DESCRIPTION: All three of these fish are closely related, and at a casual glance, each may, depending on the age of the fish in question, be mistaken for either of the other two. All three share the same body type, being ovoid and deep bodied, with a sharply pointed snout and a powerful caudal fin. All three species sport a pale greenish-yellow-gold band from eye to tail that fades in all species quickly after death. All three species are apex predators and thus obviously swim powerfully, quickly, and continuously.

Body coloration varies little between the three species. The Bluefin sports dots on its belly, but aside from that, all three species have white to blue-gray to silver bellies, gray to black to blue backs, and silvery heads.

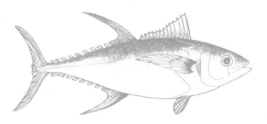

Of the three, the Yellowfin is by far the most commonly fished and the most easily distinguished. Its bright yellow second dorsal fin and anal fin are elongated and sickle shaped; the same yellow covers the back finlets, which line the top and bottom of the caudal peduncle and terminate at the tail. The pectoral fins stretch past the first prominent dorsal fin. Commercial boats target (and grade) fish weighing at least sixty pounds (headed and gutted); those weighing forty to sixty pounds (called "footballs" in the trade) typically do not merit grading and command a lower price. In the sea (swimming blissfully unaware, head and guts still intact), the Yellowfin may exceed several hundred pounds.

The Bigeye certainly seems to fit the role of middle child. Not as showy as the (slightly) smaller Yellowfin, the Bigeye has only moderately long dorsal and anal fins, and while one may see some yellow on those fins, the color appears to have been hastily and unevenly applied. The same careless paint job is in evidence on the finlets. While the Bigeye does sport larger eyes than its cousins, the difference in size does not seem great enough to merit nomenclature. Pectoral fins are as long as those of the Yellowfin. Bigeyes constitute a very small percentage of total tuna catches in the Gulf. They aren't rare so much as rarely caught (they live and hunt deeper in the water column than Yellowfins do). The commercial fleet out of Louisiana catches them rarely enough that a landing is a big deal. Bigeyes grow a little larger on average than Yellowfins, and common market size starts at around eighty pounds (headed and gutted).

The Bluefin may be recognized by its short pectoral fins, its lack of any splashy color, its mottled belly, and most of all its size (several hundred to a thousand pounds). If you happen to be looking at various whole tunas one day, you will probably not need to remember what kind of fin a Bluefin has, for size alone will tell the tale. They can be gigantic. Once, as a tuna boat was unloading, the captain mentioned that they had hooked a Bluefin, but that after it was hooked, it had been attacked by sharks and as a result was in no shape to market. While the fish was a loss, he did save the roe for me. The two lobes together weighed a little over twenty-six pounds. We've never been lucky enough to see a local Bluefin whole right out of the water and have seen commercial specimens only a few times over the years. The largest of these weighed over six hundred pounds headed and gutted, each top loin weighing about one hundred pounds.

EATING: We think tunas owe their gustatory reputation to the fact that the meat doesn't handle, cook, or taste like fish. We do not mean to imply that tuna is like terrestrial meat, either; rather, that tuna can do what no other meat or fish can do—simultaneously recall land and sea by not recalling either exactly.

Yellowfin meat requires little description, for it is the tuna we all know—red, steaky, prone to overcooking and drying out. Bigeye meat is darker, fattier, and softer. The soft texture makes it preferred for sushi, but most chefs shy away from Bigeye for other applications. Bluefin is a class unto itself. Top loins are dark red and oily (though not generally with a great deal of marbling in top loin flesh), resulting in a richer "tuna" flavor. The back of the bottom loins is the same. It is the belly meat that distinguishes Bluefin Tuna from any other fish in the sea. On adult fish, bellies are several inches thick at the thinnest spots. The meat in the fattiest section of the belly does not look (or taste) like fish at all, but rather like well-marbled beef.

Regarding the various grades of tuna, only a grade of #1 means anything, and even then, only if the grader and processor are knowledgeable enough to decide the matter. A tuna that is truly #1 will have flesh that is a certain ruby-red shade throughout, with no darker patches anywhere; the flesh will be fatty enough to rub off onto your finger in a certain way; the sun will shine through a thin sliver in a particular manner. The problem is that a #2 tuna or even a #3 may be just as fresh. The grade has to do with the attributes of a specific individual, not necessarily with freshness at all. We say: ignore grades (unless you need the fish for sashimi), and concentrate on quality.

AVAILABILITY: Gulf-caught Yellowfin Tuna does not often show up at the retail level, but, at least in Houston, it is available to restaurants—but only from the best fish-mongers. Yet even without a local fishery, Yellowfin remains the most commonly marketed tuna, so sourcing should not be a problem.

Good luck finding Gulf Bigeye Tuna.

Regarding the Bluefin, in the Gulf, only Yellowfin Tuna boats ever catch them commercially, and regulations restrict most potential catches. No boat may target Blue-fin, but it may retain one for every two thousand pounds of Yellowfin already on board. Also, commercial tuna boats are required to use "weak" hooks. These hooks are strong enough to catch Yellowfin but usually bend straight under the weight of very large fish like Bluefins, which allows the fish to escape. Together, commercial tuna boats in the Gulf bring in fewer than a dozen Bluefins a year. If you see US Gulf Bluefin Tuna, buy some and enjoy it with a clean conscience.

BLACKFIN AND ALBACORE TUNA

Thunnus atlanticus and *Thunnus alalunga*

COMMON NAME: Albacore Tuna: White Tuna

HABITAT: Both species are pelagic, blue-water travelers.

RANGE/DISTRIBUTION: The Blackfin is confined to temperate and tropical waters of the western Atlantic, including the Gulf of Mexico and the Caribbean Sea. The Albacore is a global wanderer like the Yellowfin and Bigeye and may be found alongside those fish in all warmer seas and oceans.

DESCRIPTION: Both of these species are true tunas, and as such resemble to a great degree their larger, previously described cousins, including the quickly fading band of prismatic color from eye to tail. Both of

these species are much smaller, with the Blackfin being the smallest true tuna. The Albacore's most defining characteristics are its elongated pectoral fins, which stretch for more than half the length of the body. The Blackfin looks like every other tuna but is distinguished by its color—every fin and every finlet is black—and its size.

Albacore can weigh upward of seventy pounds, though the common catch is more likely to weigh from twenty to thirty pounds (fifteen to twenty-five pounds headed and gutted). A giant Blackfin would weigh about fifty pounds; the vast majority swimming and being caught are less than twenty-five pounds live (about seventeen pounds headed and gutted).

EATING: While Albacore meat can be dark red, it's usually closer to the beige of a large jack, though with the familiar tuna shape and texture. Albacore Tuna constitutes significant fisheries across the world, and for good reason. It is the most versatile of the tunas. In the United States, vast amounts of Albacore are consumed—most of it out of cans.

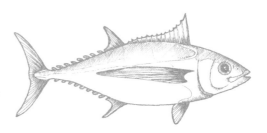

Blackfin is the wallflower among tunas: fast-living, fast-growing, and unobtrusive in its eating habits. Sometimes loins are blood red; other times they are beige, even approaching brown. If you are looking for a tuna akin to Yellowfin, look somewhere else. The taste is not exactly consistent, but it is always good. We love eating Blackfin, especially when we can get little guys weighing less than ten pounds—they are perfect for spit-roasting (a whole tuna cooked thusly is impressive, no matter the size). Both of these tunas take well to salting, smoking, and preserving.

AVAILABILITY: Albacore shows up frequently in seafood sections in supermarkets in larger cities. Sometimes it is marketed fresh, though we recommend exploring frozen forms as well—these are often better handled and stored than fresh product, whereas cut pieces of fresh tuna have a limited shelf life (see page 206 for more on frozen fish).

Blackfin, despite being the most numerous true tuna in Atlantic and Gulf waters, does not now constitute any kind of fishery. Those catches that do cross the dock are quite small and completely incidental to targeted fish. Consequently, even if you find a local Blackfin Tuna for sale, it will more than likely have suffered in handling and is probably older than it should be.

Instead, make friends with someone with a boat who recreationally fishes pelagically, and tell them you would be happy to take Blackfins off their hands. More than likely, you will find yourself inundated with fish. Or learn to catch your own, which will require access to an expensive boat.

SPANISH AND KING MACKEREL

Scomberomorus maculatus and *Scomberomorus cavalla*

COMMON NAME: King Mackerel: Kingfish

HABITAT: The Spanish Mackerel lives in shallow nearshore waters but is still very much a pelagic fish; the King, on the other hand, might visit inshore waters but is a much more common figure on reefs and around structures, in water a bit bluer.

RANGE/DISTRIBUTION: Neither species has an extensive range. The Spanish is limited to the waters of the Gulf, western Caribbean, and Atlantic coast up through New England. The King has the same approximate northern limit but is more widely spread around the Caribbean and South American coastal waters.

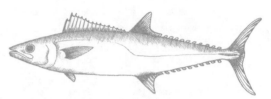

DESCRIPTION: These are closely related species—so much so that juvenile King Mackerels are almost indistinguishable from adult Spanish Mackerels. The snouts of both are pointed, and both have small heads and large mouths filled with dagger-sharp teeth. Bodies are elongated and have powerful swimming muscles. Caudal fins are deeply forked; other fins are small. Juveniles of both species have gold spots running from head to tail. These spots fade completely in King Mackerel, whereas they stay bright throughout the Spanish Mackerel's life. The best way to differentiate between these two species is size—Spanish Mackerels almost always weigh less than five pounds, and almost never reach ten pounds. King Mackerels, on the other hand, can easily weigh dozens of pounds, and very large fish can come close to one hundred pounds.

The other way to tell the difference between species is by knowing where the fish was caught. Spanish Mackerels will come close enough to shore that people fishing from piers catch them. King Mackerels do come quite close inshore in the summertime, but generally not close enough to be caught from land.

EATING: While both species are more than fit for the table, only the Spanish Mackerel enjoys a widespread reputation as a food fish. We are honestly a bit flummoxed by this, for they taste about the same. The King gets bigger, so it stands to reason that the flesh of larger Kings would taste stronger and perhaps be darker. The meat of Spanish (and juvenile King) Mackerel is much paler than one would expect for a mackerel—though not quite as pale as the Wahoo. Adult King Mackerel meat is closer to beige and sometimes translucent gray. The meat is flavorful and fatty, though not at all oily; even larger Kings don't taste fishy. Both fish are very easy to fillet, and the King cuts nicely into steaks. They are excellent fish to cook on the grill, in a pan, or in the oven.

AVAILABILITY: Both of these fish may easily be found in larger cities, though rarely to never will they come from local waters. The local King Mackerel fishery is small and inconsistent, a consequence of limited market demand and low price. No targeted local commercial Spanish Mackerel fishery exists.

Unfortunately, given the delicate nature and short shelf-life of mackerel meat, quality is always an issue with King Mackerel. It's easier to find better-quality Spanish Mackerel, but only because it is a fish commonly marketed frozen (see page 206 for more on frozen fish).

Provided one has access to the water at the right time, both of these fish are easy to catch trolling from boats or (in the case of the Spanish Mackerel) using floating midwater rigs from land. Should you try to catch your own Spanish Mackerel, we suggest that you use wire leaders (for the razor teeth of the Spanish will slice through most monofilament) and have a lot of ice ready. These are, after all, mackerel, and mackerel do not tolerate postharvest abuse.

ATLANTIC CHUB MACKEREL
Scomber colias

COMMON NAMES: Tinker, Tinker Mac, Tinker Mackerel

HABITAT: This species lives in open blue waters, coming slightly closer to shore in warmer months.

RANGE/DISTRIBUTION: The Atlantic Chub Mackerel occurs in warm temperate waters on both sides of the Atlantic, including everywhere in the Gulf of Mexico, the Mediterranean, and the Black Sea. This species is replaced in more northern waters by the Atlantic Mackerel (*Scomber scombrus*) and in Pacific waters by the Pacific Mackerel (*Scomber japonicus*).

DESCRIPTION: This is the archetypal mackerel (or at least as close as we get to it here in the Gulf): a small head, with a pointed snout and large eyes, sits atop a torpedo of a body that ends in a V-shaped tail. While a giant might weigh more than a pound, most weigh half that. The head is copper and silver, the

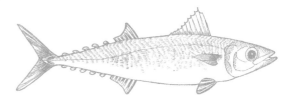

belly is white, and the back is blue green to gray (the greener it is, the fresher, and an emerald back is a sure sign of a good fish; such an emerald-colored mackerel is known in the seafood business as a "greenback").

From head to tail, irregular vertical black stripes and dots splash down the back.

EATING: We lack the superlatives with which to properly describe this mackerel. It is our desert island fish. It's also our workhorse fish. It is ridiculously nutritious and delicious. It's quite easy to fillet, but we never even do that. We grill or roast it whole, then pick the fish to bare bones.

AVAILABILITY: These fish swim in vast schools around the Gulf, but there is no commercial fishery. Very rarely, an enterprising fisher jigs a few, but the price at the dock is nowhere near enough to justify targeting these mackerels.

The Atlantic Mackerel is readily available at larger supermarkets and seafood markets in big cities. Sometimes the fish is displayed fresh at the counter, but make no mistake: almost all Atlantic Mackerel sold at the retail level has been previously frozen. At the grocery store, you might as well just buy the fish still frozen—it will be of better quality. Exceedingly few fish markets carry high-quality fresh mackerel.

WAHOO

Acanthocybium solandri

COMMON NAMES: Guajo (American Spanish), Ono (Hawaiian)

HABITAT: Though mostly known as a blue-water species, the Wahoo migrates much closer to shore during summer months.

RANGE/DISTRIBUTION: Wahoos can be found in all temperate and tropical oceans and seas of the world.

DESCRIPTION: The Wahoo looks like a giant mackerel, which it is. It is, in fact, the largest mackerel swimming the seas. Small Wahoos

weigh more than ten pounds, and larger ones can easily surpass one hundred. The head is proportionately longer and larger than smaller mackerels, and the teeth are more impressive as well. The Wahoo shares the torpedo shape common to all mackerels, though perhaps in a more perfected form. The tail is a normal mackerel tail writ large—power and grace in equal parts. Freshly caught, Wahoos have silvery bodies and bluish silver backs, with vertical black tiger stripes running from head to tail. After death, the color quickly fades to a brushed chrome, but the stripes remain.

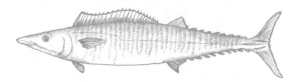

EATING: The Wahoo is much loved by all fish cooks, for the meat is mild enough to please even finicky fish eaters and fatty enough to handle some overcooking. The fillets are steaky and should be handled thusly—in other words, cook them on the grill or in the oven, but stay away from the fryer. The Wahoo has a long and muscular tail, which lends itself beautifully to steaks.

AVAILABILITY: Wahoo is commonly available at the restaurant level, less so at the retail level. At higher-end markets, you might see a fish called Ono. This is a Wahoo, just called by its Hawaiian name. Most Asian markets of any size carry Wahoo as well. Local Wahoo is seldom available—the fishery here is incidental at best. Occasionally a boat will target them during summer, but even then, the catch is only a few hundred pounds. Wahoo is a game fish of excellent repute, so if you have a boat that travels dozens of miles offshore, then you are in luck. The rest of us have to make do with occasional treats.

TUNA COUSINS: SKIPJACK TUNA AND LITTLE TUNNY

Katsuwonus pelamis and *Euthynnus alletteratus*

COMMON NAME: Little Tunny: Bonita

HABITAT: Both species are open-ocean pelagic fish, though the Little Tunny tends to be a bit more sedentary.

RANGE/DISTRIBUTION: The Skipjack swims all warm seas of the world, whereas the Little Tunny sticks to the Atlantic Ocean (where it is found up and down the coasts of the Americas, Africa, and Europe).

DESCRIPTION: These two species are typically tuna-shaped fish (though neither, common names notwithstanding, is better than a relative to true tunas). The two look much alike, though the Skipjack can reach as much as twenty pounds or more, whereas the Little Tunny usually weighs less than ten, and never more than thirty. Most commercially or recreationally caught Skipjacks and Little Tunnies weigh around ten to fifteen pounds. The bodies of both are more or less silver, and each has patterns and dots distinctive to the species. The Little Tunny has a few randomly placed black spots on the front belly near the pectoral fins, and a series of dots and swirls on the back. The patterns on the back start at the base of the dorsal fins and continue to the lateral line, where they cease abruptly. The back of a freshly dead Little Tunny is bright blue, almost turquoise; this color fades to silver within a day or two, even with the best handling. The Skipjack has a darker back, devoid of spots. Instead, bold irregular stripes run horizontally from right behind the pectoral fins, continue down the belly, and terminate at the tail.

EATING: The Little Tunny suffers from a bad (though undeserved) reputation. The meat is much darker than Yellowfin Tuna meat and is also more insipid and oilier. The dark meat is extensive and looks more like pork liver than anything else. It also has a lot of blood. All of these traits make the Little Tunny a conundrum, but a tasty one at that. The dark meat, like that of the Crevalle Jack, makes excellent jerky, and is also quite nice marinated and grilled like a piece of beef. The main muscle meat is passable when grilled but tends to dry out. Overall, wet cooking (soups, curries, even stews) or preserving (confit, etc.) are best for Little Tunny. After all, tuna salad doesn't really require tuna, just meaty, fatty fish.

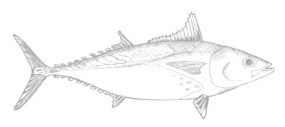

The Skipjack Tuna, while not enjoying much reputation one way or the other locally, is quite an important food fish in other waters. Most Skipjack consumed in the United States comes from the canned goods shelf. In Japan, it is used to produce *bonito*, the dried fish that is shaved into broths and over dishes. Fresh Skipjack Tuna is a spectacular table fish, almost the inverse of the Little Tunny in terms of immediate tastiness and as perfect for the grill as Little Tunny is problematic.

AVAILABILITY: Some local commercial boats might catch and cut up both of these fish for bait, but almost none would waste ice and hold space on either. The few boats that keep Little Tunny usually do so to use them as part of the crew's share of fish. (Most commercial boats in Texas don't keep a portion of the fish for the crew's personal use. In fact, almost none do, the exceptions being those boats owned, captained, and crewed by Vietnamese immigrants. The crew's share would never consist of targeted species, but always bycatch; and this share was never directly sold by the boats, but rather parceled out among the crew and their families. Unfortunately for us, the fish they always kept for themselves were the very fish we really wanted to buy.) Little Tunny is just about always available at larger Asian supermarkets, but the quality is not always what one would desire (like all fatty fish, the Little Tunny spoils quickly if not handled properly). Recreational fishers sometimes target Little Tunny for the sport of the catch or for

ATLANTIC BONITO

Sarda sarda

HABITAT: Like every other scombrid, the Atlantic Bonito is a pelagic species. Most of the fish in the mackerel family live somewhere in the top of the water column (down to about two hundred feet), and though the Bonito is certainly comfortable there, it also swims quite a bit deeper, to six hundred feet or more.

RANGE/DISTRIBUTION: This species is a straggler in the Gulf of Mexico. While reports are not uncommon, this is not a fish that exists in large numbers in our waters. More stable populations exist throughout the temperate Atlantic, as well as in the Mediterranean and Black Seas.

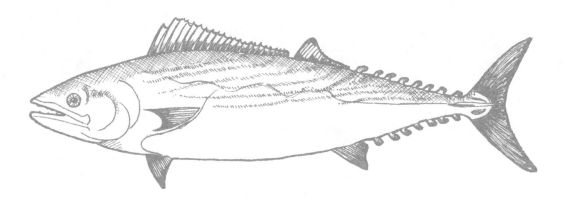

bait purposes, but almost never to eat the fish itself.

Skipjack Tuna is generally available in most larger cities, but *never* is it commercially fished in our part of the Gulf.

DESCRIPTION: The Atlantic Bonito (the name is a Spanish word; this fish has nothing to do with the Japanese dried Skipjack product of the same name [see the preceding entry]) has the snout of a mackerel and a short, cigar-shaped body. It's smaller than both the Skipjack and Little Tunny, but otherwise looks like those fish. And as with those fish, the patterns on the body are the quickest way to identify which species is which. The Bonito has thinner black stripes, less irregular than those of the Skipjack. The stripes start at about the lateral line, from which they run diagonally up at about a thirty-degree angle toward the back. Coloration tends to more muted silvers and chromes.

EATING: The Atlantic Bonito is a delight of a fish, the enjoyment of which is frustrated by the fact that it is always a sporadic catch by any boat. The meat is opaque and surprisingly pale for a scombrid. The flesh is neither too fatty nor too oily, but instead strikes a perfect balance between the two. Bonito takes to just about any method of cooking—even frying—but we prefer it with other rich, full flavors like saffron, fennel, or pepper.

AVAILABILITY: This is not a fish you are going to find easily or often. Large harvests are typical throughout this fish's range, but little of that fish reaches us. Some Asian markets carry Bonito, but only occasionally. Locally, the picture is not much better, for this is a fish rarely landed by commercial boats and even more rarely marketed. The few times we came across Bonitos, they had come off Vermilion Snapper or, less rarely, amberjack boats.

SPANISH SARDINE

Sardinella aurita

COMMON NAME: Round Sardinella

HABITAT: This species occurs in open waters from nearshore to the deep blue waters far offshore, always in schools, which can be vast.

RANGE/DISTRIBUTION: The Spanish Sardine can be found on both sides of the Atlantic: in the western Atlantic, from Argentina almost to Canada and throughout the Gulf

of Mexico; in the eastern Atlantic, from the Mediterranean Sea down to South Africa.

DESCRIPTION: Large eyes dominate an otherwise small head in this sardine. The cigar-shaped body is silver from the belly to the lateral line, where blues, greens, and grays dominate. Color is darkest on the back at the base of the dorsal fins. All fins are dark gray and unremarkable. A similar species, the Brazilian Sardine (*Sardinella brasiliensis*) also swims in Gulf waters, but it is even more uncommon than the Spanish.

EATING: Many fish claim the name "sardine." All are in the same family and are similar in appearance, but they are not equal in terms of edibility. Larger species are full of bones, and the meat is coarse (not that this deters us from eating them when we have the opportunity). The Spanish Sardine is thankfully one of the smaller species, rarely exceeding five ounces. It is bonier than the best of the sardines, but the situation is manageable. Grill these with good olive oil, or roast them at a high temperature, also with good olive oil.

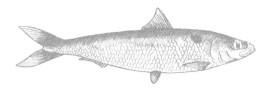

AVAILABILITY: While Spanish Sardines do swim in our waters, Gulf populations are concentrated in the eastern Gulf and beyond. At various times, commercial fisheries have existed there, but more than likely any American Gulf fishery in existence now is predominantly for bait purposes. Seafood companies sell sardines (from other waters obviously), and some grocery stores and seafood markets do as well. In Texas, sardines of whatever provenance have a limited market, so inventory tends not to move quickly, which means quality is always an issue.

GULF MENHADEN

Brevoortia patronus

COMMON NAMES: Shad, Pogy

HABITAT: The Gulf Menhaden swims in nearshore and inshore waters, sometimes in vast schools.

RANGE/DISTRIBUTION: This species is limited to the Gulf of Mexico, where it is ubiquitous.

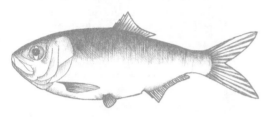

DESCRIPTION: A Gulf Menhaden hauled up in a net (and only a net, for that is the only way it may be caught) is a shiny enough little fish—chromed on the sides, with mustard-colored fins and tail. It has a single large irregular black dot right behind the head, followed down the body by other, smaller dots. While most Gulf Menhadens encountered by humans are quite small (ranging from one to several ounces), they can grow to be much more substantial. Shrimpers most often see the large ones, which can weigh close to a pound.

EATING: A member of the herring family (Clupeidae), the Gulf Menhaden is closely related to the Atlantic Menhaden (*Brevoortia tyrannus*); indeed, the two are almost indistinguishable (another Gulf species and close relative, the Threadfin Herring, looks similar as well). The flesh and roe of the Atlantic species was, at one point in the late eighteenth and early nineteenth centuries, considered well worth eating; indeed, a small but obsessively devoted roe fishery along the lower Atlantic seaboard has existed at least for several hundred years. (The Carolinian name is "mammy shad roe." In North Carolina, one can apparently still find fish markets that carry fresh roe every spring for a few brief weeks. Sometime in the past, it had been common in that part of the world to salt whatever roe could not be eaten fresh. The practice has mostly died out, but we would imagine one could find it still if one was very inclined.) For no good or discernible reason, the Gulf species never enjoyed such prestige, and most coastal citizens believe the fish to be inedible—a belief happily not shared by all of us.

With the proper preparation, Gulf Menhadens can make fine eating, though admittedly they are not to everyone's taste. They are, after all, herrings, and thus exceedingly bony and oily (the fat content of their flesh always exceeds 20 percent). Nonetheless, the smaller ones can make outstanding dried fish; the larger may be grilled, baked, steamed, or used in dishes that require fatty fish.

AVAILABILITY: Menhadens in the Gulf are targeted for the bait and reduction fisheries and nothing else. The only way to get ahold of them is to make friends with a shrimper or learn to use a cast net. Of the two options, learning to throw a net might be the easiest, though you will only catch smaller fish. Luckily, Gulf Menhadens swim everywhere inshore and may easily be caught from land. Be warned, however, that those caught from beaches, inlets, and large bays taste better than those caught in small isolated wetland pools (they are filter feeders, so they tend to really taste like where they live).

ATLANTIC THREAD, SCALED, AND RED-EYE ROUND HERRING

Opisthonema oglinum, Harengula jaguana, and *Etrumeus sadina*

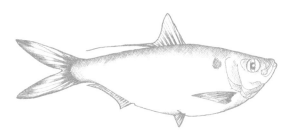

COMMON NAMES: For all species: Herring, Shad

HABITAT: The Red-Eye is the deepest dwelling of these three species, occurring in waters as deep as four hundred feet. The others live in shallow coastal waters, the Scaled in somewhat shallower waters than the Thread, but both are found in a lot of the same places: bays, estuaries, passes, inlets.

RANGE/DISTRIBUTION: All species occur up and down the American Atlantic coast, throughout the Gulf of Mexico and Caribbean Sea, and along the Brazilian coast.

DESCRIPTION: The Atlantic Thread and the Scaled look more or less like the Gulf Menhaden, which is to say they look like upside-down half circles with fins attached. All three are quite thin and small (always weighing less than a pound), the Atlantic Thread being the largest. The Red-Eye looks closer to a sardine than a herring. The Scaled Herring is silver on both its belly and back, with silver to beige to light gray fins. It bears no distinctive traits. Unfortunately, it looks almost exactly like another fish, the False Herring (*Harengula clupeola*), one of the least appetizing members of the Clupeidae family. The two fish look so similar that we tend to consign the lot to bait duty.

The Atlantic Thread is easily distinguishable by its green and turquoise back, the black dot on its shoulders, and the long thread-like filament (for which it is named) sprouting from the back of the dorsal fin.

The Red-Eye has a more compressed body and is cigar shaped. Its eyes are big and reddish.

EATING: If you like herring, you will enjoy eating all of these fish. Of the three, we prefer the Red-Eye, for reasons of size and taste. Grill these fish. Or pickle them. Or ferment them. Or make fish sauce. Do *not* boil or poach. Do not fry. Do not use in most soups.

AVAILABILITY: These species occur sporadically across the seafood supply chain, and absolutely none are from local waters. Herrings in general are marketed, but they are usually prepared in some way. Fresh herring is a little more difficult to acquire, and quality is an eternal problem. As with the Bay Anchovy, Gulf Menhaden, and lots of other fish—catch your own!

STRIPED ANCHOVY

Anchoa hepsetus

COMMON NAME: Cigar Minnow

HABITAT: This anchovy prefers shallow inshore waters, from brackish backwaters to hypersaline lagoons.

RANGE/DISTRIBUTION: The Striped Anchovy is found from the Gulf of Mexico to Maine.

DESCRIPTION: This fish looks like a fishing lure. The head appears to contain nothing more than the huge eyes and a tiny slit for a mouth. The body connected to this head has a slightly deep belly, but aside from that it is roughly rectangular. Fins are nondescript. The skin is translucent enough to see outlines of organs. The only color is the very thick polished-chrome stripe running from the back of the gills to the end of the caudal peduncle. It's a small species, even by anchovy standards, and owing to this, it has never been exploited commercially.

While we describe only the Striped in detail, several other species of anchovy occur

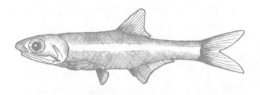

in the Gulf, all of which might end up in a net. The others are the Bay (*Anchoa mitchilli*), the Cuban (*Anchoa cubana*), and the Dusky (*Anchoa lyolepis*). A few others live close to, but not in, the northwestern Gulf. All species

taste equally good, though the Striped and Bay are the largest and easiest to process.

EATING: This is an excellent eating fish, but it is only worth frying and eating whole, bones and all (you won't even notice crunching).

AVAILABILITY: Shrimpers haul good numbers of anchovies up sometimes, but those fish rarely make it to any markets. There are no directed fisheries in the Gulf, and thus the Striped Anchovy is not available at the restaurant or retail level.

If you know where to go, you can catch your own with a cast net, bearing in mind, though, that anchovies taste like the waters in which they swim. If you catch them in a muddy bayou, they will taste like muddy bayou. So only eat them if the water you caught them in was running clear.

CHAPTER 6

SNAPPERS (LUTJANIDAE)

Anyone living within a hundred miles of the western Gulf of Mexico knows the name "Snapper." Most of the time it refers to only one species, the Red. Among commercial fishers, the word "Snapper" means *only* Red Snapper; all of the other species are called by lesser names.

Most Gulf-dwelling members of the snapper family are in the genus *Lutjanus*. A smaller number are in the genus *Pristipomoides* (of this number, only one, the Cardinal Snapper, is described here, the rest being too small or rare). Two other species, the Vermilion and Yellowtail, are in their own genus (*Rhomboplites* and *Ocyurus* respectively), of which they are the only living representatives.

Most species of Gulf snappers are highly edible, and the majority support fisheries, large or small, somewhere. Some, like the Black (*Apsilus dentatus*), Schoolmaster (*Lutjanus apodus*), Cubera (*Lutjanus cyanopterus*), and Caribbean Red Snapper (*Lutjanus purpureus*) simply do not occur in our waters in enough numbers to be caught with any regularity. We suspect they all occur somewhere in the northwestern Gulf, but we didn't describe them here.

RED SNAPPER

Lutjanus campechanus

COMMON NAMES: Snapper, Huachinango (Mexico)

HABITAT: This species swims from thirty to eighty miles offshore, in water fifty to two hundred feet deep. All snappers like structures or reefs, and the Red is no exception.

RANGE/DISTRIBUTION: Red Snappers swim throughout shallower waters of the Gulf of Mexico and Caribbean Sea, as well as down the coast of Central America and the northeast coast of South America to Brazil. They also live on the lower US Atlantic coast, though they are few and far between north of the Carolinas. Atlantic populations have always been tenuous relative to those in more southerly waters, since Red Snapper is most at home in tropical waters.

DESCRIPTION: Let us consider the Red Snapper the blueprint for all lutjanid species. Let us also admit that this is an arbitrary designation, for the Red is no more the archetype than the Mangrove (*Lutjanus griseus*) or the

Lane (*Lutjanus synagris*). But if we are at all familiar with any snapper, it will be the Red. Besides, most lutjanid species look pretty much the same. Color, size, and teeth seem to be the main points of differentiation.

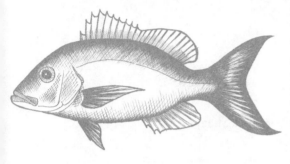

While they are only one member of the family in the Gulf, Red Snappers are the most dominant. They exist in large numbers, they are aggressive, and they live in places that are relatively easy to fish (as opposed to a snapper like the Cardinal Snapper [*Pristipomoides macrophthalmus*], which typically lives in one thousand feet of water).

The head is not particularly large, but neither is it tiny. It sports red eyes with large black pupils, as well as the full lips typical of all snappers. The body is slightly compressed, but certainly longer than it is taller. The dorsal fin is supported by long, sharp spines common to all snappers, and pectoral fins are similarly armed. A broom tail finishes the picture.

The belly is white, gradually fading into pink then red along the back and fins. Color is most concentrated along the top part of the fish, above the lateral line. Younger fish have a blurry blackish dot on the lower back directly above the anal fin, which fades with age and size.

In the mid-twentieth century, snapper boats routinely landed snappers weighing more than fifteen pounds, and around seven pounds was the average weight. By the early twenty-first century, the average size had dwindled to closer to two pounds. These days, the average size seems to be around four to five pounds, at least according to what boats are unloading in Texas waters. Recreational fishers tend to bring in larger fish (five to thirty pounds), though this might have more to do with bag limits than anything else. (If one is only allowed to keep two snappers, one might be encouraged to keep throwing fish back in hopes of catching the big one. This sounds great in theory, but considering the mortality rates of thrown-back fish, it does not make a lot of practical sense.) Away from human interaction, Red Snappers live for many decades and can weigh scores of pounds.

The skin and scales are usually quite red to red orange, though sometimes they are closer to pink; more rarely, they may be mostly white, with a faint pink sheen. According to fishers, some of the difference in coloration has to do with age, sex, and diet. While this certainly makes sense, we would do well to focus on the qualifier in that argument: "some." The overriding factor in the color of a dead Red Snapper is harvest and postharvest handling. Sun, heat, fresh water, and length of time from catch to death all have an immediate and direct effect on the color of a Red Snapper. The fish needs to come out of the water quickly; it needs to die quickly; it needs to get cold very quickly and thoroughly. (This is true for all fish and seafood of course, but Red Snapper is so common, the point is more easily made.) The red parts of the fish should look closer to a mostly ripe strawberry. Red washed out almost to the color of gray is not right. Pink is acceptable, though certainly not ideal.

EATING: The Red Snapper seems to be the apogee of accessible and appetizing fish, at least according to most of the population of the northwestern Gulf Coast. No other local fish can command the price and respect that is so readily bestowed on the Red Snapper.

Basically, anything that one can think to do with white fish can be done with Red Snapper. The cooked meat is moist and white with a large flake. While it has all the regular fish bones, it is not excessively bony. The skin is among the tastiest of fish skins (though not, perhaps, superior to that of the Vermilion Snapper).

AVAILABILITY: Red Snapper is among the easiest fish to find in Texas grocery stores; it is also among the priciest.

Pay attention to where the fish comes from. You should buy only US Red Snapper—different countries have different fisheries regulations, and US Gulf regulations provide the most sustainable management anywhere in the Red Snapper's range.

VERMILION SNAPPER

Rhomboplites aurorubens

COMMON NAME: B-liner (colloquial)

HABITAT: The Vermilion Snapper lives in water from about one hundred to close to one thousand feet and is usually associated with structures or reefs. Vermilion Snappers tend to "cloud up," or congregate, over such features.

RANGE/DISTRIBUTION: This species of snapper can be found from the northern limits of the Carolinas, through to the southern coast of Brazil. The largest populations are in the Gulf and the Caribbean Sea.

DESCRIPTION: The Vermilion Snapper is the only living representative of the genus *Rhomboplites*. As such, it hardly resembles any other snapper (except for the Yellowtail Snapper, described below, which is also the single living representative of its genus,

Ocyurus chrysurus; perhaps these genera are the modern representatives of the original "snapper" form, or perhaps the similarity is coincidence). The red eyes are relatively large and set in a small head. The fish itself is quite small, with large adults rarely weighing more than five pounds (common market size is just under two pounds). The tail is gently forked. In young fish, the body is skinny and tapered. Adult fish are rounded out a bit and have rather large bellies.

Vermilion Snappers are the exact color advertised—bright reddish orange. Thin horizontal stripes stretch from tail to head. These stripes are usually yellow, sometimes blue, sometimes green. The fins are usually vermilion, sometimes brighter red.

EATING: Vermilion Snapper is unequivocally the best snapper to cook whole and almost as unequivocally the best snapper to eat raw. Fillets might not deserve such superlatives, but they are quite lovely as well.

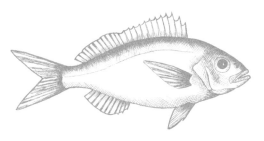

AVAILABILITY: This species is commonly available in larger markets in larger cities. Generally, such offerings are from American Gulf waters, but not always. Quality is an issue, as always. Not too many Texas boats target Vermilion Snapper anymore, and those that do are generally doing so only as an auxiliary to Red Snapper, which is the mainstay.

Beware: Vermilion Snapper is commonly sold as Red Snapper. This is fraud, whether it is intentional or not on the part of the sellers.

MANGROVE AND DOG SNAPPER

Lutjanus griseus and *Lutjanus jocu*

COMMON NAMES: Mangrove Snapper: Mango Snapper, Gray Snapper, Black Snapper

HABITAT: Both of these species live in relatively shallow waters, especially places with vegetation (mangroves in more southerly reaches, hence the name), reefs, and structures. Young fish of the species live very close inshore, with adults residing a bit farther out.

RANGE/DISTRIBUTION: The Mangrove Snapper ranges from the Carolinas through northern South American Atlantic waters, being most common in the northern Gulf of Mexico and Caribbean Sea. The Dog Snapper tends to be a more southerly species and is far more common in Mexican and Caribbean waters.

DESCRIPTION: While all snappers have teeth of some sort, the Mangrove's are prominent, and those of the Dog Snapper are downright unnerving. The Mangrove got its name from where it lives; the Dog got its name from those teeth. The teeth distinguish these snappers from others, as the rest of their bodies follow the same snapper blueprint (large lips, sharp spines, broom tail, compressed body).

Differentiating the Dog from the Mangrove, though, requires knowledge of each species' color and size. The Mangrove is usually darker and smaller. Its color runs from maroon to brown to burnt orange to black to gray, never yellow or bright orange.

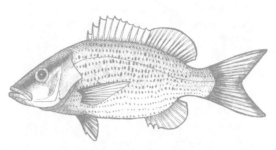

The back is darker, the belly lighter—but not white. Fins are the same rich, muted color as the body. An adult Mangrove may be the better part of two feet long and weigh more than thirty pounds (though a little more than twelve inches and somewhere between three and ten pounds is much more common). Young Mangrove Snappers are lighter and brighter and sometimes have blue stripes on their snouts and faint vertical stripes along the length of their bodies. These stripes fade with age, and a mature adult lacks them completely. Eyes are burnt orange to brown.

The Dog Snapper grows much larger than the Mangrove—it is in fact the largest snapper in our waters. Adults routinely weigh more than twenty pounds, and landings of fish weighing three times that are not uncommon. Where the Mangrove has muted colors, the Dog is painted with oranges, reds, and yellows. Fins all around are yellow or bright orange. The body itself is orange red, shot with yellow and some brown, and more burnt orange than anything else. Vertical stripes, straight or meandering, faint or stark, run along the length of the body, no matter the age of the fish. Eyes are typically red, sometimes more orange.

EATING: Maybe it is this fish's diet (heavy on shellfish and crustaceans), but Mangrove Snapper meat has a more refined taste than most of the other species, and the meat actually cooks whiter than Red Snapper. It is very lean, with very little dark meat, and fillets are the perfect width for cooking in a pan. We have always loved Mangrove Snapper.

Dog Snapper is a fine table fish, but the prodigious size of the fish means that the meat itself can be, if not tough, then certainly chewy. We do not intend criticism with this comment, for everything tastes good if you cook it right. We mention it merely to avoid unpleasant surprises. Aside from texture, Dog Snapper is as good as any other member of the family.

AVAILABILITY: One finds Mangrove Snapper rarely to never in grocery stores. It is a bit more available at the restaurant and distributor level, but any landings in Texas are always bycatch. During warmer months, you can sometimes catch a nice batch of Mangrove Snappers without ever getting on a boat. Just go down to the coast, find a jetty, walk out as far as you can (you will want a longer jetty, like those at Surfside Beach and Freeport, Texas), and start fishing. We suggest doing this near high tide. You can fish on the surface or a few feet down. You might have to let some go before you get one large enough to keep (there are no state size limits for Mangrove Snapper, but you don't want to be keeping babies).

Dog Snapper has been targeted in more southerly waters for a long time, and for that reason one does find it available from time to time at the retail level. At the restaurant and distributor level, Dog Snapper tends to be a placeholder or substitute for Red Snapper and has thus experienced a diminution in reputation. It is delicious for what it is, but a Red Snapper it certainly is not.

Beware: Both of these species are commonly sold as Red Snapper. This is fraud, whether it is intentional or not on the part of the sellers.

LANE SNAPPER

Lutjanus synagris

COMMON NAME: Candy Snapper

HABITAT: The Lane Snapper prefers reefs and grassy, sandy bottoms, from about fifty to one thousand feet of water.

RANGE/DISTRIBUTION: The species is found throughout the Gulf of Mexico and Caribbean Sea down to the northern Atlantic coast of South America. It is common enough in our part of the Gulf, but more so in more southerly waters.

DESCRIPTION: The Lane Snapper is the smallest of commercial snappers in the Gulf, with few landed fish weighing more than four pounds. The body is pale pink red fading to a white belly, with six or seven thick, bright yellow horizontal stripes running from the snout to the caudal peduncle (the fins and tail are identical in shape and color to those of the

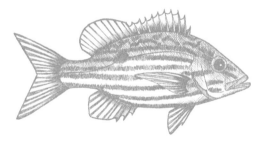

Red Snapper). A large dark blurry dot decorates both sides of the lower back, just below the back dorsal fin. Eyes are red.

EATING: Not only is the Lane Snapper the smallest commercially important snapper; it is also the softest. The meat can gape to the point of falling apart, which is a key reason why Lane Snappers have never garnered a very decent price. The meat itself is a beautiful translucent pink, but fillets are notoriously fickle.

But don't let the soft meat deter you from eating this fish. Simply cook it whole. Because the fish is relatively small, and tends to be quite thin, it's great for frying whole in a pan (or, preferably, a wok).

AVAILABILITY: This fish is common enough at larger Asian markets, though rarely does it come from local Gulf waters. It's a bit easier to find from seafood companies, but again not locally, as Lane Snapper is imported in large quantities from southern Gulf and Caribbean fisheries. Recreational catches off Texas waters are rather sporadic.

Beware: Lane Snapper is commonly sold as Red Snapper. This is fraud, whether it is intentional or not on the part of the sellers.

MUTTON SNAPPER

Lutjanus analis

HABITAT: This species is generally associated with reefs and structures and is found in a hundred feet of water or more.

RANGE/DISTRIBUTION: The Mutton Snapper is an oddball in our waters. It is much more common in the southern Gulf of Mexico and eastern Caribbean Sea.

DESCRIPTION: The Mutton Snapper resembles the Dog and Mangrove Snappers more than other members of the family, though it lacks the oversized teeth. It is a medium-sized fish, reaching perhaps thirty or forty pounds at maturity. Eyes are orange to light red. The belly, pectoral, and anal fins are pink white; this color fades into dark orange, olive, brown, or green all the way to the top of the back. The dorsal fin and tail are orange red.

EATING: We admit our knowledge of this particular fish is limited to a very few

specimens. One of those was a freak catch by a reputable Vermilion Snapper boat, and the fish weighed only about fifteen pounds. We found it delightful on the grill, even if it was a bit coarse (like a large drum). Then

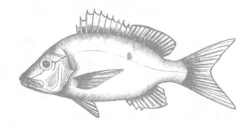

we sliced it into thinner pieces, and it fared much better in clear soup. The other times we saw Mutton Snapper it had arrived from afar in Styrofoam without enough ice packs and so was not worth the bother.

AVAILABILITY: Mutton Snapper is fished commercially in other parts of its range, and most of that catch is either consumed locally or exported as an economical alternative to Red Snapper. It is hard to find a Mutton Snapper worth eating in Texas.

Beware: Mutton Snapper is commonly sold as Red Snapper. This is fraud, whether it is intentional or not on the part of the sellers.

YELLOWTAIL SNAPPER

Ocyurus chrysurus

HABITAT: This species occurs in tropical waters and is frequently associated with reefs in twenty to two hundred feet of water.

RANGE/DISTRIBUTION: The biggest populations (and fisheries) of Yellowtail Snapper are in southern Florida and throughout the Caribbean Sea. In the Gulf of Mexico, populations are sparse and dependent on the presence of appropriate reefs, and the northwestern Gulf has few such places. It is an extremely unusual fish for the northwestern Gulf.

DESCRIPTION: In shape, this fish most resembles the Vermilion Snapper. Do not assume, though, that the two species are ever mistaken for one another. The Vermilion, as described, is red to orange, whereas the Yellowtail is light blue to gray, speckled with neon yellow along the body. A stripe of that same yellow starts at the snout and stretches down the body, increasing in size until it engulfs the tail fin entirely in gleaming yellow.

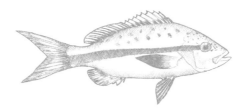

EATING: Unfortunately, the Yellowtail is a soft fish—much softer than the Lane Snapper even—and does not age well at all. As much as we hoped otherwise, we never found this fish to be anything more than satisfactory. Stick to cooking it whole.

AVAILABILITY: The Yellowtail Snapper is available in those areas where it is a targeted fish. In Texas, you will only find this fish occasionally as a sale or special item, in which case there is probably a more predictable fish for sale. Over our time of fishmongering, we saw fewer than five landed by local boats.

BLACKFIN AND SILK SNAPPER

Lutjanus buccanella and *Lutjanus vivanus*

COMMON NAMES: Blackfin: Hambone Snapper; Silk: Yelloweye Snapper

HABITAT: Both species live in deeper waters (down to several hundred feet) on or around reefs and rocky bottoms.

RANGE/DISTRIBUTION: These two snappers occur in the Gulf of Mexico and the Caribbean Sea, both being most common in the eastern Caribbean and Bahamas, with smaller populations in the southern Gulf. Any commercial catches in the northwestern Gulf are stragglers from other waters or from protected reefs.

DESCRIPTION: The Blackfin Snapper is so named because of a ham-shaped black splotch right at the base of the pectoral fins. Aside from that mark, the Blackfin closely resembles the Red Snapper in shape if not in size (the Blackfin at its largest is half as large as an equivalent Red). It tends to be more richly colored, almost scarlet, and the color spreads to the belly. The tail is yellow orange, and the fish has pale yellow eyes.

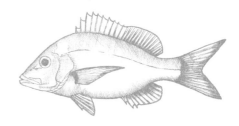

The Silk is painted bright orange from snout to tail, including fins. The very tip of the tail is fringed in black, but this fades after death and is thus not always a useful way to identify the fish. The eyes are the key. They are lemon yellow, noticeably larger than shallower-water snappers, with relatively small pupils. The fish doesn't get to be very big, reaching no more than twenty pounds at most, and usually half that. Whether it has to do with diet or something particular to the species, the Silk is rounder than most snappers—not fat or fatty, just bigger around.

EATING: All snappers taste good, but deep-water snappers taste even better. These two species are somewhere in between. They have all of the flake and white-fish taste one expects from, for example, Red Snapper, with the sweetness of deep, cold-water fish. They are perfect for any snapper dish, whether grilled, fried, baked, or served raw.

AVAILABILITY: No local fisheries exist, and those few fish landed are caught incidentally while targeting Vermilion or Red Snapper. Larger seafood markets and seafood departments sometimes carry these fish, but they are always imported (generally from Caribbean waters).

Beware: Both the Silk and the Blackfin Snapper are commonly sold as Red Snapper. This is fraud, whether it is intentional or not on the part of the sellers.

CARDINAL SNAPPER

Pristipomoides macrophthalmus

COMMON NAMES: Mahogany Snapper, Bigeye Snapper, Wenchman

HABITAT: This is the deepest-dwelling snapper described in this chapter—from six hundred to more than fifteen hundred feet down, nearing the deep end of the continental slope, and mostly in rocky areas.

RANGE/DISTRIBUTION: The species is most common in the southern Gulf of Mexico and Caribbean Sea, but potentially substantial populations live in the deeper waters of the northwestern Gulf as well.

DESCRIPTION: The Cardinal Snapper may grow quite large, but all the specimens that we ever saw weighed less than six pounds. We suspect it is a smaller species. The Cardinal more resembles the Vermilion than the Red, though the body is stouter and the fish itself bigger. The large eyes are the color and luminosity of gold. The body itself is a bright pink orange, flecked with golds and silver, then fringed all around with subtle blue along the base of its fins. Fins are bright neon orange. Some fish are also studded with small bright blue dots. All in all, it is a stunning fish.

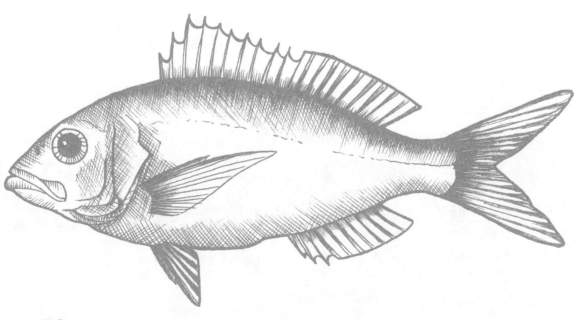

EATING: The raw flesh of most snappers (and indeed most white fish) is pink white and translucent. The flesh of the Cardinal is snow white and opaque, with almost no dark meat. It is excellent eaten raw, but even better cooked as gently as possible (fillets are usually thin enough to cold poach). The meat is sweet, tender, and delicate. This is not a fish to be fried or grilled.

AVAILABILITY: On rare occasions, bottom longline boats targeting Yellowedge Grouper and Golden Tilefish will bring in several hundred pounds of Cardinal Snapper as bycatch. Once we saw a boat unload almost a thousand pounds; catches this big are rare, however.

Yellowedge Grouper and Golden Tilefish like sandy and muddy bottoms, so that is where boats usually lay their lines, typically avoiding rocky areas (ideal Cardinal Snapper grounds) when possible due to the potential for lost gear. Also, these are snappers, and snappers cloud up in schools when feeding (as opposed to groupers and tilefish, which are more solitary ambush hunters). So, a bottom longline, stretching for a mile or more in a straight line, is great for catching solitary fish like groupers. But the same longline isn't as handy for fish that school and move up and down the water column.

We were told on more than one occasion by more than one old salty fisher that this species is quite abundant, enough so that a small-scale fishery is theoretically possible (and potentially lucrative). Unfortunately, the most effective way to fish Cardinal Snappers would be to use vertical gear (bandit rigs used commonly for most snappers), and such gear is awkward in a thousand or more feet of water. So, this wonderful fish remains tantalizingly unavailable at any level. The best analog would be the Hawaiian fish called Opakapaka (*Pristipomoides filamentosus*), a closely related species. It is not as good as the Cardinal Snapper, but it has the distinction of being commercially available.

Forget about recreational fishing, unless you have access to a deepwater boat with deepwater hydraulic reels.

QUEEN SNAPPER

Etelis oculatus

COMMON NAMES: Ball Bat, Silky, Onaga (erroneous—Onaga [*Etelis coruscans*] is in the same genus, looks very similar, but only lives in the central and western Pacific)

HABITAT: This species is associated with rocky bottoms in waters deeper than six hundred feet (though juveniles are often caught in water half that deep).

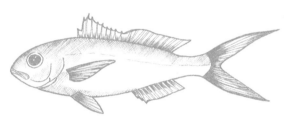

RANGE/DISTRIBUTION: The Queen Snapper is found throughout the Gulf of Mexico and Caribbean Sea, down to Brazilian waters. It also ranges as far north as the Carolinas, though it is quite rare that far north.

DESCRIPTION: The colloquial name Ball Bat gives an indication of what this fish looks like, with the "handle" of the bat being the caudal peduncle (attached to which is a large extravagant V-shaped tail). The head is oversized, rounded, and equipped with red eyes twice the size of any other snapper. The fish tapers severely from head to tail, and its scales are large. The back down to the lateral line is cherry red; below that line the color fades to mostly white, but the belly scales are mottled with both colors. All of the fins and the tail are cherry red. The majority of Queens we ever came across were between four and twelve pounds, though they can get much bigger. We saw a few over twenty, and more than one that pushed forty pounds.

EATING: All Queen Snappers have sweet white flesh with a huge flake, and the meat is famously versatile. The giants still provide tasty meat.

AVAILABILITY: Local harvests are inconsistent at best. As mentioned above, only when grouper boats fish in difficult-to-fish waters do Queen Snappers get brought to dock.

Catches may be decent enough, occasionally approaching a ton, but those catches happen maybe a few times a year. The limited local catch is funneled into restaurant sales and never makes it to grocery stores.

A very close relative to the Queen is the Onaga (the two are almost indistinguishable, though they swim in waters separated by a continent and half an ocean). Onaga is more commercially available and will work for any recipe in which you want to use Queen Snapper.

As for recreational fishing, the distance necessary to get to this fish's grounds, and the specialized equipment required to fish in water that deep, keep opportunities rare.

GROUPERS AND SEABASS (SERRANIDAE)

Almost all of these fish have fine white flesh with a large flake and very little fat. Almost all are highly esteemed table fish. Most are also targeted fish, which means that they show up regularly on menus and in grocery stores. In the Texas market, one generally sees Yellowedge or Red Grouper (the former is from our waters, the latter only from the eastern Gulf).

All groupers are bottom fish, and for the sake of fisheries management, are further divided into shallow and deepwater species. "Seabass," in the context of serranid fish, is just another word, and does not signify any relation at all to any real bass, fresh or saltwater.

Most serranids have large, bulky heads and deep bodies; most also have large lips, pronounced underbites, and sharp dorsal spines. Groupers all start life as females, and usually change sex at some point in their lives (while this is not particularly unusual or even impressive relative to all the life in the sea, it is a neat fact). Most groupers change coloration as they mature, sometimes dramatically so.

The northwestern Gulf, by and large, is not the best environment for groupers, most of whom prefer the hard and rocky bottoms farther east and south. A few species, though, have carved out niches and thrive in the muddy bottoms of our part of the Gulf. They are the Warsaw, Snowy, Yellowedge, Misty, and, to a lesser extent, Scamp and Gag. Most of the groupers in this chapter are less common here, and commercial catches are sporadic and small.

Provenance is particularly important with regard to groupers. A Yellowfin Grouper from a Texas boat, for example, is from a tightly regulated fishery and thus in a larger sense is sustainable. That same species of grouper from other American waters is just as sustainable. However, that fish from *any other fishery* is part of an overfished population that is still experiencing overfishing.

YELLOWEDGE GROUPER

Hyporthodus flavolimbatus

HABITAT: This grouper lives on the muddy and sandy bottom from about three hundred feet to a little more than one thousand feet. It is most common in the northwestern Gulf of Mexico, which provides more ideal habitat than the rocky southern and eastern regions. It is generally caught at least seventy miles offshore.

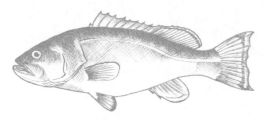

RANGE/DISTRIBUTION: The Yellowedge Grouper ranges from the mid-Atlantic through the Caribbean Sea and beyond.

DESCRIPTION: Commercially, Yellowedge Groupers are marketed as small (less than four pounds), medium (four to eight pounds), and large (eight pounds and up), though the majority caught certainly fall within the "large" range, and a forty-pound Yellowedge, while not common, is also not really newsworthy.

The Yellowedge Grouper is tan to light brown, with a whitish underside; it has the large lips and stout dorsal fins common to most fish in the genus. The tail is rounded, not forked. The dorsal, pectoral, and ventral fins are all edged in brilliant yellow—hence the rather prosaic name. On a freshly dead fish, the yellow is so bright as to appear painted on.

EATING: The meat is mild and sweet, with large flakes. It is very lean of course, so overcooking can be an issue when dealing with fillets from larger fish (and again, most of the fish caught are larger, so this is always an issue). The meat from some groupers tends to seize up when cooked; not so that of the Yellowedge. Look for Yellowedges weighing between three and six pounds, but all sizes can be grilled, roasted, stewed, or sautéed with ease.

AVAILABILITY: This is the main commercial species of grouper in the northwestern Gulf, making it also the most available species of grouper in Texas. Since 2009, all commercial grouper and most tilefish species in the Gulf have been regulated under the Individual Fishing Quota (IFQ) system.

Larger grocery stores usually carry some kind of grouper, and here it will be Yellowedge (or Red, which, again, is only fished in the eastern Gulf). While it is not cheap, Yellowedge Grouper is increasingly popular at Texas restaurants, as Red Snapper prices have skyrocketed in recent years.

Short of having a suitable boat (or renting a spot on a suitable charter), this is not a fish most anglers catch.

SCAMP AND YELLOWMOUTH GROUPER

Mycteroperca phenax and *Mycteroperca interstitialis*

HABITAT: These two species live around rocks, reefs, structures, and other hard bottoms, in fifty to about three hundred feet of water.

RANGE/DISTRIBUTION: They occur in the western Atlantic from the Carolinas through Florida, as well as in the entire Gulf of Mexico and Caribbean Sea.

DESCRIPTION: All of the fish in the genus *Mycteroperca* are on the sleek side, at least relative to other groupers. This is not to imply that they are skinny, but rather that they lack the full belly and bulge of, for example, their *Hyporthodus* cousins.

Exactly two features easily distinguish the Scamp from the Yellowmouth. The first is that the Yellowmouth has more yellow on its mouth than the Scamp, and its dorsal,

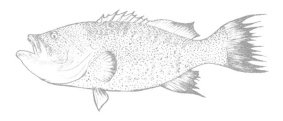

caudal, and anal fins have splashes of yellow along their edges (the Scamp's yellow is limited to its upper lip). The second is the short trailing filaments at the top and bottom of the Scamp's caudal fin.

Other than that, there are few physical differences between these species. Both grow to around twenty pounds (the Scamp grows a little larger). Sometimes they are brown, with darker areas around fins. Sometimes the brown is more red than brown, and other times the background color is shot through with thousands of small dots. At still other times, odd shapes called "cat's paws" appear to be stamped all over their bodies. The variations are due not to geography or diet, but to age, for both of these species change color and patterning as they grow older.

EATING: The Scamp and the Yellowmouth Grouper have the best meat-to-carcass yield of any grouper, with a smaller flake and whiter meat than most. Were they more consistently available, every restaurant (that could afford them) in the state would have them on every menu. They are easily the mildest of the groupers.

AVAILABILITY: These species are regulated under the same catch share program as all groupers in the Gulf of Mexico. They are "shallow water" groupers, which means most catches are incidental during Red Snapper trips (the Texas grouper fishery targets predominantly deepwater species with bottom longlines, whereas Scamp and Yellowmouth are usually fished with bandit rigs). So these are not easily or consistently available fish.

GAG AND BLACK GROUPER

Mycteroperca microlepis and *Mycteroperca bonaci*

HABITAT: Both of these species are associated with offshore rocky bottoms and reefs, in waters sixty to several hundred feet deep.

RANGE/DISTRIBUTION: The Black Grouper occurs in southern and eastern Gulf waters, throughout the Caribbean, and along the Atlantic coast between Florida and the Bahamas; the Gag occurs in these places as well, and also in the northeastern Gulf (populations in our waters are limited mostly to protected reefs and sporadic rock or reef outcroppings elsewhere).

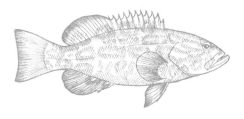

DESCRIPTION: The two species of fish look so similar that captains, dock workers, and seafood companies unintentionally misidentified Gags as Black Groupers (and vice versa) for years. These days, Gags are sold as Gags.

Regardless, both the Gag and the Black Grouper look like larger, stockier versions of the Scamp (and Yellowmouth Grouper).

Both have broom tails, and both are tan to brown. The Black usually has square patterns across the body and dark to black dorsal, anal, pectoral, and caudal fins. The Gag is the same dull brown to tan color as the Black, but usually without the spots, patterns, and stark fins—though sometimes it does have them. And, of course, we are describing just the adult fish, those one generally encounters on the hook or at the store. Juveniles complicate the situation so much as to be beyond the ken of such as ourselves. Gags grow quite large, sometimes reaching seventy or more pounds. Black Groupers can grow more than twice as large.

EATING: They are both tasty and unremarkable.

AVAILABILITY: Texas commercial catches are so small and inconsistent that they make up a tiny percentage of groupers on the market. If a fishmonger tells you they get Texas Gag or Black Grouper on a regular basis, said fishmonger is either lying or ill informed. Admittedly, these are marketed species in Texas, both at the restaurant and the retail level, but they almost always come from elsewhere. Some come from Florida; the rest are imported from Mexico or the Caribbean.

YELLOWFIN GROUPER

Mycteroperca venenosa

COMMON NAMES: Fireback Grouper, Firecracker Grouper, Fire Grouper

HABITAT: The Yellowfin Grouper lives around rocks and reefs in one to several hundred feet of water.

RANGE/DISTRIBUTION: It occurs from southern Florida through the southern Gulf and throughout the Caribbean, and also in Bermuda, where it is a highly targeted species. In the northern Gulf, populations are almost exclusively limited to eastern waters. Commercial catches in the northwestern Gulf are very rare and small—rarely more than a fish or two caught at a time, and months pass between catches.

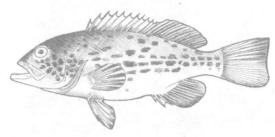

DESCRIPTION: In terms of body shape, the Yellowfin looks just like the Gag and the Black Grouper, though it is a smaller fish, perhaps half the size of the Gag. Its markings look like jigsaw pieces or illustrations of continental drift.

From its belly to the lateral line the body itself is gray to tan to brown. Orange dots entirely cover the body, but not the fins. The pectoral, dorsal, and anal fins are fringed in lemon yellow. All of this is pretty enough but pales next to the color of the back, which is cherry red—not red like an actual cherry, but red like the color of a sports car. The red is so thick, overwhelming all the other colors and patterns, that it looks artificial.

EATING: As with so many creatures from the sea, color does not necessarily correlate to tastiness. The Yellowfin is good, like the Black and the Gag, but that is the most that may be said about it.

AVAILABILITY: In Texas, it is occasionally available, at both the retail and restaurant levels, as an exotic species. If you know for sure that the fish is a product of American Gulf fisheries, then by all means indulge. If you cannot verify provenance, stay away from this fish, as it is severely overfished throughout much of its range, and overfishing is still occurring.

WARSAW, SNOWY, AND MISTY GROUPER

Hyporthodus nigritus, Hyporthodus niveatus, and Hyporthodus mystacinus

COMMON NAME: Misty Grouper: Convict Grouper

HABITAT: All three occur over rocky bottoms from about two hundred to more than seven hundred feet of water. The Warsaw is found in deeper waters than the other two species.

RANGE/DISTRIBUTION: All three species are concentrated in the Gulf of Mexico and the Caribbean Sea, with outlying populations ranging up to the Carolinas and down the northern Atlantic coast of South America.

DESCRIPTION: Fish in this genus share the common grouper features, but their bodies are slightly compressed, bellies are substantially deeper, and tails are fan shaped. All three species have drab dark skin—browns and grays. The Misty and Snowy tend more toward brown; the Warsaw, toward gray.

The Snowy Grouper, the smallest of the three groupers described here, is so called because of the white spots that decorate its sides. The dots are bright when the fish is young, fade with age, and by the time a Snowy is thirty pounds or so, the dots might have disappeared altogether. It reaches at most slightly under a hundred pounds, and, like most groupers, can live quite a long time.

Once the Snowy has outgrown its dots, it's almost a dead ringer for its cousin the Warsaw. Three features distinguish the two fish: (1) the Warsaw gets much larger; (2) the Warsaw is gray, not brownish; (3) the Snowy has proportionally larger eyes than the Warsaw. Admittedly, comparing eyes is

only useful if you have at least one of each animal in front of you. Size and color are more predictable indicators. The Warsaw is also the giant among commercial groupers in the Gulf of Mexico. (The Atlantic Goliath Grouper [*Epinephelus itajara*], also a Gulf of Mexico native, can weigh up to one thousand pounds or more. It dwarfs the Warsaw. However, the Goliath is protected throughout its American range, and no commercial harvest is possible anywhere [even the recreational fishery is catch-and-release only]. We don't cover the Goliath in this book because we

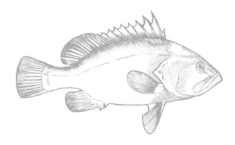

have never and will never eat one, and we hope you won't either.) Landed fish routinely weigh several dozen to over a hundred pounds—the biggest one we ever handled weighed 324 pounds. PJ cut that fish up, and it was, to say the very least, awkward.

The Misty Grouper, which can weigh over two hundred pounds, is easy to spot. It looks like the Warsaw and Snowy in shape. Its most obvious feature, however, is the set of thick vertical stripes that run from the belly to about halfway up the dorsal fin (hence the sobriquet "Convict Grouper"). Almost always the stripes are black, or at least darker than the brown background; occasionally they are a paler shade of brown than the background color. The stripes are distinct when the fish is young; as it matures the stripes blur a bit, but they remain throughout the fish's life.

EATING: These three species are great eating fish, but unfortunately they are the least valuable (and thus least fished) groupers in the Texas market. The thick, meaty flesh defies expectations, and most chefs and restaurants prefer to stay away from it entirely. The Misty and Snowy have the most traditional grouper taste and texture, but all three depart from grouper territory by the time they are about fifty pounds. At that point, they taste more like chicken than fish. Which is not a bad thing at all—unless you're expecting to eat fish. So, don't expect fish, just expect something good.

Big, giant groupers swim in warm temperate and tropical waters throughout the world. Across vast swathes of that range, lots of people in lots of places, speaking lots of languages, have found lots of ways to cut, cook, and eat them. The head of a decent-sized Warsaw, for example, can feed a family a couple of times over (we know this from repeated experience).

Any an old fishmonger can tell you about the pleasures of eating a five-pound Warsaw Grouper, just over the legal size limit.

AVAILABILITY: At the retail level, Asian markets (specifically catering to East and Southeast Asian tastes) generally carry some kind of big grouper. They are not always local fish and not always local species, but these three are common enough. The local Warsaw Grouper fishery, small though it may be, exists because of such local demand. Sport fishers like to target these species, we assume, because the fish are big.

SPECKLED HIND AND MARBLED GROUPER

Epinephelus drummondhayi and *Dermatolepis inermis*

COMMON NAMES: Speckled Hind: Calico Grouper, Kitty Mitchell (this is our preferred name—see below)

HABITAT: Reefs and rocky bottoms are the dwelling places for these two fish. They are found in dozens, if not hundreds, of feet of water—sometimes around shallower reefs as well.

RANGE/DISTRIBUTION: The Speckled Hind occurs only from Bermuda to the Carolinas, all around Florida, and in the eastern Gulf of Mexico. The Marbled Grouper has the same northern limit as the Speckled Hind, but extends throughout the Gulf, the Caribbean Sea, and down to Brazil. Both of these fish are rare in the northwestern Gulf, the Marbled much more so.

DESCRIPTION: The Marbled Grouper is an altogether arresting fish—from snout to tail, from dorsal fin to belly, its skin is painted with browns, white, grays, black, oranges, reds, and yellows, all fading and merging into one another in a mesmerizing jigsaw fashion. It doesn't look exactly like marble, but it's close enough to understand the name of the fish.

A very small head gives way to a tall, high-shouldered body, which is quite compressed and relatively thin (though the highly muscled shoulders provide quite a bit of meat). Pectoral fins are quite large. If you are lucky enough to get ahold of one, you will immediately know what you have.

The Speckled Hind is sometimes colloquially called the Kitty Mitchell Grouper (mostly by older fishers). An old fisherman first shared the name—and the legend behind it—with us, and it has stuck ever since. Since we have not been able to confirm details of the legend (and since Kitty Mitchell was apparently a real person), we shall not repeat the anecdotal information we have. We will confirm that it is a great story.

That aside, the Kitty Mitchell's body is much like a Warsaw's, but it has a much smaller head. The large belly and rounded back give it an oval shape. Aside from the standard spiny dorsal fin, the rest are rounded; the caudal fin is broom shaped. The lower lip, belly, and pectoral fins are solid pink. The rest of the body is brown to maroon to rust and festooned everywhere with small brilliant white dots. Even the fins are covered with these dots.

EATING: In our experience, and according to every customer who ever tried these fish, the Marbled Grouper is the most delicious of our local Gulf groupers. The meat is pale and bright and absolutely sweet. The Kitty Mitchell is a close runner-up.

AVAILABILITY: Don't bother your fishmonger about these fish, for the experience will only disappoint you and flummox your fishmonger.

One occasionally sees Kitty Mitchell for sale at stores and seafood companies in Texas (sold always as Calico Grouper or Speckled Hind). Very rarely will a Marbled Grouper pop up in these places.

If you should serendipitously find one of these fish for sale, always ask where it was caught. If the fish came from fisheries in the American Gulf, then buy away. Unfortunately, the few Marbled and Kitty Mitchell Groupers that make their way into the local market are almost always imported from Caribbean waters. In general, grouper from the Caribbean Sea is not a good idea—most populations are overfished, and overfishing is still occurring.

ROCK HIND, RED HIND, AND GRAYSBY

Epinephelus adscensionis, Epinephelus guttatus, and Cephalopholis cruentata

COMMON NAME: Red Hind: Strawberry Grouper

HABITAT: These three groupers occur around reefs and rocks, from one to five hundred feet of water.

RANGE/DISTRIBUTION: All three species occur from waters off the Carolinas through to Brazil and everywhere in between, with the largest populations occurring around Florida, the eastern Gulf, and the Caribbean Sea. They are less common in the northwestern Gulf (our part of the Gulf doesn't have enough of the right kind of bottom).

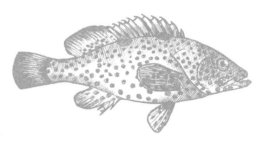

DESCRIPTION: These are smaller species. The Graysby is the smallest, usually weighing about a pound. The Rock Hind isn't a lot bigger, but occasionally weighs over five pounds. The Red Hind can grow to more than forty pounds but is more commonly less than ten.

The Graysby is green gray with red-orange dots; the Rock Hind is lighter gray with orange dots, and a yellow fringe runs along the dorsal fin; the Red Hind is red orange with red dots (its caudal and back dorsal fins are fringed in black).

EATING: All groupers like to eat crabs and other crustaceans, and of all the groupers, these three species might eat the most crabs and crustaceans. As a result, the meat is sweet and redolent of tasty critters in hard shells.

Most often, you will want to cook these fish whole. We usually crust them in salt and bake. Grouper skin isn't that great, so you're not losing much.

AVAILABILITY: The three species are commonly available at larger Asian markets and high-end seafood markets. They are not commercially targeted by Texas boats—only landed as bycatch from Vermilion Snapper and occasionally Yellowedge Grouper boats. Provenance is important—if you know the fish is from a US Gulf fishery, by all means indulge. But *only* if you know where it's from. Other fisheries are not regulated the same way, and those fisheries are overfished and experiencing overfishing.

LONGTAIL BASS

Hemanthias leptus

HABITAT: The Longtail Bass prefers rocky and hard bottoms in deep water (two to more than nine hundred feet).

RANGE/DISTRIBUTION: It is found in the Gulf of Mexico and Caribbean Sea, down to South America along the entire Brazilian coast.

DESCRIPTION: The genus *Hemanthias* contains only three species, all of which look almost the same. One is our Gulf Longtail Bass; the other two (the Damsel Bass and Splittail Bass) occur only in the neighborhood of Baja California. The Longtail, like its cousins, looks as if it belongs in a taxidermy

shop. The colors are too bright (every single color is neon), and the eyes are too gaudy.

The full lips and upturned mouth (the only typically serranid features) are orange to orange red, as is the head. The eyes are yellow ringed by orange. The back is orange

with yellow highlights; a faint orange stripe runs from the back of the eye along the lateral line. A yellow stripe runs below this orange stripe. The belly tends to be white or close to it.

The first spine of the primary dorsal fin is highly elongated and feathery, extending six inches or more. Pelvic fins are even longer than the dorsal fin, stretching up to a foot off the fish. All of the fins are orange shot through with yellow dots and squiggles. The Longtail Bass has a broom tail, as opposed to its Pacific cousins with their forked tails. It never grows to be a giant, weighing at most four or five pounds.

EATING: Most Longtail Bass weigh around two pounds. And while fillets are easy to collect (and quite versatile), this is another fish to cook whole (admittedly, we can't think of many smaller fish that aren't better cooked whole).

AVAILABILITY: The Longtail Bass is not commercially targeted anywhere in at least its US range, though there may be commercial fisheries in other waters. They are commercially landed in American Gulf waters as bycatch by boats targeting various groupers and snappers. In Texas, most catches come from Vermilion Snapper and Yellowedge Grouper boats (catches from the latter tend to be bigger). So, it is not completely unusual to see Longtail Bass for sale at the restaurant level. Try catching your own, but you'll need a boat.

ATLANTIC CREOLEFISH

Paranthias furcifer

COMMON NAME: Rosebud Seabass

HABITAT: This species occurs in reefs and associated areas, in a few to almost a thousand feet of water.

RANGE/DISTRIBUTION: It ranges on both sides of the Atlantic but is most abundant in the west from Florida throughout the Gulf of Mexico and from the Caribbean Sea to Brazil; in the east, it is limited to mid-Atlantic islands and the Gulf of Guinea. In our local waters, Creolefish don't have a lot of ideal habitat, as we don't have as many reefs.

DESCRIPTION: The Creolefish has a thin ellipse of a body, a small head with a little mouth, ruby-red eyes, and a large and gracefully forked tail. The fish overall is orange red to ruby red, the color fading to pastel pink toward the belly and under the head. Occasionally the tip of the caudal fin might be fringed in white or black or gray. The base of the dorsal fin is red like the rest of the fish; the tip is fringed in yellow or green or a combination of both. Scales are tiny and firmly embedded in the skin.

EATING: The Creolefish tastes exactly like it looks—unassuming yet surprisingly complex. It is delicate enough to poach, hardy enough to cook in a pan or in a fryer, and firm enough to grill or roast. Normally we would recommend cooking a fish this size whole. And we do like cooking the Rosebud whole. However, this is one of those fish seemingly built to fillet—fast, with no fuss. If you want to fillet the Creolefish (and there is no reason not to), don't even think about scaling it. You will get maybe a third of the scales off. Just cut the fish, cut off the skin, and rinse the fillets in salted water.

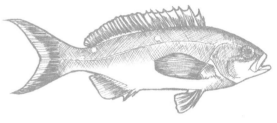

AVAILABILITY: In American Gulf waters, this is not a targeted species. Commercial catches, consisting of one or two to several hundred pounds, have always been bycatch from Vermilion Snapper boats. Vermilion Snappers cloud up when they feed, and Rosebuds get caught in the mix. The two species look superficially similar, enough so that cheating boats occasionally have lumped the species together and called the whole lot Vermilion (a trick that has never worked, as the deception becomes clear when the fish are sorted at the dock). These days, with fewer local Vermilion Snapper boats working, fewer Creolefish are landed. The few available at the restaurant level undoubtedly come from American Gulf fisheries.

SAND PERCH AND SPANISH FLAG

Diplectrum formosum and *Gonioplectrus hispanus*

COMMON NAME: Sand Perch: Sand Seabass

HABITAT: Habitats overlap a bit here. The Spanish Flag prefers deeper waters down to almost a thousand feet, whereas the Sand Perch is found down to depths of only three hundred feet or so. Both fish occur on sandy and vegetated bottoms and around reefs.

RANGE/DISTRIBUTION: The two species range from the Carolinas throughout the Gulf of Mexico and Caribbean Sea to the northern Atlantic coast of Brazil. The Sand Perch is apparently less common in the Caribbean.

DESCRIPTION: These are both small fish, never weighing even a pound. The Spanish Flag looks like a tiny grouper. From the top of the dorsal fin down to the belly, and from the eyes to the caudal fin run alternating horizontal bands of yellow and red (which are the inspiration for the common name). On the lower face, these bands break up into yellow dots on a red background. Pectoral fins are white to pink; anal and secondary dorsal fins fade at their tips to pink; pelvic fins are pastel purple. Every Spanish Flag has a large red regular dot on each side at the front of the anal fin.

The Sand Perch is so named because the fish resembles lowly freshwater perch—it looks like it would be more at home in a shallow lake than in the sea. That said, it is most certainly not a perch. It is roughly cigar shaped and sized, being shorter than an outstretched hand. It has modest fins all around. The background color is drab, from tan to light olive. Thick, undefined dark stripes run vertically from the tips of the dorsal fin to about halfway down the body, while a thick dark stripe runs horizontally from the snout through the eye to the tail. This horizontal stripe is accompanied by up to several smaller and better-defined lines, which are green or blue or black or brown.

EATING: The Sand Perch is great to eat, especially fried. It is way too small to fillet unless you have a specific reason for doing so.

As for the Spanish Flag . . . the taste is acceptable enough, though not memorable. The texture, on the other hand, is rather hard to overcome, as it calls to mind not fish, but the soles of old shoes. It is a tough fish. It is a rubbery fish. We have no idea why this would be so.

We always enjoyed giving them away to unsuspecting chefs. In fact, for us it became an informal test of a new customer. If the chef came back raving about the delicate texture, we could draw some very accurate conclusions (e.g., the chef had never cooked the fish and was just showing off and might not be a good fit for our business model); if the chef came back and admitted to a rather negative reaction to the fish, we could draw some rather more favorable conclusions about said chef. The test was highly accurate.

AVAILABILITY: Neither species is targeted for food anywhere in the American Gulf. Commercial landings (always bycatch) are tiny and wildly unpredictable. They are rarely sold anywhere.

CHAPTER 8

OFFSHORE REEF, RUBBLE, AND ROCK FISH

In all, well over a hundred species live around the reefs and rocks of the northwestern Gulf of Mexico. In this chapter (and those concerning the snapper, grouper, and jack families), we describe a few. This chapter covers both reef fish and reef-associated fish, along with other bottom fish that prefer hard places to just sand and mud. Most are pretty fish that live near rocks and eat things growing on rocks (arthropods, worms, and some vegetation); those that aren't exactly attractive are showy or exotic, and sometimes fierce. They exist on a spectrum of tastiness. On one end of this spectrum lie the tiny strict vegetarians, dining on the algae and plankton growing on the rocks and corals. Marine vegetarian fish as a rule are not as predictably good to eat, in contrast to freshwater vegetarian fish, which are almost always delicious. Closer to the other end of the spectrum is the Great Barracuda, whose meat is also a crap shoot, but for different reasons.

The largest reef area in the northwestern Gulf, the Flower Garden Banks, is not only off-limits to commercial fishing, but commercial boats are prohibited from fishing within fifty miles of it. Other areas are similarly protected, and because those areas represent the overwhelming majority of northwestern Gulf reefs, commercial vessels bring in fewer of these types of fish.

Some species venture far away from reefs, which is why we have a Red Snapper fishery in our part of the Gulf. Most of the fish in this chapter are found just as easily around structures as reefs. Commercial boats certainly are allowed to fish off structures (intentionally sunken objects like oil rigs, or wrecks, or just rock piles), and the fish they encounter there we describe here.

We also describe a few fish—like the Guaguanche and smaller tilefish species—that seem to be happy on, near, or even quite a distance from reefs and structures.

KNOBBED AND WHITEBONE PORGY

Calamus nodosus and Calamus leucosteus

COMMON NAME: Whitebone: Silver Porgy

HABITAT: Both the Knobbed and the Whitebone Porgy are offshore bottom fish, rarely found in less than fifty or more than five hundred feet of water. The Whitebone is more at home on soft bottoms, whereas the Knobbed sticks to rocky areas.

RANGE/DISTRIBUTION: These two species are more or less confined to the Gulf of Mexico, with only minor populations and catches elsewhere in contiguous waters.

DESCRIPTION: The Whitebone is a typical porgy. It has a compressed head and face, coupled with an oval body upon which sits a prominent and spiny dorsal fin. The body is mostly silver, with some dark pink and gray running down the back and irregular and faint black splotches overall. Fins, including the caudal, are grayish brown. Though they are not in the same genus, the Whitebone is similar in appearance to the Scup (*Stenotomus chrysops*) found on the east coast. You will rarely catch or find a Whitebone weighing more than three pounds.

The most distinctive member of the Gulf faction of the family Sparidae (and also, alas, the most uncommonly caught) is the Knobbed Porgy. Most porgies look like ovals of some sort, to which have been attached small heads on one end and tails on the other. The Knobbed, by contrast, looks more like a right triangle to which has been attached a tail at the tip of the smallest angle, and a triangular head at the right-angle end. The head appears to have been ill chosen, maybe hastily assembled. The top of the body (upon which is perched a typical porgy dorsal fin) seems to overhang the head itself, resulting in a fish that appears to have a hump. The eyes are polished gold, and a bony ridge, like a stubby visor, runs over both. The fins are all shades of blue and a little gray. The lips are yellow, and the face itself is covered with tiny yellow dots. The metallic scales, which catch the light like prisms, are silver, their edges painted many colors, resulting in a body that is at once silver and blue and yellow and green and platinum and orange. A stunning fish.

EATING: When the subject is fish, there is, as we have written already, no correlation between beauty and edibility. So, the Knobbed Porgy is a happy coincidence—the flesh is superb, the best of the Gulf porgies. Fillets are large (thanks to that weirdly shaped body), pale, and just fatty enough.

The Whitebone usually gets big enough to provide fillets worth the effort. But we strongly recommend steaming this fish whole instead.

AVAILABILITY: Both of these species are inconsistent bycatch from Vermilion Snapper boats, or sometimes Snapper boats fishing in deeper waters. Neither has been or is now targeted. The most widely available porgy in Texas markets is either the Sheepshead (described in chapter 2) or the Scup (from the east coast). At the retail level, any porgy aside from the Sheepshead will have come from other waters.

BIGEYES: ATLANTIC BIGEYE, SHORT BIGEYE, AND GLASSEYE

Priacanthus arenatus, Pristigenys alta, and *Heteropriacanthus cruentatus*

COMMON NAME: All three species colloquially: Storm Snapper

HABITAT: In general, most species of bigeyes live around reefs and structures (more commonly on the former), in a few to many hundreds of feet of water. Commercial fishers call them all Storm Snappers because the fish tend to school close to the surface right after bad weather.

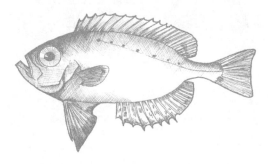

RANGE/DISTRIBUTION: The Short Bigeye is limited to US Atlantic waters from the Carolinas to the Gulf of Mexico and Caribbean Sea and the northern Atlantic coast of South America. The Atlantic Bigeye roams a bit farther and is common in tropical and warm temperate waters on both sides of the Atlantic. The Glasseye occurs throughout the world, wherever the water is warm and the reefs are plentiful.

DESCRIPTION: Most members of the family Priacanthidae (including all from the Gulf) are a shade of either red or orange; some have elaborate patterns painted atop this background. Most members look roughly the same: bodies are somewhat compressed and

thin, and the secondary dorsal and anal fins are longer close to the caudal fins, which are themselves broom shaped.

All of this is minutiae, however, for every bigeye has an unmistakable face. The namesake red, large-pupiled eyes are huge (the Glasseye has strange deep-set pupils that look like marbles, which explains its name also). The mouth is severely upturned, so much so that it is situated where the nose is on most fish. When the mouth is closed, the large, bony lips interlock like the legs of a folding chair.

The Short Bigeye is the smallest of our local species. Its body is highly compressed, with large fins all around. Its eyes are even larger (proportionally speaking) than other bigeyes. It rarely weighs more than a pound.

The Atlantic Bigeye's body is less compressed than that of the other two species and is generally a paler red as well. The Glasseye, on the other hand, is as big as the Atlantic, with the body of the Short Bigeye. Both of these species can weigh as much as six pounds, but around half that is more common. The Glasseye is the prettiest of the three.

EATING: All three species have white flesh, mild and sweet, as befits a deep-dwelling fish that eats mostly small critters. Only the largest are worth filleting (remember the fish is thin); all the rest we cook whole in salt. Don't try to scale them, in any case, for you will wind up with nothing but a weary soul and scarred fish. Most of the scales come off, but those that remain are stubborn.

Should you stumble upon a nice fat specimen, by all means try it raw. The Glasseye surpasses the other two species as a raw fish and is in fact fished for the sashimi and sushi market in Japan, where it is called Kintokidai.

AVAILABILITY: The Glasseye is marketed by seafood companies catering to sushi restaurants, but the fish is never from our waters. Local catches—very small and unpredictable—are always bycatch from Vermilion Snapper or Yellowedge Grouper/Golden Tilefish boats.

PINK PORGY

Pagrus pagrus

COMMON NAMES: Red Porgy, Red Bream, Sea Bream, Silver Snapper (erroneous—this is *not* a snapper)

HABITAT: This species is associated with sandy, grassy, and rocky bottoms, in water a few dozens of feet deep to more than six hundred. Practically speaking, in this part of the Gulf, the only Pinks found in waters less than one hundred feet deep are juveniles and stragglers.

RANGE/DISTRIBUTION: The Pink Porgy is found from the Mediterranean Sea to European, North American, and South American Atlantic waters; in the Caribbean Sea; and in the Gulf of Mexico. This fish gets around—at least when it is very young, when it floats on open ocean currents for a bit (according to Alan Davidson, in his brilliant-from-start-to-finish *North Atlantic Seafood: A Comprehensive Guide with Recipes*).

DESCRIPTION: The blunt head makes up a small part of the whole length, and the face looks slightly compressed; the body is oval, a trait common to all porgies. Eyes are golden, sometimes with flecks of blue or pink. A band of turquoise blue runs over the eyes, with patches of bright olive between the eyes and the gills.

Describing the color of the Pink Porgy is a surprisingly difficult task, for the fish changes color depending on age, and to a greater degree than many fish described in this book. No matter the particular shade or color, it is always metallic and always sparkles and shifts hue in bright light. A young Pink Porgy (less than a pound) is mostly metallic orange and pink, with a shadow of copper along the back; dorsal and pectoral fins are pink, whereas the caudal fin is orange. As the fish gets older (from more than a pound to about four or five pounds), it becomes a brighter pink, the belly becomes paler (though still sparkling and shot through with other colors), and blues over the body become more obvious. By the time the fish is mature (more than five pounds), the back has started to turn a dull gold-tan color, which eventually dominates. At any age, the lateral line is prominent, and it is sometimes traced down the body by a series of turquoise dots.

EATING: This fish has delicious sweet flesh, easily filleted from the body. Unfortunately, Pink Porgy flesh will start to gape just a few days out of the water. The closely related Pacific Red Seabream (*Pagrus major*) is called Madai in Japan, where it is highly regarded.

AVAILABILITY: There is no targeted fishery in the Gulf. Porgies are landed as bycatch from Vermilion Snapper or Yellowedge Grouper boats; the former land smaller fish, and the latter land porgies exceeding six pounds. Restaurants these days have access to a small amount of local product (inconsistent though it may be). Some markets in larger cities predictably carry porgies, but those tend to be Scups, an inferior species fished off the mid to upper east coast. Pink Porgies are not easy to fish recreationally. Your best bet is to catch some Sheepshead (more on that in its description, page 21).

Beware: Pink Porgy was formerly (and occasionally still is) sold as a species of snapper. This is fraud, whether it is intentional or not on the part of the sellers.

BLACKBELLY ROSEFISH, SPOTTED SCORPIONFISH, AND SPINYCHEEK SCORPIONFISH

Helicolenus dactylopterus, Scorpaena plumieri, and Neomerinthe hemingwayi

HABITAT: All members of the Scorpaenidae family, including these three, are groundfish. The Spotted is the shallowest dwelling of the three species, living on or around reefs in at most a few hundred feet of water. The Spinycheek swims in deeper waters to about six hundred feet, over hard bottoms and around reefs, while the Blackbelly likes soft bottoms in a hundred to around three thousand feet of water.

RANGE/DISTRIBUTION: The Blackbelly occurs almost everywhere in the Atlantic, from Canada to the Gulf of Mexico, the Caribbean Sea, and Venezuela in the west; and from Iceland through the Mediterranean Sea to South Africa in the east. The Spinycheek and Spotted have a much smaller range, from mid-Atlantic US waters through to the Gulf and the Caribbean.

DESCRIPTION: Several species of scorpionfish live in the Gulf, the Spinycheek being one of the largest, often weighing more than

two pounds and measuring more than twelve inches. The skin is a fiery shade of orange, shot through with multicolored spots. Fins are edged in bright yellow. In terms of color, it is one of the prettiest Gulf fish—in terms of everything else, it is a frightful-looking animal. The Spinycheek appears to be permanently scowling, partially a result of the large, bony brow. The mouth is wide and covered with fleshy lips, which are more pronounced by what appears to be a stubborn underbite. The head is quite large and covered from snout to gills with spines. These spines are small and not always conspicuous, but they can easily slice the hand of an unwary human. The dorsal spines are no friendlier.

The Blackbelly is a much smaller species, hardly ever reaching a pound. Its lemon-yellow eyes, located high on the head, give it a frightened expression. The fins are red, and the body itself is alternating red and orange. Its name comes from the internal lining of its gut cavity, which is completely black.

Of the three, the Spotted Scorpionfish is without question the best for the table. It is also the most uncommonly caught. Its skin, browner than orange, is mottled with black, white, and red. It gets about as big as the Spinycheek. It is the sternest appearing of any fish, with a large, boxy head.

EATING: Once one gets past the head of these scorpionfish, one finds a fish not only worth eating but one of the finest eating fish in the Gulf of Mexico. Scorpionfish are prized table fare the world over, so we should perhaps not be too surprised that our local varieties are also delectable. Raw fillets are sometimes translucent pink, sometimes opaque white; cooked, they are snow white.

AVAILABILITY: No targeted fishery exists for any scorpionfish in the Gulf of Mexico. They are sometimes caught by longline boats fishing for grouper and tilefish, but even then, catches are unpredictable at best, as the best grounds for grouper and tilefish are not necessarily the best grounds for scorpionfish. Given that those are the directed fisheries, and that it is easier to fish on sand than mud, it is no surprise that scorpionfish are infrequently landed. Catches are far more common east of the Mississippi into Florida, where rocky bottoms abound.

GOLDFACE AND BLUELINE TILEFISH

Caulolatilus chrysops and *Caulolatilus microps*

COMMON NAMES: Goldface: Goldeneye Tilefish, Silver Tilefish; Blueline: Gray Tilefish

HABITAT: Both of these fish are found in several hundred feet of water (the Goldface in slightly deeper water than the Blueline), though not as deep as the Golden Tilefish (*Lopholatilus chamaeleonticeps*, described elsewhere). Both species favor rock, sand, and rubble bottoms.

RANGE/DISTRIBUTION: The Blueline Tilefish is limited mostly to the Gulf of Mexico and contiguous waters up to about the Carolinas. The Goldface may be found in those waters as well, and also throughout the Caribbean Sea and the northern Atlantic coast of South America.

DESCRIPTION: Humans tend to anthropomorphize other animals and to do so more when continuously confronted with lots of animals of the same general type. PJ occasionally succumbs to this temptation. With that in mind—if *Goodfellas* had been made by fish, the Blueline would have been one of the big tough guys introduced with a voiceover and given a moniker like "Tommy Blueface" or "Johnny Blue Stripes." It doesn't get nearly as big as the Golden (it almost never exceeds fifteen pounds), but it is the meatiest of tilefish; while it shares the same tapering shape typical of all tilefish, the fillets are thick at the head and thick at the tail (and those pin bones aren't nearly as pernicious). Silver eyes (sometimes flecked with brilliant blue) are small relative to the large head and are set high up in the head.

The Blueline is so named for the bright

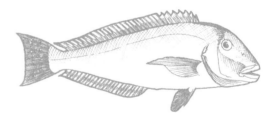

blue stripe that runs from the snout to the bottom of the eye. Sometimes this is a double stripe, with the two stripes running parallel. Sometimes a few other smaller stripes, or perhaps dots or splotches, accompany the stripe(s). Pectoral and anal fins are a more muted, lighter blue. Aside from these splashes of color, the Blueline is a drab fish. The body is gray to olive and always paler at the belly than at the back. Dorsal and caudal fins are the same color as the body;

sometimes the former has a dark splotch nearer the head, though this is not always present.

The Goldface is the smaller of the two species, reaching no more than seven or eight pounds. A thick lemon-yellow stripe, splashed across the face under both eyes, is the only bright coloring on the fish. The rest of the body is covered in muted, blurred colors. The back is gray to light brown; around the lateral line, from head to tail, runs a faint yellow stripe; below this is perhaps another faint stripe, maybe of blue, terminating in a pale belly, only the very bottom of which is snow white. Fins overall are the same color as the parts of the body to which they are attached, though sometimes you can see a bit of yellow on the front or tips of the dorsal fin.

EATING: Honesty compels the admission that we much prefer either of these species to the more marketable Golden Tilefish. We assume that differences in diet are at least partly responsible for the superior taste of these species.

AVAILABILITY: The Goldface and Blueline Tilefish are occasionally available at the restaurant level, and they are unusual in that Texas market offerings are generally local product (at least from American Gulf waters). Retail sightings are rare indeed. They are Yellowedge Grouper bycatch when the boat fishes on rock; Vermilion Snapper bycatch otherwise. Recreational fishing is a possibility, but all the deepwater caveats apply.

SAND TILEFISH
Malacanthus plumieri

HABITAT: The Sand Tilefish prefers slightly shallower waters than the other Gulf tilefish, from a bit over one hundred to more than five hundred feet down. Like the Blueline and Goldface Tilefish, the Sand is more

common on sandy bottoms with a lot of rubble.

RANGE/DISTRIBUTION: This species ranges from the northern Atlantic coast of South America through the US mid-Atlantic coast, though it is most common in the Gulf of Mexico, Caribbean Sea, and more southerly waters.

DESCRIPTION: Maybe this is the prettiest tilefish. It is certainly the smallest of the Gulf tilefish, weighing at most three or four pounds. It is also the most distinctive, for it only vaguely resembles its cousins. A small head with pointed snout and small eyes attaches to a long, tube-shaped body, which ends in a large caudal fin, the top and bottom of which trail off in filaments. The dorsal fin is delicate, soft, and continuous from head to tail.

The back is sometimes yellow, sometimes tan, sometimes olive or brown; usually it is a combination of all of these, one color fading into another. The belly is white, and the gradual change of color between back and belly starts around the lateral line. The face looks tattooed with parallel meandering blue lines and blue dots, though this display fades quickly after death. Lips and snout are a faded yellow. Almost all the fins are white and plain, with the exception of that caudal fin, which is usually a combination of all the colors appearing elsewhere on the body.

EATING: The Sand Tilefish is a tasty fish, easy to fillet and quite versatile. And it makes a dramatic whole-fish course (as long as you don't have too many guests).

AVAILABILITY: Despite the quality of the flesh, this is a fish that is all too unlikely to grace your table. It's a minor enough fish that it is not even included in the tilefish catch share regulations. Any catches are bycatch from Vermilion Snapper boats. Landings can be measured in individuals caught, not in pounds per year.

ATLANTIC SPADEFISH

Chaetodipterus faber

HABITAT: Juveniles of this species swim everywhere inshore. Adults live around rocks and structures in shallow offshore waters less than one hundred feet.

RANGE/DISTRIBUTION: The Atlantic Spadefish is found from the mid-Atlantic US coast, throughout the Gulf of Mexico, and into the Caribbean Sea to Brazil.

DESCRIPTION: The body is highly compressed, resulting in an almost round shape. The head is small, as are the eyes. The mouth is quite small with small teeth, obviously not capable of eating large prey. The first dorsal fin and the pelvic and pectoral fins are small. The triangular second dorsal and anal fins, which extend almost to the tips of the caudal fin, are, by comparison, gigantic. The discreet caudal fin is something of an anticlimax. All fins are ridged in black, and the body is silver gray. Thick black vertical stripes run from back to belly. These stripes sometimes fade with age; death improves neither the clarity nor the color of the stripes.

EATING: Fillets of Atlantic Spadefish are more or less comet shaped and quite thin. The meat is gray to white, almost translucent. While you can certainly fry the fillets, you will lose the delicate flavor specific to Atlantic Spadefish. Poach them instead in a slightly spiced white broth.

AVAILABILITY: Seafood markets right near the coast will sometimes have an Atlantic Spadefish or two for sale. While you can be assured that such fish are local, quality is always suspect, for no commercial boats target these fish, and most boats fish in deeper waters than the Atlantic Spadefish swims in. And, for some reason, Atlantic Spadefish is one of a small group of fish considered by most commercial fishers to be beneath contempt. Apparently, this contempt is internationalized, for the Atlantic Spadefish is at best an incidental catch throughout most if not all of its range. Basically, there is no consistent retail or restaurant availability.

This is one of the few offshore fish that are within reach of anyone who can get a boat a few miles out in the Gulf. Atlantic Spadefish love oil rigs, and even the rig nearest to shore will almost certainly have more than a few. Small pieces of cut squid are the

best bait. Use a small circle hook and a cork or bob to keep the baited gear about three feet under the surface of the water.

Bear in mind that other fishers in the vicinity might mock you. Pay them no mind. Keep fishing, secure in the knowledge that while you might not bring home a trophy fish or an impressive photo, you will certainly bring home dinner. Your antagonists will more than likely not.

BERMUDA SEA CHUB

Kyphosus sectatrix

HABITAT: While it isn't typically found in waters more than a couple hundred feet deep, the Bermuda Sea Chub occurs everywhere in shallower waters more than a few dozen feet deep. It is common over grasses, vegetation, reefs, sand, mud, rock, and structures.

RANGE/DISTRIBUTION: This chub occurs on both sides of the Atlantic in warm temperate to tropical waters: in the eastern Atlantic, from France to the Gulf of Guinea, though it is not common in the Mediterranean Sea; in the western Atlantic, from Brazil to at least the mid-Atlantic US coast, including the Gulf of Mexico and Caribbean Sea.

DESCRIPTION: The Bermuda Sea Chub's body is a pointed ellipse with an insignificant tail. The mouth is small, as are the eyes and indeed the entire head. Fins are silvery gold or golden silver. The entire body is covered in alternating stripes of gold and silver, and the head is a mix of these two colors, mostly gold. None of the colors are metallic or bright—less like jewelry and more like model paint.

The Bermuda Sea Chub is opportunistic in its eating habits. It eats vegetation and small things in shells, as well as little fish and bits of larger fish.

EATING: Despite a very poor reputation, the Bermuda Sea Chub is tasty enough. It leaves no lasting impression one way or the other. It is best suited for cloaking in a heavy batter, frying in lots of hot oil, and eating with a spicy sour-and-sweet sauce.

We confess that it took us a while to warm up to this fish. Its feeding habits, including allegedly feasting on dolphin feces and vomit, can be off-putting. Then again, chickens are disgusting creatures, and chickens taste good.

AVAILABILITY: This fish is rare or never to be had at either the restaurant or retail level. Vietnamese boats would occasionally bring some in, but even then the Bermuda Sea Chub was a tertiary fish. You can fish it yourself, at around the same spot at which you'll find, for example, the Atlantic Spadefish. Use the same gear and bait.

FRENCH ANGELFISH

Pomacanthus paru

HABITAT: The French Angelfish is associated with reefs in shallow waters down to a few hundred feet.

RANGE/DISTRIBUTION: It can be found in all of the waters around Florida, the entire Gulf of Mexico, the Caribbean Sea, and down to the northern tip of the Brazilian Atlantic coast (obviously, populations in the northwestern Gulf are small). Smaller populations occur in the eastern Atlantic, around Senegal and other parts of extreme West Africa.

DESCRIPTION: The French Angelfish is shaped much like the Atlantic Spadefish. The rounded second dorsal and anal fins are

even more voluminous, and the filament tips of the fins extend past the caudal fin. The mouth is small and shaped a bit like a beak (though the lips are not fused), and teeth look like baleen (or at least they look like pictures we have seen of baleen). The body is quite thin and as tall as it is long. The small gold eyes are ringed in bright yellow. The same color of yellow fringes the pectoral fins and the tips of the rest of the fins. The body itself is matte black. Scales along the sides of the body are not entirely black—the rearward-facing edges of each scale are yellow, resulting in the sides of the fish looking like a constellation of crescent moons in a dark sky.

EATING: We are told that angelfish make fine table fare. This has not been our experience, but our data sample is limited to a few specimens over several years. Angelfish in general eat algae and plants growing on reefs. Sometimes they eat little animals, but the majority of their diet consists of green matter. Vegetarianism among fish is not unusual, and we can think of dozens of delightfully tasty species—but not the angelfish. The few we've eaten tasted of old algae. We would love to be proven wrong.

AVAILABILITY: This fish is just about never for sale anywhere and is definitely not fished in American waters. You can try to catch your own. Your best bet is probably a spear gun, though we have no experience whatsoever in that area. (Aside from the beach and shallow waters, we do not go directly into the ocean itself. Apple can't swim, and PJ has a paralyzing fear of the infinite.)

PRINCESS PARROTFISH, STOPLIGHT PARROTFISH, BLUELIP PARROTFISH, AND OTHERS

Scarus taeniopterus, Sparisoma viride, and *Cryptotomus roseus*

COMMON NAME: Most species are simply called Parrotfish, with no differentiation.

HABITAT: Parrotfish are almost always on or very close to reefs, which means, in the northwestern Gulf, far offshore. They are far less common in other places.

RANGE/DISTRIBUTION: All three species occur in temperate to tropical reef-bottomed waters from Florida to Brazil, including the Gulf of Mexico and the Caribbean Sea. All species are most common in the extreme southern Gulf; the entire Caribbean; and between south Florida, the Bahamas, and Cuba.

DESCRIPTION: We won't dwell much on the defining traits of each species, mostly because these fish are so rarely encountered on land or caught at sea, and also because we are not familiar with them ourselves, having seen each species only a handful of times over the years.

They are all members of the wrasse family (Labridae) and are brightly colored, or at least brightly marked, fish. All have large scales. The distinguishing trait of this group of fish is the mouth, which is tiny and, together with the snout, molded into a beak (the better for scraping bits of food off of reefs). Most parrotfish are oval shaped, but some are cigar shaped: all have gently rounded fins, which are as colorful as the rest of the body.

EATING: At its best, parrotfish has a taste and texture that almost, but not quite, recalls lobster. At its worst, parrotfish meat tastes like old algae. Because we've eaten so few (and we've never had these kinds of parrotfish from other waters), we can only assume that, as in the case of the Striped Mullet, diet determines everything.

AVAILABILITY: These species are very occasionally caught by Vermilion Snapper boats. Your best bet for any of them would be to buy a boat, get spearfishing equipment, learn how to use said equipment (and how to drive the boat), then go hunt your own. They are sometimes imported from countries around the Caribbean Sea and the Pacific and Indian Oceans. Beware of these fish. Parrotfish don't

travel well under the best of circumstances, and they don't stand prolonged storage very well. In seafood industry parlance, they "don't have legs," which means, after the circuitous route they take from their country of origin, they are probably not worth the money you will pay for them.

The wrasses are fish similar to the parrotfish and are commercially exploited in some parts of the world. These tend to be higher

quality. One species of wrasse, the Hogfish (*Lachnolaimus maximus*), is a highly commercial species. Alas, while commonly caught in eastern Gulf of Mexico and southern US Atlantic waters, it is pretty much nonexistent in northwestern Gulf waters. As for other wrasses, see the preceding paragraph.

SQUIRRELFISH AND LONGSPINE SQUIRRELFISH
Holocentrus adscensionis and *Holocentrus rufus*

COMMON NAMES: Colloquially, both species are called Daggerfish, Razorfish, and Soldierfish.

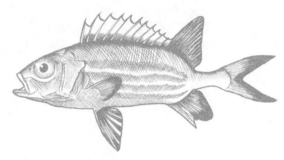

HABITAT: These two species prefer reefs and shallow waters to more than three hundred feet.

RANGE/DISTRIBUTION: They can be found in Gulf of Mexico and Caribbean waters, as well as in immediately contiguous waters.

DESCRIPTION: Both species are rectangular, with small heads, very large red eyes, and very prominent fins. The sharply forked tail fin is taller than the fish itself, the second and anal fins run parallel to the tail, and the pelvic fins drag far beneath the fish. The bright yellow front dorsal fin is tall and spiny. The body is mottled white and cherry red and orange. The only difference between the two species is the length of the bodies; the Longspine Squirrelfish is less compressed.

We don't know where or why the name Squirrelfish was born, but the other common names refer to the wicked gill plates and sharp dorsal spines of these species. The edges of both the front and back sections of the gill plates (the preoperculum and operculum, respectively) are razor sharp. While most fish possess such gill plates, in the Squirrelfish they are weaponized. PJ has sliced his hand open on more than one occasion with Squirrelfish, each time reminding himself that he isn't even as smart as a dead fish. There are half a dozen more Gulf species of squirrelfish than we describe here. All look similar, and all are well armed.

EATING: Both of these fish taste good enough, but they are also both exceedingly bony. They are too small to fillet but great to fry—if you don't mind lots and lots of small bones.

AVAILABILITY: These two squirrelfish are almost never available commercially.

FLYING GURNARD

Dactylopterus volitans

COMMON NAME: Flying Searobin

HABITAT: The Flying Gurnard swims around rocks and reefs in waters as deep as a few hundred feet.

RANGE/DISTRIBUTION: It occurs on both sides of the Atlantic; along almost the entire coasts of both North and South America, including the Gulf and the Caribbean; in the eastern Atlantic from Angola to England; and in the Mediterranean.

DESCRIPTION: This fish looks almost exactly like its inshore searobin cousins, except its pectoral fins are much, much bigger. Each

fin, fully extended, forms slightly more than a semicircle. The body is drab brown to tan to olive to orange, sometimes with spots or patterns. The pectoral fins are fringed in blue. This is the largest searobin in our waters, reaching more than twenty inches in length and weighing up to five pounds.

EATING: The Flying Gurnard is utterly delightful to eat, even better than the inshore searobins. Fillets are easier to cut as well. If you happen to get one of these (and, more importantly, if you already have some large and small scorpionfish), we would hope you would make Bouillabaisse.

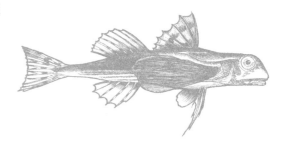

AVAILABILITY: Unless you catch your own, you will not see this fish from local fisheries. On the other hand, very closely related species are fished in the waters off New Zealand and marketed here in the United States. We only saw this fish once from local waters, and it was in poor shape.

GREAT BARRACUDA

Sphyraena barracuda

COMMON NAME: Kaku (Hawai'i)

HABITAT: Great Barracudas are associated with reefs and structures down to several hundred feet but are not limited to bottom waters, being usually caught much higher in the water column.

RANGE/DISTRIBUTION: The species is found worldwide in tropical and semitropical waters—anywhere warm enough for reefs to thrive.

DESCRIPTION: The Great Barracuda has a pointed snout, covering a mouth (which cannot fully close because of the large spiked teeth sprouting at odd angles), attached to a large, heavy head that is, with the snout, more than twice as long as it is tall. The rest of the elongated body is no bigger around than the head. Dorsal, pelvic, pectoral, and anal fins are unimpressive. The caudal fin is broom shaped and about twice as tall as the body. Large metallic silver scales cover a body that is silver from belly to back, head to tail. Sometimes black or gray triangular stripes run down the back, and sometimes black dots pepper the sides of the fish. The Great Barracuda certainly appears to be an animal confident of its place in the food chain.

EATING: Barracuda can be delicious; it can also at times be slightly unpleasant. We have a few assumptions about why this is, but nothing more than that. But you will not have to taste it to find out—appearance alone tells the tale.

A Great Barracuda with pink, firm flesh will be delightful. If, however, a barracuda has gray meat, don't even consider it. Please note that we assume that both fish are equally fresh. Once PJ took an ill-advised gamble on a couple hundred pounds of barracuda (they had been caught by a handline boat targeting amberjack and Vermilion Snapper). He sold quite a bit. Then the phone calls from disgruntled customers started, followed by return trips to pick up all the fish. The complaints were identical: some fish were good, others terrible. After filleting all the fish, PJ was no closer to discerning the difference in external appearance between a good and a bad barracuda. The smaller fish were less affected by gray meat, but even that was not a defining trait.

The FDA designates dozens of species of Gulf fish as potentially ciguatoxic, including *all* snappers, groupers, and jacks, among others. However, because we have so few coral reefs, the risk (at least in the northwestern Gulf) is negligible as long as certain elementary steps are taken in harvesting (for example, commercial boats follow strict protocols to eliminate any such hazard). Barracuda is probably as safe to eat as those other species, but given the feeding habits of this fish, the distance it can travel, and the painful consequences of ciguatera poisoning, we recommend staying away from any Barracuda larger than seven pounds.

AVAILABILITY: There are no local directed fisheries for Great Barracuda. It used to be caught as bycatch by Vermilion Snapper and amberjack handline boats, but there are fewer boats like that these days. Larger markets serving Southeast Asian, Latin American, Caribbean, West African, and South Asian communities might carry imported barracuda. Seafood companies sometimes sell barracuda at the restaurant level, but this is also product from other waters, either imported from or fished in Hawaiian waters. Hawaiian barracuda tends to be a decent choice, but avoid most others.

GUAGUANCHE AND SENNET

Sphyraena guachancho and *Sphyraena borealis*

COMMON NAMES: For both species: Tenaga Kamasu (Japan), Lesser Barracuda

HABITAT: Guaguanches are generally found over sandy and muddy waters, though they are a semipelagic species that does travel considerable distances sometimes. Sennets sometimes swim in the same areas as the Guaguanche but are also found around reefs and structures.

RANGE/DISTRIBUTION: The two species range along the eastern seaboard of the United States south of Massachusetts and all throughout the Gulf, the Caribbean, and southern Atlantic waters.

DESCRIPTION: The Guaguanche and Sennet are almost identical (the former is more commonly caught than the latter, so we focus on that species). The Sennet is slightly smaller and has a tan caudal fin as opposed to the black caudal fin of the Guaguanche.

They both look like a very small barracuda because that's what they are. The bodies are long, round, and needle shaped. Snouts end in a sharp point, and the mouths are filled with rather unpleasant-looking teeth, some of which grow so long as to prevent the fish from completely closing their mouths. Both species are metallic silver with irregular series of black dots and blotches. All of the fins are rather small, but the streamlined

bodies are powerful, as befits an ambush predator.

EATING: To say that these two fish are very good to eat is an understatement. The meat is quite white when raw, with a fine flake when cooked. Guaguanche in particular has a delicate flavor, but both stand up to just about any kind of cooking. They are great whole, but the fillets are very easy to get at. Analogous species in the eastern Mediterranean are prized food fish (a friend from Lebanon, who is also a longtime Gulf Coast resident, waxed poetic about the fish, which he called Malifa, and could not believe that he had been living "next door" to his favorite

fish for years). An almost identical species is used for sushi and sashimi in Japan, where it is called Kamasu (this seems to be a common name for possibly more than one species of barracuda, for we have found no definitive information one way or the other).

Because these species prefer grassy and sandy areas, there is no known ciguatoxic risk.

AVAILABILITY: Commercial boats targeting Vermilion Snappers sometimes bring in a few dozen. Unfortunately, very few boats target Vermilions anymore, and these fish are rarely caught aside from that. Alas.

If you should find yourself in a good Japanese restaurant, and you see Kamasu on the menu, do yourself a favor and order it.

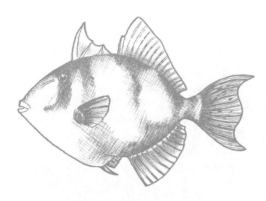

GRAY TRIGGERFISH

Balistes capriscus

COMMON NAMES: Trigger, Turbot (Jamaica)

HABITAT: This is not a deep-dwelling species, as it rarely occurs below three hundred feet. It is associated somewhat with grass beds, but mostly with rocks, structures, and reefs.

RANGE/DISTRIBUTION: This fish can be found on both sides of the Atlantic, from Argentina and Angola in the south to Massachusetts and at least the Mediterranean in the north. In the Gulf of Mexico, Gray Triggerfish has traditionally been considered more of an eastern Gulf species (that part of the Gulf having much more favorable conditions for it).

Western Gulf populations have always been, outside of a few areas, sparser. According to some old fishermen we knew, the triggerfish population in the western Gulf increased relative to the decline in the Red Snapper population (this might have been due both to the triggerfish taking advantage of filling an ecological niche and to a lack of predation by Red Snapper on juvenile triggerfish). The same has been true, in reverse, as the Red Snapper population has bounced back. When we started in the fish trade in 2007, the catch share system had just started,

and the Red Snapper had not even started recovery. Landings of triggerfish back then were common enough. As the Red Snappers have come back, triggerfish catches in our part of the Gulf have declined.

DESCRIPTION: The Gray Triggerfish is gray and white, and sometimes black and tan also; sometimes it is a solid color, and other times it has colors interlocking over the whole body in a tessellated design resembling a coral reef. The face is mostly solid gray, with high-set eyes and a very small mouth equipped with scraggly triangular teeth. Sometimes the fins and face under the eyes are tinged with a bit of turquoise, which fades quickly after death. The caudal fin is vaguely broom shaped, with filaments at the top and bottom tips of the fin extending up to several inches behind the tail. Anal and second dorsal fins are rounded but roughly triangular. A small Gray Triggerfish is slightly under a pound, and a giant is over ten; most are between two and five pounds.

The first spine of the dorsal fin is thick and elongated and stands independently with only a small bit of fin webbing stretching to the next dorsal spine, which is maybe a quarter of the length of the first. A third spine stands behind this second, and this third spine marks the end of the front dorsal fin. The front dorsal spines are hinged, able to fold back flush with the back and also extend perpendicular to the body. The first dorsal spine, when extended all the way, locks into position. The spine will snap before it folds down. However, a slight amount of pressure on the small third dorsal spine unlocks the first spine and allows the whole assembly to fold into the closed position. Hence the "trigger" in triggerfish.

The Gray is anchor shaped, like all triggerfish, with the head forming the crown. The arms are formed by the first dorsal spine, and also by the large bone that runs from the mouth almost to the vent (this bone is formed by the fusion of the pelvic fin spines). When being pursued by predators (and the triggerfish has many predators, from tunas to snappers to groupers and beyond), it will wedge its head into a crack in nearby rocks and extend its dorsal spine. Predators have a great deal of difficulty in dislodging it after that, and its thick skin helps to protect its lower body from predators' teeth.

EATING: Nothing tastes like triggerfish. The fillets look like white fish, but the flesh is firm and redolent of shellfish. The flake is also quite unusual, pulling apart almost like frog meat rather than fish. Any cooking method is great for this fish.

Traditionally Gray Triggerfish had been a favorite (and economical) white fish in the eastern Gulf, common at fish shacks and white-tablecloth restaurants alike. Only in the last two decades did it gain such popularity in the northwestern Gulf.

Cutting one is a simple affair, as long as you treat the skin with the respect it requires. First, take a pointed blade and poke through the skin right at the shoulder. Then insert the knife into the hole and cut through the skin all the way around the fillet. You will want to insert the knife with the blade up rather than down and cut the skin from the inside. Trust us. The ribs and pin bones are soft and small, so the fillet can be cut with one fluid motion. After the fillet is off the bone, just pull the skin off the meat (the skin is thick—it will come off in one piece).

After you fillet the fish, do *not* throw away the head! Peel the skin off the head (by hand, no tools required), then pull the collars away from the head. Or just cook the whole head and take the meat off.

Or, don't fillet the fish at all. Cut and peel the skin off the fish. You can peel every bit of skin off easily. After that, grasp the dorsal fin with one hand and the fish with the other,

and pull. The dorsal fin will pull off in one piece (it always reminds us of peeling the rind off an orange). Repeat this process with the anal fins. Pull off the caudal fin and the pectoral fins. You now have a perfect whole roasting fish. Of course, it looks like a tadpole with a lamb's head, but it is quite tasty.

Lastly, prepare the liver. We don't know why some fish livers taste so good, and some so bad. We *do* know that Gray Triggerfish liver is a delight, good enough even to use in fish charcuterie.

AVAILABILITY: A decade ago, Gray Triggerfish was so common at the dock that we sometimes couldn't sell it all. These days, landings are not nearly as common and are always small. As mentioned above, Gray Triggerfish had been a ubiquitous restaurant fish in parts of Florida. Then it got overfished in those waters (an old Florida fisherman told PJ once about a pair of Gray Triggerfish skin boots he had made during the halcyon days of the triggerfish fishery). In recent years, commercial catches have been dramatically curtailed. A few years ago, commercial boats had only size, but not catch, limits on Gray Triggerfish. Currently, a commercial vessel may not possess or land more than fourteen Gray Triggerfish per trip.

Fishing for Gray Triggerfish is fun. Use the same rig and bait as for Atlantic Spadefish, and fish in the same places.

THE OTHER TRIGGERFISH: QUEEN, OCEAN, ROUGH, AND BLACK DURGON

Balistes vetula, Canthidermis sufflamen, Canthidermis maculata, and *Melichthys niger*

COMMON NAME: Black Durgon: Black Triggerfish

HABITAT: All of these species live near reefs and associated areas, as well as rocks and

structures. The Queen is found in deeper waters (down to more than six hundred feet); the other species typically swim in waters no more than half that deep.

RANGE/DISTRIBUTION: The Rough Triggerfish occurs worldwide in warm seas. The other three species are limited to the eastern and western Atlantic in most temperate and tropical waters. The eastern Gulf of Mexico and the Caribbean Sea boast substantial populations of all four species.

DESCRIPTION: All of these species are obvious variations on a theme of triggerfish, and they all grow to be at least as big as the Gray. The Queen is most similar in shape to the Gray and is certainly the showiest of the Gulf triggerfish. The body has a background of solid gray, upon which flashes of turquoise and green and yellow play. The rear of the belly is gray, which fades into a custard yellow to pumpkin-flesh orange that covers the throat up to the mouth. The mouth is encircled with a thick band of blue or turquoise, and two thick lines of the same color stretch from pectoral fin to pectoral fin over the eyes and above the mouth, resulting in what looks like two hastily drawn fake mustaches, the lower intersecting the blue band around the mouth. There are one or two blurred but bright blue bands around the caudal peduncle. Dorsal, anal, and caudal fins are fringed in blue.

The Ocean is longer and less compressed than the Gray. Its second dorsal and anal fins retain the typical triangular shape, but are larger and straighter and extend perpendicular to the body itself. It is gray like the Gray, with occasional black flourishes on the tips of the caudal, dorsal, and anal fins. It also has a slightly more pointed snout.

The Rough isn't remarkably rough, at least not relative to other triggerfish. It has the long body and fins of the Ocean, with a more rounded snout. Usually it is gray to dark gray. Younger fish are covered with irregularly shaped and sized white spots; these usually fade as the fish gets older, but not always.

The Black Durgon is not as compressed as the Gray but is less elongated than the Ocean. Dorsal and anal fins are prominent but rounded and follow the shape of the tail. Bright white stripes run along the base of the dorsal and anal fins. Aside from those stripes, the entire body is completely matte black. It is a stunning fish.

EATING: All of these species are uncommon, so we have only been able to try them sporadically. The Queen has always been our least favorite, the meat being coarse and sometimes having an unpleasant taste. The Ocean and the Rough are slightly coarse as well, but taste very nice, at least as nice as the Gray. The Black Durgon is almost indistinguishable from the Gray in terms of taste and texture.

AVAILABILITY: These species are never landed in appreciable numbers by commercial boats in Texas. All four are eternally oddball fish sold with other oddballs as a lot.

FILEFISH: UNICORN AND SCRAWLED

Aluterus monoceros **and** *Aluterus scriptus*

COMMON NAME: Filefish (rarely caught, so all species tend to get lumped together)

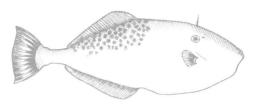

HABITAT: Unicorn and Scrawled Filefish swim on or around reefs, occurring in waters as shallow as a few dozen feet and as deep as several hundred feet.

RANGE/DISTRIBUTION: These two species occur worldwide in tropical and tropically influenced waters. Other Gulf species (which we do not describe here) are limited to local waters.

DESCRIPTION: Imagine a fish getting run over by a steamroller, like in the old cartoons. That more or less describes all filefish. The bodies are elongated and severely flattened (not as flat as the Moonfish or Lookdown but impressive nonetheless). Filefish have larger eyes and smaller mouths than their trigger-fish cousins.

The Unicorn is so named for the first dorsal fin spine, which is quite elongated and thin (it does indeed stick up from the forehead, but the overall effect calls to mind a narwhal, not a unicorn). The body of the Unicorn is triggerfish shaped and uniformly gray, and the skin is smoother than that of the triggerfish (though it is just as thick and tough). Occasionally, a few blurred black dots occur along the back of the fish.

The Scrawled Filefish gets its name from the meandering blue stripes and black dots that cover the body. The body is shorter than the Unicorn's but otherwise recognizable as a filefish. The caudal fin is very large, about twice the height of the body.

EATING: We have seen each of these species exactly once. We have therefore only cut

them up and eaten them exactly once. We got lucky, as both of the fish were on the larger size. They were fine eating, but we can see the difficulties involved with processing smaller specimens. They are more or less like Gray Triggerfish, but a bit finer in texture.

AVAILABILITY: Don't count on it. Due to their feeding habits, habitats, and small mouths, these fish are almost never caught by either commercial or recreational boats.

SMOOTH PUFFER AND THE REST OF THE PUFFERS

Lagocephalus laevigatus et al.

COMMON NAME: Smooth Puffer: Rabbitfish

HABITAT: The Smooth Puffer prefers shallow to deeper waters on sand and mud bottoms. Other puffers live over rocks and reefs.

RANGE/DISTRIBUTION: This species occurs on both sides of the Atlantic, from north to south; puffer species in general are globally distributed in temperate to tropical waters.

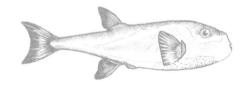

DESCRIPTION: Puffers generally don't have scales (or if they do, they are tiny enough to elude notice). Heads are large, as are the eyes. Mouths are tiny. Front teeth are usually fused together into structures called beaks. Bodies taper significantly toward the tail; all fins are small. The skin on the bellies is barbed, and the bellies themselves are white.

The Smooth Puffer in particular is golden everywhere except the belly. Even the eyes are golden. Some puffers are small; the Smooth Puffer can weigh several pounds.

If you happen to come across an ungutted puffer fresh out of the water (but not alive), impress your companions by blowing it up like a balloon.

EATING: We only describe this species and its Tetraodontidae cousins because we saw a few over the years. We have never eaten any puffer from the Gulf.

Some species of puffers are famously toxic, though no species of puffer actually produces toxin. Rather, they accumulate toxins (called tetrodotoxin) through their diet (the poison does nothing to the fish itself). Over time, more and more toxins accumulate in the fish's body (in the guts and skin). Some species of puffer have a different diet and are thus less or not at all toxic (the Northern Puffer [*Sphoeroides maculatus*] of the east coast is an example). Other puffers are safe to eat, as long as the fish is harvested only from certain waters and processed in a specific way so as to avoid contaminating the meat (the Japanese Fugu, for example). Still other puffers are completely toxic and cannot be eaten at all, no matter the degree of processing.

The Smooth Puffer is apparently one of the least dangerous of the puffers, and it is marketed in northern Gulf coastal areas of Mexico. However, those fish are harvested elsewhere, and no accurate and timely information exists concerning toxicity of this or other Gulf puffer species.

Tetrodotoxin is a toxin for which there is no antidote. Treatment consists of secondary support but no direct treatment. It can mean a slow, paralyzing death. It can be a one-way street. So, we stay away from these and all puffers, except under very specific circumstances.

AVAILABILITY: No American Gulf fisheries exist at all for Smooth Puffer, but some local fisheries can be found in northern Mexico.

Fishing puffers for your own table is a very bad idea.

GOATFISH: YELLOW, DWARF, AND SPOTTED

Mulloidichthys martinicus, Upeneus parvus, and Pseudopeneus maculatus

COMMON NAMES: The Dwarf is occasionally imported from Brazil and erroneously marketed as Rouget, aka Red Mullet.

HABITAT: These three goatfish prefer rocky areas, reefs, and seagrass meadows in nearshore waters. The Dwarf swims deeper than the others, down to maybe a few hundred feet. However, all three are common in shallower waters.

RANGE/DISTRIBUTION: These are tropical fish, and all are confined to the western Atlantic, roughly between the southern United States and Brazil, as well the Gulf of Mexico and Caribbean Sea.

DESCRIPTION: If you have ever seen or eaten the fish called Rouget or Red Mullet, then you know what these fish look like. They are small, never reaching a foot in length, and are generally half that size. They are kind of comet shaped (not unlike tilefish, though the two families share no close ancestry), with steeply angled snouts terminating in downward-facing mouths accompanied by barbels. The Spotted is apparently drab, at least compared to most goatfish; the Dwarf is red, but not the red of its regal Mediterranean cousins; the Yellow is appropriately yellow, though mostly in the form of thick horizontal stripes running from snout to tail against a white background.

EATING: We confess here that, aside from an unfortunate experience with a disagreeable Brazilian specimen, we have not eaten these species. We include them only as a further (and we hope not gratuitous) illustration of the tapestry of edible Gulf fish. We do, however, routinely enjoy delightful Rouget, to which we are lucky enough to have access thanks to a local fishmonger of impeccable repute.

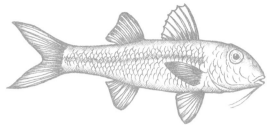

Few can match the majesty of goatfish. Almost no fish is better to eat. This is not our opinion alone—the goatfish enjoy a culinary reputation stretching back thousands of years. The meat is pure white and as succulent as fatty crab. Goatfish have no more bones than most other white fish, but the size of the fish themselves means that the bones are small, so a bit of practice is needed to master the filleting process—or perhaps more than just a bit of practice, for we know many chefs who recoil at the thought of Rouget in their kitchens.

Cook this fish whole. If you perchance get ahold of a particularly pristine goatfish, consider grilling it whole, scaled but ungutted.

While the famous Mediterranean Rouget is indeed a goatfish, it is emphatically not the same fish as the Dwarf Goatfish (superficial appearances aside). The former is admittedly superior to the latter, though any goatfish in the world tastes great.

AVAILABILITY: Traditionally, shrimpers have been the only boats ever to catch any Gulf goatfish. All of these, it seems, were returned to the water and have never been marketed whatsoever.

CHAPTER 9
DEEPWATER GROUNDFISH

Of all the fish in this chapter, only the Golden Tilefish is targeted locally. Of the rest, some, like the Barrelfish and Driftfish, are marketable bycatch; others, like the Beardfish, are destined to remain low-dollar, third-tier fish; still others, like the Crimson Rover and the Slimehead, are rarely caught, and then only in small numbers, which makes marketing them impossible.

In that last category, we could include dozens more species from a vast swathe of deepwater Gulf of Mexico fish that remain inaccessible. In the Gulf, as discussed at the beginning of the book, commercial finfish may only be taken by hook and line in federal waters. Hook-and-line methods, however, are effective only for some kinds of fish and only in certain environments; they are not as well suited for use in more than two thousand feet of water. Furthermore, no sustained work has ever been done on assessing and exploiting these potential fisheries. Commercial fishing boats, for their part, do not have the time or money to go out to sea time after time, looking for new species and new grounds (which is a good thing in the end).

The most effective fishing method would be trawling, but that is, of course, strictly illegal, and no one in fisheries management is looking to change the situation. We do not find fault with this stance, for it is better to restrict in the beginning than try to catch up with a decimated fishery afterward.

For a partial list of Gulf fish not currently targeted by any commercial vessels, see appendix I, page 281.

GOLDEN TILEFISH

Lopholatilus chamaeleonticeps

COMMON NAME: Great Northern Tilefish

HABITAT: The Golden Tilefish prefers muddy, sandy bottoms in deep waters from several hundred to more than a thousand feet. This is the same type of bottom preferred by Yellowedge Grouper (though it lives in slightly shallower waters), and this is why both species are targeted by the same longline boats on the same trips.

RANGE/DISTRIBUTION: This species is found in western Atlantic waters from southern Canada through northern South America. The largest commercial fishery in American waters is on the mid-Atlantic coast off of New York and New Jersey.

DESCRIPTION: The Golden Tilefish has a heavy head relative to its tapering body, which ends in a modest broom tail. The head alone (with collars and all meat attached) makes up around 25 percent of the weight of the fish. The brushed-gold eyes are large but not overly so, and the heavy lips seem to be settled in a perpetual frown. On the top of the head, right before the beginning of the dorsal fin, is a fleshy bright yellow bit—the equivalent, we've always hoped, of a rooster's comb (though not as grand).

Overall the fish is gray, though speckled with bright yellow dots everywhere on the body from snout to tail. Pectoral fins are pale gray to white; the rest are all fringed with the same brilliant yellow.

Commercially caught Golden Tilefish range from two to fifty pounds, though the majority are between four and twenty; those caught by recreational fishers tend to be on the larger side.

EATING: The meat yield is famously low (around 30 percent, as opposed to around 43 percent for Red Snapper), owing to the tapering shape and the firmly anchored pin bones running from head to tail. Aside from this marketing flaw (a flaw because it leads to a higher fillet price than the fish actually merits), the Golden Tilefish is a tasty, if rather insipid, fish. The flake is large and the flesh very lean. In other words, it is a highly accessible fish.

AVAILABILITY: Golden Tilefish local fish are more and more common in restaurants, thanks to current management, which has resulted in modest year-round catches. (Golden Tilefish, Goldface Tilefish, and Blueline Tilefish are managed together under a catch share system; see page 82 for more information.) Outside of coastal areas of the Gulf, Golden Tilefish is more likely to come from boats unloading in New York or New Jersey (together, these two states unload more than half of the American catch of Golden Tilefish).

As for recreational fishing, the same requirements and caveats apply as for Queen Snapper, Cardinal Snapper, and all deepwater groupers: a long-distance boat, adequate hydraulic gear, and money to make those things work.

BARRELFISH AND BLACK DRIFTFISH

Hyperoglyphe perciformis and *Hyperoglyphe bythites*

COMMON NAME: Both species traditionally (and erroneously) were called Barrel Grouper.

HABITAT: The Barrelfish and Black Driftfish inhabit all kinds of bottoms in five hundred to more than thirteen hundred feet of water. They are apparently benthopelagic, meaning they roam far and wide in the ocean, staying closer to the bottom than to the surface. They do not stay right on the seafloor (like, for example, a Golden Tilefish), but rather swim some distance above.

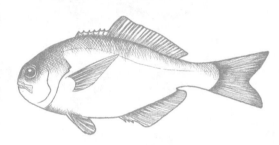

RANGE/DISTRIBUTION: These fish are more at home in temperate waters. Hence, although both species occur throughout our waters, the Gulf is the southernmost limit of their range. More than likely the largest populations are elsewhere.

DESCRIPTION: We admit we might have some difficulty in differentiating these two fish. Both have deep, stout oval bodies with gently forked tails. The eyes are large and expressive, the Black Driftfish's being larger than those of the Barrelfish. Their snouts are severely blunted, so much as to appear disfigured. Mouths are small, with discreet teeth. While the Barrelfish is slightly larger

than the Driftfish, both can easily weigh as much as thirty pounds or more. Both fish are more or less monochromatic, with only the slightest fading at the belly. The Driftfish is brownish black, and the Barrelfish is green gray. Both can also be completely gray. Scales are large but start to slough off after the fish dies.

EATING: Because their meat is white, sweet, tender, and flaky, these species were sold as "Barrel Grouper" for years by Gulf Coast docks and seafood companies. No one was interested in a weird fish with a weird name, but everyone knew grouper, so the name stuck. And the fish was cheap, so it sold well. To be clear, though, in no way are either of these fish members of the grouper family.

Both the Barrelfish and the Black Driftfish are easy to cut and large enough to provide fillets weighing at least a couple of pounds each but not so large as to be unwieldy or unappetizing. The skin is edible, but it's not the kind of skin one just fries up. The head is large and meaty.

AVAILABILITY: Traditionally, these two fish constitute a minor, nontargeted fishery here in the Gulf. In other words, the Barrelfish and the Driftfish have never been sought out by commercial boats, but some boats (in our waters, bottom longliners targeting Yellowedge Grouper and Golden Tilefish) catch some incidentally, and the flesh is marketable enough, so they are kept and unloaded at the dock.

In recent years, thanks to accurate marketing campaigns, the Barrelfish has become a more or less common, if inconsistent, catch (a practical effect of which has been an across-the-board price increase from dock to restaurant of around 100 percent). They are still not easily available at the retail level, aside from seafood markets.

Two very similar species, occurring in the western Pacific, are both targeted commercially and enjoy considerable table reputations. One is the Bluenose (*Hyperoglyphe antarctica*, alternately called the Bluenose Warehou and the Bluenose Cod), fished off Australia and New Zealand; the other is the Pacific Barrelfish (*Hyperoglyphe japonica*), fished off Japan, where it is called Medai.

ATLANTIC BEARDED BROTULA

Brotula barbata

COMMON NAMES: Hake (erroneously), Cusk, Sugarfish

HABITAT: The Atlantic Bearded Brotula lives in deep waters down to two thousand feet or more (though it is most common at half that depth). It sticks close to the bottom and prefers sandy and muddy bottoms.

RANGE/DISTRIBUTION: It is found on both sides of the Atlantic: in the west from Florida to Brazil, including the Gulf of Mexico and Caribbean Sea; and in the east from Senegal to Angola.

DESCRIPTION: The Atlantic Bearded Brotula is a member of the family Ophidiidae, the cusk-eels, but no fish in the family is actually an eel—that name was applied to these fish because of rough similarities to true eels. In truth, cusk-eels are more closely related to the family Gadidae (the cod family).

Like all members of the family, the Atlantic Bearded Brotula has no tail—the body just tapers to a point, with the small dorsal and anal fins running all the way to the end. It has a small head, small mouth, small eyes, and no pelvic fins. It can exceed twenty pounds, but ten or a bit under is more common. It is a uniform brown to light brown, sometimes with some pink, paling toward

the belly. Both the scientific and common names derive from the prominent barbels hanging down from the mouth.

EATING: If you like cod, you will like this fish. It yields a pale white fillet, thick at the shoulder (though too thin at the tail end), with little taste and nice flake. Obviously, it is perfect for frying (maybe the best frying fish in this book). It is also great cooked in a

pan or steamed. The head is delicious fried also. Filleting is easy—just like a cod, except for the tail (and just like a cod, the backbone is small and floats between the fillets). And if you should find yourself with dozens of Atlantic Bearded Brotula, by all means cut out and fry the "tongues," which are not tongues at all, but instead the fleshy patch of meat under the chin (see page 197 for more about fish tongues).

AVAILABILITY: Atlantic Bearded Brotula is a bycatch species from the bottom longline fishery. Traditionally, at least in the eastern Gulf, brotula was considered part of the crew's catch, that part of the catch the crew took back to their families.

Catching your own is possible—if you have the time and the boat and the gear. Just fish on the bottom (assuming you know where to fish; we don't).

BEARDFISH AND STOUT BEARDFISH

Polymixia lowei and Polymixia nobilis

HABITAT: These species are found over soft, muddy, and hard bottoms in several hundred to more than two thousand feet of water.

RANGE/DISTRIBUTION: Two species are described here, and both range throughout all waters of the Gulf of Mexico and the Caribbean Sea, up the Atlantic coast through the mid-US coast, and down to Brazil. The Stout Beardfish also occurs in the eastern Atlantic, from Angola to Senegal.

DESCRIPTION: The "beard" in "Beardfish" comes from the long barbels that hang from the bottom of the mouth. The differences between these two species are negligible. Neither species is large—at most they weigh four or five pounds. Their eyes are large and silver. None of the fins are striking, including the fork-shaped tail. The bodies are dark blue to dark gray, and scales are bright metallic silver.

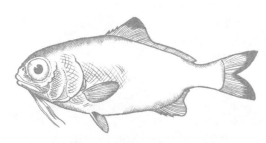

EATING: Beardfish is good, but not for everyone. The fish is a snap to fillet (don't mess with scaling it, for the skin isn't that great), but the fillets themselves are riddled with several rows of awkward pin bones. Pulling out the pin bones isn't a great option, as they are embedded in the skin.

The best way to attack a Beardfish is by cooking the fish whole, then picking the meat. This has the added benefit of keeping the fillets from drying any more than need be, for the flesh under the best circumstances tends to be dry. The flesh doesn't flake so much as pull apart in threads, much like crab or lobster claw. This is a nice coincidence, because the flesh happens to have a distinctly crab-like taste.

AVAILABILITY: Both species of Beardfish are bycatch from Yellowedge Grouper and Golden Tilefish bottom longliners. Catches by these boats are small, and landings smaller, for the Beardfish is not now, nor will it be, a targeted fishery, at least in American waters. It is rarely even available at the wholesale and restaurant level (remember that dry flesh and those bones).

CRIMSON ROVER

Erythrocles monodi

COMMON NAME: Atlantic Rubyfish

HABITAT: This is a schooling bottom fish, found close to (but not on) muddy and sandy bottoms, in three hundred to more than a thousand feet of water. It is not quite a sedentary species (meaning it migrates to some extent, as opposed to most fish in this chapter, which pretty much stay in one place).

RANGE/DISTRIBUTION: The Crimson Rover ranges on both sides of the Atlantic in warm waters. In the northern Atlantic, it occurs from the Carolinas to Senegal, and from Brazil to Angola in the southern Atlantic. Populations are smaller and inconsistent in the Gulf of Mexico.

DESCRIPTION: The Crimson Rover is more or less torpedo shaped. The pointed snout lies atop bony lips that can, when fully extended, stretch a couple inches from the mouth. Eyes are red and large. The dorsal, pectoral, anal, and pelvic fins are small and delicate; the caudal fin is severely forked. The head and fins are indeed crimson, as are the lips. The body is crimson— light, dark, or shot through with greens, yellows, and purples—from the back to a bit below the high-set lateral line, right above the pectoral fin. The few we've seen weighed between one and three pounds, which is apparently the average size.

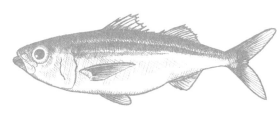

EATING: Of course, this is a great fish to cook whole, scaled or not. Any method is applicable here. The pale white fillets come off the bone easily. It is delicious.

AVAILABILITY: Superficially, the Crimson Rover resembles the Vermilion Snapper, and both fish sometimes hang out in the same places, which means a few Crimson Rovers will inevitably get caught by boats targeting Vermilions. Catches are always small and incidental, and, frankly, a lot of hands touching the fish throughout the supply line don't necessarily catch the difference, so sometimes restaurants and seafood markets end up selling Crimson Rover as Vermilion Snapper. This is not intentional fraud of course, nor is it a loss of value, for the Crimson Rover is at least as good as the Vermilion, but it is still not the same fish. The point is, this fish is rare at any level of the seafood chain—at least here in the northwestern Gulf. The species is apparently targeted off the central West African coast (Senegal to Angola) for local food fisheries (where it has a good table reputation) as well as reduction fisheries

(meaning fishmeal and fish oil). Large, sometimes vast trawlers can process dozens of tons of product per drag; these are almost always foreign vessels operating (legally or not) within the Exclusive Economic Zone of one or more central West African countries.

DARWIN'S SLIMEHEAD

Gephyroberyx darwinii

COMMON NAMES: Slimehead, Roughy, Big Roughy, Darwin's Roughy

HABITAT: A schooling fish, Darwin's Slimehead is found (sometimes in dense clouds) over rocky or hard bottoms, sometimes on sand, in deep water along the continental slope (down to at least four thousand feet). This slimehead is pelagic, moving sometimes over long distances in search of food, but always close to the bottom.

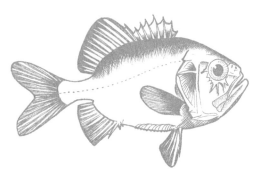

RANGE/DISTRIBUTION: Darwin's Slimeheads occur worldwide: in the Atlantic Ocean on both the west and east coasts, from top to bottom, including the Gulf of Mexico and the Caribbean Sea; in the Pacific, the largest populations are from Australia through the Philippines and throughout the Indian Ocean.

DESCRIPTION: Darwin's Slimehead is more or less comet shaped, with a tall, thin broom tail. The head is rounded and covered with a mask of bony plates. The eyes are silver gold. The mouth is large, with protrusible lips. The body is monochromatic—sometimes dark pink, sometimes pink red, sometimes red orange—with fins slightly darker than the body. It's not a big fish, weighing at most a few pounds and reaching a little more than a foot in length.

EATING: Like the Orange Roughy (*Hoplostethus atlanticus*), the darling of expensive restaurants in the 1980s and middle-of-the-road restaurants in the 1990s, this fish is a member of the Trachichthyidae, or slimehead, family. Orange Roughy is famous for its snow-white flesh, nice flake, and almost complete lack of flavor.

The Darwin's Slimehead is more watery and insipid than the Orange Roughy, but it's not bad. The skin is edible, though the firmly embedded scales make it difficult to get it in usable shape. The fish is easy to fillet, but if you get the chance, use it whole—it's a mighty impressive whole fish to bring to the table. If you fillet the fish, it's best to salt the fillets for ten minutes, as taste and texture will be much improved.

AVAILABILITY: No targeted fisheries exist in the Gulf or in most places in the fish's range. In some areas, the Darwin's is targeted for reduction purposes, but not for the table. In the Gulf specifically, a fishery is impossible due to both gear restrictions (trawling for finfish is illegal here) and the lack of a local deep-sea fleet. It is occasionally taken as bycatch by bottom longliners or, more rarely, by Vermilion Snapper boats fishing in unusually deep waters.

GULF HAKE (WHICH IS NOT A NORMAL HAKE) AND THE OFFSHORE HAKE (WHICH IS)

Urophycis cirrata and *Merluccius albidus*

HABITAT: Both species live in deep water to at least two thousand feet. The Gulf Hake lives on muddy bottoms and is quite sedentary; the Offshore Hake tends to travel a bit more and is found over mixed bottoms.

RANGE/DISTRIBUTION: The Gulf Hake occurs throughout the Gulf of Mexico and the Caribbean Sea and in the North Atlantic down to Suriname; the Offshore Hake shares the same southern distribution, but also occurs as far north as Canada.

DESCRIPTION: These are both obvious Gadiformes (cod-like fish). The Gulf Hake has a small head; sad, tired brown eyes; and a slightly downturned mouth (with the requisite gadiform barbels). The pelvic fin spines are fused into a single thin, long thread, which hangs below the fish several inches. As far as cod-like fish go, this is not a big species, weighing at most six or seven pounds (and most commonly less than half that). It is a dull tan all over, with black fringe on the dorsal, caudal, and anal fins. Pectoral fins are dark brown. The fish is very soft, and its scales are deciduous.

The Offshore is perhaps the more familiar, if only because it is of secondary commercial importance on the US Atlantic coast. The snout is pointed; the eyes are large; and the mouth is filled with small, transparent needle teeth. It is dark silver on the back and lighter silver on the belly, while all of its fins are dark gray to light brown or yellow. A dark streak runs along the lateral line from head to tail.

EATING: The Offshore Hake is an accessible fish. It is easy to fillet and even easier to split down the back and smoke. The flesh is firm

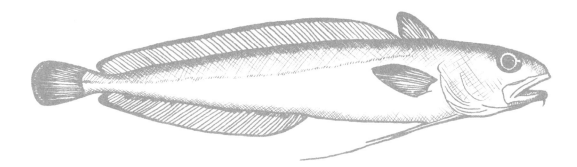

and pale. Fry it, steam it, put it in a soup. Scale it first, though, for the skin is a delight.

The Gulf Hake is a little more difficult. As noted, it is a soft fish—very soft. Without a very sharp knife and a knowledge of the fish, filleting can sometimes be tricky. But it is not that difficult.

The fillet, freshly cut from the fish, is watery and tends to fall apart when cooked (and it doesn't taste like much). Solve both of these problems by salting the fillets. Put the fillets in a single layer on a pan and sprinkle them liberally with salt. Let stand for no more than ten minutes, then wash off the salt and dry the fillets. You will be surprised at the difference. Incidentally, this technique may be applied to a great many fish with some success.

AVAILABILITY: Offshore Hake is rare in the Gulf of Mexico, so catches are few and far between and always bycatch (from Vermilion Snapper boats fishing in deep waters or from bottom longliners). It is occasionally available at seafood markets and upscale grocery stores (though the fish are from New England, never the Gulf). Gulf Hake is a low-dollar fish, however, so it tends to get battered and forgotten.

CHAPTER 10

ASSORTED BLUE-WATER PELAGIC FISH

This group of fish varies widely in appearance, from the archetypal Swordfish to the otherworldly Opah to the surreal Mola. They all, however, are blue-water fish, mostly staying closer to the surface than the ocean floor (the glaring exception to that is certainly the Swordfish); most travel sometimes spectacular distances. They are mostly, but not all, large fish.

Aside from the Swordfish and the Dorado, which on account of their predictable and convenient daily and seasonal routines are easily fished, these species are bycatch or oddballs or extreme rarities. Very few of them are targeted species in large fisheries.

These are not the only pelagic species in the Gulf—all members of the tuna and mackerel family are pelagic, as are most sharks and several jacks. Those fish, however, fall conveniently into other chapters.

The Opah is included because we have heard of exactly three ever being caught by Gulf pelagic longliners. Having never heard of anyone catching or landing the Louvar (*Luvarus imperialis*), we do not include it.

We also do not include the billfish (Istiophoridae): Blue Marlin (*Makaira nigricans*), Atlantic Sailfish (*Istiophorus albicans*), Sailfish (*Istiophorus platypterus*), Marlin (*Kajikia albida*), and Longbill Spearfish (*Tetrapturus pfluegeri*). Commercial harvests of these fish are prohibited, and recreational catches are strictly regulated.

BIGSCALE POMFRET AND KEELTAIL POMFRET

Taractichthys longipinnis and *Taractes rubescens*

COMMON NAME: Bigscale Pomfret: Sickle Pomfret (though this is slightly erroneous)

HABITAT: Both species are oceanic pelagic fish, generally staying in the middle of the water column but also venturing into much deeper water—eighteen hundred feet or more. Both are also solitary fish, a fact that makes targeting them commercially difficult.

RANGE/DISTRIBUTION: The Keeltail Pomfret occurs around the world in tropical and warmer temperate oceans and seas (including, obviously, the Gulf of Mexico). The Bigscale is limited to the Atlantic but occurs basically everywhere there and in contiguous waters.

DESCRIPTION: The Bigscale is tall and rounded, with a blunt snout. The head is small, the eyes black and large with pupils like marbles. The upturned mouth gives the fish a petulant look. The sickle-shaped anal and dorsal fins are tall and hard, extending perpendicularly two or more inches from the body. Except for a whitish fringe on the back of the forked caudal fin, the fish is completely black. The scales are large, giving the fish a glossy look.

The Keeltail Pomfret looks like a Bigscale Pomfret that has been slightly flattened and then elongated. The snout is more pointed, though the upturned mouth is retained. Dorsal and anal fins are triangular, long, and firm. Whereas the Bigscale has a smooth caudal peduncle, that of the Keeltail is covered in smooth scutes. Coloration is the same as the Bigscale.

A few other species of pomfrets occur in the Gulf, but it seems as though humans only ever encounter the Bigscale and the Keeltail. The others are the Caribbean Pomfret (*Brama caribbea*), the Lowfin Pomfret (*Brama dussumieri*), the Tropical Pomfret (*Eumegistus brevorti*), and the Atlantic Fanfish (*Pterycombus brama*). We assume these all taste similar to the pomfrets described here.

EATING: Both species taste and look about the same, and both are delicious. While pomfrets are not as familiar to diners in most parts of the United States, they have a superb food reputation throughout most of their range, and they always command good prices. The fillet has the shape of a pompano fillet—thin, tall, and wide. Despite the odd rib structure, the belly is thick enough to save with the fillet. The meat itself is white and barely translucent. It is not gelatinous, but it looks as if it would be.

Few fish are better in a soup. Then again, not a lot of fish steam better than pomfrets.

Don't try to fry it. It will taste all right, but all of the delicate taste and texture will have been lost in the process.

AVAILABILITY: In the Gulf of Mexico, and in most places in the world, these species are bycatch from pelagic longline boats targeting tunas or Swordfish. They are not common anywhere—a boat might make several trips without catching any pomfrets at all. Sometimes a Gulf pelagic longliner brings in a few, which go to seafood companies, then to restaurants, but almost never to grocery stores.

A very similar species, the Sickle Pomfret (*Taractichthys steindachneri*), lives in the Pacific Ocean and is a slightly more common bycatch from the tuna fleets based in Hawai'i. It is sold as Monchong and is available by special order from most seafood companies and upscale seafood markets.

MAHI AND POMPANO DOLPHINFISH

Coryphaena hippurus and *Coryphaena equiselis*

COMMON NAMES: Mahi: Dorado, Dolphin, Dolphinfish

HABITAT: Both species are highly pelagic blue-water species. They swim fast and far. They live near the surface, seldom swimming deeper than a few hundred feet down.

RANGE/DISTRIBUTION: The two species range through all temperate and tropical oceans and seas of the world.

DESCRIPTION: The Mahi does everything fast. It swims fast. It eats fast. It grows faster than just about any fish. It reaches sexual maturity in less than six months, whereas snappers and groupers sometimes take decades to mature. It lives and dies quickly (few Mahi anywhere in the world even reach four years of age). It is a long (up to five feet or more) and thin baseball-bat-shaped fish. The front and second dorsal fins in both species are connected and run down the back from head to tail. This combined dorsal is several inches tall, and the spines are delicate; the anal fin is similar. The tail is tall and deeply forked. Commercially caught Mahi on average weigh between ten and twenty-five pounds; their maximum size, though, is perhaps four times that weight. The species exhibits a modest degree of sexual dimorphism. The male is larger and has a prominent bony crest on its head, making it look somewhat like a piscine cassowary. The female has a round head, lacking any ostentation.

The Pompano Dolphinfish looks exactly like a young female Mahi. It attains a maximum length of maybe three feet and can weigh up to ten pounds (though less than two feet and under three pounds is the average). We assume that it grows as fast and frenetically as the Mahi.

Both species boast extravagant coloration. When they first come out of the water, it's all neon colors: green, blue, and yellow, in varying patterns and combinations. The colors are so bold as to appear artificial, but they start to fade even a few moments after death.

EATING: The Mahi's most marketable characteristics are its long fillets that lack awkward bones, its neutral flavor, and its global abundance (making it an economical fish).

Pompano Dolphinfish is just as handy.

AVAILABILITY: Though their meat might not be glamorous, their life histories mean that both species are decent enough fish to hunt (populations can replace themselves in a timely manner, even with fishing pressure). Unfortunately, while Mahi is widely available at the retail level across the country, it very rarely comes from American Gulf waters (commercial catches in the Gulf are incidental).

Pompano Dolphinfish is not targeted ever, though probably a great many are unknowingly caught by boats targeting pelagic species. They are rare at the restaurant or retail level.

Both species are easy to catch in blue waters offshore. The most effective method seems to be drift-fishing or jigging. You just need a boat to get you there.

ESCOLAR AND OILFISH

Lepidocybium flavobrunneum and *Ruvettus pretiosus*

COMMON NAMES: Escolar: Butterfish, White Tuna (erroneous), Walu (Hawaiʻi)

HABITAT: These two species swim in deeper waters far offshore, sometimes closer to the surface (within a couple hundred feet), but more often farther down in the water column, up to two thousand feet or more. Apparently, the Escolar migrates vertically to a greater extent than the Oilfish.

RANGE/DISTRIBUTION: Both species probably occur all over the world in all temperate and tropical oceans.

DESCRIPTION: First, the easiest way to tell these species apart is the skin. Telling them apart is important, as shall be made clear shortly. The scales on both are fused to the skin. Escolar skin has a smooth, pebbled texture (like alligator luggage). Oilfish skin is covered from shoulder to tail with tiny barbs. The barbs are less than half an inch apart and run in orderly rows down the body. Each barb is actually a modified scale, composed

of several small hooks sprouting from a common base. Each individual barb faces a slightly different angle, but all are oriented toward the tail. We advise respecting them.

Aside from that, both fish look basically the same. They are about the same size, reaching several feet and weighing up to one hundred pounds or more at maturity. Both have pointed snouts enclosing mouths lined with small but impressive teeth. The eyes are typical of fish that spend a lot of time hunting in deep water—large and black, with gray-green marbles for pupils (if you should ever see a freshly caught Escolar or Oilfish, please take a moment to peer into the eyes—but only a moment, for any more than that and you are in danger of falling into the abyss). The bodies are cigar shaped, the Escolar being slightly more oval than

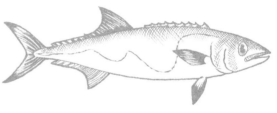

the Oilfish. Both fish are matte gray black at maturity (they are more of a chocolate color when younger). The lateral lines on both species are unlike any other, meandering and looping all over the sides of the body. Neither species has very impressive fins at all. The dorsal fin on the Oilfish is set slightly farther back than that of the Escolar. The Escolar has a more sharply forked tail.

A related fish, the Roudi Escolar (*Promethichthys prometheus*), looks more like a Snake Mackerel (which is neither a snake nor a mackerel). Edibility is unknown.

EATING: Both fish are, in their own setting and context, fantastic. The meat on both is almost white and completely opaque. It may be cut like a steak and grilled, or it may be eaten raw. For Escolar, poaching isn't the best way to go, especially if the broth is to be consumed along with the fish. It is fatty, but nothing like Bluefin Tuna. The fat just fades into the meat.

The Oilfish is quite good, but it requires special treatment. The meat must be cut into large pieces and then boiled in *three* changes of water. Then it can be used in soups or fried dishes. Even then, limit intake to four ounces at a time. We need to stress: if you want to cook Oilfish, DO NOT omit the blanchings and never eat more than a few ounces at a time.

Small portions and blanching procedures are necessary because of the hazard of gempylotoxin poisoning. Gempylotoxin, despite the name and FDA designation, isn't really a toxin at all. It is a name, basically, for certain wax esters, which, though not very toxic to humans, produce significant embarrassing side effects. Bear in mind, though, that some people are more sensitive to wax esters than others.

WE ADVISE QUITE A BIT OF CAUTION WHEN EATING EITHER OF THESE FISH.

AVAILABILITY: Both of these are sometimes caught as bycatch by Yellowfin Tuna and Swordfish longliners in Louisiana (and sometimes Texas). They are also taken as bycatch in the Hawaiian tuna fisheries, where they are called Walu.

OPAH

Lampris guttatus

COMMON NAMES: Moonfish, Sunfish

HABITAT: The Opah inhabits blue waters, from near the surface to almost two

thousand feet down. This is a solitary fish, swimming endlessly across the seas.

RANGE/DISTRIBUTION: It is recorded from tropical and temperate seas and oceans all over the world.

DESCRIPTION: The Opah belongs to the order Lampriformes, which is made up of just a few species, all of which are strange, magical fish with metallic-orange to silver-blue skin and neon-orange fins. It is the only member of the order that commonly encounters humans (the rest are even more secretive and solitary).

It is a big fish, shaped like a finned coin, with the distended belly making up half of the circumference. The fish might be up to six feet across and weigh five hundred pounds or more, but it is never more than a few inches wide. The head is small and mostly occupied by the large silver eyes and large gill plates. The mouth is small, the lips fleshy and full. Triangular pectoral, pelvic, and dorsal fins are elongated, hanging from the body a foot or more. The caudal fin is unremarkable.

The area across the back is orange, which fades at the lateral line into blue silver. The fins are solid orange. Numerous white dots pepper both sides of the body.

EATING: Neither in appearance nor taste does Opah resemble any other fish. The meat is orange, near the color of salmon, and is usually cut into loins, like tunas. The top loin looks familiar enough, and is best treated like Swordfish or tuna, or maybe a nice jack. The bottom loin is a large triangular flap, terminating in a small loin. This part of the fish is quite fatty. It is best served raw or smoked.

AVAILABILITY: Opah apparently pass in and out of the Gulf, so catches are exceedingly rare. More commonly they are caught by Hawaiian pelagic longline boats ("Opah" is the Hawaiian name for the fish). It is always bycatch, regardless of where it's caught.

WHITEFIN SHARKSUCKER, AND OTHER SHARKSUCKERS AND REMORAS

Echeneis neucratoides et al.

HABITAT: These fish are everywhere one finds large marine fish and mammals, as well as near reefs.

RANGE/DISTRIBUTION: This particular species of sharksucker is limited to the Gulf of Mexico, the Caribbean Sea, and surrounding waters, though other Gulf species occur throughout the world.

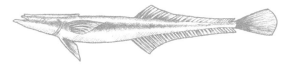

DESCRIPTION: The Whitefin Sharksucker is shaped like a tiny, skinny Cobia (to which it is related), with a suction cup on its head. It is maybe two feet long at its biggest and weighs only a few pounds. The suction cup is a series of ridges shaped so as to adhere when the pad is pressed against a solid

surface. This cup looks manufactured and is highly efficient. It also functions long after the fish is dead (a fact that has in the past delighted not only our children but professional cooks across Texas).

EATING: There is not a lot of meat on a sharksucker—the yield is less than 15 percent. The meat itself resembles Cobia in appearance and taste.

AVAILABILITY: Most likely, you will never see any species of sharksucker or remora for sale.

COBIA

Rachycentron canadum

COMMON NAMES: Ling, Lemonfish

HABITAT: Cobias are solitary fish that may be found from nearshore all the way to blue water. While they are somewhat pelagic, they are generally associated with reefs, structures, rocks, and floating debris (most notably the fields of Sargassum so common in the Gulf).

RANGE/DISTRIBUTION: This species ranges in temperate and tropical waters around the world.

DESCRIPTION: The Cobia looks, at first glance, like some kind of shark or maybe a long-lost relative of the catfish. It is neither, but rather a distant cousin of sharksuckers and remoras (a fact that becomes glaringly obvious when they are compared side by side). The head is large and slightly flattened on top, with prominent lips. The body is more rounded than flat (more like a shark than a snapper, for example), ending in a muscular fan-shaped tail. The top of the head and body are a dark brown, fading into gray or yellow up to the snow-white belly. Cobia can get very big, occasionally exceeding one hundred pounds and more than five feet in length. Recreationally caught specimens are usually on the larger side; those from commercial boats are usually less than forty pounds.

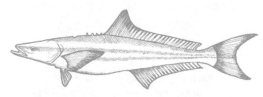

EATING: Cobia is a favorite eating fish—at once meaty, flaky, firm, and unctuous. Fillets vaguely resemble Swordfish in appearance (though Cobia meat is more compact), so steaks are a better idea than anything else. The meat is pinkish white when raw, and slight marbling is not uncommon.

For those who like to eat fish heads, Cobia is probably king.

AVAILABILITY: Commercially, Cobia is most effectively targeted with nets rather than hooks; however, only hooks are legal in US Gulf waters, thus fewer Cobia are caught. Additionally, state and federal regulations allow only small incidental catches. Cobia are also not commonly caught recreationally (they have a reputation for canniness). Grocery stores, restaurants, and seafood markets (with access to imported fish) are the best bet for finding them, but then there is the problem of quality. Very little of the Cobia available at the retail level is actually wild-caught US Gulf fish.

Cobia is also one of the best candidates thus far for aquaculture, a fact we hope will be embraced by Gulf authorities sooner rather than later.

THE MORASS OF FLYINGFISH

Hirundichthys spp.; *Cheilopogon* spp.; *Cypselurus* spp.; *Exocoetus* spp.

HABITAT: Flyingfish swim in open blue waters, rarely coming closer to shore.

RANGE/DISTRIBUTION: All of these species occur in temperate and tropical seas the world over. Some species occur worldwide, while others are limited to specific waters. If a species occurs in one part of the Gulf, it occurs in all parts.

DESCRIPTION: There are about thirteen species of flyingfish in the Gulf. They all look pretty much the same: big eyes set in blunt-snouted heads attached to cigar-shaped bodies terminating in V-shaped tails. All species have extraordinarily voluminous pectoral fins, which they use to glide above the water for dozens of yards at a time (they do not actually fly). Most species reach less a foot in length. All are chrome silver; some have stripes or spots or patterns, always black.

EATING: They look a bit like herrings, so one might think that flyingfish are quite bony. On the contrary, once the long row of pin bones is removed, the fillets are mild and sweet. In those countries where flyingfish are commercially fished and marketed, most are sold spatchcocked, similar to a boneless, headless, tailless Rainbow Trout.

AVAILABILITY: We assume any commercial fishery would require the use of nets, which, as we discussed previously, are prohibited. We do not know how one would target them commercially otherwise. We got two over the years from commercial boats. On both occasions, the fish had accidentally glided onto the deck of the boat.

SWORDFISH

Xiphias gladius

HABITAT: Swordfish swim in blue waters, from the surface (where they "bask" during the day) to depths of at least half a mile (and probably more), where they feast on squid, shrimp, and fish at the bottom of the ocean, at crushing depths.

RANGE/DISTRIBUTION: They occur in all of the temperate and tropical oceans and seas of the world. Swordfish are highly migratory, and individuals will cover vast areas of that range.

DESCRIPTION: The Swordfish is at once quotidian and magical. It is common enough to have become a stereotypical image along with the men who fished it and magical enough to somehow not seem like just another animal. We all know the sword, the improbable weapon mounted right on the animal's snout. It seems familiar enough, but landlubbers (like ourselves) usually fail to consider just how large this sword can be (we have one in our living room that is just over four feet long). It is a huge weapon, affixed to an animal many feet longer. The body of the Swordfish is, after the snout and before the tail, essentially cylindrical. This part of the body can easily be more than five feet long, with the tail section adding another couple of feet. The dorsal fins are relatively small, even dainty. The pectoral fins are large and powerful, as one would expect from a swift pelagic fish. The tail is likewise large and strong.

The eyes of the Swordfish are like those of no other fish: large and completely black, and wonderfully evolved for life up and down the water column. The gills are also quite different. Instead of the filament-like appearance of most fish gills, Swordfish gills are paler and almost spongy.

EATING: Swordfish seems to have evolved for the grill, and no other fish tastes as good that way. The flesh does tend to dry out if overcooked, so diligence is required no matter the method. It is also quite good fried in a pan or baked in the oven.

Sometimes Swordfish will find a particularly good source of food and will gorge on it. Usually this is fish or squid. In the Gulf of Mexico, Swordfish sometimes gorge on shrimp instead (and specifically, if old fishers are to be believed, *Sicyonia brevirostris*, the Rock Shrimp). When that happens, the flesh of the Swordfish starts to take on an orange color, just like wild salmon, and for the same reason. When these fish are caught on the Atlantic coast (which is rare), they are referred to as "pumpkin" Swordfish. Here in the Gulf, they are called, appropriately, Peachbelly Swordfish—and they are more of a seasonal seafood treat than anything else. Peachbelly meat is as moist as the fattiest farmed fish. The belly in particular is quite rich, enough to even allow curing and smoking.

AVAILABILITY: Most fishing communities around the Gulf coast cannot target Swordfish year-round. The exceptions are in eastern Louisiana, a spot that allows fishing for Swordfish and tunas for most of the year. However, these catches make up only a tiny bit of the overall US Swordfish catch, so don't expect to see Gulf Swordfish all the time in grocery stores. It does happen, though, and a very few fishmongers proudly carry only Gulf Swordfish.

OCEAN SUNFISH

Mola mola

COMMON NAME: Mola

HABITAT: The Ocean Sunfish is a wandering giant, generally found in far offshore waters. Usually it swims near the surface, though it does sometimes move through the water column as deep as fifteen hundred feet or more.

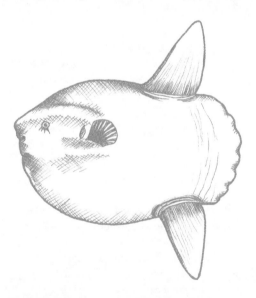

RANGE/DISTRIBUTION: The species occurs in all of the temperate and tropical seas, gulfs, and oceans of the world.

DESCRIPTION: Without a doubt, the Ocean Sunfish is the most otherworldly fish described in this book. It is gigantic and looks like half a fish—after the dorsal and anal fins, the body seems to simply stop. It has no tail, no caudal peduncle, no caudal fin. Instead it has a clavus, which is basically just a stub. The fish can be as long as ten feet and can weigh five thousand pounds. It is the largest bony fish in the world, even if its bones are flimsy and small. Its head is insignificant, it has large eyes, and a bony ridge runs between them to the snout. The mouth is always ajar, open in a perfect circle. All of this combines to create a comically tragic face.

The triangular dorsal and anal fins are very long and extend perpendicularly from the top and bottom of the fish. As the Ocean Sunfish has no tail, it uses those long dorsal and anal fins to locomote throughout the ocean. It usually swims upright, sometimes close enough to the surface that its dorsal fin pokes out of the water. It also basks on its side on the surface of the water (apparently a behavior that allows scavengers to clean the parasites off its skin). Oddly, it has no swim bladder.

EATING: The one time we saw an Ocean Sunfish (more on that below), we took advantage of the situation to cut it up and try it out. As Ocean Sunfish go, ours was small—only 411 pounds—but too large for any cutting table. Thus, it was disassembled on a large fish vat. The skin was easy to cut through but very thick. The meat itself looked a bit like very firm, opaque snow-white jelly—or maybe like raw lobster meat (though devoid of color). Perhaps it was more like the chalky fletch from a massive halibut. The skeleton was surprisingly small for the size of the fish, and the bones were softer than those of a Swordfish (though harder than those of, say, a Mako shark). We didn't eat it raw. Maybe we should have, but the numerous parasites deterred us.

The meat, when cooked, contracted dramatically—as much as 75 percent, depending on how the meat was cooked (poaching or boiling resulted in the most extreme shrinkage). The taste was beyond bland, almost like jellyfish, but without the good texture. It was not much of anything, kind of like Chilean Seabass (itself an unimpressive fish) that had been soaked in warm tap water for a day or two.

AVAILABILITY: No one targets this fish. Or rather, we are aware of no Ocean Sunfish fisheries anywhere in the world. In fact, the one time a local boat brought one in, the fish was an object of much conversation as well as controversy.

The boat that brought it in was a bottom longliner that had been out for deepwater groupers and Golden Tilefish. Given that Ocean Sunfish never really feed where and how groupers feed, and given that they generally have no interest in baited hooks, the crew was mystified. The fish had been hooked in the lip (the hook was still embedded when the fish was unloaded), exactly where the other fish were hooked. In other words, the Ocean Sunfish had, contrary to its recorded habits, taken the hook. The assumption was that it had gotten hooked near the surface, then had been dragged down to the seafloor, along with the rest of the set. It was, in other words, a freak catch.

Some commercial fishermen hanging around the dock that day were slightly horrified, for an old superstition held that bringing an Ocean Sunfish on a boat was like killing an albatross—an invitation to the worst kinds of bad luck.

CHAPTER 11
ON THE SUBJECT OF GULF MARINE EELS

We won't dwell on the subject of Gulf marine eels very long.

The Gulf of Mexico has dozens, maybe hundreds of species of eels. Some of these (or maybe even most) are deepwater species, encountered by scientists, not fishing boats. We won't enumerate the species or even the genera. These deepwater eels are quite long for their size, sometimes to the point of ridiculousness. Some of them have overly large mouths. From a human point of view, most of them have little to no direct uses. They are very large or very tiny, or they have little flesh, or their flesh is bony or watery. Unfortunately, we have none of the immediately tasty saltwater eels found in other parts of the world (except for the mostly freshwater American Eel [*Anguilla rostrata*], covered elsewhere in this book).

Some kinds of eels regularly come into contact with humans, most of whom are in commercial fishing boats. Bottom longliners (targeting groupers and tilefish) routinely haul up various species. These eels are invariably large (up to seven or more feet long and, at their thickest, seven or more inches in diameter). Some species like mud and sand, while others prefer rocks and reefs. Boats generally don't bring eels to dock, but instead use them for bait (the meat and skin are both very tough and can't be easily torn off the hook by a fish). Most eels caught by commercial boats are in one of the following three families (other representatives also swim thousands of feet down):

- Congridae: Conger eels. These species are typically large and always monochrome gray or light brown.

- Ophichthidae: Snake eels, also called worm eels. All species are drab colored, mostly browns and tans and grays. Some species, like the Shrimp Eel, are found closer to shore and are regularly caught by shrimpers. Most dwell in mud and

sand and rocks far off-
shore. The King Snake Eel is
one of the biggest of these
species, reaching as much
as twelve feet or more in
length and weighing more than a hundred pounds.

- Muraenidae: Moray eels live near rocks and reefs. They have rounded, shriveled faces and snouts. They are generally brightly colored. A large Moray can be more than six feet long and weigh dozens of pounds.

EATING: All of these species are bony to the point of being of limited use in the kitchen (with the partial exception of the conger, whose bones, while numerous, are slightly easier to deal with). Fillets have at least several rows of pin bones, all of which are firmly anchored in the flesh and skin. If you can find the rows, you can cut strips of meat. That is the only convenient way to go about it. If you want to preserve the fillet shape, then be prepared to make row after row of careful V-shaped cuts, taking out the bones sometimes one by one. (A Japanese technique for dealing with marine eels involves making hundreds of cuts down the flesh in a hatch pattern. We've neither the skill nor the patience for such a task.)

Also, the meat is tough. It cannot be cooked quickly, unless you enjoy the texture of sandal rubber. Slow cooking is the only answer. A few hours of braising in the oven does wonders. But again, you'll have to see to the bones first. And the average size of these eels makes that kind of work difficult. If you really want to pursue cooking a big roast of marine eel, we suggest the recipe in the *River Cottage Fish Book*. We can attest that the result is impressive, having tried it on a conger ourselves.

Possibly the best use of these species of eels might be the soup or stock pot, for any of them give fish soup a nice savory base. Or, these eels may be used, with considerable success, to make a stock with enough body, color, and taste to use in meat dishes.

Of them all, the congers are by far the best eating.

AVAILABILITY: You will have to rely on your wits to catch your own. Or get your fishmonger to convince a boat to keep one.

CHAPTER 12

RAYS, SKATES, AND SHARKS (ELASMOBRANCHS)

This chapter is intentionally small, for we really shouldn't do a lot of eating of these animals. Sharks (and their cousins rays and skates) cannot withstand much fishing pressure—their biology prohibits it. They grow very slowly, mature even more slowly, and they birth only a few young at a time. There are dozens more species of sharks in Gulf waters besides those we describe here. Some are edible, some are toxic; most are not eaten by humans.

There are today no directed shark or ray fisheries in the northwestern Gulf, but elsewhere in the Gulf and beyond, sharks are targeted to some extent (the most lucrative shark fisheries of course are for fins—certainly the most despicable fishery on the planet). The only time that we saw or sold sharks was when they were bycatch, and had been hauled up in no shape to be returned to the water—and even then we were never totally comfortable with it.

Anyone fishing recreationally in the Gulf of Mexico has at one time or another encountered a shark or ray, even if it was only a baby Bonnethead caught while fishing for something else. Most of them tend to swallow hooks, so fishers simply cut the line as close to the hook as possible, though this means that the fish returns to the wild with what is probably a mortal injury. One may try to get the hook out, but this is rarely accomplished without injuring the animal even more. *If the fish has swallowed the hook and is already bleeding profusely as it comes out of the water, there is no more dilemma, for the fish has been fatally injured. Kill it quickly.*

PJ loves to eat an accidental ray or skate. If he catches more than a couple, though, he either stops fishing or changes gear and fishes differently to avoid catching any more.

The same goes for sharks. While a small Bonnethead or Blacktip Shark tastes wonderful, we really try to avoid catching sharks at all.

Shark and ray meat can develop an ammonia off-taste (due to anatomical peculiarities unique to these animals). While that might be appreciated in some culinary traditions (the famous Icelandic Hákarl, for example, or the typical treatment in classic French cuisine, in which skate was routinely hung and aged like wild game until it had become slightly "high"), we have never developed such an appreciation.

If you should catch one of the fish in this chapter, and want to keep it for your table, you will want to do the following: kill it quickly, cut the head off, and gut it right afterward (making sure that you scrape out the kidneys completely), then rinse the gut cavity completely—the water in which the shark was just swimming will work fine. Rinse it until all blood and gut odors have dissipated. It might take a couple of minutes of soaking and rinsing. Make sure you get out every scrap of gut. Ice the fish immediately. This will do wonders.

We do not describe the various species of sawfish (*Pristis* spp.). They are endangered and highly protected. We also do not describe the Basking Shark (*Cetorhinus maximus*), though it is theoretically edible after lengthy processing to remove naturally occurring toxins fatal to humans. Also not described is the Tiger Shark (*Galeocerdo cuvier*), which is commonly caught by recreational beach anglers (and which has been responsible for more than one fatal attack on humans wading in the surf). It doesn't apparently make the best eating but is rather caught for the manly sport of it all. We prefer to leave such fish alone.

STINGRAYS (SOUTHERN, ATLANTIC, AND BLUNTNOSE)

Dasyatis americana, Dasyatis sabina, and *Dasyatis say*

HABITAT: All three of these species live on sandy, grassy, and silty bottoms in shallow coastal waters—especially in bays and along beaches and inlets.

RANGE/DISTRIBUTION: The Southern and Bluntnose occur from around the US mid-Atlantic coast to at least Brazil, including the Gulf of Mexico and the Caribbean Sea. The Atlantic has the same northern limit, but only occurs as far south as the Gulf. All three of these species are caught in the same areas.

DESCRIPTION: All three species are flat, disc-shaped fish, with bodies about as wide as they are long. The Southern and Atlantic Stingrays have pointed snouts; the Bluntnose, perhaps unsurprisingly, does not. From a bird's-eye view, one can clearly see the harder cartilage skeleton enclosing the torso and head; the highly modified pectoral fins sprouting off that trunk resemble wings, which is what they are called (hence the market name for these kinds of fish: "skate wing," as only the wings are marketed). Stingrays swim close to the bottom, but they also walk along the seafloor using their wings as feet.

These flat bodies, along with the two large breathing orifices (called spiracles) on the top of their heads, allow stingrays to half bury themselves in the sand and lie in

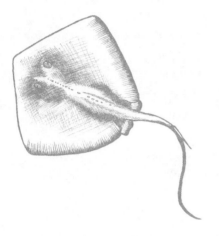

wait for unsuspecting prey to wander along. Tails are about as long as the bodies themselves, and all come equipped with a single serrated barb right near the base of the tail. These barbs are only used for defensive purposes (the barb, when extended, points straight up), and can deliver a painful and memorable wound, one that aches for hours afterward, but that is rarely fatal unless vital organs are involved (almost all stings are to feet and hands).

All three are dull brown, with the Bluntnose being the darkest and the Atlantic the lightest. The Atlantic is the smallest of the three, weighing at most twelve pounds. The Bluntnose weighs a bit more—as much as thirty pounds. The Southern Stingray is the giant, often weighing dozens of pounds, and sometimes as much as two hundred or more.

EATING: These fish make for quite nice eating. The smaller specimens may be cooked whole (we suggest steaming or poaching). Slightly larger stingrays are easily filleted. Or the wings may be cut off, then skinned, then cut into chunks, then cooked like ribs. The largest fish have to be filleted.

The flesh is composed of long strands of muscle, arranged in such a way as to resemble corduroy. Frying works well if the fillet is thin (simply cut the fillet in half horizontally if it is too thick). It is also very good cooked in a pan or baked. We must admit that the flesh of a large stingray can be a little coarse, and only smaller fish produce fillets comparable to those from skate (the gold standard for this kind of fish). Because of its cartilaginous skeleton, stingray makes an excellent addition to *fumet* (fish broth), adding depth and body. If you have stingray carcasses, you can even make aspic (simmer the bones in plain water, strain the broth, reduce it by two-thirds, then cool).

AVAILABILITY: No one in the US Gulf of Mexico commercially catches or sells any of our local stingray species. In coastal towns with seafood markets, you might sometimes see them as bycatch from shrimp boats, but don't expect that. Some fishmongers and seafood markets sell various species of skate (wings only, of course), which are close relatives of these rays (as mentioned, most skate species are held in rather higher regard than any ray). Marketed skates come from the Atlantic or Pacific Oceans—about a dozen skate species in total are fished in those waters.

All three species are very easy to catch on your own, though, and certainly at the beach. Have ready a stout pole, a strong line, and a decent-sized circle hook. Fish on the bottom and cast out to the back side of one of the sandbars (basically the spot a few feet farther out from where the waves crest).

Stingrays seem to hang there, stuck fast to the bottom, waiting for lunch.

Once hooked, they use their pectoral fin to simply back up. They don't fight hard—but they do have a knack for simply sticking in one spot and not moving at all. You'll more often than not snap your line if you try for a contest of brute strength. It is best to give the line some slack, then wait for the fish to relax its grip, then reel in fast.

COWNOSE, SPOTTED EAGLE, AND BULLNOSE RAYS

Rhinoptera bonasus, Aetobatus narinari, and *Myliobatis freminvillei*

HABITAT: These three species are migratory, moving up and down the water column and throughout different parts of their range according to the season, food sources, and mating cycles. All three migrate in their own schools, which are spectacular—hundreds or thousands of rays packed on the surface of the water in tight interlocking geometric perfection. During migrations, these species travel through much deeper waters in the middle of the water column; nonetheless, they all more or less stay in shallow coastal waters, the Cownose usually in the shallowest.

RANGE/DISTRIBUTION: The Spotted Eagle occurs worldwide in tropical waters; the Cownose ranges from the mid-Atlantic US coast to northern South America, as well as to East Africa, in the waters off Senegal and Mauritania if not farther; and the Bullnose only occurs along the US mid-Atlantic, in the Gulf of Mexico and the Caribbean Sea, and along the northern tip of South America.

DESCRIPTION: These three species are myliobatids, meaning they are members of the family Myliobatidae, the eagle and manta rays. The only manta ray confirmed in the

Gulf is the Giant Manta (*Mobula birostris*), which is a giant indeed, weighing up to three tons or more, with a wingspan over twenty feet. No one commercially or recreationally catches manta rays in the American Gulf, and no one should. Thus, we don't cover them here. For the same reason, we don't cover the Whale Shark (*Rhincodon typus*), another giant Gulf resident.

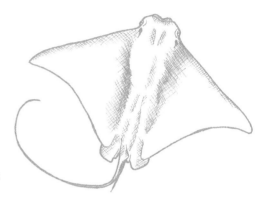

Eagle rays are parallelogram shaped, and all have slender trunks with differentiated snouts off of which sprout triangular wings, slightly curved back, with the rear-facing edge being slightly concave. All have very long (up to several feet), thin whiptails. All three of these species can reach considerable size.

The Cownose Ray's triangular wings are the most swept back of the lot. The name comes not really from the shape of the nose, but that of the head, which, looked at from a certain angle, does resemble, if remotely, a cow's nose. The small eyes are mounted on the side of the cartilaginous ridge at the front of the head. The Cownose is a monotone brown on top and mostly white underneath (sometimes the bottoms of the wings are light brown). A mature Cownose can weigh over two hundred pounds and measure several feet across.

The Spotted Eagle Ray gets its name from its curious pointed snout, offset at the bottom rather than the middle of the head. Eyes are just behind the snout, on the side of the head. In profile or when viewed from above, the snout resembles a bird's beak (though from the bottom, the snout looks like a pig snout). We think it looks more like a finch than an eagle, but that is neither here nor there. All eagle rays have long tails, but the Spotted Eagle has one of the longest, spanning several feet. The fish is snow white underneath, with a back of magnificent navy blue. White spots and designs, much like a leopard's, cover the entirety of the back. It's the largest of these three species, weighing up to five hundred pounds, with a wingspan of more than eight feet.

We do not see the resemblance between the Bullnose Ray and the actual nose of a bull. We contend it is more like a catfish head (a contention bound to go unchallenged, as the name is settled). Either way, the head is blunt and rounded and sticks out ahead of the junction of the wings and body. Eyes bulge from the sides of the head. It is dark brown on top, occasionally with dark spots on the wings. The Bullnose is a smaller species, with a wingspan less than four feet.

EATING: We have never gotten ahold of a large Cownose or Spotted Eagle Ray, and we hope we never do. Some fish are just better in the sea.

Having said that, these three fish are delicious if they are small enough. As long as the wingspan is no more than four feet from tip to tip, the meat is fine, compact, and at least as good as any species of skate. In fact, these rays are superior to skate, for none of them have barbed skin, and all are easier to fillet. As with all skates and rays, each wing has

two flaps of meat—one above and one below the cartilage layer of spines.

AVAILABILITY: These species are never commercially fished, at least not from US Gulf waters. Only commercial shrimpers catch them, and even then, catches are sporadic, small, and never sold up the supply chain. Due to their migratory lifestyles, they are also difficult to target recreationally. Spawning migrations happen in the fall, so that would be the best time to luck into a school on their way to somewhere else.

ATLANTIC GUITARFISH

Pseudobatos lentiginosus

HABITAT: Atlantic Guitarfish live in shallow waters down to about a hundred feet. They are associated with structures and reefs, though they are also found over grassy and sandy bottoms.

RANGE/DISTRIBUTION: This species is found along the US Atlantic coast and through the Gulf to Mexico.

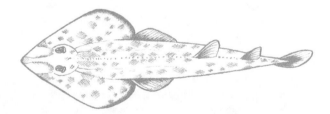

DESCRIPTION: With its flat spade-shaped head and thin tapering body, the Atlantic Guitarfish is an altogether arresting animal. It does not get very big, almost always measuring less than four feet long. Coloration is muted and monochromatic, mostly tans and browns.

EATING: The meat on the "wings" of the head are like skate; the body meat is similar to the tastiest of sharks.

AVAILABILITY: This fish is rarely encountered in the waters of the northwestern Gulf. You won't see local Atlantic Guitarfish for sale, but sometimes imported fish is sold in specialty fish markets.

SPINY AND SMOOTH BUTTERFLY RAYS

Gymnura altavela and *Gymnura micrura*

HABITAT: These two ray species stay close to or at the seafloor, mostly on or very close to mud and sand. They are sedentary ambush predators. Both swim only in shallow coastal waters—beaches, larger bays, passes, and inlets. The Spiny Butterfly swims a little deeper, to one hundred feet or more.

RANGE/DISTRIBUTION: The Spiny Butterfly occurs on both sides of the Atlantic, everywhere from north to south. The Smooth Butterfly is found on both Atlantic coasts as well, but in a smaller range, from the US mid-Atlantic coast to Brazil, and from Senegal to Angola.

DESCRIPTION: Both of these fish are shaped like flattened wedges, and both have small eyes set atop their heads. Being ambush predators that typically lie in wait on the seafloor, they also have spiracles, but theirs, unlike those of the stingray, lie flush against the top of the head, with no accompanying hard ridges. Both also have the short, stubby, thin tails typical of fish in their family (Gymnuridae), though only the Spiny's tail is armed (the spine is small and apparently not venomous). Both species look quite similar, enough so that the easiest way to tell them apart is by their snouts: the Smooth Butterfly

has a very slightly pointed snout, whereas the Spiny Butterfly Ray's is rounded.

The Spiny is the larger of the two species, reaching more than four feet in wingspan and weighing as much as one hundred pounds or more. The Smooth is a little more than half that size. Typical catches of both species, however, are closer to three to seven pounds (the larger fish tend to stay out of the way of humans).

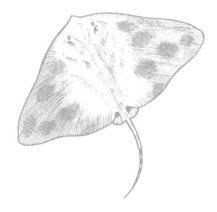

Both tend to have drab coloration. Their bottom colors are light tan to white, while top colors can range from mahogany to olive to tan to chocolate to almost yellow. The back of the Spiny is generally accented with dots, spots, or other camouflage patterns.

EATING: Butterfly and eagle rays are equally good to eat, though the former is slightly meatier.

AVAILABILITY: Like the eagle rays, the butterfly rays are also never commercially targeted. And like the eagle rays, they are incidentally caught by commercial shrimpers. These are not migrating rays, though, so you are slightly more likely to catch one on your own. Fish in the same places as you would if you were fishing for stingrays—beaches, sandy and muddy bays, and similar locales.

BLACKTIP AND BULL SHARKS

Carcharhinus limbatus and *Carcharhinus leucas*

HABITAT: These are coastal sharks (especially the Blacktip) that sometimes venture far out to sea, but more commonly they do the opposite, going far into bays and even into brackish and fresh waters (especially the Bull).

RANGE/DISTRIBUTION: Both are found worldwide in tropical and temperate oceans, seas, and brackish waters.

DESCRIPTION: They look like stock photos of sharks, with gray bodies overall and paler undersides.

The Blacktip has distinct markings on all its fins (the tips, shockingly, are black), a sharper snout, and a more torpedo-shaped body than the Bull. The Blacktip can grow as long as nine feet and weigh more than two hundred pounds. The average size is closer to five feet and less than one hundred pounds.

The Bull Shark is bigger, as long as thirteen feet and weighing up to around seven hundred pounds (most Bulls encountered by humans are smaller, only six to eight feet and a hundred or so pounds).

EATING: As far as sharks go, these are both acceptable enough to eat. They are steaky

fish, to say the least, and can become dry if you overcook them by more than a few seconds. Also, if not cleaned properly immediately after capture, these sharks (and sharks in general) have a slight ammonia taste.

AVAILABILITY: There might not be any commercial fishers in Texas targeting these or any sharks. We certainly don't recall any. Regardless, sharks are not easy to come by in a commercial setting, which is a good thing.

If you are so inclined, these are both easily caught in shallow waters just a few hundred feet from shore and are almost as easily caught by fishing off the beach. We sometimes catch small ones on our surf rod rigs, but never intentionally.

You might have seen eager young men fishing on the beach, at dusk or dawn, with very large gear cast very far out (they are almost universally young men, for everyone else has more sense). For more information on fishing from the beach for big sharks, look elsewhere, for we have none.

ROUNDEL SKATE

Raja texana

HABITAT: The Roundel Skate lives on or near the seafloor. It is sometimes found inshore (especially younger fish), but adults are typically offshore, in water as deep as five hundred feet. We have about sixteen species of true skates in the Gulf. This Roundel Skate (along with the Clearnose [*Raja eglanteria*],

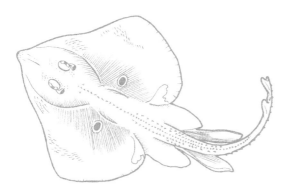

BRAZILIAN ELECTRIC RAY

Narcine brasiliensis

HABITAT: This ray occurs only in shallow coastal waters, on sand and mud bottoms, especially in areas close to rocks and structures.

RANGE/DISTRIBUTION: It ranges from the Brazilian Atlantic coast, through the entire Gulf of Mexico, and along the lower US Atlantic coast.

DESCRIPTION: The Brazilian Electric Ray has a round, flat disc for a head. That head is attached to a tapered fleshy tail that ends in a small caudal fin. At the junction of tail and head sprout the fan-shaped pelvic fins. The head is as long as the tail and as wide. This is a small ray, usually slightly under two feet in length and weighing less than two pounds.

an eastern Gulf species) is the only one that ever occurs in less than several hundred feet of water.

RANGE/DISTRIBUTION: The Roundel Skate is limited to the southern US Atlantic coast and the Gulf of Mexico. The Clearnose Skate shares the Roundel's southern limit, but it occurs farther north as well.

DESCRIPTION: The Roundel Skate is small. Like the Clearnose, the Roundel has a sharp, translucent snout and a body shaped like a thick but flat wedge. Its color ranges between shades of brown, with a prominent dark circular spot on top of each wing. The spot is surrounded by at least one lighter-colored halo (sometimes several, arranged concentrically).

EATING: This fish is usually too small to mess with, but when it's big enough, it is quite nice to eat. On the rare occasions when we've had one of these, we have just cooked it whole.

AVAILABILITY: This skate is occasionally caught as bycatch by a White Shrimp boat, but it is less common than other rays and skates. Those caught that way tend to be smaller, as the boats don't typically fish in deep water.

The word "electric" in the common name is not intended as a literary flourish, for this fish is bioelectric, that is, it generates and stores electricity in its body (its head, in this case). It uses this electricity for offensive as well as defensive purposes, delivering a shock to anything that touches it or even comes near it (salt water being an excellent conductor). There are several electric rays in the Gulf, but only this species has any possible food value.

EATING: This is a decent enough fish, but due to its diminutive size, one that is best cooked whole. The tail (which vaguely resembles that of a monkfish) has a bit of meat clinging to both sides of the central bit of cartilage running throughout. The head is mostly concerned with electrical generation and storage, so there's not as much there to eat.

AVAILABILITY: No one targets this fish, and no one wants to. Its shock is not fatal, but it is enough "to knock a grown man down" (we don't know why, but that seems to be the universal unit of measurement for the strength of electricity produced by animals). Shrimpers who catch one incidentally (for that is the closest this fish comes to commercial exploitation) just want to get it back in the water. We're told it retains its gathered electricity for hours after it dies.

Targeting the Brazilian Electric Ray recreationally is neither feasible nor desirable. If you should catch one, don't let your curiosity get the best of you. Try to get the hook out remotely, or just cut the line. If you really want to take it home, you'll have to keep it separate from the rest of your catch, as it is possible to get a shock just reaching into the cooler.

BONNETHEAD AND ATLANTIC SHARPNOSE SHARK

Sphyrna tiburo and Rhizoprionodon terraenovae

HABITAT: Both of these species are coastal sharks. The Bonnethead sticks to shallow waters, usually less than seventy-five feet deep, over seagrass and sand and, less commonly, hard bottoms and rocks as well. Sometimes it ventures into very shallow waters in back bays and marshes. The Atlantic Sharpnose likes slightly deeper waters—larger bays, beaches, and nearshore open water. While it is far more common in shallow water, it has been recorded down to several hundred feet.

RANGE/DISTRIBUTION: The Atlantic Sharpnose is found from Brazil to Canada, including the Gulf of Mexico and the Caribbean Sea. The Bonnethead is truly an American fish, occurring along both the Atlantic and Pacific coasts of the Americas—and nowhere else. In the Pacific, it can be found from Baja California to Peru; in the Atlantic, from Brazil to the Carolinas.

DESCRIPTION: These are both small species. Neither gets much bigger than four or five feet and about thirty or forty pounds. Both species are a drab light gray, with pale undersides. The Bonnethead is closely related to the hammerheads and has a similarly unusual head—flat and molded

into a semicircle, with eyes placed in a fashion similar to the hammerheads. The fins are unremarkable. The top lobe of the caudal fin is elongated and notched near the tip. For its part, the Atlantic Sharpnose has a pointed snout and the same elongated caudal fin, this time notched with a slight bump above. These sharks are both slim bodied.

We should mention here an altogether astonishing (if slightly tangential) fact about the Bonnethead shark. Based on research conducted in the past few years, it appears that the Bonnethead is the only known omnivorous shark in the world. Researchers have observed Bonnetheads eating seagrass in the wild, and know, based on experiments, that the vegetation does not merely pass through the sharks' bodies, but is utilized as efficiently as it would be by an herbivore.

EATING: If we are going to eat shark, we always want it to be one of these two species. Even at their largest, they are hardly steaky. Their meat is not like white fish of course, but it is not really like shark either—almost like the offspring of an amberjack and a triggerfish. The meat flakes firmly and is sweet. Of the two, the Bonnethead is superior.

AVAILABILITY: Like most of the fish in this chapter, these two sharks are rarely to never fished, landed, or marketed in most American Gulf waters. You can catch your own. Fish off of jetties or piers. Use a stout rod and a rig that keep the bait off but close to the bottom. Obviously, you will want to use a wire leader.

THRESHERS: COMMON AND BIGEYE

Alopias vulpinus and *Alopias superciliosus*

HABITAT: These are oceanic sharks, at home far offshore and throughout the water column. Both species are found as deep as two thousand feet but also spend significant amounts of time much closer to the surface. The Bigeye Thresher prefers deeper waters.

RANGE/DISTRIBUTION: Both are circum-global in temperate and tropical waters.

DESCRIPTION: Both species have small mouths and small teeth (although they are numerous and razor sharp). The Common has a short, pointed snout; long pectoral fins; small eyes; and a torpedo-shaped body. The Bigeye meanwhile has the same long pectoral fins; a very blunt rounded snout; eyes at least twice as big as the Common's; and more prominent, bulging gills. It also has a deeper belly. Both species reach the same approximate size—thirteen to twenty feet long, weighing up to almost half a ton.

The caudal fin distinguishes these two species (and a relative—the Pelagic Thresher [*Alopias pelagicus*], which only occurs in the Indian and Pacific Oceans)—from all other sharks. The top lobe of the caudal fin is wide and elongated to a ridiculous degree. It extends at almost a forty-five-degree angle from the body and is almost as long as the rest of the body.

The thresher sharks get their name from the way they use their long tails. Threshing is the act of separating the edible parts of grain

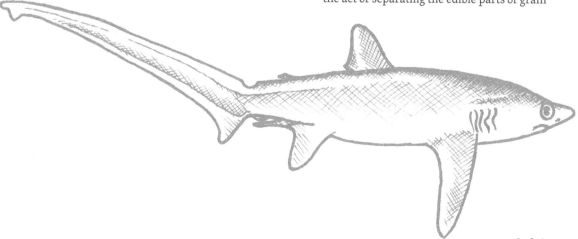

from the rest of the plant, a process sometimes traditionally accomplished by beating bundles of harvested stalks against the ground or a hard surface in order to loosen the seed pods. When a thresher is attacking a school of fish, it uses its tail as a bludgeon to strike and stun its prey. The action is said to call to mind threshing. We are not convinced.

EATING: The meat of these two species is as good as that of other large sharks but no better. All of the regular shark recipes can apply.

AVAILABILITY: Neither species is targeted in the northwestern Gulf, but sometimes they are in the east and south. They are sometimes caught as bycatch by pelagic (tuna and Swordfish) and bottom (deepwater grouper and tilefish) longliners, but it is pretty unusual.

Recreational fishing is difficult. The distance to their grounds and the depth at which they swim makes targeting either of the species difficult for most boats and equipment.

SHORTFIN MAKO

Isurus oxyrinchus

COMMON NAME: Mako

HABITAT: The Shortfin Mako lives in offshore deep, open waters, usually down at least a hundred, if not a thousand, feet or more, though it is sometimes found at the top of the water column close to the surface.

RANGE/DISTRIBUTION: This fish is found all around the world in temperate and tropical waters.

DESCRIPTION: A larger shark species, the Shortfin Mako can be more than fourteen feet long and weigh over half a ton. The underside is pure uninterrupted white, while the back, including all fins, is navy blue to gunmetal gray. The sharply pointed snout gives way to a terrifying mouth, filled with hundreds of teeth, arranged in rows curling back into the jaws. We have a few Mako jaws in our house, and we've tried counting the teeth, but we've not yet been successful. There are just too many. We estimate that there are over 250 teeth in one set of jaws in our cabinet. The front teeth are

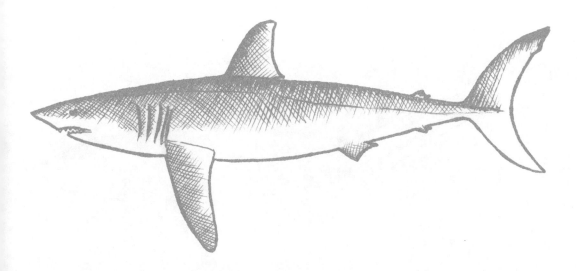

large and mature; behind those are several teeth in various stages of formation, getting ready to replace a front tooth whenever it is lost. Such a teething arrangement is not uncommon among sharks of course (most species produce thousands of teeth in their lifetime); we've merely seen more Shortfin Mako jaws than any other.

The body is the standard shark shape, with a pronounced, but not protruding, belly. First dorsal, pectoral, and caudal fins are large and triangular, while all other fins are tiny. The top lobe of the caudal fin is longer than the bottom and more scythe shaped.

EATING: The taste of this fish is unique among sharks. The meat certainly looks like that of a shark, but the taste and texture closely resemble Swordfish.

AVAILABILITY: Shortfin Mako is sometimes taken as bycatch by northwestern Gulf pelagic and bottom longliners. It is commonly marketed along the Gulf Coast but is almost always harvested from other waters.

INVERTEBRATES

Having dealt with at least a few of the edible fish in the northwestern Gulf of Mexico, we turn our attention to the invertebrates—bivalve shellfish (oysters and clams), snails, cephalopods (squid and octopus), and crustaceans (shrimp and crabs). Taken together, this is a huge group of animals, but we focus only on a few dozen of the most edible and accessible.

Perhaps the word "invertebrates," though accurate and concise, is not the most eloquent word, at least for our purposes. Traditionally, in the US seafood industry (but to a lesser extent today) the word "seafood" colloquially meant all edible marine animals *except fish*, thus the phrase "fish and seafood." While it's not perfect, we like the division, because "seafood" sounds a lot more appetizing than "invertebrates." (Although we generally use the term colloquially, in places throughout this book we occasionally use the term "seafood" as an inclusive term for both fish and invertebrates. We cannot excuse the inconsistency—but it remains as our nod to seafood industry arcana.)

We've struggled before to describe the sense of frustration we feel when pondering the (edible) Texas marine invertebrates. The Gulf of Mexico contains thousands of species of crustaceans and shellfish, but aside from a few commercial species—the Blue Crab, the Eastern Oyster, and various shrimp—too many Gulf Coast residents are unaware of the fact. We dream of the day when these treasures are more properly appreciated.

CHAPTER 13

BIVALVES, GASTROPODS, CEPHALOPODS, AND ODDBALL INVERTEBRATES

Bivalves are creatures with two hinged shells, the most iconic of which in the Gulf of Mexico is undoubtedly the Eastern Oyster. It is fished and eaten everywhere along the Gulf coast. Lesser known are the dozens of Gulf species of clams and mussels, most of which are not only edible but delicious. In an ideal world, we would all be able to eat these local treasures at our favorite restaurants and buy them at our favorite markets. Alas, no commercial fisheries exist here for any of these critters. Some harvesting and cultivating are done in the eastern part of the Gulf, but not at all in Texas, aside from the aforementioned oysters. In Texas, to legally harvest these animals for commercial purposes, one would need a commercial "Clam and Mussel" license. To obtain such a license, one would need to find a current holder and buy said permit from them (this is because of the moratorium on issuance of new commercial fishing licenses in general). As of a few years ago, there were fewer than five such active permits left in the state (if the licenses are not renewed yearly, for a fee, they expire). Once these licenses expire, it will be impossible even theoretically for fishers to commercially harvest these animals.

Animals that have one large shell are gastropods, commonly called snails. Most marine snails are edible, and the majority of those taste very nice. While no special license is needed to commercially harvest snails in Texas salt waters (other than a commercial fishing license of course), no one fishes any snails in Texas. The Texas

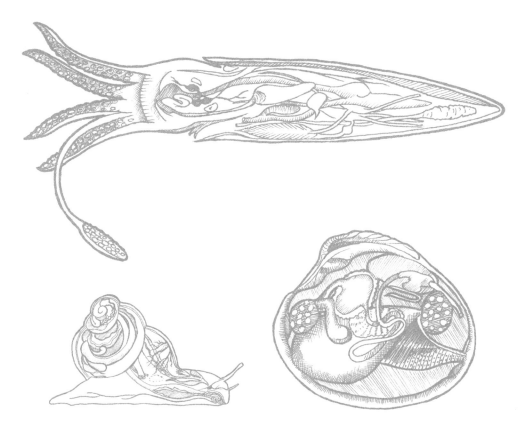

Department of State Health Services (TDSHS), the Texas shellfish regulator, does not regulate snails, only bivalves, and Texas commercial fishing regulations don't say much about snail harvesting. These factors result in a regulatory gray area, and because neither fishers nor game wardens want to gamble with legality, almost no snails are commercially landed.

At first glance, one would perhaps not assume a close (or any) relationship between an oyster and a squid. Nonetheless, they are, along with snails, all mollusks. Aside from the various species of nautilus (which we do not cover here), cephalopods all have internal and highly modified shells. In the case of the octopus and the squid, the shell is a tiny atrophied structure hidden deep in the body. The cuttlefish (an altogether delectable animal we do not cover here) has an internal shell as well, which is thick and chalky (dried cuttlefish shell is a common sight in pet stores, where it is sold to bird owners as "cuttlebone").

As far as most of these animals are concerned, we now must be content with gathering our own, which we do whenever we have a chance and the fisheries are open. The trick lies in knowing where, how, when, and under what legal circum-stances one may obtain them. Details on species follow. For more on harvesting oysters and foraging for shellfish, see page 17. We must rely on markets for our cephalopods. Catching your own squid is unlikely unless you have a boat and a squid jig—and know how to use both.

EASTERN OYSTER

Crassostrea virginica

HABITAT: This oyster lives in marshes, bays, inlets, and all other coastal waters. While some oyster reefs are situated in shallow waters exposed by the Gulf of Mexico's pal-try tides, most are found in slightly deeper waters, from a few feet to more than twenty.

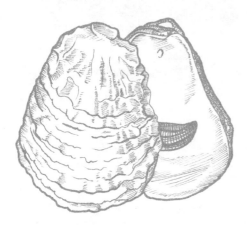

RANGE/DISTRIBUTION: The Eastern Oyster occurs from Canada through to Brazil. Every oyster farmed or dredged from Gulf or east coast waters is this same species (Pacific oys-ters are an entirely different species, which is why the possession of live Pacific oysters in Texas is illegal—they pose an invasive risk).

DESCRIPTION: Everyone knows the hinged-rock look of an oyster. The soft animal inside is a tan to gray mass, inside of which are all of the soft organs. As a result

of our mild winters, Gulf oysters tend to be quite large relative to their east coast cousins (oysters only grow when the water is warm enough, which means a longer period of dor-mancy every year for colder-water oysters).

EATING: It's probably not necessary to describe the delights of oyster eating, as this is a subject that has been covered by hundreds of better-informed (and more eloquent) sources for literally thousands of years. Concerning our Gulf oysters, perhaps a few words may still be said.

When the weather cools off (always a dicey proposition along the Gulf coast), and the bay waters feel more like tap water than a hot shower, it is time to eat raw oysters. In our opinion, our waters produce some of the most superior raw oysters in the country. On both east and west coasts, oysters are small, skinny, very salty, and expensive. Ours are large, fat, only slightly briny, and one-half to one-quarter of the price of those from other coasts. The oyster eaters on the Pacific and Atlantic coasts insist that a small oyster is the best oyster to eat raw. They insist our oysters are too big to eat raw. This makes no sense to us. We eat an Olympia Oyster, or a fine east coast oyster, and before we have even begun to relish the exquisite flavor and texture, it is all gone. On the other hand, a nice Gulf oyster sometimes won't even be taken in a single bite; one has to snack on it, like a fruit. Gulf oysters, which are mostly wild and harvested from reefs rather than cages, allow us the pleasure of savoring all of the different tastes and textures. Gulf oysters are never very salty (usually less than 20 ppt), a characteristic that allows more mineral and metal notes to shine through, notes that are sorely lacking in oysters from less favorable climes.

Unfortunately, warmer waters mean not only big oysters but also more frequent occurrences of foodborne illness. In the Gulf, the most common pathogen is *Vibrio vulnificus*. *Vibrio* loves heat and very salty water, and Texas summers (and springs, and sometimes falls) provide plenty of both. Lots of people eat raw Gulf oysters in warm months, but that doesn't mean it's a good idea. Healthy adults usually don't get sick from *Vibrio*, but that is hardly enough of a guarantee. Instead of eating oysters raw during hot months, try roasting, grilling, or frying them. While a cooked oyster in June is not as delectable as a raw oyster in February, it is still better than most other foods on the planet.

A caveat, though: because all Texas and most Louisiana oysters are wild (and therefore scraped up from reefs on the seafloor) and sold as commodity product, quality varies considerably from oyster to oyster. Also, the shells are muddy and encrusted with barnacles (unlike farmed oysters raised in cages).

AVAILABILITY: Texas oysters are harvested from two types of waters: public and private leases. Private leases are open year-round, and oysters may also be harvested year-round. Public lands may only be fished from November 1 through April 30. The TDSHS can and does close some or all grounds throughout the year (whether due to natural outbreaks like *Vibrio* or human activity).

Oysters, either in the shell (called shellstock) or shucked are generally available year-round from local grocery stores and seafood markets. This is a local seafood that is very easy to find.

Or you may harvest oysters yourself. If you choose to do this, remember that in the state of Texas, one must have a saltwater fishing license, and one must be harvesting in an approved area (see page 17 for more information). Almost all commercial oysters are harvested in several to more than twenty feet of water, meaning most legal areas are too deep to just wade in and forage. However, a few spots do remain where oysters may be taken in less than three feet of water, and most of these spots are abundant oyster grounds. Low tide will assist in the search.

If you find yourself out searching for oysters in low-tide areas, you might notice lots of small tracks, vaguely hand shaped, with long claws. Raccoons famously prowl around oyster reefs at low tide, gobbling up all the young oysters and spat they can find. They are so closely associated with this behavior that "cooning" is a common colloquial term for harvesting oysters by hand in low-tide flats. Predictably, oyster fishers are not particularly fond of raccoons.

If you are shucking your own oysters, you will notice that the insides of the shells, though usually pale white, are sometimes shot through with browns, purples, blues, and yellows. Our advice is to seek out oysters with great coloring in the shell—the colors come from trace minerals, which add complexity to the taste. The darker the inside of the shell, the better the oyster—so says Jim Gossen, a Gulf oyster connoisseur if there ever was one.

For decades, Jim has been one of the strongest advocates for Gulf of Mexico seafood, and he has also been instrumental in the establishment of the Louisiana oyster farming industry, which is these days producing the finest farmed oysters in the country.

LIGHTNING WHELK

Busycon perversum pulleyi

COMMON NAME: Perverse Whelk (on account of its left-handedness, about which see below)

HABITAT: The Lightning Whelk is associated with shallow waters of bays and marshes, usually right near the water's edge. They are particularly drawn to piers, channels, and structures. If you see a whelk in the water, pay attention to the appearance of the shell and how it appears to be moving. If the shell is pale monochrome white or appears to be walking on the bay floor, then you are looking at a hermit crab, not a living whelk (see the separate entry for hermit crabs for more on eating these unlikely animals). If the shell

is half buried in the sand or appears to be slowly trudging through it, leaving a trail like that of a sloppy snow plow, or is on an oyster reef, then you are looking at a living whelk.

RANGE/DISTRIBUTION: The Lightning Whelk ranges from the Gulf of Mexico and western mid-Atlantic up through the Carolinas.

DESCRIPTION: If you were to conjure up images for the word "seashell," the whelk might be one of the first images to cross your mind. The knobby shell has a short spire and a large whorl, all radiating (in a beautiful illustration of the golden ratio) from a central point, the tip of the spire. The spiral terminates in a large aperture (the opening of the shell), the outer lip of which curls back only slightly. The narrow bottom tip of the shell, the siphon canal, is elongated and well developed. When the animal is alive, the shell is yellow to purple to maroon to light brown, with darker or lighter bands or splotches. The outer lip and siphon canal are yellow to gold to pink to brown to purple, fading to snow white farther inside the shell. Like all whelks (and most snails), the Lightning is equipped with a bony plate, the operculum, that attaches to the foot and is used to seal up the shell after the animal has retracted completely.

If you should see a living Lightning Whelk in situ on the bay floor, you might be surprised at the size of the soft body. When the snail is moving or feeding (it is a highly carnivorous animal), its soft tissue fills with water and swells so much it seems impossible that all of that fluffy flesh could fit into the small hard shell to which it is attached. Pick that whelk up and turn it over, and you will see how it all works. Basically, it will appear as if the whelk is urinating on you. After getting rid of the excess water, the body is a fraction of the size and as firm as a boot. Its body, with the long siphon (which it uses both to breathe by pulling water over internal gills and to smell out prey), will retract completely into the shell, which it seals up entirely.

A few other closely related species share the same waters with the Lightning Whelk. They all look similar, but as the Lightning Whelk is by far the most commonly encountered, we only cover that species. However, all are edible and legal for the taking. These other species are the Pear Whelk (*Busycotypus spiratus*), Shouldered Pear Whelk

(*Busycotypus plagosus*), and Splendid Whelk (*Busycon candelabrum*). We shall not waste words describing the differences in appearances between these latter three species, as they are small and insignificant; all three together, however, share one characteristic that easily differentiates them from the Lightning Whelk. They are right-handed, whereas the Lightning Whelk is left-handed. No, none of these snails (or for that matter any snails in the world) have hands. Handedness in snails refers to which way the aperture points, and most snails, evidently, are right-handed.

All whelks are carnivores, preying on oysters, clams, mussels, other snails, crabs, and detritus. They are slow but determined and deadly hunters—essentially enveloping their prey then working through their victim's shell by crushing it or simply rasping their way inside.

EATING: Whelks are excellent to eat. The meat is, of course, small relative to the size and weight of the shell; nonetheless, it is a superior seafood. The taste recalls the best of mollusks, with a texture similar to abalone. This is a seafood not nearly as appreciated as it should be.

There are two ways to get at the meat of a whelk. The first produces raw meat and requires nothing more than a hard surface, a hammer, and a small amount of brute strength. The second involves blanching. Bring salted water to a boil, add the whelks, and cook for just under ten minutes. Shock in cold water, and then winkle out the soft tissue.

The foot is the part most often eaten (the size of the whelk makes its guts slightly less appealing), and recognizing and detaching it from the viscera is easy. The cooked foot is a vague round stump, black on the outside and light brown on the inside. After the foot is separated from the viscera, it can be sliced or chopped and used in a further cooked dish. Alternately, the cooked foot can be sliced and served as is, with just a little lemon juice and olive oil for dressing.

AVAILABILITY: Asian markets and very good seafood markets in larger cities carry or can get ahold of Lightning Whelks harvested on the US east coast. There are no large directed whelk fisheries anywhere in the Gulf. Small oyster boats used to bring some in as bycatch, but not so much anymore. In Mexican waters, small fisheries, serving mostly local and regional markets, thrive here and there.

Harvesting Lightning Whelks yourself is quite easy, once you find where to look (bottoms around piers, rocks, canals, and oyster reefs). The recreational fishery in Texas is tightly regulated, so bear in mind the rules, especially concerning daily limits.

ANGELWING CLAM

Cyrtopleura costata

HABITAT: This clam can be found burrowed about two feet into clay and mud at the edges of bays.

RANGE/DISTRIBUTION: It occurs all around the northern Gulf of Mexico through the lower Atlantic states (similar species exist throughout the Caribbean Sea and mid-Atlantic down to at least Brazil).

DESCRIPTION: While strolling along a Texas beach or bay, you might see the shells of the Angelwing scattered around: delicate brittle shells (usually bone white), looking almost sculpted, almost riddled, with radiating patterns. The shells are tall and narrow, and pretty obviously come in pairs (even if finding an intact set is rare). Usually the shells are just fragments, because they break under the slightest pressure. You might wonder what lived in such a shell, and how it possibly survived inside its fragile armor.

Young Angelwings find a spot in a sturdy area on the bay's edge (a spot with lots of mud and even more clay), then they burrow. They keep burrowing until they are an arm's length down in the clay and mud (though we doubt they measure the distance with that unit). Then they excavate a small hole all the way back to the surface. They do this with their ridiculously long siphon, which can stretch from the burrow to the surface (walking along a bed of Angelwings you can see their siphons poking out like the galaxy's most pitiful Exogorths).

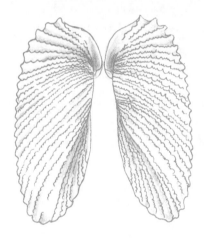

Once the Angelwing has established its burrow, it never leaves again. It grows into the mud and clay, and actually uses the sturdy walls of its burrow to buttress its own shell. The shell of the adult cannot even fully close. Angelwings rarely get much bigger than about six or seven inches in shell length, and each one weighs only a few ounces.

EATING: This clam is rightly considered a delicacy in some countries along the Angelwings' range but is pretty unknown as a food item here. Angelwings are indeed a treat—if they have been allowed to purge (more on that below). The gut (that part of the animal that is mostly protected by the shell) tastes at least as good as any east coast clam. The siphons compare favorably to geoduck (in taste and texture, not in size).

AVAILABILITY: This is not a critter you will be able to buy, at least not in the United States. If you want to eat Angelwings, be prepared to do a little work. We assure you the effort is worth the prize.

To find them, walk along the margins of an approved open bay (see page 17 again for shellfishing advice). You will want a bay with a lot of clay and mud. As you walk, keep looking for holes in the mud and clay. The holes will be the approximate diameter of a pencil or Sharpie and will be located in only an inch or two of water (assuming you have come to the bay at low tide). The holes must be in the water; those on dry land contain crabs, not clams.

To get at them: Once you have located a hole, start digging a hole straight down about four inches away from the hole. You will, of course, have had the forethought to bring a thin spade along with you for the purpose of digging this hole. Be very careful as you dig, for the Angelwing is easily crushed, and if crushed, is difficult if not impossible to use. After the hole is a bit more than elbow deep, stop with the spade and start with your hands. As you excavate, start working closer to the burrow's shaft. Do not start digging into the shaft, but rather, once you locate it, make sure you are digging close. As you get down to about shoulder deep, gingerly work your way toward the shaft. If you go slowly, you will find the burrow. Carefully excavate around the animal, bearing in mind the fragility of the shell. Once you have dug around the shell, slowly remove it from the hole. The siphon will have retracted back into the shell, so you only have to worry about that shell.

After you have successfully brought the Angelwing to the surface, take a few minutes to fill back in the hole you dug. You're not going to leave the spot unblemished, and the path of destruction will remain. But at least you're not leaving holes in the ground. And always take only one for every ten you see.

Now for the purging. Angelwings tend to be exceedingly gritty, too gritty to enjoy right out of the ground. There are two ways to get around this problem, three if you count just ignoring the clay (we don't recommend this). Obviously, both of these methods pertain only to freshly foraged Angelwings. If you should be so lucky to find them in the market (and you almost certainly won't in this country), purging the meat is probably not necessary.

The first way to clean out the grit is to cut the meat out of the shells (just like you would an oyster), then slice the long siphon lengthwise. Cut the guts into strips, then put all the meats into a bowl of iced salt water. Let everything sit for a few minutes, agitate the water somewhat, then rinse off each piece of meat. This will work, but it takes a lot of effort for so little meat, especially as the delicate gut meat tends to shred into nothingness the more you mess with it.

The second way we find much easier and more effective, even if it does take a lot more time and a little specialized equipment. Fill up a small Igloo cooler with beach water. Put a small bait pump in the cooler and get it aerating. After you harvest your Angelwings, place them gently in the Igloo. Keep the Igloo in a cool place, and let the pump run for a

couple of days. You will want to strain the water through a coffee filter at least twice during the process. Afterward, you will find your Angelwings have purged perfectly.

SLIPPER SHELL AND STRIPED FALSE LIMPET

Crepidula fornicata and *Siphonaria pectinata*

COMMON NAME: Slipper Shell: Slipper Limpet

HABITAT: Both of these snails (which they are, despite appearances) live in coastal waters, on rocks, jetties, and piers. The Slipper Shell is, like the oyster, a suspension filter feeder: it takes in large amounts of water, strains out all the good microscopic bits of food, and passes out the water, which is afterward cleaner than when it went into the animal. It is perhaps not surprising, then, that Slipper Shells are often found not only in the vicinity of oysters but also anchored directly to them. This is not a parasitic arrangement, for the oyster is in

no way harmed or affected by the much smaller Slipper Shell. They are so common on oyster reefs that if you have ever shucked a sack of Texas oysters, you have certainly (if unknowingly) thrown at least a few of them away. Though they are more common on oyster reefs in less than thirty feet of water,

Slipper Shells are sometimes found in waters three times that deep.

False Limpets prefer smooth rocks and piers (concrete especially), right at the edge of tidal waters. They breathe air, so they camp out as close as possible to the high-tide mark to take advantage of the algae, on which they graze. Because they require a specific environment, they tend to live in loose clusters.

RANGE/DISTRIBUTION: The False Limpet occurs in temperate Atlantic waters, on both sides, including the Mediterranean Sea and the Gulf of Mexico. The Slipper Shell is endemic to temperate coasts of North America but was accidentally introduced to US coastal Pacific and European Atlantic waters (it is considered invasive in both of those regions).

DESCRIPTION: The limpet is a squat cone, with radial lines all around to the aperture (the bottom of the cone). It is only an inch, maybe two, across. The aperture has no operculum with which the snail could protect its soft body, so it spends its life with its foot firmly anchored on the rock upon which it lives. It moves a bit here and there and migrates somewhat with the seasons, but it never leaves its rock.

The Slipper Shell is more sedentary. As a young, free-floating larva, it finds suitable substrate, settles down, and moves very little after that (recall that it is a filter feeder).

It is not unusual to find several Slipper Shells stacked on top of one another. This is a reproductive strategy. Like most mollusks (and sea life in general), Slipper Shells are broadcast spawners, meaning sperm and egg are broadcast in the open water. For this strategy to work, the animals need to be close to one another. So Slipper Shells stack on top of one another, thus ensuring the smallest possible distance. While Slipper Shells have both female and male sexes, they are also sequential hermaphrodites, meaning they can change sex as required by environmental conditions. In the aforementioned stack, one snail is a female. The rest are male. If that female dies, one of the males changes sex, and life proceeds.

An adult is small, with a shell less than three inches in length. The shell, which is tan to white to tan and white to a faded brown with white and tan stripes, looks a bit like a flattened hat, the sort worn by a troll or a Smurf. The aperture is half covered by a very thin shell.

EATING: Neither of these animals is very large, so bear that in mind when deciding on a meal consisting solely of either. For both, the meat is easy to get to—simply turn the animal upside down and scrape out the disc-shaped foot (for the Slipper Shell, first tear away the operculum, which is delicate; then you can scrape out the entire meat). Both species are delightful raw, simply scraped from their shells, sprinkled with at most a bit of lime juice. They may also be grilled very briefly, aperture side up. Cooking takes at most a minute or two, and eating requires nothing but fingers, a towel to hold the hot shell, and maybe, if one is being ostentatious, a toothpick.

It takes a great many live limpets to yield a pound of meat. Nevertheless, if you should find yourself with an abundance, by all means blanch and pick the lot, then use the meat as you would whelk or even abalone meat.

AVAILABILITY: There are absolutely no fisheries, recreational or commercial, anywhere along the Gulf. Very rarely, limpets are sold by high-end seafood companies, but these always come from distant waters. In Normandy, France (where Slipper Shells are highly invasive), a small fishery has grown up seeking to fish the snails out of existence.

The shucked meats are sold frozen, marketed as Berlingots de Mer.

For both species the best bet, at least for home consumption, is to hunt them yourself. Don't expect to find many Slipper Shells, for they are difficult to spot.

Limpets, on the other hand, are more visible: small cones sticking on smooth rocks right at the high-tide line. However, hunting them is not simply a matter of grabbing shells off rocks—you will need a thin-bladed knife and a bit of stealth. After having spotted a limpet on a rock, sneak up on it and quickly dislodge it by running the blade of the knife between the shell and the rock. You will only get one chance before the limpet seals its shell to the rock. If that happens, only a hammer will dislodge it. The whole operation is simple enough, but remember that limpets live on slick rocks at the water'e edge, so a bit of foolhardiness is required.

ATLANTIC BAY SCALLOP

Argopecten irradians

HABITAT: This scallop species is found in shallow and relatively calm bays, in a few inches to a few feet of water. It prefers sandy bottoms with good amounts of seagrass.

RANGE/DISTRIBUTION: The Atlantic Bay Scallop occurs along the US Atlantic coast to the entire Gulf of Mexico and the Caribbean, though it is far more common and abundant in the northern part of that range. In the southern parts of its range (and Texas falls within that area), the winters are not predictably cold enough to produce large, stable, and fishable populations. Some years (usually a season or two after a cold winter), scallop populations swell, but successive warm winters can wipe out all the increase. In Texas, we have always found more scallops in southerly waters, due apparently to their preference for saltier waters (south Texas bays are famously hypersaline), though they are nowhere consistently abundant.

DESCRIPTION: Everyone knows the shape of the Bay Scallop shell. It has a big hinge at the base, deep grooves running radially, and is always less than four inches across. The body inside looks like a typical clam, except that the adductor muscle is quite large. Around the rim of the aperture, on the fringe of the body, there is a series of turquoise dots. These are not decorations, but true functioning eyes—the scallop has dozens of them.

EATING: Only the adductor muscle of the scallop is marketed, for scallops, unlike oysters, mussels, and other clams, do not survive long out of water. If you get ahold of the live animal, we suggest eating the whole thing. You will be happy you did, for the scallop is, after all, just a clam.

AVAILABILITY: This species is the same as that harvested in US mid-Atlantic waters, shucked and tubbed, and sold across the country. Similar species in western Pacific waters are fished in much greater numbers and exported, the result being that the majority of Bay Scallops bought and sold in the United States are imported from elsewhere.

There is no scallop fishery in Texas, nor in most parts of the Gulf. Florida is the only exception, and even there commercial harvests are relatively puny. A closely related species, the Atlantic Calico Scallop (*Argopecten gibbus*), lives farther offshore (in more than thirty feet of water) and was historically the focus of trawl and dredge fisheries on both sides of Florida, as well as Georgia and South Carolina, but those fisheries have always been boom-or-bust, as the scallop populations don't tolerate heavy fishing pressure or uncooperative weather. This white-and-pink-shelled scallop does exist in all Gulf waters but has never been commercially fished locally. When the weather has been right, small fisheries pop up here and there in northern Mexican Atlantic waters. Those fisheries, however, are tiny, and all of the harvest passes directly into the local economy, never leaving the region, much less the country. The same happens in Florida, to a much smaller degree.

Instead, go hunt your own. Find a shallow clear bay, with lots of seagrass, and walk slowly. If they're there, and if you're patient, you'll find some. They'll be resting right on the surface of the bay floor, and will occasionally hop or even swim around, though never very far or fast.

COQUINA, OR THE BEAN CLAM

Donax variabilis

HABITAT: Coquinas occur throughout the intertidal zones of beaches. They migrate daily along with the tide, pitching their bodies up or down the beach, depending on the movement of the waters. They also migrate seasonally, going into subtidal waters during winter. Warmer weather brings them back into shallow waters, right onto the beach. They are most commonly seen in late spring

and throughout the summer, when millions, or even billions at a time, crowd the margins of the beach as far as the eye can see. When they are most abundant, they appear as small pebbles right at the water's edge. Only upon close inspection does one see that they are actually tiny clams. They live within the top couple of inches of the seafloor.

RANGE/DISTRIBUTION: Coquinas range from the upper US Atlantic coast to the entire Gulf of Mexico. Closely related species live in eastern Atlantic waters and the Mediterranean, as well as throughout the Indian and Pacific Oceans.

DESCRIPTION: It is called a Bean Clam because of its size—never even an inch long, and usually half that. The shell is triangular. The "*variabilis*" in the scientific name refers to the variety of shell colors and patterns. No matter how many Coquinas you might ever see, you will never see two identically colored and patterned. Some are white, others are pink, purple, red, tan, gold, green, or yellow; still others are hybrids of these colors. Some have one radial stripe, others have several. Likewise, some Coquinas have one stripe running anterior to posterior; others have several. Finally, some have both kinds of stripes, which may or may not be the same color. In short, the Coquina shell is endlessly fascinating.

EATING: There's not a lot of meat in a Coquina, and what little there is, is more than a little sandy. One can certainly purge

Coquinas (see the Angelwing entry for more on this process), but such a process dilutes the taste of their nectar, and the nectar might be, at least from a gustatory point of view, the best thing about the Coquina. The meat is delightful, but we've never had the patience to eat more than a plate or two at a time.

AVAILABILITY: There are no commercial harvests of Coquina at all, at least domestically. (In the waters of the Mediterranean and western Pacific, small commercial fisheries do thrive. We have no doubt that informal fisheries exist everywhere Bean Clams congregate.)

Harvesting your own is quite simple. Take an empty oyster, crawfish, or onion sack and a shovel. When you spot Coquinas—and if you see one, you will find many—dig up a clod of the surrounding beach. You will come away with hundreds or even thousands of clams. Dump the whole mess in the oyster sack, then repeat. Fill the sack up, then tie it off tightly, drag it out into the surf until it is well underwater. Gently agitate the bag in the water for about a minute, then bring the sack back in, being careful not to drag it. You will emerge from the water with a sack of Coquinas washed of sand and mud and ready to be cooked.

Bear in mind, as always, regulations concerning the harvest of clams. Open beaches are a gray area as far as clam regulations go.

AGGRAVATING MUSSELS: SOUTHERN RIBBED, HOOKED, AND TULIP MUSSEL

Geukensia granosissima, Ischadium recurvum, and *Modiolus americanus*

HABITAT: Ribbed Mussels live in exceedingly shallow intertidal grasses and mudflats, especially around *Spartina* grasses, around whose bases they cluster. The Hooked prefers hard substrate in slightly deeper waters, to about thirty feet; the substrate upon which they typically settle is oyster reef. The Tulip also lives on substrate, though it prefers coral to oyster reef. Tulip Mussels are not common in Texas inshore waters, though we've found more than a few over the years.

RANGE/DISTRIBUTION: All three are warm temperate to tropical species. The Ribbed has the largest range, being found farther north than the other two. The Hooked and the Tulip are more at home in the Gulf and waters to the south.

DESCRIPTION: None of these mussels look exotic. The Ribbed is the largest (up to five inches long) and is covered in radial grooves. The Hooked is similarly grooved, but the shell bends halfway along the shell at an angle as sharp as forty-five degrees. It is a smaller species, hardly ever reaching more than an inch in length. The Tulip is larger than the Hooked and smaller than the Ribbed. Its shell is more rectangular than the other species. All three mussels are brown to black.

EATING: Oh, the heartbreak. The Hooked, though abundant and common, is generally too small to enjoy as a mussel and too bland to make a good broth. The Ribbed, also abundant and very large as well, is only marginally edible and rarely tasty. Maybe one out of ten Ribbed Mussels provides an experience worth repeating, and even that one leaves little memory one way or the other. The Tulip fares better on the scale of edibility but is not common enough in shallow waters to easily access. None make an acceptable broth.

AVAILABILITY: These mussels are never ever fished anywhere commercially. You can hunt your own, but your time would be better spent hunting more easily edible critters.

MARSH PERIWINKLE

Littoraria irrorata

HABITAT: The Marsh Periwinkle is found along the edges of shallow, protected bays and throughout saltwater marshes—it is almost ubiquitous wherever cordgrass grows. While intimately associated with saltwater areas, periwinkles always stay dry. When the tide is up, and marsh shores are lapped with water, you will find periwinkles clinging to stalks of cordgrass everywhere (from a distance they almost look like growths on the cordgrass itself). When the tide is out, periwinkles will cluster around the base of cordgrass plants. They are easy picking either way. A related species, the Zebra Periwinkle (*Echinolittorina interrupta*), lives on jetties, but it is a small species, almost never big enough to be practically edible (snails don't make great broth).

RANGE/DISTRIBUTION: The Marsh Periwinkle occurs all along the northwest Atlantic and through to the Gulf. This species (and others closely related) may also be found in northeastern Atlantic waters.

DESCRIPTION: Periwinkles are quite small, with very big specimens being less than an inch long. The shells are dull tan, with small ridges covering the external part of the shell. The inside rim of the shell is orange and smooth as glass.

EATING: Periwinkles are a delight to eat, but perhaps not for people unwilling to work a bit. Cooking (usually boiling) is the easiest, though some work with a toothpick is required to fish out the tasty morsels (the verb for getting the meat out of a periwinkle is "winkle"). Alternatively, one may clip the pointed end of the shell off before cooking, which makes the meats fall out quite easily. However, the thickness and size of the shell make this route kind of inconvenient.

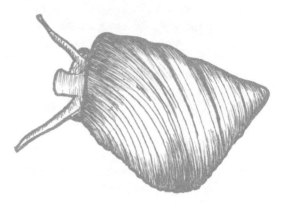

AVAILABILITY: Large Asian markets will generally stock live periwinkles, but these are harvested on the east coast, never from Gulf waters (the species is the same). If you want local periwinkles, your only choice is to hunt them yourself. The hunting is quite pleasant, though—just go to a saltwater marsh, walk near the water where the cordgrass grows, and pick as many as you like (you *will* of course need a valid saltwater fishing license and you must also be harvesting in approved waters—see the Eastern Oyster entry for more details).

MOON SNAIL AND FALSE MOON SNAIL

Neverita duplicatus and *Neverita delessertiana*

COMMON NAMES: Moon Snail: Shark Eye; False Moon Snail: False Shark Eye

HABITAT: These two snails prefer soft, sandy bottoms in coastal waters, from twelve feet down to one hundred feet.

RANGE/DISTRIBUTION: They are found along the US Atlantic coast and in the Gulf of Mexico.

DESCRIPTION: The Moon Snail (as well as its "False" cousin) has a shell like that of a land snail: rounded and mostly spherical, with an operculum and without pointed spires. The shell is tan, usually banded with olives and browns, though always with an aperture dominated by a large black splotch, with only a fringe of white around the edges. It grows to at most a touch over three inches in length. It is a predatory snail, preying on clams and mussels by drilling a hole in their shells and sucking out the insides.

EATING: Like most snails, these are excellent to eat and may be used in any snail recipes. Because of their size and shape, they are perfect (along with five of their fellows) for a classic escargot treatment. Always cook snails with garlic.

AVAILABILITY: Boats targeting White Shrimp just offshore usually haul in some Moon Snails as bycatch, but, like all the rest, they are tossed overboard, never marketed. Apparently they are not marketed elsewhere in the United States either.

Catching your own is difficult, given the distance and depth offshore required to get to suitable habitat.

SAWTOOTH AND STIFF PEN SHELLS

Atrina serrata, Atrina rigida, and *Atrina seminuda*

COMMON NAMES: Fan Clam, Tairagai (Japan)

HABITAT: Sandy soft bottoms, generally in or among seagrasses, are the pen shell's preferred habitat. It lies in the sand, buried almost all the way, with only its posterior visible to the world. It is common in very shallow bays, and just as common in deeper bays and near offshore waters. Other species live on offshore bottoms attached to rocks and structures, but these are rarely encountered by humans.

RANGE/DISTRIBUTION: All of these species live along the Atlantic coast of the Americas but are most abundant in warmer waters.

DESCRIPTION: We describe these species together and do not differentiate between them, for they all may be found in the same waters, and they are all equally common and abundant.

Imagine a giant mussel with a shell measuring a foot or more in length and weighing over a pound; then you will have a fair idea of the appearance of a pen shell. The outer shell layers of all of these species are brown to gray to black to olive. Underneath the drab layer lies another, this one of nacre more beautiful than any oyster or abalone shell. All pen shells have a long beard, or byssus, at the terminal end. This is not in itself unusual, for all mussels and quite a few clams have such beards. The threads of the byssus help anchor the animal in place and protect it from the buffeting of waves and weather. In the case of the pen shell, the byssus is unusually long—up to several inches—and the individual threads are as fine as human hair. These threads, once washed, then treated with lemon juice and allowed to dry in the sun, shine exactly like gold (once upon a time in the Mediterranean, pen shell byssi were used to produce one of the costliest fabrics in history: sea silk).

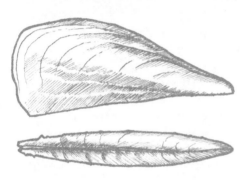

Pen shells seem to produce pearls easily and often. These pearls are chocolate to gold in color and are generally no bigger than BBs.

EATING: The soft internal body of a pen shell is large, filling the shell entirely. The most conspicuous part is the adductor muscle, which is huge (on an average pen shell, it is about as big as a U-10 shucked scallop). While it's not a common seafood product in the United States, the adductor muscle is marketed elsewhere and is highly regarded. A secondary adductor is located right next to the primary one and is just as good. The rest of the organs taste good, but texture makes for difficult eating. It's best to chop them up and use them in chowders and stuffing.

AVAILABILITY: They are not fished in US waters, though pen shells compose a fishery around the Bay of Campeche in Mexico.

Harvesting pen shells is easy, as long as you know where to look. The animal is not readily visible, as it is almost totally buried in the sand. It is also a solitary creature, so you must search for what appears to be a slightly open mouth sticking out about an inch from the sandy bottom. Taking your time over shallow sandy flats, look for such objects. When you spot one, run your hand all the way to the terminal end, which will be located a foot or more down in the sand. Work the terminal end free and extract it, making sure not to tear the byssus as the pen shell is dislodged.

OYSTER DRILLS

Stramonita haemostoma and *Stramonita canaliculata*

COMMON NAMES: *S. haemostoma*: Florida Rock Snail, and *S. canaliculata*: Hay's Rock Snail are the widely accepted common names. But the only colloquial name we have found in Texas is Oyster Drill, occasionally shortened to just Drill. In coastal Louisiana, the common name for both species is Bigano, an Acadian corruption of "*birgorneau(x)*," the French common name for periwinkle. Oyster Drills in France are called Bulots.

HABITAT: Sometimes great swarms of Oyster Drills will cover jetties and rocks right at and under the tide line. More commonly they are found on shell substrate in shallow waters, where they will be preying on all the young oysters and mussels they come across.

RANGE/DISTRIBUTION: Oyster Drills occur on both sides of the central Atlantic: from the Mediterranean to Angola in the east, and from the Carolinas to the Gulf of Mexico in the west.

DESCRIPTION: Both species of Oyster Drills grow to at least three inches, with the Hay's getting a bit bigger, to at most five inches. While they both share the same general shape (a tall spire attached to a fat central whorl that ends in a wide aperture), the Hay's has a double row of nodules (rounded spikes) on its shoulders (the widest part of the whorl right under where the spire begins), whereas the Florida has smooth

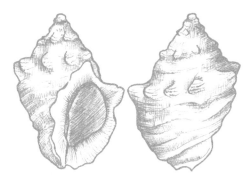

shoulders with faint bumps rather than nodules. Also, the Florida has a rounded aperture; that of the Hay's is angular. These distinctions are important if you decide to go foraging for your own.

Oyster Drills are always some shade of brown, usually monochromatic. The inside rim of the aperture is yam orange, which fades into white farther into the shell.

EATING: As for all snails, the foot is the main muscle (and also the most edible bit), along with the guts, which, while edible, are not for everyone.

In Louisiana, Oyster Drills are sometimes added to the crab boil, or a boil is made of them alone. The technique, spices, and seasonings are the same. The meats are then winkled out and eaten right away or picked

for later use in pasta sauce. In France, where they are served as cold *fruits de mer*, the cooking liquid is white wine, red wine vinegar, some herbs, and a few peppercorns.

Alternately, the Oyster Drills can be cooked and picked, then used for escargots. Or the chopped meat may be used in stuffing. Perhaps the most superior way to prepare them, though, is by breaking the shell right at the shoulder, right off the living animal, then picking out any relevant bits. We prefer this method, for the raw muscle is much more versatile than the cooked. It may be braised or fried (after being pounded to a suitable thickness).

The snail's hypobranchial gland is a green to brown tube-shaped organ located at the junction of the shoulder and the spire. The contents of this gland, once extracted, smeared on a flat surface, and exposed to oxygen and sunlight, will change in color from bile green to radiant purple. For thousands of years in the Mediterranean, relatives of the Oyster Drill—most importantly the Purple Dye Murex (*Bolinus brandaris*)—were harvested to produce dye, which in turn was used to produce purple textiles. The process was so tedious that only the wealthiest of ancient Mediterranean elites could afford such purple clothing. The color was and is known as Tyrian purple. The first known manufacture of such fabrics was by the Phoenicians, and they were doing it as much as three thousand years ago. The word "Phoenicia" itself was an ancient Greek exonym deriving from the word for that shade of purple. If you find yourself with a surfeit of Oyster Drills, try it out. You won't really be able to produce a dark dye, but if you extract the glands, smash them, expose them to sunlight until they turn purple, then mix with a little bit of water, you might be able to dye a pair of children's socks a pale pastel. We once managed to do so. Our kids, very young at the time, were absolutely delighted that they had snail-gut socks.

AVAILABILITY: Occasionally someone harvests a few Oyster Drills and sells them somewhere in Louisiana, but aside from that, no fisheries exist in US waters. Drills can be the bane of both oyster and crab fishers, for they prey on young oysters and foul crab traps. While both fisheries would welcome the opportunity to market drills, they are prohibited, at least in Texas, by ambiguities in TPWD regulations and fears of trouble with game wardens.

Harvesting for your table is both legal and easy. However, TPWD regulations prohibit taking more than two Florida Rock Snails per day, and no more than fifteen snails combined per day. This is where the distinctions between the Florida and the Hay's become relevant.

PURPLE-SPINED SEA URCHIN

Arbacia punctulata

HABITAT: This sea urchin is most common near the bottom of rocks and structures but is also found on seagrass beds and shell substrate. It is a shy urchin, rarely venturing away from nooks and crannies during the day, only grazing on algae and seaweed at night. Typically, this species sticks to shallow waters. Lots of other species of urchins live in the Gulf of Mexico, but they are all offshore and usually deepwater species.

RANGE/DISTRIBUTION: The Purple-Spined Sea Urchin lives in tropical Atlantic waters, the Gulf of Mexico, and the Caribbean Sea.

DESCRIPTION: It is small, no more than a few inches across, including spines. It is also adorable, but only the largest specimens are worth harvesting for the table (and the

largest should certainly be left alone so they can make babies).

EATING: We've tried these a couple of times, but we'll not be repeating the experience. The species is a smaller one, with not much room in its shell (which is called a "test")

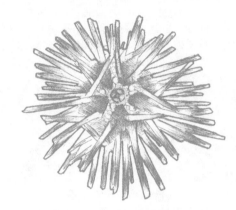

for any decent amount of tasty bits. Also, it is much more common in the southern part of the state, where harvests are prohibited during the spawning seasons.

AVAILABILITY: The Purple Sea Urchin (*Strongylocentrotus purpuratus*) and the Red Sea Urchin (*Strongylocentrotus franciscanus*) and the Green Sea Urchin (*Strongylocentrotus droebachiensis*) are the US commercial species. The first two species are found in and fished in California. The third is found and fished in Maine.

GIANT COCKLE AND BLOOD ARK

Dinocardium robustum and *Lunarca ovalis*

COMMON NAMES: Blood Ark: Blood Clam, Blood Cockle

HABITAT: Both of these clams (for both cockles and arks are clams) occur in very low intertidal to subtidal waters, always in soft sand, where they stay at least half submerged in the silty substrate. Both species are found in subtidal areas along beaches, passes, and larger sandy bays, as well as in near offshore waters down to one hundred feet or so, in the same kinds of sandy bottoms.

RANGE/DISTRIBUTION: The Blood Ark is found from northern South American Atlantic waters up to New England and everywhere in between. The Giant Cockle tends to be found only in the central northern part of that range.

DESCRIPTION: The Giant Cockle, with a shell length of up to five inches, is, not surprisingly, larger than the Blood Ark, which is three inches at most. Both look like nondescript deep-bodied clams, with dozen of rows of radial grooves running from the hinge to the lips.

The Giant Cockle is tan, light brown, dark yellow, or umber, sometimes with darker stripes running perpendicular to shell grooves. The Blood Ark has a white shell, but this is usually hidden by a gray-brown furry periostracum (which is the soft coating on the shells of some bivalves).

EATING: Both are excellent to eat relative not only to other seafood in general but to other clams specifically. Cockles have a unique depth of taste, unlike any other. The meat tastes like clam, of course, but the notes of iron, iodine, metals, and minerals make it incomparable. Cockles are hands-down Apple's favorite clam. The Blood Ark produces hemoglobin, which is responsible for the occasionally shocking sight of a freshly opened specimen oozing what appears to be blood.

AVAILABILITY: Both species are commercially exploited, to some extent along the US Atlantic coast, though not in the Gulf outside of highly localized and informal fisheries in Mexico. Better fishmongers and most large Asian markets will carry some kind of cockle, as will most seafood companies. All of these cockles will come from elsewhere.

Harvesting your own is difficult. In other parts of their range, these cockles are enthusiastically foraged by recreational fishers. But those places have dramatic tidal movement, which exposes subtidal areas. In the Gulf, of course, we have almost no tidal movement. Unless it's a freakish low tide and seas are flat, you will have to blindly tong, which is hit-or-miss as well as cumbersome, considering you will be tonging in several feet of water off the beach. If you do find some, purging is necessary but easily accomplished, for these species filter water quickly. See the Angelwing Clam entry for more on purging.

SOUTHERN SURF CLAM

Spisula raveneli

HABITAT: The Southern Surf Clam can be found burrowed in sandy bottoms, from subtidal flats right off the beach to more than two hundred feet down, but rarely to never in bays.

RANGE/DISTRIBUTION: It ranges all down the Atlantic coast from southern Canada through the Gulf of Mexico.

DESCRIPTION: The pale to white triangular shell grows up to six inches or more. Tiny parallel ridges run from the hinge to the lips. Some ridges may be dark, but more typically the shell is more or less white.

EATING: Like all clams that live buried in wave-tossed sandy waters, the Southern Surf Clam is overwhelmingly sandy. It is so sandy that the only part considered edible and thus marketed is the foot, a shark-tooth-shaped muscle, pale tan at the base, fading into pink or purple or brown or red.

Extracting this muscle is a simple task, for it is so large it barely fits in the shell, and it, along with the leathery adductor, is the only muscular part of the animal. The rest of the animal is soft tissue, which makes a decent, if cloudy, broth.

AVAILABILITY: Seafood companies carry frozen cleaned feet, and higher-end establishments occasionally sell live Southern Surf Clams. Large Asian markets carry both. Surf Clams are fished along the upper US Atlantic coast and elsewhere in the world.

Harvesting your own is fraught with challenges, all of which are summed up in the Giant Cockle and Blood Ark entry. Bear in mind also that Surf Clams live in deeper waters than the cockles do.

QUAHOG CLAMS: SOUTHERN AND TEXAS; RANGIAS: BROWN AND ATLANTIC

Mercenaria campechiensis and *Mercenaria texana; Rangia flexuosa* and *Rangia cuneata*

HABITAT: The quahogs lie buried in sandy and soft muddy bottoms, usually (at least in Texas) near seagrasses. They are found from intertidal areas to one hundred feet or more below the water's surface. They prefer high-salinity conditions, as one finds in bays with limited water exchange. The rangias, on the other hand, do not tolerate salinity as well, preferring lower-salinity bays and brackish waters. They, too, bury themselves in sand and soft bottoms.

RANGE/DISTRIBUTION: The Southern Quahog more or less overlaps the southern range of its cousin, the Northern Quahog (*Mercenaria mercenaria*), and occurs much farther south as well, throughout the entire Gulf. Apparently, the Texas Quahog (which is, to laypeople, identical to the Southern) is a hybrid species. The rangias are endemic to the Gulf.

DESCRIPTION: The Northern Quahog is more commonly known under a variety of market names—Littleneck, Topneck, Cherrystone, Chowder, and others—all of which indicate specific sizes of the same animal. The Southern is the Northern's doppelgänger, differing only in size. The Southern may have a shell up to six inches or more in length and may weigh the better part of two pounds. The thick outer shell is white to tan to brown, with one or a few or no stripes running from anterior to posterior. The Texas Quahog is slightly smaller than the Southern, but don't expect to tell the two species apart.

The rangias look exactly like the quahogs, except for the chocolate- to olive-colored periostracum.

EATING: There is no finer edible thing in the northwestern Gulf than the raw foot of a Southern Quahog, consumed minutes after the animal was harvested from its sandy bed (the rest of the organs taste just as nice, but are a bit big to be enjoyed in a gulp). Alas, once the meat comes close to heat, it tends to get very tough. It's best to gorge on as many feet as you care to cut off, and then make clam chowder with the rest. Once the meat is chopped, the firm texture stops being an impediment. Bear in mind that even though the meats are huge, the shells are that much bigger. You might be surprised at how little the end yield is.

We include rangias even though we have never knowingly eaten one. Because they prefer low-salinity waters, they tend to grow very close to places where humans live and work, which means the danger of contamination (be it pathogen or pollution) by humans is much greater. This means that there is no place in the state where rangias grow that is also open for the harvesting of shellfish. We consider this a great shame, as rangias were the preferred shellfish of the indigenous inhabitants of the area, who themselves were, if the literal mounds of archaeological evidence are to be believed, great connoisseurs of our region's coastal bounty. We can only imagine the delights of the rangia.

AVAILABILITY: Quahogs, fished along the US Atlantic coast, are easily available from seafood companies and at better fishmongers and Asian markets. Outside of small and specialized cultivation operations in the far eastern Gulf, there are no commercial clams from US Gulf waters. In Texas, any potential clam fishery is prohibited by permitting issues, regulations, and a lack of recognized market demand.

We've harvested many hundreds of pounds of quahogs by ourselves over the years. During our rare extreme low tides, when the bay floors become mud flats, you will see the hinges barely poking up from the sand. If you are lucky enough to be at the bay on a day without wind, you'll be able to slowly wade in the water and gather as many as the law allows.

STOUT RAZOR CLAM

Tagelus plebeius

HABITAT: This clam prefers sandy or muddy bottoms in shallow coastal waters down to dozens of feet. It is particularly abundant in Texas near the shore in small muddy bays, on beaches, and in passes.

RANGE/DISTRIBUTION: Stout Razor Clams are found from Argentina to Massachusetts and everywhere in between.

DESCRIPTION: The rectangular shell has rounded edges and is at most four or so inches long. This species is much thinner and wider than the commercial species fished in Atlantic and Pacific waters. The white shell is covered with an olive brown periostracum.

EATING: It's a razor clam. It is delicious, if a bit muddy.

AVAILABILITY: This species is commercially fished in the Chesapeake Bay, but harvests are inconsistent from year to year. That is the only fishery for this species in the United States.

Hunting your own Stout Razor Clams is frustrating. It may also be rewarding. If you find them on the beach, the burrows are marked by a rough figure-eight opening; if you find them on a muddy bay shore, look for a more rectangular opening. On the beach, simply pour some salt into the opening, wait for the clam to violently jump out of the hole, and grab it quickly. Don't pull back your hand immediately, as the clam's muscle, still clinging to the hole, might get torn off. Wait until the clam has relaxed, then extract. On a muddy shoreline, you'll have to dig as you would for an Angelwing Clam (see that entry for more details on digging and purging). Its burrow might be a couple of feet down.

FLORIDA HORSE CONCH

Pleuroploca gigantea

HABITAT: This species is found in intertidal to subtidal waters on sand, mud, seagrass, and weedy bottoms. It normally occurs near large bays, jetties, offshore structures and rock bottoms.

RANGE/DISTRIBUTION: The Florida Horse Conch occurs along the US mid-Atlantic coast and throughout the Gulf of Mexico.

DESCRIPTION: This is a giant snail, certainly the biggest in the Atlantic, and one of the largest in the world. Its shell (including its tall spire) may grow up to twenty-four inches long from tip to tip. The flesh is bright orange. It is a predatory species, hunting and eating other shellfish, mostly large clams and even larger snails.

EATING: The Florida Horse Conch enjoys a fine table reputation in northwestern Gulf areas of Mexico. We do not know of other places where it is routinely fished and marketed. It does make fine eating, but a bit of work with a meat mallet is recommended. After that treatment, the muscle may be sliced and grilled to great effect.

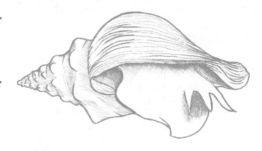

AVAILABILITY: The Florida Horse Conch is rarely available commercially in the United States. Conch meat, imported from other waters, would be its closest substitute, but we cannot suggest that, as commercial fishing pressures have decimated populations. You can try to hunt your own. Be prepared to hold your breath.

ARROW AND LONGFIN INSHORE SQUID

Loligo pleii and *Loligo pealei*

HABITAT: The Arrow and Longfin Inshore Squid are both pelagic species, and both typically do not venture great distances offshore.

RANGE/DISTRIBUTION: They range along the mid- to northwest Atlantic coast and are usually found in shallower (less than several hundred feet) water. These squids are common in the Gulf of Mexico and southern Caribbean, but absent from Cuba and the Caribbean islands.

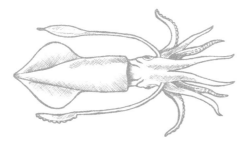

DESCRIPTION: Both species look exactly like what most of us think of when we think of squid: a bulbous body, with two short fins at the tapered end; a small head, sporting enormous black eyes, sprouting from the open end of the body; a mass of tentacles of various sizes. Neither is a large species, ranging from twelve to twenty inches (from tip to tentacle tip). Like their other cephalopod cousins, these squid change their color and the patterns of dots on their bodies minute by minute in remarkable visual displays that pretty much defy belief. Freshly dead, the body itself is pure white, covered with a thick membrane of pink to purple skin, in which are contained all pigments and chromatophores. After a few days out of the water, the body skin turns pink to purple, a result apparently of the ink leaking throughout.

EATING: If you've ever eaten squid in a restaurant, you have eaten one of these species.

AVAILABILITY: If you're looking for these squids fished by Texas boats, you are out of luck, unless you know someone who works on an offshore Brown Shrimp boat. And even if you know a friendly shrimper, the boat is fishing for shrimp, not squid. No commercial boat in the state goes after squid. So appreciable catches of squid are few and far between. This does not, however, stop a great many unscrupulous fishmongers from claiming that they have consistent local sources. Squid is targeted in Florida for the bait industry, but don't assume that bait squid is handled as well as table squid.

The Longfin Inshore Squid is fished heavily on the US Atlantic coast, especially out of Rhode Island. Large numbers are caught, processed, and marketed domestically. We suggest you rely on those rather than waiting on dubious Gulf catches.

Like shrimp, squid do not age well. We always buy our squid frozen, because it was frozen at the peak of freshness. Days-old fresh or thawed squid, on the other hand, are almost always at least on the downside of the quality curve, if not at the bottom.

ATLANTIC BRIEF SQUID

Lolliguncula brevis

COMMON NAME: Finger Squid

HABITAT: The Atlantic Brief Squid inhabits shallow coastal waters down to around seventy-five feet or so. It is common in bays during the summer. It is a midwater pelagic species, so it is found over all kinds of bottoms.

RANGE/DISTRIBUTION: Its range includes warm temperate and tropical waters of the western Atlantic, from the lower US coast to Brazil.

DESCRIPTION: Reaching at the very most six inches in length, and usually little more than half that, the Atlantic Brief Squid is a small species. Its two longest tentacles, which are

flattened like spatulas, only have suckers at the tips. The body is short, and the terminal end is rounded and blunt. It is a paler squid than the two described previously, its coloration being limited to purple to brown spots. Eyes are rimmed with hazel green and yellow, which fade within hours of death. Like most cephalopods, this squid is capable of impressive visual displays. The death throes of the Atlantic Brief Squid, while not something we celebrate, are nonetheless mesmerizing.

EATING: By far the best squid in the Gulf, the Atlantic Brief Squid is one of the better squid we have ever eaten from any waters. With its humble appearance and even humbler name, the Brief Squid pales in reputation and price next to the splashier-attired and -named Firefly Squid (*Watasenia scintillans*); were the former graced with a better paint job and a more catchy moniker, we do not doubt it would rank at least as highly as the latter.

Cleaning takes a little while, on account of the small bits. Still, two people working together can clean a few pounds in an hour. If those two people have children of their own, or access to children, the job goes even faster. Cleaning squid is a dirty job, so kids usually enjoy it.

No squid is better lightly battered and fried than the Atlantic Brief Squid. The tubes are so thin that a higher-than-usual frying temperature, approaching four hundred degrees, is perfect. The tentacles may be fried the same way, after cutting them into at least two pieces.

Apple likes to fry them whole and then pick out the beak, organs, mantle, and other bits as she works her way through—just as she would a fish or a chicken. On the rare occasions when these squid make their way into Chinatown restaurants in Houston, they are generally served the same way.

AVAILABILITY: This squid is caught as bycatch from the few White Shrimp boats still fishing, as well as by bait shrimp boats. Sometimes the catch will be two pounds; more rarely, it will be two hundred. Very little makes its way to the larger Texas seafood supply chain. Most is sold for bait. Insignificant amounts are sold in smaller restaurants and markets.

COMMON OCTOPUS

Octopus vulgaris

HABITAT: The Common Octopus lives in, on, or around rocks, structures, reefs, wrecks, debris, or anything else capable of supplying camouflage and refuge. It is also found in seagrass meadows and on sandy and soft bottoms, though never far away from the safety of shelter, and in coastal waters and along the continental shelf to more than three hundred feet deep.

RANGE/DISTRIBUTION: This species occurs all around the world in warm temperate and tropical waters. This is *the* commercial species globally.

DESCRIPTION: If you should ever see an octopus in the northwestern Gulf, it will be this species. It is a fiercely intelligent animal, with the most amazing adaptive camouflage ever devised by nature.

EATING: Everyone loves octopus, and so do we. It has come a long way in terms of acceptance. Two decades ago, octopus was a hard sell in most restaurants. It is so common today that it sometimes escapes notice on a menu.

AVAILABILITY: The only octopus fishery in the Gulf is in the Bay of Campeche, and that is a highly seasonal fishery, open only a month or two during the year. Most commercially available octopus is fished either by Spanish vessels in the central Atlantic or by vessels flying various nations' flags in waters surrounding Southeast Asia. By far the better product is that from the Atlantic.

The only suitable octopus habitat in the northwestern Gulf is small and scattered, and noncontiguous as well. This means any octopodes (our preferred plural of the octopus) in our part of the Gulf are stragglers, not part of stable breeding populations. White Shrimp boats very occasionally catch an octopus, and almost invariably that octopus is curled up in a piece of maritime debris (an old can, for example). Our part of the Gulf is just too flat and sandy, lacking the structures so necessary for an octopus to live and thrive.

MUSHROOM AND CANNONBALL JELLYFISH

Rhopilema verrilli **and** *Stomolophus meleagris*

COMMON NAME: Cannonball Jellyfish: Cabbagehead Jellyfish

HABITAT: These two jellyfish live anywhere deep enough to float. Mostly, though, they are found in deeper inshore waters and offshore.

RANGE/DISTRIBUTION: The two species range through North and South American waters, mostly in the temperate waters of the Atlantic.

DESCRIPTION: We should be clear here: we are well aware that jellyfish are not shellfish, but we had no other place to stick these odd creatures.

The Cannonball is a sturdy jellyfish. It looks like an opaque straw mushroom. The actual Mushroom Jellyfish is almost transparent. It looks sort of like a flattened mushroom.

EATING: *DO NOT* go and grab a jellyfish and start eating it. We catalog these creatures because we live here, they live here, and their cousins are eaten elsewhere. We've only prepared Cannonball Jellyfish once (and the process involved dissuaded us from trying it again). At best it was jellyfish, which is to say it had an almost pleasant texture and nothing else.

AVAILABILITY: At one time, in the eastern Gulf, scientists and at least one or two commercial fishers attempted to capture the local jellyfish market. They were able to catch the jellyfish, but no one anywhere in the world wanted to pay much for it. So that was it for the nascent Gulf jellyfish fishery.

CHAPTER 14
SHRIMP, CRABS, AND OTHER CRUSTACEANS

This group of animals is commercially represented by very few species—less than a half dozen shrimp and an even fewer number of crabs. Hundreds or thousands more swim in the shallow and deeper waters of the Gulf of Mexico, though, and we suspect that the majority are at least edible. We only cover a few.

Also absent from this chapter are those crustaceans, such as the spiny lobsters and slipper lobsters, that are either absent entirely from our waters (the former) or rarely encountered by humans in this part of the Gulf (the latter).

While the Blue Crab may be the sole commercial representative of the group, several other species of swimming crabs—like the Lesser Blue (*Callinectes similis*) and the Iridescent (*Portunus gibbesii*)—ply the shallow waters of the Gulf coast. They are very rarely caught. If you should happen upon one or a few, treat them as you would the Blue Crab.

Though we would love to describe the joys of eating the Blue Land Crab (*Cardisoma guanhumi*), we've yet to find one to eat.

We do not cover the constellation of smaller noncommercial crabs either. While they are all fascinating, their uses in the kitchen are rather limited, and they are hard to catch in numbers. Among these crabs are various species of spider crab (*Libinia* spp.), purse crabs (*Persephona* spp.), porcelain crabs (family Porcellanidae), mud crabs (families Panopeidae and Xanthidae), box crabs (*Hepatus* spp.), and box and fiddler crabs (family Ocypodidae). All of these species may be used in soups and fumets, or they may be pickled with either vinegar or fish sauce (see the recipe with crawfish on page 251). Should you be lucky enough to find any of these species right after they have molted, you may enjoy a true delicacy: tiny soft-shelled crabs. But don't count on this ever happening.

The same is true for lesser-known shrimp species. We do not discuss the various

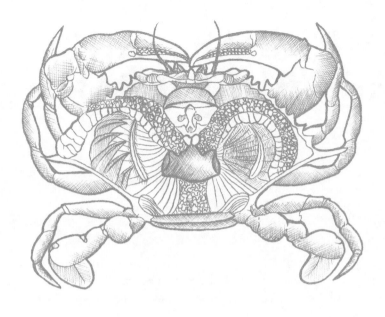

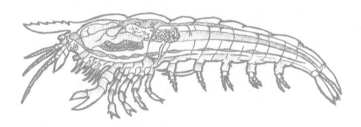

snapping shrimp (family Alpheidae), or the grass shrimp (family Palaemonidae), or the ghost shrimp (families Callianassidae and Ctenochelidae). They are small and difficult to get in any usable quantities (though they all are acceptable fried whole and good in soups). We also do not cover denizens of the deep sea, like the magnificent Scarlet Shrimp (aka Scarlet Prawn, Cardinal Prawn, Carabinero; *Plesiopenaeus edwardsianus*), simply because these species have never been explored, much less exploited, in the Gulf of Mexico.

Concerning the farming of shrimp, we have this to say: the technology and the industry have both come a long way in the past couple of decades. We have eaten some excellent farmed shrimp and look forward to what the future holds.

The last entry in this chapter is for the crawfish, which is not in any way a saltwater animal. We include it in this chapter because it is a crustacean.

We did not describe the most unassuming crustaceans in the Gulf of Mexico—the barnacles (Cirripedia). While most if not all species are entirely edible, they are also generally small and difficult to impossible to harvest. While the northwestern Gulf of Mexico boasts a few representatives of the genus *Lepas* (the gooseneck barnacles), they are all quite small, and all are associated strictly with floating debris. The Giant Purple Barnacle (*Megabalanus tintinnabulum*), though it is a nice size, is limited to offshore waters and only rarely washes up on beaches (after bad weather).

THE COMMERCIAL SHRIMP: BROWN, WHITE, ROCK, PINK, ATLANTIC SEABOB, AND ROYAL RED

Farfantepenaeus aztecus, Litopenaeus setiferus, Sicyonia brevirostris, Farfantepenaeus duorarum, Xiphopenaeus kroyeri, and *Pleoticus robustus*

HABITAT: All shrimp (and these are no exceptions) live in, on, or right over the seafloor bottom. These species, like most shrimp, prefer sandy, silty, and muddy areas (of them all, Atlantic Seabobs are the most common inhabitants of mud, especially near river outlets).

Juveniles of all these species live in shallow estuarine waters like bays and marshes. Adults move farther offshore. Atlantic Seabobs live in the shallowest waters, close to the mouths of rivers down to about one hundred feet or so. Pink Shrimp, who sometimes occur almost a thousand feet down, are more often fished in one hundred feet of water or less. White Shrimp can live farther out yet, migrating from a few dozen feet of water down to three hundred feet, with most catches made in waters around one hundred feet or less. Brown Shrimp occur in one hundred to six hundred feet of water. By far the deepest-dwelling of these species is the Royal Red, which can live as far down as six

thousand feet (it is most abundant between seven hundred and fifteen hundred feet).

Of course, the caveat is that all shrimp migrate throughout their life cycles from shallow to deeper waters, and most species migrate from spot to spot and area to area throughout adulthood as well. This makes exact delineation of habitat and terrain difficult, at least for nonscientists like us.

RANGE/DISTRIBUTION: These species are all limited to the Gulf and Atlantic waters of the Americas, and all occur at least to the central US east coast. They are most abundant around the Gulf and in close contiguous waters. The Atlantic Seabob and Brown Shrimp have the southernmost range, to at least Brazil. Pink Shrimp are specifically a southeastern Gulf and southern US Atlantic species, rarely venturing into the western Gulf. In the Gulf, Atlantic Seabobs are most prevalent in the near offshore neighborhood of the mouth of the Mississippi River. Royal Reds are rare in the northwestern Gulf—the gently sloping topography means that deep enough waters are very far offshore, almost outside of our immediate region. Rock Shrimp are limited mostly to the Gulf of Mexico, with smaller populations extending up to the waters of the Carolinas.

DESCRIPTION: These species all have the typical shrimp body: an overly large head and

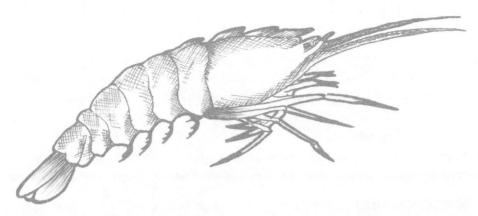

trunk section called the carapace (enclosing all of the guts, and from which sprout the walking legs), equipped with a large central horn above the eyes (the rostrum), two smaller horns (the antennules) emerging from a point just under the eyes, and long threadlike antennae; and a tail section, attached to the underside of which are two rows of swimmer legs, and to the end of which is a tail (called the telson). Along the top of the tail, right underneath the shell, from the telson to the carapace, is the organ usually called the "vein." In reality, it is not a vein at all, but instead it is essentially an intestine (in accordance with common usage, we use the term "vein" throughout the book).

The Brown Shrimp is less brown than a deep brown orange with bright orange swimmer legs. Reaching more than seven inches in length, it's the largest of all of these species, barely edging out the Pink and the White. The antennules and rostrum are short. The tail is longer relative to body length than the tails of other shrimp.

The White Shrimp is more translucent gray than white, with a tail edged in green and red, occasionally with white dots. This shrimp reaches almost seven inches in length. The rostrum and antennules are short. The carapace is bulky and large.

The Pink Shrimp is the color of watered-down pink lemonade. It grows to be a decent size, though it's slightly smaller than the Brown. The tail is thin where it meets the telson, and the long rostrum is oriented slightly upward.

The Atlantic Seabob is distinguished not by its faded orange color but by its long swimming and walking legs, short carapace, and very long antennae. It is rather shorter than the previous species, reaching at most around six inches.

The Rock Shrimp is well armored, with a thick shell on both carapace and tail. The tail is mottled white-and-red stripes, as are the antennae. The carapace is red maroon. The tail is almost as big around as the boxy carapace and is almost twice as long as the rest of the body. Total length is less than six inches.

The Royal Red, from antennae to telson, is the color of maraschino cherries. Like the Rock Shrimp, the Royal Red is unmistakable.

EATING: Where to start with Gulf shrimp? All species described here are excellent, and all rank favorably with any equivalent product anywhere in the world. Americans and even residents of the Gulf Coast region tend to take Gulf shrimp for granted, and far too often don't even pay attention to the shrimp on their plates and in their shopping baskets.

Because the fisheries are so large, we all tend to forget what an amazing resource we have in the Gulf.

In contrast to the rest of the US Gulf Coast, the Texas market by and large prefers Brown Shrimp. The tails are sweet and plump and don't get grainy when overcooked, traits that endear themselves to a cooking culture more afraid of undercooking than ruining all taste and texture. Brown Shrimp have a noticeable iodine taste that is not to everyone's liking, but it is a good shrimp to peel and eat, to grill, or to stuff.

White Shrimp is the preferred commodity species from Louisiana through Florida. The pale meat is not as sweet as that of the Brown, but it has a purer shrimp taste. The meat is delicate but turns to rubbery mush if overcooked. Correctly prepared, it has the perfect amount of sea flavor. White Shrimp is often available truly fresh in other Gulf states, but less commonly so in Texas.

We admit, we've never been as impressed by the Pink Shrimp. It seems halfway between the White and the Brown, with none of the defining characteristics of either. Still, it is better than most other shrimp in the world.

We challenge you, dear reader, to find a more exquisite shrimp than the Rock Shrimp. The taste is unique not just among Gulf shrimp but shrimp in general. Only the peeled tails are marketed. The shell is so hard that for years the Rock Shrimp avoided being targeted by shrimpers—they were just too difficult to peel. It was only with the invention of a peeling machine that the fishery took off.

The Royal Red ranks only slightly below the Rock in terms of taste. Because it is generally marketed whole, head on, it has a far more glamorous appearance than Rock Shrimp.

We love smaller shrimp. The Atlantic Seabob is such a shrimp and a fine one at that.

AVAILABILITY: Every year, a couple hundred million pounds of shrimp (or more) are harvested out of American waters of the Gulf of Mexico. Our shrimp fisheries don't just produce good shrimp, they produce massive harvests as well. Brown and White Shrimp account for the overwhelming bulk of landings (over one hundred million pounds and more than eighty million pounds, respectively). Atlantic Seabob, Royal Red, Pink, and Rock Shrimp account for only a few tens of million pounds combined.

Brown and White Shrimp are available everywhere in Texas. The other species are also available from finer fishmongers and seafood companies, usually through special order and always according to seasonal availability.

Shrimp are highly perishable, so the Gulf fishery is by and large a frozen fishery. This is a good thing. Shrimp handle the industrial freezing process quite well, with little to no adverse effects. Buy frozen and be confident in what you are getting (see page 190 for more on frozen fish).

THE COMMERCIAL CRABS: BLUE AND STONE

Callinectes sapidus and *Menippe adina*

HABITAT: These two crabs are associated with very shallow coastal waters, generally less than thirty feet deep. Stone Crabs stick to shallower waters than Blues, but aside from that, both species are found in the same general areas.

RANGE/DISTRIBUTION: The Stone is more or less a Gulf species. The Blue ranges throughout the Gulf and up through the middle of the US Atlantic coast (where it is the iconic Chesapeake Bay crab).

DESCRIPTION: Both species wear the standard-issue crab uniform: a large central carapace from which sprout six legs and two large front-facing claws.

The Stone is dark red brown on top, light tan underneath, with black on the tips of both claws. The carapace is squat and vaguely rounded, quite small compared to the claws, both of which are massive. The Stone Crab looks like a bodybuilder who spent too much time on the arms while completely neglecting the rest of the body. Put together, the claws are larger than the carapace. The larger claw is the "crusher" and the smaller is the "pincer." Stone crabs are handed, meaning some have the crusher on the left side, and some have it on the right. The legs are small and meant for walking on the seafloor. At its largest, the Stone Crab is less than eight inches wide in the carapace.

The Blue Crab is a member of the family Portunidae, the swimming crabs. While it certainly walks here and there, it is also an accomplished swimmer, and its back legs are formed almost into flippers, like other portunids. The carapace is roughly semicircular, the face and claws attached to the bottom front of a semicircle. Either side of the carapace extends out and ends in a sharp point, giving the shell a pinched look. The carapace is olive brown to blue on top and pale tan underneath. Claws are that same brown on top, with cobalt-blue and snow-white sides and bottoms. Legs are all white and pale blue. Male Blues are larger than the females, with more prominent claws; females are easy to identify by their claws, which are always tipped with bright orange red. Female Blue Crabs have a large rounded skirt (the hard flap of movable shell on the back underside of the carapace); the males' is small and pointed.

EATING: Stone Crab claws are best on their own (cold or hot) with a very simple sauce.

Everything else in between does not seem to do justice to these crabs. Do not attempt to dress up an already magnificent beast.

The Blue Crab is not just a good crab. It is part of the culture from Mexico to the Chesapeake Bay. While Blue Crabs are best simply boiled whole, then picked and eaten with friends, such an approach is not always practical or possible. Grocery stores and markets almost always sell picked meat, both fresh (always the first choice) and pasteurized (it'll do in a pinch if absolutely nothing else is available, and if you have no choice at all in the matter, and if you must use crab meat or suffer dreadful consequences).

Of all crustacean delights, certainly one of the finest is softshell crab. Along the Gulf and American Atlantic coast, softshell crab means Blue Crab. In Southeast Asia, it means another Blue Crab (*Portunus amatus*, formerly *P. pelagicus*). Wherever it may be, softshell crab *always* connotes some species of swimming crabs, for only swimming crabs have the right body, shell, and life cycle to make such a treat possible. When the time comes for the crab to molt (during warmer months), its joints change color, from pale olive to red. When all the joints are red, the crab is about to molt; at this stage, it is called a "buster." When crabbers find busters in their traps, they set those crabs aside. Later, back at the boathouse, the busters are placed in a holding tank. From then on, the busters are checked every fifteen minutes around the clock. As soon as the crab starts to slough off its old shell, it is immediately removed from the tank, and the rest of the shell is peeled off. Constant monitoring of the tanks is necessary because once a crab has shed its old shell, its new shell hardens within a matter of minutes (for in the wild it cannot be defenseless for long). If the crab stays in the water with its new shell, it will cease being a softshell; if removed from the water, though, the hardening process stops. A crab left in the water just a few seconds too long will no longer be totally soft but still entirely edible (such a crab is called a "papershell").

AVAILABILITY: A word on Stone Crab fisheries in general: they are possibly the most sustainable fisheries in existence. The animal is never killed, it is merely relieved of a claw and released back into the water. It will grow a new claw very quickly and may continue to grow claws as often as needed. Some readers might recoil at the thought of such a barbaric fishery, wherein an animal is mauled, disfigured, and tossed away. It might be a mistake, though, to anthropomorphize the crab and its regenerating claw.

Most Stone Crab claws come from Florida, where the fishery is well established and produces consistently high-quality (and graded) product. While Stone Crabs abound in Texas, and commercial harvest is legal, actual catches are mostly limited to bycatch from the Blue Crab fishery. The very few crabbers who mess with Stone Crab claws usually sell them ungraded and raw. We do not recommend buying raw Stone Crab claws; they must be cooked very soon after harvest, or else the meat gets grainy and sticks to the shell.

Catch your own. If you happen to spot a Stone Crab, it is quite easy to catch it with a net. Or they can be tempted into traps as well. We've always had better luck just poking around debris and piles of rocks, net in hand and ready for action. If you catch one, bear in mind only one claw may be retained, and that claw must be at least two-and-a-half inches from the tip of the claw to the first joint. Always take the crusher claw, the largest of the two.

Regarding Blue Crab, we have a thriving fishery here in Texas, and whole crabs are sold every day at the retail and restaurant level. But almost all of those crabs are female, and the few males are young and small. The large males (designated in the industry by the grade #1) do not typically enter commerce anywhere along the Gulf coast. Instead, they are boxed up live, trucked to the airport, and sent to Maryland, for demand in the Chesapeake region far outpaces local supply. Crab-laden trucks drive to the airport every day of the year, sending away the biggest and fattest crabs Texas has. Respectable fishmongers and seafood companies can certainly source #1 male crabs for you. Expect to pay three to four times the price you would otherwise pay for common Texas market crabs.

Picked Gulf Blue Crab meat is widely available at grocery stores and seafood markets. It is almost always from Mexico, much more rarely from Louisiana or Alabama. There hasn't been a picking house in Texas for a few years now. Mexican Blue Crab meat has an excellent reputation and is honestly more consistent than domestic product. Although a fair amount of Mexican Blue Crab meat is sold fresh, perhaps the lion's share is pasteurized.

If you want fat crabs, you will need to go hunt your own. If you have the time, use a trap. If you don't, just get some chicken

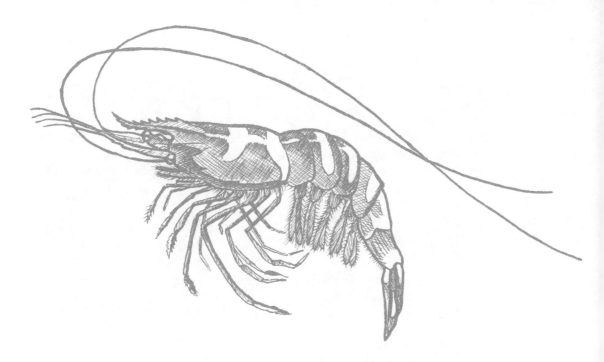

necks, a few lengths of string, and a net. Find a spot (most anywhere in bays at least a few feet deep, though places influenced by tidal action are perhaps best), tie the necks to pieces of string about ten feet in length, toss in the necks, and wait. When you see a crab bothering the neck, slowly pull in the string. The crab will follow it and grab on. Pull the neck slowly out of the water, slide the net underneath, and let the crab drop. Always be sure your crabs are at least five inches from carapace spine to carapace spine. If you should pull up a berried female (that is, a female with a cluster of eggs hanging off the bottom of her carapace), immediately return her to the water, for possession is illegal. Aside from that, there is no daily bag limit.

THE LOOMING SPECTER OF THE BLACK TIGER SHRIMP

Penaeus monodon

HABITAT: This species lives near the seafloor, in just a few to more than three hundred feet of water.

RANGE/DISTRIBUTION: It is found in the Indian and Pacific Oceans, from Pakistan to Australia and Japan. The Black Tiger Shrimp was accidentally introduced into the Gulf decades ago, and now is consistently reported, in very small numbers, throughout the northern Gulf to at least Freeport. Shrimpers catch one or several at a time, and often they catch none. It has significant potential as an invasive species in the Gulf.

DESCRIPTION: This is the giant among shrimp, weighing up to almost a pound each. The body is a dirty brown with alternating white and black vertical stripes running down the length of the body. Swimming and walking legs are dark red.

Specifically in the context of the Gulf, because Black Tigers are predatory shrimp, they not only potentially outcompete native species but could, in theory, decimate native shrimp populations.

EATING: Wild Black Tiger Shrimp are fantastic; those raised in ponds are less predictable. We avoid farmed Black Tiger Shrimp in most cases.

AVAILABILITY: Black Tiger Shrimp are fished and farmed all over their native range. We include them in this book because the invasive population in the Gulf seems to keep slowly growing every year, and little to nothing can be done to control it, except for eating them whenever possible. Should Black Tiger Shrimp find the Gulf of Mexico to their liking, we could, within a few years, even start seeing small commercial harvests. With luck, that won't happen.

MANTIS SHRIMP AND ITS COUSINS: DARK-BANDED MANTIS SHRIMP AND LESSER MANTIS SHRIMP

Squilla empusa, Lysiosquilla scabricauda, and *Gibbesia neglecta*

COMMON NAMES: For all species: Sea Lice, Sea Scorpion

HABITAT: These shrimp prefer relatively shallow waters, from coastal areas to a few dozen miles out.

RANGE/DISTRIBUTION: They range from the upper eastern US coast, throughout the Gulf of Mexico to at least Brazil. Related species live in tropical and temperate seas and oceans around the world.

DESCRIPTION: The Mantis Shrimp looks more or less like a shrimp (though the two are only distantly related), but with a much-extended abdomen and long front claws that resemble those on a praying mantis (hence the name). The coloring is not very striking, being mostly tans, browns, whites, and a few splashes of bright yellow. It is a carnivore, mostly feeding on bivalves, snails, and other creatures in hard shells (all species of mantis shrimp are extraordinarily powerful). It reaches a moderate size, at most five or six inches.

The Dark-Banded Mantis is quite a bit larger, reaching maybe ten inches or more. It has larger arms and black bands around its abdomen. The Lesser Mantis is, well, lesser in size. To be clear, all three species are encountered in the same places, and differentiation between species isn't really practical or necessary. They all taste the same.

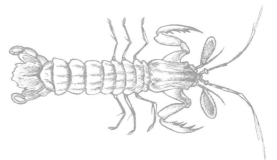

EATING: In other parts of the world (specifically the Mediterranean and throughout Southeast Asia), Mantis Shrimp not only form viable fisheries but also command quite high prices. The meat has the taste and texture of something between lobster and shrimp (with more of the lobster sweetness and less of the shrimp iodine and mineral taste). The shell and meat turn vermilion to purple rather than red or orange when cooked. All in all, Mantis Shrimp is one of the finer eating crustaceans in the Gulf of Mexico.

AVAILABILITY: Alas, there are no targeted Mantis Shrimp fisheries here in the Gulf. The only commercial fishers who encounter them are shrimpers, and very few shrimpers here want to mess with them (Mantis Shrimp can strike faster than the human brain can detect movement, and they are often able to draw blood). We have been on shrimp boats when the nets came in and can attest that if one fights with a Mantis, one usually loses. A few pounds are unloaded, mostly for bait.

THE HUMBLE HERMIT CRAB

Various genera and species in the family Diogenidae

HABITAT: Hermit crabs live on the borders and in the shallow waters of bays.

RANGE/DISTRIBUTION: We will not go into species-specific information here. Suffice it to say that hermit crabs are found everywhere where the water is salty and it doesn't get too cold.

DESCRIPTION: Outside of the shell, which is, after all, just a temporary home, the hermit crab is a poor-looking creature. Its claws

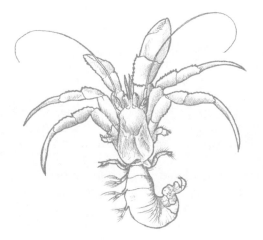

are big enough to wave around but not big enough to do any real damage to a human. The hard carapace ends abruptly after the head, and the rest of the animal is more or less like a worm. Hermit crabs are rarely more than an inch or two long.

EATING: The whole animal is edible, but we suggest eating only the soft tail. It tastes like crab.

AVAILABILITY: Gas stations near the beach sell live hermit crabs for pets. That is the closest you will find to a fishery. Finding hermit crabs in the wild is very easy. Just look for old snail shells in the water.

CRAWFISH

Procambarus clarkii and *Procambarus zonangulus*

COMMON NAMES: Mudbugs; outside of the southern United States and throughout the rest of the English-speaking world, Crayfish is the accepted common name for these animals.

HABITAT: Crawfish live in ponds, rivers, streams, ditches, low-lying ground, lakes, and stock tanks. If there's no water, crawfish simply build a nest and wait. They are always and only found in fresh water.

RANGE/DISTRIBUTION: The famous Red Crawfish (which makes up most harvests) occurs from Mississippi to Texas and a bit farther north. Other crawfish species occur throughout the temperate areas of North America. Still other species range throughout Europe.

DESCRIPTION: Red Crawfish have very large claws and thick red-and-black shells. Other crawfish (which make up less than 30 percent of harvests) have thin brown shells and small claws.

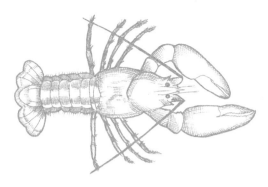

EATING: These animals taste like little fantastic freshwater lobsters. While the crawfish boil is the most well-known method of cooking and eating the mudbugs, that is certainly not the only way.

Historically, crawfish were highly esteemed throughout western Europe, and especially in France. Glancing through pages of old French cookbooks (especially those focusing on La Grande Cuisine), one cannot help but be struck by the ubiquity of crawfish. Unfortunately, while that tradition lives on somewhat in France (PJ remembers cleaning crawfish in Provence), it has been largely forgotten in the United States.

Crawfish are excellent for use in soups and stir-fries, where the whole animal is used, and also very good pickled in fish sauce (a technique brought to Texas by Lao and Khmer immigrants). The tail meat is basically good for anything from sauce to eating straight out of the bag.

AVAILABILITY: From about January to almost June, crawfish are ubiquitous in Houston and the southeastern part of Texas. The best time to buy them is right around March. Picked meat is available frozen year-round (only buy picked crawfish meat from Louisiana—we highly recommend staying away from imported crawfish meat).

While we understand the allure of softshell crawfish, we have never been as impressed with the actual reality.

CHAPTER 15

A FEW WORDS ABOUT EDIBLE PLANTS FOUND CLOSE TO THE WATER'S EDGE

The spectrum of edible wild plants along the coastal areas of the Gulf Coast region is large enough to easily merit a book by itself. Edible plants thrive along the beaches themselves, along bay and marsh shores, in the sandy patches behind dunes, at the edges of the dunes themselves, in wetlands and scrub brush. We certainly cannot describe them all here.

Instead, the following is a *very* incomplete list of edible plants that can and do grow within at most three miles of the Gulf itself. All are easily spotted and easily gathered. We have not included any difficult-to-identify species, nor any potentially dangerous species (so no mushrooms). Also, all the plants listed here are immediately useful; we include no grains or nuts or other products requiring lengthy or awkward processing. Almost everything listed below is directly usable, and it all tastes good with seafood. Most of these plants are easy to use in informal situations such as cookouts and camping trips. A few of these plants just make good snacks.

Do not rely on this list of plants to judge the edibility of any wild plant. For more on native plants, we recommend the sources on page 287.

AMARANTH (*Amaranthus*): Shoots, young leaves; arid dry areas everywhere in the state

BEACH WATERMELON: Watermelons make popular beach snacks, and seeds naturally fall here and there, then are further dispersed by wind and bird. Sometimes these seeds land in just the right places, close enough to at least some fresh water to sprout. Usually that will be a spot near a seawall or close to, in, or behind a dune. These plants are scraggly, producing only enough leaves and stems to stay alive. Maybe one long tendril winds ten feet, always in search of water that just isn't there. Rarely, one of these plants will muster enough energy to produce a fruit. This fruit is stunted, half the size of a market watermelon. The skin is pale, the flesh white with a hint of pink throughout. It is insipid but edible. And it is salty.

DEWBERRY (*Rubus* spp.): Berries; scrubland, continuously dry borders around bays, everywhere in Texas

DOCK (*Rumex chrysocarpus*): Young leaves; right where sand gives way to dirt, then everywhere in the state

DOLLARWEED/PENNYWORT (*Hydrocotyle* spp.): Leaves; dry sandy soil especially right near beaches, and common very far inland as well

GLASSWORT (*Salicornia* spp.): Stalk and leaves; at the very edge of the tide line along shallow bay and marsh shores

PEPPERWEED (*Lepedium virginicum*): Seed pods, which taste like hot radish; everywhere

PRICKLY PEAR (*Opuntia* spp.): Fruit (after the skin is peeled off!); not on beaches, but never very far away

PURSLANE (*Portulaca oleracea*): Shoots and leaves; beaches to dunes to marsh shoreline to inland areas

SALTWORT (*Batis* spp.): Leaves only, stalks being woody; like the glassworts, at very edge of high tide in shallow marshes

SARGASSUM (*Sargassum* spp.): Finely chopped as an addition to other dishes, also for cooking fish; far out to sea, close to the beach, and washed up on the beach—best is freshly washed up

SEA LETTUCE (*Ulva* spp.): Versatile seaweed; low tide around rocks and especially jetties

SEA PURSLANE (*Sesuvium portulacastrum*): Leaves and shoots; beaches and adjacent sandy dry areas

SEA ROCKET (*Cakile* spp.): Leaves; on the beach and in sandy areas around bays and marshes

SPIDERWORT (*Tradescantia micrantha*): Leaves; wet marsh shoreline

WILD ONION (*Allium* spp.): Root bulb, green stem; like dock, where sand becomes dirt

CHAPTER 16
SOME HONORARY FRESHWATER INCLUSIONS

All of these animals live in areas backing up to, and in at least two cases, spilling into, salt water. Of course, some of these animals also live thousands of miles from the ocean. Either way, we include them because it feels strange not to. We do not include the Atlantic Sturgeon (*Acipenser oxyrinchus*), partially because its presence in Texas waters is unverified, and partially because it is a highly protected species. We never eat turtles, so we don't describe them here.

ALLIGATOR GAR

Atractosteus spatula

HABITAT: This is a freshwater species that lives in rivers and lakes but occasionally wanders into salt waters.

RANGE/DISTRIBUTION: It ranges throughout the central to southern Mississippi basin and along the northern Gulf coast.

DESCRIPTION: The Alligator Gar has a cylindrical body with rounded fins all about. The snout is long, pointed, and toothed very much like an alligator. Overall it is a drab olive brown, lighter on the belly. The skin is incredibly thick, and the scales are completely fused with the skin. One cannot scale the fish, one must skin it. To skin it, one needs a cleaver (or a hatchet) and a mallet. This fish has a pretty ancient lineage.

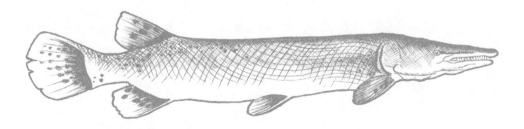

EATING: There is nothing fishy about this fish. We use it for pot roasts. PJ loves to clean Alligator Gar.

AVAILABILITY: Alligator Gar is commonly available. If you buy it in any market in Texas, it will always have been fished in either Louisiana or Texas. While it does have fans and devotees, this fish has a less than spectacular table reputation.

AMERICAN BOWFIN

Amia calva

COMMON NAMES: Choupique, Shoepick

HABITAT: The American Bowfin is found in freshwater lakes, swamps, and vegetated waterways.

RANGE/DISTRIBUTION: It occurs in the eastern half of North America. Texas is at the westernmost edge of the American Bowfin's range.

DESCRIPTION: This is another fish from the past. The head is strangely armored, and the body tapers gently to the tail. Dorsal and anal fins are long and continuous down the body and tail. The Bowfin is gray black from snout to caudal fin.

EATING: Bowfins are not closely related to Sturgeons, but both fish have ancient lineages, and both happen to produce the same kind of roe. Bowfin caviar is undoubtedly the most popular and valuable food product made from Bowfin. (It is such a good product in fact, that the majority of Bowfin caviar produced in the United States [mostly in Louisiana by a very few producers] does not stay here but goes to Russia. A few years ago, at any rate, almost ten thousand pounds a year went from Louisiana to Russia.) The meat is very soft, making fillets difficult to impossible. Instead, the meat is generally

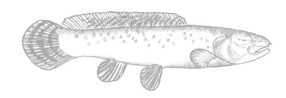

scraped off the bone with a spoon, then is used for fish balls, fish cakes, and other dishes requiring ground fish meat (in fact, during the spawn season, after the roes have been extracted, the carcasses are generally further processed to remove all meat, which is then sent to various Asian grocery chains in California). The taste is quite nice.

AVAILABILITY: The caviar is commonly available, whether directly from the source or through a reputable fishmonger. The only practical way to get ahold of Bowfin meat involves fishing.

AMERICAN EEL

Anguilla rostrata

HABITAT: Males of this species live within about one hundred miles from salt water; females can live ten times as far away. All eels are born in the ocean, spend their lives in fresh water, then return to the ocean to spawn and die.

RANGE/DISTRIBUTION: One can assume that eels could be in any large body of fresh water in the northern part of North America.

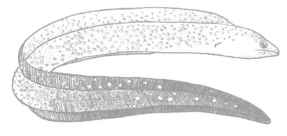

DESCRIPTION: The American Eel has a rounded head and a snakelike body, with a delicate dorsal fin running from the head to the tail, which is itself rounded. It is yellow gold on the bottom, nondescript brown on the top.

EATING: Oh, to live in a world where we could eat fresh eel every day. Alas, that is not our reality in the twenty-first century. We eat eel maybe once a year, usually less often than that, and we buy one live eel for the family.

AVAILABILITY: This is a fish we really shouldn't eat very often. Wild populations are tenuous, for both local and global species; farmed product isn't farmed at all, but rather ranched, which is no better than wild fishing.

AMERICAN BULLFROG

Rana catesbiana

HABITAT: American Bullfrogs live in swamps, ponds, lakes, rivers, and any other permanent body of fresh water.

RANGE/DISTRIBUTION: They are found throughout the eastern part of North America and have been introduced in the rest of the United States and around the world.

DESCRIPTION: Bullfrogs range in color from green to olive to brown on top, sometimes with marks, splotches, or dots. The underside is tan to yellow to gold to gray. The eyes, perched atop the head, are golden and accusing.

EATING: The back legs are famously tasty. The front legs and top of the body are just as tasty, though there is less meat, and it requires slightly more work. The skin (which peels right off the frogs in one easy piece) makes a superior crackling. Of the guts, we only discard the stomach and gallbladder. Frog eggs (and oviduct, the structure attached to the eggs) are excellent. The head we don't have much use for.

AVAILABILITY: Bullfrog meat is most available only in the form of frozen cleaned legs. They come one pair per little plastic bag, the pair of legs still joined, as it were, at the hip. The meat is opaque tan. We cannot stress enough that this is a bad, unworkable, untenable product. It was raised and slaughtered far away in dubious conditions and has been frozen for a long time. Frog meat should be pink, not tan. It's better not to eat frogs at all than to eat inferior nonsense.

Frogs are commercially harvested in Louisiana. Cleaned Louisiana legs go for about six to seven times the price of the inferior imported product. We *never* buy cleaned frogs. Luckily, Houston has several markets that sell them live.

AMERICAN ALLIGATOR

Alligator mississippiensis

HABITAT: Alligators inhabit slow-moving or still fresh waters, such as lakes, ponds, swamps, and rivers.

RANGE/DISTRIBUTION: They range throughout the southern United States, from

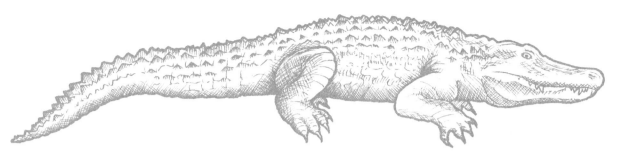

the Carolinas through Texas. In Texas, they are very rare past the southeastern part of the state.

DESCRIPTION: If you don't know what an alligator looks like, and are confronted by one someday, we trust that will not stop you from reacting appropriately.

EATING: Alligator, like crocodile and rattlesnake, is good enough to eat, rather like poultry mixed with shark and pork, but there isn't very much to say beyond that.

AVAILABILITY: Wild harvests are extremely regulated in Texas and Louisiana. So if you are eating alligator from either of these states, rest assured it was harvested legally.

NUTS AND BOLTS

After having described or at least touched on more than two hundred species of edible marine life from the northwestern Gulf of Mexico, we now get into practical aspects of procuring, processing, and storing some of these animals (and, of course, everything in this part of the book was written to be applicable to fish and seafood everywhere).

As we've indicated elsewhere, our assumption is that you, our reader, will be buying, rather than catching, most of your seafood, so we have attempted to walk you through the whole process, from the fish market to final storage in your home.

We start with what you should expect from your fishmonger, and how to pick a good one. From there, we cover at least part of the spectrum of product forms, from whole fish to picked crab meat.

But knowing the lingo is not sufficient on its own, so we provide some basic information about quality, how to choose the best, and when to walk away from dubious product.

From there, we cover processing, from whole fish preparations, to cutting a fillet, to cleaning shrimp, to shucking an oyster, to picking crab meat.

We finish this part with tips on storing fish and seafood in a home kitchen.

CHAPTER 17

FINDING, BUYING, AND PROCESSING SEAFOOD

FINDING YOUR FISHMONGER

We assume most readers will not have access to the various boats and rigs necessary to harvest all of the animals covered in this book; we further assume that our intrepid readers will be getting most of their seafood from vendors of whatever sort. Depending on where one lives, this might be a grocery store, a specialty market, or a fishmonger. We've had great, mediocre, and ghastly experiences at all three kinds of establishments. Find a good one and stick with it.

Good fishmongers are honest about their inventory. They will tell you where the fish came from, when it was delivered to them, and any other relevant details you might wish to know. They will not claim to have Texas amberjack during the closed season; they will not claim to have live Texas softshell crabs in the dead of winter. They will be able to tell you what has been frozen and what is truly fresh, and they will know which of the two is best for you.

The good fishmonger will know the rules and regulations and will abide by them. If they have something unusual, they will know why they have it. They will know what quality is and why it's important.

Talk to your fishmonger, not just about what you're buying at the moment, but about fish and seafood in general. Good fishmongers are warehouses of fish knowledge and trivia. And *every* good fishmonger, no matter what they sell or on what continent they work, loves talking about fish; the best among them can keep even the most disinterested listener entranced.

A good fishmongers' shop will be clean and well lit. It might smell of fish and seafood, but it will never stink of rot and low tide. If you catch a faint whiff of cleaning products, all the better, for it means that the establishment is serious about sanitation. (On the other hand, if the stench of cleaning products is overwhelming, you should be suspicious, for the only thing that can cover the stench of rotten fish is bleach, and a lot of bleach might mean a fair amount of old fish is on hand.) The display cases will be clean inside and out, with no rusty or moldy spots. The floors will be clean. The cutting tables and equipment will always be well maintained, never rusty or slimy. All employees will take pride in their products.

Most importantly, a good fishmonger will love to eat fish. *Never, ever, under any circumstances, trust one who doesn't. If you take away only a single thing from this book, let it be that!*

BUYING FISH WITH A COMPUTER

While we are sure online seafood purchasing can be fun and exciting and can bring to one's fingertips products hitherto only dreamed of, we generally don't trust the experience.

FETISHIZING FRESH AND DENIGRATING FROZEN

First—and this is crucial—in the seafood trade, "fresh" technically only means that the product is not frozen *at the time of the sale*. Almost every shrimp sold in the United States has been frozen. (About 90 percent of shrimp on the US market is imported, and almost every single bit of that is frozen; among US fisheries, frozen is far and away the common product form.) Chances are, the piles of fresh shrimp at your favorite market have been frozen at least once, and maybe more, depending on the level of processing (peeled and deveined shrimp will have been frozen and thawed several times during their voyage from the water to the retail case). To be clear, you can find truly fresh shrimp in some coastal areas of the country (on the Gulf coast, Louisiana by far dominates the fresh shrimp fishery), but don't believe the sign just because it says so. Ask questions.

Fish and seafood are the most perishable of all human foodstuffs. Freezing prolongs shelf life; lets fishers maximize the profit from their catches; allows uninterrupted supplies of commodity products; and, in some cases, maintains quality in a way that would be impossible if the product were kept fresh. If all the fishery products in the world were stored and distributed only fresh, supply would be cut by three-quarters at least, and most of the seafood that came out of the water would be dumped right back in after it spoiled on the docks.

There is nothing at all inherently wrong with frozen fish and seafood. In fact, though we opt for fresh fish and seafood in most situations, we sometimes insist on frozen product. For example, unless we see it unloaded off the boat (or we trust our source absolutely and completely), we never buy fresh whole shrimp or fresh whole squid. Those products deteriorate quickly, and unless meticulously handled, are usually a shadow of their former beauty in as little as forty-eight hours after harvest (and most seafood takes *at least* a week or more to reach you, the end user). Frozen shrimp and squid are frozen almost immediately after harvest. Unless you trust your fishmonger at least as deeply as you trust your dentist, and unless said fishmonger has truly fresh and beautiful whole shrimp and squid, it is better to buy frozen and have, in essence, a fresher product than "fresh."

Freezing takes several forms. The best, from the viewpoint of quality, is Individually Quick Frozen (IQF). Most fish and fish fillets these days, at least at the retail level, are IQF, as are most shrimp. A "block frozen" product is frozen in batches according to weight. This form is more typical with boxed frozen product—squid tubes, shrimp tails, and frozen-at-sea boxed fish fillets. Sometimes, as in the case of shrimp, some quantity of salt brine is added, so a five-pound box of shrimp might weigh between seven and eight pounds (which will yield five pounds of thawed shrimp, no more no less). As with everything else, ask questions about the frozen seafood at the market.

THE MYTHOLOGIES OF FRESHNESS AND FISH AGE

The modern seafood business grinds on every hour of the day, every day of the week, so in 2019 no particular day of the week is automatically better than another to buy fish. The fishmongers' wares are perhaps no fresher on Friday or Monday or Wednesday. It all depends on when they got the latest shipment and how old the fish was before it got on the truck (or plane). This is especially true for local seafood products—boats go fishing when weather, regulations, and finances allow and necessity dictates; the day of the week doesn't necessarily enter into calculations at all.

Fishmongers the world over insist that they sell only the freshest fish. The languages and phrases might differ, but everyone seems to have the best. In reality, for too many fishmongers, the "freshest" fish is whatever they need to sell. We have seen, more times than we care to recall, unwitting consumers buying obviously inferior fish solely on the deceitful claim of freshness.

Freshness or, more accurately, the length of time a given fish has been dead, is important. But it is not the only variable. Just as important, if not more so, is the way the fish is handled from hook (or net) to fishmonger. Improperly killed or gutted fish does not age well. Nor does fish that sat too long on the deck of the boat. Fish that was stored in containers without drainage might have sat in water for hours or days, and standing water is just about the worst thing that can happen to a dead fish. If the fish wasn't stored in ice continuously, the shelf life and quality are dramatically affected.

Time, temperature, and handling make the difference between dinner and an inedible mess. We've seen fish twenty-four hours out of the water that was not fit to eat, and we've seen three-week-old tuna that was still beautiful and enchantingly red.

BUYING GULF, BUYING AMERICAN GULF, AND BUYING TEXAS GULF

The adjective "Gulf," when used to modify any word associated with seafood, does not necessarily mean what most consumers think it means. Snappers and groupers, and White and Brown Shrimp, for example, are harvested in the Gulf waters of both the United States and Mexico (the border between the two countries being, of course, imaginary, only existing on maps and thus irrelevant to both fish and shrimp, who have little interest in either international lines of demarcation or maps in general). Respectable Texas restaurants proclaim "Gulf crab" on their menus, and naturally diners assume that Gulf crab means Texas crab. But if it's picked crab meat, it's not from Texas—the last in-state crab processor closed down years ago, and market conditions continue to make the enterprise unprofitable. If Texas retail and food service consumers pressed the issue (and were willing to pay about twice the current price—or more—for a pound of jumbo lump), that might change, but we don't expect anything of the sort. Almost every bit of picked Gulf crab meat comes from Mexico, and most of the fresh product is of good to superior quality. (We cannot endorse canned crab meat; it is, at best, a pale imitation of a delicious seafood. Better, in our opinions, is to forego crab meat until you can find fresh.

Currently, high-quality canned meat is almost as expensive as fresh, and sometimes it is even pricier, so there are neither economic nor gustatory grounds for purchasing canned meat.) We don't fault restaurants for the omission; the point is that the single word "Gulf," in the context of provenance, is of little use.

If a fish is labeled as a product both of the USA and of the Gulf, then you are on much firmer ground. A Red Snapper from American waters of the Gulf is always, without exception, preferable to a Red Snapper from Mexican waters. The fish are exactly the same wherever they swim, but American fisheries are better regulated (in terms of effectiveness of management systems) and, on average, produce a better-grade fish (due to fishing and icing practices, as well as a shorter supply line). (Incidentally, we do not denigrate the work of Mexican fisheries officials and fishers—we have certainly seen a great deal of beautiful Mexican seafood and have been lucky enough to meet some fishers and fishmongers doing excellent work in Mexico. However, on the whole, US infrastructure is, at least at the time of writing, superior.) In an ideal world, fishers on both sides of that imaginary line would be working together, as would fisheries officials and governments from both countries.

But even "American Gulf" needs some context. Five US states share the Gulf coast, and fish populations are not the same throughout. Red Grouper is a substantial fishery in Florida, where around ten million pounds are caught commercially every year; it is completely absent, however, from Texas waters. If you see "Gulf" fish or seafood at the market or in a restaurant, make sure you know what you're buying.

GULF FISHERIES TO FEEL GOOD ABOUT

Monterey Bay Aquarium's Seafood Watch (seafoodwatch.org) is not necessarily the bible, but they have high standards, based on scientifically rigorous methods. They're a good source in general, even if they at times paint with too broad (and vague) a brush to be practically useful. Around a decade ago, there didn't seem to be a lot of "green" or "yellow" Texas and Gulf seafood in the Monterey Bay Aquarium Seafood Watch guidebook, but there certainly was some "red." These days, at least some (though not all!) US Gulf fisheries for snappers, groupers, tilefish, Black Drum, shrimp, oysters, and crabs are rated "good alternatives."

CHAPTER 18

THE ABCS

FINFISH

CONCERNING ROUGH CATCH AND SASHIMI GRADE: THE UBIQUITY OF THE FORMER, THE AMBIGUITY OF THE LATTER

"Rough catch," in the context of most American fisheries, is not a pejorative designation. It merely signifies that the fish is killed and processed according to American commodity methods (which usually means the fish die just from being out of the water, with no stunning or slaughter). We discuss elsewhere (see page 15) fish slaughter and the steps necessary to produce a fish of superior quality.

While most very fresh fish (and seafood) can be eaten raw in ceviches and poke, be skeptical when you see "sashimi" or "sushi" grade fish for sale. Ask why the fish was assigned such a grade and remember that freshness alone *never* qualifies. (That beautiful Red Snapper you caught this morning might be impeccably fresh, but unless you slaughtered, bled, and iced it appropriately, *it is not sashimi grade*. We are forever indebted to two of our favorite fish people, Shinobu Maeda and Horiuchi Manabu, for their steadfast insistence on this point.) If it's a whole fish, ask some questions, especially about how and when the animal was killed and how it was stored. If a fillet of fish is advertised as sashimi grade, be very suspicious.

VARIATIONS ON WHOLE FISH

Seafood terminology tends to be labyrinthine, esoteric, colloquial. A complete mastery of the lingo isn't necessary for most of our readers, but a few terms and general information on product forms might come in handy.

A "round" fish (or a fish "in the round") is a whole, ungutted fish. Small and farmed fish are generally sold this way, as are others, depending on where the fish was caught and who the target customer is. Locally, Black Drum and flounder are usually sold round as well. Offshore fish (including snappers, groupers, and tilefish) are gutted on the boat—always (except if the snapper is a Vermilion Snapper destined for California, in which case it will be round, as the market there for that fish apparently demands that form). A gutted fish should have all viscera as well as the swim bladder removed, although the heart and a bit of the throat, being difficult to extract, might still be attached near the head (this is not preferable, but it is inevitable with current American fisheries standards).

A "G&G" fish has been gutted and has had its gills removed. Very few American fisheries regularly produce gilled and gutted fish. We have always suspected this form evolved as an excuse to remove the gills from aged fish, though in reality the gills on fish for export markets are also often removed during gutting to reduce shipping weight. If you see a Red Snapper (or a grouper or a tilefish) for sale, and the fish is lacking its gills, yet the fishmonger claims it comes from an American fishery, be suspicious.

An "H&G" fish is headed, gutted, and (usually) tailed on the boat at capture. This is the standard commercial form for most large Highly Migratory Pelagic Species (HMPS)—tunas, Swordfish, Wahoo, Dorado, Escolar, Opah, and others. In the Gulf, only such pelagic species may be headed at sea.

CUT FISH AND FISH PIECES

Every fish has two fillets, no more no less (except the rays and skates, who, one could argue, have four—though we would counter with apples and oranges). The two fillets are completely symmetrical. Each fillet, viewed from the cut side, is obviously composed of two separate lengths of muscle, called loins. At the joint of the two loins, on the skin side of the fillet, you will find the pin bones (at least on most fish—a few fish, like herrings, have several rows of pin bones) and also the dark meat. The common term for dark meat on a fish is "bloodline," which is nonsensical. There is no such structure in fish or beast. Fish dark meat is the same thing as chicken dark meat: tougher muscles used continuously for support and locomotion (as opposed to white meat muscle, which is only used for short bursts of activity). Do not cut the dark meat out of a white fish fillet. Cut out but *never* discard the dark meat on a red fish loin. One does not buy a whole chicken just to throw away the thighs and drums.

The loin closest to the back is the top loin; the bottom loin includes the belly. White fish and smaller fish are usually cut into fillets and sold that way. Fillets are skin on or off, depending on the edibility of that species' skin and the preference of the customer. Also, the fillet may be "pin bones in" or "pin bones out." If the latter, the bones are generally cut out of the fillet in a V-shaped piece. With the exception of salmon, with their floating pin bones, most fishmongers in the United States will cut, not pull, pin bones (pulling is always best in theory, but not all fish bones cooperate). You won't need to remember many fillet specifics—your trusty fishmonger can take care of the details.

Among white fish, only a few flatfish are sold in loins rather than fillets, and even then, not always. (Of course, the labyrinth of seafood industry terminology demands that a halibut loin is not called a loin, but rather a fletch. A large flounder may also be cut into loins, in which case the loins are also called fletches; on the other hand, small flatfish like sole are often cut into loins, yet are sold as fillets.) For our part, if the fish is bigger than a pound, no matter what kind or species, we always cut it into loins. They are handier to use, and the pesky pin bone situation takes care of itself.

A steak is a bone-in cross section of the fish. A whole fish can be cut into steaks from shoulder to tail. Of our local fish, tunas and mackerels work best.

Fish houses generally break down larger pelagic fish—especially tunas—into loins. The top loin (almost always cut into boneless steaks of the sort we all know) is more practical for most home cooks and restaurants, as the shape is the same from head to tail, the only variation being the diameter of the loin. The back half of the bottom loin is shaped more or less like the top.

The front part of the bottom loin of a fish, essentially adjacent to the guts, is the belly. On all but the largest food fish, bellies are essentially flaps of skin that hold in the guts. White fish rarely have bellies muscular enough to bother with, and most of those that do aren't impressive. A one-hundred-pound Warsaw Grouper has a substantial flap of boneless belly meat, but it is no different from the rest of the meat in either taste or texture. Most white fish are rather lazy, only leaping into action to eat or escape being eaten. And most species don't generally stray far from home unless compelled to by hunger or procreation.

Only continuously active fish like tunas and large jacks—and not even all of those—have bellies worthy of special treatment. Jacks over sixty pounds, Yellowfin and Bigeye Tunas over eighty pounds, Bluefin Tunas over one hundred pounds, Wahoo over sixty pounds, Cobia over fifty pounds, and Swordfish over one hundred and twenty pounds—all yield good belly meat. Tuna belly is rightfully regarded as a delicacy, though we have always found the fattiest tuna belly to be a bit too decadent and rich. (Of all fish bellies, the Bluefin Tuna's is the most coveted, so much so that all species are fast being driven from the oceans of the world. The belly of the Bluefin is typically broken down according to Japanese practice: *chu-toro* is the darker, leaner, less-marbled meat near the back of the belly; *o-toro* is the pale, incredibly fatty front piece.) Peachbelly Swordfish (see the Swordfish entry for more on Gulf of Mexico Peachbellies) might have better belly meat than most tunas and is unctuous without being heavy. Regarding most other fish bellies, honesty compels us to admit that we find them to be somewhat fetishized.

The "collar" is the part of the fish from the seat of the gills to just behind the pectoral fin. It is mostly bone, but the pieces of meat are large and easy to dislodge. It is also the piscine equivalent of the chicken wing, not only in reputation and utility but also somewhat in structure, for what becomes a wing in a chicken becomes a pectoral fin in a fish. People generally cook and eat collars the same way they cook and eat wings. Chicken wings were originally slaughterhouse scrap, sold cheap; now they are as expensive as breast meat. Meanwhile, probably well over 90 percent of collars trimmed from whole fish go into the garbage, which does seem a great waste.

Cheeks are just as advertised: the boneless scallops of muscle on both sides of the face. If the fish is smaller than ten pounds or so, don't waste time cutting out the cheeks, just cook the whole heads, for only larger fish yield decent cheeks. The shape of cheeks varies from species to species, but with a little practice, the common themes become quite apparent.

The bits of muscle that connect the dorsal and anal fins to the body are called feather meat (flounder feather meat is called *engawa* in Japan, where it is much appreciated). While all fish possess this kind of meat, only in flatfish is it so large and pronounced. The texture is indeed unique—just chewy enough to be pleasant. We don't know if it's objectively better than fillet meat, but it is a nice treat.

Fish have bony tongues, pretty much devoid of meat in even the larger groupers. What is sold as "fish tongue" is not really the tongue at all, but rather a triangular patch of boneless meat attached to the underside of the bottom jaw. Some fish, like snappers, have withered tongues; others, like groupers, have full and meaty tongues and are absolutely worth the effort. We don't recommend buying a fish just for its tongue, but we suggest you always check to see if it's worth eating.

Generally speaking, "roe" refers to the actual intact two-lobed egg sac; caviar is a lightly salted preparation of individual eggs, after they have been liberated from the egg sac. (Purists might dispute our broad definition of caviar, for technically caviar refers only to the salted eggs of a sturgeon in the genus *Acipenser*. We use the word colloquially to refer to the process rather than the species. Until a suitable English equivalent comes along, we shall continue to use the word "caviar.") The milt, or soft roe, is the male gonad. *Not all roes and milts taste good. Try a little out before you make grand plans.*

The swim bladder is an opaque white organ located at the top of the abdominal cavity, attached to the backbone. It is used to keep the fish neutrally buoyant (the bladder fills with gas according to where the fish wants to be in the water column). Not all fish have swim bladders, but most do. In some fish, like the Vermilion Snapper, the bladder is small and delicate; in others, like the Black Drum, it is thick and substantial. We typically slice and fry bladders, after which they look and taste like chicharrones. Sometimes the fried bladder is an ingredient in other dishes like stir-fries and soups (if you have had "fish maw" at a Chinese restaurant, you have eaten swim bladder).

Some fish organs taste terrible, some are passable, and fewer numbers are quite nice. None (at least none in this book) are delicacies. Triggerfish, mullets, drums, and croakers all have tasty livers. The mullets have true gizzards, and their long intestines can be washed and fried like chicken intestines. Beyond that, we don't do a lot with fish guts—which is not to say there aren't things to do with them (a specialty of southern Thailand, *tai pla*, is made by salting all of the soft organs of white or red fish and letting them cure for a few days or weeks. The resulting juicy wet mass smells very strong and tastes even stronger. Happily, it is generally used only in a diluted form, and only as one ingredient in a dish, as in the eponymous curry [*gaeng tai pla*]. Such a method of preservation is not unique to southern Thailand; undoubtedly analogs exist at least throughout the archipelago nations of Southeast Asia).

The tails (or, more precisely, the caudal peduncles) of large pelagic fish such as tunas and reef fish like large jacks can substitute for turkey necks. Simply hack off the caudal fins and remove the skin. The backbones of these same fish yield a salty treat: spinal jelly. In the words of our friend Ricky Sucgang (and from his blog *Science Based Cuisine*, food.drricky.net):

> [Spinal jelly] is neither neural tissue nor marrow—it's mostly the cartilaginous intervertebral disc that separates the bones to enable the backbone to flex. If you've heard of people having a slipped disc—that's the analogous body part in question. Basically, it's like a pillow of fluid between the bony segments, and when compressed on one side, the other side expands to permit the whole structure to bend.

BIVALVES, GASTROPODS, CEPHALOPODS

Shellstock refers to bivalves (and less commonly gastropods) alive and intact in their shells, sold by count or weight. Half-shell bivalves are those that have had their top shell removed and lower adductor muscle cut. The term is appropriate for any bivalve, not just oysters. A shucked bivalve is one that has been removed entirely from its shell. Most oysters on the market are shucked.

A live gastropod is simply a live gastropod. Snails aren't shucked. Instead, they are cooked (boiled or steamed) and the meat picked; though the entire soft body is edible, most cooked snail meat is cleaned, with all viscera removed.

Almost every single squid bought or sold in this country is frozen. Truly fresh squid is rarer than truly fresh shrimp. A "dirty" squid is whole, completely intact; this form represents only a small fraction of squid on the market, limited to bait, low-quality commodity, and, ironically, high-grade sashimi. In general, though, dirty squid are processed into more ready-to-use forms. First the mantle (the "tube") is separated from the head (the "tentacles"), then the thin, translucent skin is peeled off. The tubes are peeled and eviscerated. The gladius, the transparent vestigial shell located in the tube, is also removed. (Even though we've seen thousands of them, we are still captivated every time we pull a gladius from a squid. So named because it resembles a sword, the gladius also looks completely artificial. It is as transparent as a piece of plastic packaging.) The heads are generally not peeled, but the eyes and beaks are removed. The most common processed forms are:

- Tubes and Tentacles (cleaned and separated, packed together)
- Whole Tubes (cleaned)
- Rings (sliced tubes)
- Tentacles
- Steaks (a specialty form: oval steaks stamped out from large commercial squids like the Humboldt Squid (*Dosidicus gigas*); needless to say, our local squid species are not nearly large enough to cut into steaks)

Octopodes have relatively few market forms. Most are sold whole, either raw or cooked. Raw octopus might or might not be tenderized (generally a mechanical or physical, rather than a chemical, process). Cooked whole octopus is sometimes treated with sulfites or other agents to maintain color (see the following pages as well for more on sulfites). Cooked tentacles are an increasingly popular form, sold ready to eat. Octopodes are sold according to size, that is, the number of individuals per kilogram.

CRUSTACEANS

Crabs, shrimp, lobster—all of these (and thousands of other marine species) are arthropods. They are, in other words, bugs. Like most bugs, they tend to be pretty hard to kill (with the partial exception of shrimp), so live crustaceans are a mainstay at fish markets. Lobsters and most crabs are kept in tanks; Blue Crabs, inexplicably, are not afforded that respect, mostly being displayed at markets in open bins (which are always too hot and too dry for live crabs). You can find live Gulf shrimp only at bait camps on the coast, where they are sold as bait. Live crawfish keep well and easily, despite the rough treatment to which they are usually subjected.

Cleaned crabs (and lobsters) are those that have been partially processed. This usually entails removing the organs and part of the shell and halving or quartering the animal. Depending on the species and market form, cleaned crabs and lobsters may be cooked or raw.

Picked meat is by far the most common market form of Blue Crab. Jumbo lump is the bit right at the junction of the carapace with the two swimming legs. It is the largest, most prestigious (and most expensive) cut. Lump is the meat at the junction of the carapace with the walking legs. While the chunks of meat are half as big as jumbo, regular lump meat is almost as expensive. Claw meat is the picked meat from the claws and knuckles. Fingers are partially picked claws, with only the immobile large claw shell still attached. A far less common market form is the lollipop, which is jumbo lump with the leg still attached. For whatever reason, fingers are sold in twelve-ounce containers; the rest are sold in one-pound increments.

THE ARRAY OF SHRIMP

Head-on shrimp are whole shrimp, shells and bodies completely intact. By a considerable margin, however, the most common form of shrimp sold in the United States is frozen tails. Shrimp tails are sold according to size, product form, and method of freezing or packing; size is determined not by weight of an individual shrimp, but by how many make a pound. The largest predictable size of Gulf shrimp is U-8 (or under eight to the pound); the smallest size—"popcorn" shrimp—is around 91/100 (between 91 and 100 shrimp to the pound).

The amount of processing determines the ultimate product form:

- "Tails" are shell-on, head-off shrimp
- "Tail-on" shrimp have been partially shelled, leaving the telson and flipper
- "Tail-off" shrimp are completely shelled (sometimes deveined, sometimes not)
- "P&D" means that the shrimp have been peeled and deveined
- "PUD" is a peeled, undeveined shrimp (this is mostly for small shrimp)
- "Butterfly" shrimp are either tail on or tail off, and are not just deveined, but split almost all the way down the middle

Bear in mind that with all but the smallest sizes, shrimp are frozen once whole (usually, but not always, on the boat), unloaded at the processor, and then thawed at least partially to further process or pack.

A NOTE CONCERNING PROCESSING CHEMICALS

Melanosis, Sulfites, and 4-Hexylresorcinol: Get one live Gulf shrimp. Kill it immediately in iced salt water. Store it in completely optimal conditions, which is to say, completely and continuously buried in finely shaved ice. In two days, usually much less, the shell and skin will start to turn brown, then black. This condition is called melanosis (colloquially "black spot"). The discoloration is not, contrary to popular belief, due to "bacteria," but rather to the presence in shrimp shells of polyphenol oxidase, an enzyme that causes discoloration when exposed to oxygen. The same enzyme is present in potatoes, avocados, bananas, and apples, and is responsible for their "browning." Quality and taste are not affected, but aesthetically the shrimp are not appetizing, which makes marketing and selling difficult. Melanosis occurs most often in thin-shelled, shallow-water tropical shrimp—which most of our Gulf shrimp are.

For decades, sulfiting agents have been used on Gulf shrimp to combat black spot. If used according to manufacturer's specifications, sulfites are considered by the FDA to be "Generally Recognized As Safe." (This designation, familiarly called GRAS, is defined by the FDA as follows: "A substance may be GRAS only if its general recognition of safety is based on the views of experts qualified to evaluate the safety of the substance. GRAS status may be based either on a history of safe use in food prior to 1958 or on scientific procedures, which require the same quantity and quality of evidence as would be required to obtain a food additive regulation.") However, workers exposed during processing to strong concentrations of sulfites can suffer serious side effects. On the other end of the supply chain, some people cannot tolerate sulfites in food, whether because of allergies (about 1 percent of the population), sensitivity associated with asthma (3–10 percent of asthmatics, according to the National Institutes of Health), or other issues. Altogether, this is a very small subset of the population, but reactions can be fatal.

In recent years, another chemical, 4-Hexylresorcinol, has started to gain popularity. It is safer in general and is nonallergenic. Unfortunately, it is also more expensive than sulfites, which has stopped it from being more widely adopted. Too few Texas shrimpers and shrimp processors use 4-Hexylresorcinol. If sulfites are used in processing, that fact must be stated on the label.

Sodium Tripolyphosphate and Other Processing Chemicals: All living things lose water after they die. Such a fact of life is accounted for in the seafood trade when, for example, a fish house, loading a truck for a cross-country delivery, puts about 2 percent more fish in the vats than they put on the invoice. By the time the fish arrives, it will have lost about that much weight in water, and the actual weight will match the invoice. In the same way, shellfish and crustacean processors might add certain chemicals during the processing of shrimp or scallops in order to slow down the loss of water (for shucked and clean shellfish lose water at least twice as fast as fish and unprocessed seafood). The practice is entirely legal (and understood throughout the industry), and per FDA regulations, products thus treated must be properly labeled. While these chemicals do impede water loss, they can also adversely affect texture and quality. We don't really buy seafood that uses these types of chemicals—not because we fear the chemicals in question, but because we really don't care for the texture of the end product.

CHAPTER 19

BUYING AND STORING SEAFOOD

PICK A GOOD FISH

First, and most importantly: quality is not binary, it's a spectrum. A fish is not good one day and magically spoiled the next. The final judgment should be based on the whole animal, not on one or two cherry-picked criteria. When adjudicating the condition of a fish, use all your senses. We do not mean this figuratively. Even your ears can sometimes tell you a thing or two about the quality of a fish—if you pick up a fish by the tail, and you hear the staccato snap of the back popping in several places, then you know that the fish is on its last legs.

GILLS

A fish with impeccable gills is almost always an impeccable fish, but the converse is not necessarily true. As an example, Scamp Groupers often flare their gill plates as they die and are sometimes packed in the ice on the boat in that position. As a result, the gills can come into direct contact with ice, which, as it melts, bleaches the gills. We've seen Scamp dead for less than forty-eight hours, in full rigor mortis, with crystal eyes . . . and the gills of a twelve-day-old fish. At the same time, some fish, like tilefish, can have red gills sometimes even after the meat has gone bad.

On a living fish, the gills are fire-engine red, tinged with crimson; the individual filaments are plainly visible and feathery; and only a very thin layer of slime covers the whole. After about three to six days (assuming correct handling and depending on species), the gills are closer to scarlet, the filaments less differentiated, and the slime more conspicuous. By about eleven days, the gills are closer to puce, and the slime is thick and viscous. As we have shown, a fish out of the water for eleven days can still be not only acceptable but even of legitimately high quality. But don't expect perfect gills.

EYES

The eyes can't be faked, and a fish with good eyes is always good enough to eat. The eyes should ideally be clear, and they should seem to peer at you accusingly (they should, in other words, appear lifelike). For most fish, the pupils and irises should have crisp, clean borders, and the color should be bright. Looking at the eyes from a bird's-eye angle, you should see the convex curve of the eye lens. If the lens is concave, the fish has either been out of the water for a few days, or it wasn't iced properly along the way—though sunken eyes alone are not necessarily indicative of a bad fish. In some fish (mostly deepwater groupers and other deeper-water groundfish), both eyeballs might look as if they had exploded out of the head—a result of their swift ascension from the seafloor. In these cases, the eyes tell you less. Also, some fish eyes just cloud over easier than others. Jacks in general can have cloudy eyes only a very few days out of the water, while the rest of the body, and the meat, will still be beautiful. And, regardless of the species, every fish will get cloudy eyes if its head sits in standing water during storage.

Finally, if the pupils themselves look like little white marbles, the fish was previously frozen.

THE BODY

Look at the color. The colors and patterns on the skin should be bright and sharp, never faded and blurred. Pay attention to the scales; they should glisten, *never* look dried out. On most fish, the scales should be firmly attached to the fish, not lying in a pile around it; and if half the scales are gone or if the fish looks dry, you should wonder why. (The exceptions here are small oily fish like sardines and mackerels, members of the cod family, among others. These fish have deciduous scales, meaning scales that slough off quickly after the death of the fish.)

THE SMELL

If your fishmonger allows you to smell the fish (and they should), smell the gills, the abdominal cavity. If the fish isn't yet gutted, and you are really good friends with your fishmonger, ask them to do it so you can take a whiff.

The gills and cavity should smell like fish and the sea. The smell is unmistakable, but it is not unpleasant in the least. It should remind you of a good late-spring day at the beach. The gills should have only a light smell, while the guts will have a more pronounced aroma. If the smell of the gills causes an involuntary (and negative) reflex, then don't bother smelling the gut cavity, and don't even think about buying the fish. Smell is the single most important indicator of freshness.

THE FEEL

This last is a bit tricky, for you must feel a lot of fish. In fact, you need to feel the same species over and over again, and then repeat the process for every fish you come across. Always try to feel the fish, any fish, all the fish. You need not pick up each one and cradle it. Simply run your finger down the body from head to tail, right above the lateral line. Don't press very hard, but enough to feel the meat under the skin. As you move your finger, pay attention to how the flesh reacts before, during, and after your finger passes. It should be supple, almost like a thick mushroom. Your finger should leave no indentation that remains.

Each species of fish is different. Some fish, like the Southern Hake and Ladyfish are just soft; others—snappers among them—have springy flesh; still others, like tunas, are about as firm as a flexed bicep. Learn the differences.

FILLETS, LOINS, FLETCHES, AND OTHER BONELESS BITS

Quality and age are more difficult to ascertain when the bones and head are gone, which is why we encourage you to buy whole fish when possible (even if you have the fishmonger fillet it for you).

Though there are a very few exceptions (cod, for example, and, in this book, the Cardinal Snapper and Escolar), most white fish fillets should be pinkish white and almost translucent at the edges (especially the feather meat). The dark meat should ideally be fire-engine red, though after only a few days on the bone, it turns more maroon. If the meat is opaque white, and the dark meat brown, either the fillet is old, or it was poorly frozen, poorly thawed out, or stored somewhere along the way in standing water.

Red fish meat (that from tunas, mackerels, and such) is another kettle of fish altogether. Meat color in these kinds of fish is highly variable, dependent on species and postmortem treatment. Yellowfin, Bluefin, and Bigeye Tunas should be a lustrous shade of dark red, while Albacore and Blackfin are generally paler (though some populations of Albacore have deep red meat, which only serves to confuse the entire situation). Tuna loins should always be firm to the touch. The meat should be crisp and compact.

No tuna swimming in the world has flesh the color of pink bubblegum. If you come across a piece of tuna thusly colored, know that it was treated with carbon monoxide. (Essentially, the cut fish is placed in a sealed environment filled with carbon monoxide. The gas preserves and exaggerates color in fish, which explains the bubblegum effect. The practice is done to mitigate the aesthetic consequences of freezing.) This safe and completely legal practice is not only commonplace but is actually industry standard for some types of frozen products; and though it does not alter the taste at all, we have always found it to be somewhat devious and under-handed.

Relative to white fish, most pelagic red fish are powerful swimmers, and they tend to fight longer and harder on the line. Such frantic muscle use builds up lactic acid in the flesh of the fish, which can affect the quality of the flesh. Luckily, com-mercial fishers figured this out long ago (with the considerable help of fisheries scientists along the way), and good-quality tuna is these days caught and handled in such a way as to reduce concentrations of lactic acid. Look at the cross section of a tuna loin under direct light; a slight rainbow sheen on the surface of the meat indi-cates an excessive amount of lactic acid. (The phenomenon is called birefringence, which has to do with refraction of light waves by certain crystalline structures.) Though this meat is still entirely edible, it is best reserved for recipes in which it will be cooked.

Sometimes fillets will develop tears in the meat itself, a condition known as gaping. At best, this just means that the fillet was slightly mishandled during cutting or display, so flavor and texture are not affected. At worst, the fish was improperly caught and slaughtered; or the fillet is old, or it has been moved around too much, too indelicately, and has almost reached the end of its shelf life.

FROZEN FISH

We once ate sashimi-grade Golden Tilefish that had been dead for 110 days. The skin and meat were virtually indistinguishable, in both texture and taste, from a fresh fish caught only a few days before. Even the eyes were clear as glass. It had been frozen and stored in a superfreezer at a constant temperature of -76°F (that is at least 80°F colder than a home freezer, and at least 50°F colder than most restaurant freezers).

Of course, had it been frozen in a regular home or restaurant freezer, the fish would have been gray and mushy after that amount of time, which demonstrates the limitations of freezing fish.

While good frozen fish does exist, the chances of finding it at the market are slim. To maintain its quality, fish needs to be stored at a much colder temperature than crustaceans, and while seafood companies can generally maintain the required storage conditions, most stores and restaurants cannot.

So, we have rather less confidence in frozen fish. Having established that, we recommend that you take advantage of frozen fish whenever quality permits.

Whole frozen fish should have bright eyes and skin; they should appear almost alive (albeit very, very cold). The absolute best frozen fish tends to be mackerels and the like; they are often cooked whole, and their flesh is sturdier than, for example, cod. Frozen fillets should have bright red bloodlines, and the meat, while slightly more opaque than the fresh version, should nonetheless be closer to pink than beige.

Beware of technicolor fish— fillets are often gassed with carbon monoxide before freezing. Just as with tuna, gassing is harmless and safe. But gassing can also cover up some defects as well.

CHOOSING THE BEST SHELLFISH

In the case at the market, bivalves should be displayed by themselves, not near or under fish or other seafood. If you see fish juice or melting ice dripping onto the oysters, then by all means stay away. Bivalves should be on ice; ideally, they should be displayed in a perforated pan, buried in ice. If you see bivalves in standing water, stay well clear. Fresh water is terrible for bivalves—it can kill the animal and provide a perfect place for pathogens to grow.

Properly stored, bivalves can stay alive, out of the water, for up to three weeks. We suggest buying as fresh as possible, and not buying anything that's been out of the water more than two weeks.

Your fishmonger can tell you the harvest date and harvest area for any live bivalves they sell, because bivalve shellstock bought and sold for commercial purposes must be accompanied by a shellfish tag, which states the primary processor's name, address, and license number, as well as the date and location of harvest. Seafood markets do not need to give these tags to retail customers, but they are required to keep the tags for ninety days after the sale of the shellfish. Better fish markets always display the tags along with the product. If you see some bivalves for sale, ask for information. And also ask to see the tag. If the market cannot or will not show it to you, the bivalves in question are not worth buying.

APPEARANCE AND SMELL

Live oysters should never have open shells. The shell is either snapped shut tight, or you throw it away. Never buy oysters that are sitting in a market display with their shells ajar.

On the other hand, clams and mussels routinely open their shells out of water. They are not necessarily dead or even dying; a tap to the shell will cause them to close up again. If, however, the meat inside appears shriveled and dry, and if you should see strands of a mucus-like substance, the animal is almost certainly dead and not worth buying. When in doubt, do not buy.

Just to sow confusion, there are some notable exceptions to the general rules about bivalves, for some species either cannot or do not close their shells after harvest. Boring clams do not attach to substrate like oysters and mussels or lie just under the sand like quahog clams; instead, as juveniles, they dig a burrow, move in, and never move again. Eventually, the juvenile grows into an adult and fills the burrow entirely. This group of boring clams includes a few well-known species, like razor clams and geoducks, as well as some relative strangers covered in this book (Stout Razor and Angelwing Clams). As a rule, these types of clams do not live very long after harvest, and while a two-week-old oyster might be edible and tasty, we recommend not buying any boring clam out of the water more than seven days.

Scallops also have a limited life out of the water. They are the most mobile of shellfish, and though they can close their shells tight, they usually elect not to. Scallops fare even worse than boring clams. Rarely are live scallops worth the money. With very few exceptions, it is better instead to buy shucked "dry" scallops. A dry scallop has been treated with no preservatives (i.e., sulfites, sodium tripolyphosphate, or the like—by law, a scallop product containing more than 83 percent water is considered "processed"—remember that sodium tripolyphosphate is used to retain moisture). If your fishmonger doesn't know whether the scallop is wet or dry, then don't take a chance.

Shucked scallops should never be pale white, and should never have soft, rounded edges. A good shucked scallop will be peach, pink, or even pumpkin colored.

Live marine snails, displayed out of water, typically seal up their shell, so all that is visible is the dark bony operculum. This is a good sign, for it means the animal is alive and healthy. Some larger snails, especially predators like Whelks and Oyster Drills, spend part of their time in the display case sealed up in their shells; the rest of the time, they are slowly moving about, trying to find an exit or a meal.

Live, fresh bivalves smell like metallic saltwater spray and nothing else really. If they smell of something else, they are not worth eating. Live snails smell a bit musty, like mushrooms and low tide (but not in an unpleasant way).

Shucked oysters should be sitting in clear, slightly viscous juice. You can eat these raw, but the processor assumes shucked oysters are going into po'boys and fried seafood baskets. Shucked oysters work in a pinch for a raw snack, but no matter how fresh, they have still been dead for a few days. When possible, buy live oysters and shuck them yourself.

The frozen bivalve is a decent enough product, but we never get excited.

CEPHALOPODS

We highly recommend purchasing squid and octopus frozen. Cleaned squid (tubes, tentacles, etc.) should be white, with maybe a little purple on the edges of the mantle and fin. Cleaned squid that is closer to yellow is old or has been improperly stored (i.e., not kept completely frozen). Pink cleaned squid means the squid was old before it was even cleaned and frozen. Whole frozen squid should also have completely white meat, though that fact will be somewhat obscured by the skin (you will nonetheless have no difficulty spotting the color of the muscle underneath).

If you insist on buying fresh squid, the skin should be clear, with all patterns crisp and vivid. The meat itself (including, most importantly, the tentacles) should not be pink or purple at all. The squid should not be at all slimy, and should smell like salt water. You will rarely find fresh squid that passes this test (clever fish markets often buy premium frozen squid, then thaw it for the retail display, where they sell it as "fresh").

Raw octopus should resemble the surface of the ocean floor in coloration and markings. Its underside should be white. Cooked octopus is a dicey proposition—in order to produce an aesthetically pleasing and tender (yet not mushy) frozen end product, most processors rely on harsh practices and liberal amounts of several processing chemicals; while the result is safe and edible, we cannot say much beyond that.

CHOOSING THE BEST CRUSTACEAN

As noted above, we recommend buying frozen shrimp most of the time. The most expensive frozen shrimp (i.e., spot prawns and head-on, U-8 US Gulf whites) are IQF, as are, paradoxically, the worst (highly processed farmed popcorn shrimp of dubious provenance). The rest are block frozen. Of the two types, block frozen is more consistent in quality, because the brine protects the shrimp quite effectively against temperature fluctuations and freezer burn, which is, of course, why the shrimp are brined in the first place. IQF shrimp have a shorter freezer life and are very prone to burn during storage. If your fishmonger is as good as ours, then you need not worry about such things, for you will never be sold inferior product. If you should not be so lucky, then take a good long look at IQF shrimp before you buy. If the shrimp look dry, or if you see pale patches of discolored shell, they are already burned, and nothing can really bring them back from that.

Live Blue Crabs need to be kept in a cool but not cold (around 45°F) environment with a good amount of humidity, which is difficult to maintain in a retail display. Until Texas retail fish markets start keeping their Blue Crabs in tanks rather than in bins, we won't be buying.

Regardless of the species and how it is stored, a live crab should be angry about its captivity. It should be trying to escape and should fight any effort to take it by tong or by scoop. Rarely will you see a retail Blue Crab this alive. Most are listless and reeking and, with a bubble or two leaking out of their mouths, at the last moments of their existence. Find out when the crabs are delivered by the crabbers and plan your shopping trip accordingly. As we wrote earlier, if you are in Texas, you will only see females and small males at the retail level (see the Blue Crab entry for more). *Never, ever, ever buy a dead crab. The best environment for live crabs is also a great environment for pathogens.*

Softshell crabs should be plump, colorful, and obviously alive. They should never be on full display in the case but rather covered somewhat (they are exceedingly delicate at this stage of the molt). Ideally, they'll be kept in the back of the shop, in a more suitable environment. Take your chances with frozen softshell crab if you want, or, for that matter, with frozen softshell crawfish and softshell shrimp—we have never been impressed with frozen softshells of any sort. Buy them fresh, and you'll be buying them when they are best.

Unless you know your fishmongers well, we do not recommend buying prepared dead crabs, like those sold as "gumbo" crabs. These have often been cleaned after they died in the live bin. While we applaud the fishmongers' thrift, we don't usually trust the result. It doesn't matter if it's fresh or frozen—an old fresh crab is the same as a frozen crab that was old when it was put in the freezer.

In the (refrigerated) display case, crab meat should be at least half buried in ice. Don't buy crab meat that is not both in ice *and* in a refrigerated cooler. The person behind the counter helping you should never reach in the case with bare hands and grab a container of crab meat. If they're not wearing gloves when they handle crab meat, question the wisdom of the purchase. Pay close attention to the pack date (it is written on every container of fresh crab meat—some crab packers use a variation of the Julian dating system, so be prepared to calculate). Don't buy meat packed more than seven days earlier. You probably won't get sick if you do, but the age will be apparent in the taste. Don't ask to smell the crab meat—it is a ready-to-eat product. No one wants to buy crab meat that has been breathed on by strangers.

Almost 100 percent of the fresh crab meat in Texas is from Mexico. As we wrote earlier, there is no such thing as Texas crab meat, unless the restaurant or market has bought live crabs, cooked them, and picked the meat (if you are told otherwise by a market or restaurant, be suspicious. It's possible, but just barely). Fresh Mexican Blue Crab meat is of excellent quality. Mexican crab meat from the Pacific side is slightly inferior (at least the product that makes it to Texas is). We strongly recommend against pasteurized. We also recommend against imported product from Southeast Asia.

ON STORING FISH AND SEAFOOD

We have no talismanic advice here, just some thoughts about methods and tricks that have served us well.

- **WHOLE FISH AND WHOLE COOKED CRUSTACEANS**: If your refrigerator is under 40°F, and you are storing overnight only, then just wrap the fish in some damp newspaper or kitchen towels, and place it in a food storage container, casserole dish, or the like. For longer storage (or if your refrigerator runs warm), always, always use ice. But never, never use ice in a container that cannot drain. Fish corpses do not like standing water, and the effect on the quality of the meat is significant. A very fresh fish, kept in suitable conditions, can still be good to eat more than a week after purchase.

- **FILLETS**: The same goes for fillets, bearing in mind that standing water is even worse for fillets. Never ice fillets directly. Always place the fillets in a sealable food storage container. If the fillets are under ice, they need to be in sealed plastic bags. *Do not let fillets get wet.* Fresh fillets, stored appropriately, last for up to a week.

- **LIVE CRUSTACEANS**: By the time a live crustacean makes it to your kitchen, it has been out of the water for a while, so the most important points are these: do not keep live crustaceans in sealed plastic containers or sacs; do not store them in standing fresh water; cover them with a wet towel and never let them dry out; and do not let them get too cold. If it's going to be more than twenty-four hours before you will be eating the crab, we suggest cooking it and then storing it the way you would a whole fish.

- **PICKED CRAB MEAT**: The plastic containers in which crab meat is sold seal quite well. Always keep fresh crab meat buried in ice in the refrigerator (in a container that can drain). You don't want things dripping on crab meat, especially raw meats.

- **LIVE MOLLUSKS AND SNAILS**: As with live crustaceans, cover these with a wet towel to keep them moist, and store them cold, but not too cold.

- **SHUCKED OYSTERS**: Treat these as you would picked crab meat.

ON THE THAWING OF SEAFOOD

The ideal way to thaw (the preferred seafood industry term for "thaw" is "slack"; rarely to never does one hear the word "thaw" in a fish house) any frozen food is by letting it slowly defrost in the refrigerator (stored in a container that can drain, of course). This method does take a day or two, depending on the item being thawed, so planning is essential. Thawing seafood under running water might be acceptable, but only if the water is cold, and only if the seafood in question is in a sealed plastic container or bag (you do not want the thawing seafood to come into direct contact with the water). Thawing at ambient room temperature might be acceptable, as long as the product in question is small, and the room is less than 70°F. Always remember that even the highest-quality frozen fish is easily destroyed through careless thawing.

CHAPTER 20

CUTTING FISH, SHUCKING OYSTERS, AND CLEANING CRABS

We have found that only two things are necessary to successfully cut a fish: experience and a sharp knife.

We've seen countless poor fish destroyed by expensive knives wielded by cooks and chefs who apparently believed that spending a lot of money was equivalent, in some way, to actual experience. Choose whatever knife suits you and learn to use it very well.

We use only black-handled Victorinox scimitar knives to cut fish, for we have found them to be the most reliable and cost-effective knives around (that they are preferred by professional butchers and fishcutters leads us to believe we are somewhat justified in our choice). We do not use any other Victorinox product aside from the black-handled models, and we don't use other brands of scimitars. We use cleavers of various sizes for pretty much everything else. We have a couple of whittled-down boning knives for little fish.

Knives need to be very sharp—always. Learn to sharpen your knives. There is no mystery, no magic, in the honing of a knife.

Buy a cut-resistant glove and wear it when you are cutting up any whole fish. It should go without saying, but the glove is worn only on the hand not holding the knife, so you may hold the fish firmly without fear of slicing through the hand holding the fish. Do not underestimate the importance of a cut-resistant glove.

Gloves do not protect your arms, though. The human arm has several rather important blood vessels, some of which lie close to the surface of the skin; these are easily pricked by a blade. Be careful.

FISH

SCALING

It's not always necessary to scale a fish, but when we need to do so, we usually use a Japanese-style scaler (the Japanese name is *urokotori*, and you should never buy any scaler except for this one; they are easy to find and inexpensive) or a spoon. We don't mean a specialized or modified spoon, or a big spoon, just a regular table spoon, oriented so that the concave surface scoops the scales off. Regardless of the tool, scale from the tail to head. You do not have to scale furiously; smooth firm strokes are better. Very large fish require sturdier tools or a sturdier hand, but the idea is the same.

GUTTING

The process is the same for most fish (the exception being the flatfish, which require a cut made between pectoral and pelvic fins). Locate the anal vent and insert a knife with the blade facing away from the fish, toward the head. Using the least amount of pressure possible and keeping the blade of the knife angled so as to cut the skin but not the guts beneath, cut from the vent to the pelvic fins. Here you will need to cut through the fins or around them (we prefer the former, though it takes a bit of practice). Either way, get past and continue to the point where the body meets the gills (basically making a straight line on the underside of the fish). Open the cavity and find the terminus of the guts, which is right at the anal vent. Tear that bit first, then, working toward the head, pull out the guts. Take the time to loosen them gently from the belly wall as you go, rather than just yanking in a mad fury. If it's a quality fish, the swim bladder will pull out with the rest of the guts; if the fish has seen a few days, the bladder will tear, and you might not be able to get it all out. After you have loosened all the guts, pull them out and, if necessary, cut the esophagus that connects the guts to the head. After removing the guts, find the kidneys and remove them also. There are two of them, of course, located where kidneys usually are—right at either side of the backbone. The kidneys are quite elongated and look almost more like thick blood vessels. You'll have to scrape them out (we find a skewer or a toothbrush or the blade of a knife works well).

GILLING

Both sets of gills are connected. Locate where and how the gills are moored to the body. If the fish is less than about five pounds, just take firm hold of the gills and pull. The whole gill mass should come out with a satisfying crunch. We would advise you to take care in handling the gills, for they are covered in bony needles called rakers that can shred the skin on your hand. If you are being sensible, you will, of course, have on your cutting glove; in which case, grab the gills with your gloved hand. If the fish is larger, you will need to trace the outline of the gills, cutting away all the connective membranes first, and then sawing or chopping through the junctions at the tops and bottoms of the gills.

HEADING

With the fish lying on its side, belly toward you, find where the skull meets the fillet. Make a cut from there to the bottom of the fish, cutting behind the pectoral fins and ending at the belly behind the pelvic fins. Make sure you cut all the way to the bone and through the belly. Repeat this process on the other side of the fish. Then stand the fish upright in a swimming position. Place your knife at the point where you started the first cuts, and hack straight down, cutting through the bone to the spine. If the fish is less than a couple of pounds, you should be able to cut through the spine as well. If it's a bigger fish, stop at the back bone. Then grab the fish firmly with one hand, and the head with the other, and jerk the head sharply down. The spine will snap in two, and the head will slide away from the body. We recommend grabbing the fish head by its eyeballs, as you would a bowling ball.

THE COLLARS AND CHEEKS

After you have taken off the head, remove the collars and cheeks if the head is big enough to bother with them. To get at the collars, cut the membranes that connect them to the gills. Then pull the collars away from the head until you see where they are still connected, right at the very top of the head. Hack through this bit, and you have your collars. Wash them well, as they are located right next to blood- and fluid-rich parts of the body. The cheeks (again, worth removing only if the fish is big enough) are located just where they are on a human. Press under and to the back of the eye until you feel a soft spot. Trace this soft spot wherever it goes, and soon you will have the outlines of the cheek. Angling the tip of your knife inward, saw the cheek out of the skull.

FILLETS

You will want to develop your own way of filleting a fish. The only measure of success is getting intact meat off the bone, with as little as possible left on the carcass. The following is a decent enough primer, if nothing else, and the technique works on any white fish, most steak fish, and even flatfish.

Position the headed and gutted fish so that its tail is pointing toward you and the belly side points away from your knife. Make an incision right along the top of the back, near the head end, right where the dorsal fin meets the body. Continue the incision to the tail. From this beginning, cut until you meet bone, then follow the bones. In wide strokes, keep cutting the fillet away from the bone. Always try to keep the knife blade more or less parallel, rather than perpendicular, to the backbone of the fish. When you come to the backbone, cut around and past it, always slicing through whatever connective tissue you see. Once past the backbone, you will be able to continue much the same way near the tail, until the back of the fillet is completely liberated from the body.

The front of the fillet is a little trickier, for the ribs connect to the backbone at the same spot as the fillet. With practice, you will learn to recognize this junction. Cut the fillet away until you encounter the ribs. With the head end of the fish facing away from you, place your knife right at the junction of rib and backbone. Grab the tail with your other hand, and with one swift and firm stroke, cut through all of the ribs at once. The fillet is now detached. Repeat the process with the other fillet. You now have two fillets, and both still have some bones. (A slightly more refined way involves leaving the ribs intact on the carcass and trimming the fillet from them instead. While we prefer this method, it is a bit more difficult to learn and substantially more difficult to explain in writing.)

To remove the rib bones, slide your knife between the ribs and the meat, and gently cut, following the bones and making sure not to cut through the belly. The ribs will come off in one sheet, usually saving at least a good part of the belly (though some fish, like the Striped Mullet, have no belly meat to speak of, so you are left with a notched fillet).

For the pin bones, cut the fillet into two loins, following the lines already there. If you do so, then just trim away the pin bones after you cut the fillets into loins. Otherwise, find where the bones are, and pull them with tweezers or cut them out in a strip (you will lose a little meat this way).

There will be some blood, maybe some scales, on the fillets. We suggest you either use salted water to rinse the fillets or wait until moments before you plan to use them before washing them in fresh water.

TUNAS

If the tuna is a tiny Blackfin, it may be filleted like a standard white fish; if it's a tuna bigger than about twenty pounds, first recall that tuna is cut into loins, not fillets. Further recall that loining a tuna is considerably more difficult than filleting a fish. A great deal more knowledge is required. Recall even further that unless you are in a restaurant or seafood company, you really don't need a whole tuna.

Should you have a tuna loin, simply carve it into steaks or chunks, depending on the recipe.

A PEEK AT WHOLE FISH FORMS

If you intend to cook your fish whole, you will at least need to gut and gill it (described above). We advise you not to skip the gilling step. Depending on the recipe, you may or may not need to scale the fish as well.

However, the category of "whole fish" need not be limited to just the gilled and gutted animal. Here we describe a few complementary forms, though only in the barest of outlines. You will need to fill in the blanks with a lot of practice. We firmly believe that one only learns how to cut a fish by cutting a lot of fish. We have never seen any evidence to the contrary.

Always wash your whole fish inside and out in iced salted water after you finish processing it.

- **WHOLE FINLESS**: this just adds a touch of class to your whole fish and makes getting at the meat slightly easier. With a pair of scissors, cut off the pectoral and pelvic fins at their bases; trim the caudal fin close to the tail. Next you will want to make a shallow cut along the back, from head to tail, on both sides of the dorsal fin. These cuts should be made right next to the dorsal fins, and if done right, will allow you to pull out the entire dorsal fin, along with the pesky small bones connecting the fins to the body. Repeat the process with the anal fins.

- **WHOLE BONELESS**: Proceed as for **WHOLE FINLESS** above; then, taking care not to cut through the fillet at either the tail or head end, proceed as if you were filleting the fish. When the fillets are freed completely, snip the backbone right at the tail and at the junction with the head. Pull out the backbone, and you have a boneless whole fish. Turn the fish more or less inside out, pull the pin bones with tweezers, and make sure the ribs have all been removed.

- **WHOLE BONELESS, BELLY INTACT**: For this preparation, you will need an ungutted fish. Proceed as for the **WHOLE BONELESS** above, cutting through the back, but do not cut through the bottom of the fish or the belly. Once the backbone has been extracted, the fish can be gutted and washed. This is the ideal form for stuffing.

- **SPATCHCOCKED**: This is essentially a combination of the above two methods. After gilling, scaling, and gutting the fish, cut off all the fins. Leaving the fillets attached at the head and tail, cut out the bones, *starting at the belly rather than the back*. You will want to keep the skin and meat attached at the back, so after cutting to that point, cut the backbone at the tail and head and gently tease out the bones. Flatten the fish with the skin facing down. Tweeze pinbones as needed and remove the ribs.

- **WHOLE PEELED**: We've found that this technique requires a fish with thicker, relatively elastic skin and firm rather than delicate flesh. Jacks, tunas, and other pelagic fish, as well as groupers, tilefish, and some snappers handle the treatment well. Remove the fins as you would for a whole finless preparation. Then make a skin-deep incision from the top of the fillet to the bottom. We recommend that you orient your knife so the blade point is up, thus splicing the skin from the bottom and keeping the flesh intact. Working from the shoulder down, gingerly separate the flesh from the skin, using the knife only when the flesh tears. If the process is performed correctly, you will not need your knife at all, for the skin will peel directly from the flesh. Work toward the tail; when all the skin has been removed from the rest of the body, cut the last shred at the tail.

SHELLFISH AND CRUSTACEANS

SHUCKING OYSTERS

You will need a decent oyster knife, of which there are scores of varieties. We recommend, for Gulf oysters anyway, a slightly thicker blade; we always hone the tip just a little, not to sharpen it so much as to make it small enough to get in between the lips of the hinges.

Using a folded kitchen towel (to protect your hand from an accidental jab with the shucking knife), hold the oyster in such a way as to make the hinge of its shell visible and accessible (the hinge should more or less be facing you). Wedge the oyster knife in the middle of the hinge, then twist the blade so as to force the hinge apart. The oyster shell will pop slightly as the hinge is broken. Wedge the shell open slightly, and with your oyster knife, cut through the adductor muscles that hold the shells together. Remove the top shell, and you now have an oyster on the half shell. Cut the adductor muscle on the other shell and you have a shucked oyster. Do not be a dummy and use a regular knife; that is how trips to the hospital happen. *Never* use too much force. Slow and steady wins the race. Once you learn how to shuck one oyster, you are fast on your way to becoming an expert.

SQUID

A squid head is easily divorced from its body. Grasp the body in one hand, the head in the other, and pull. It won't take much effort. To clean the head, find the beak opening at the underside of the head and squeeze. The beak will pop out right away. Eyes are removed in much the same way, by squeezing behind each eye. We advise that this operation be performed over the sink, and that the eye being squeezed is pointed down (there is ink in the eye sacs, and squid ink tends to stain).

The tube is an easier affair to clean. Reach in the opening of the tube and feel around for the gladius. When you find it, wiggle it a little to free it, then gently pull straight out. Feel around in the tube again and pull out remaining soft bits, which are the guts. Finally, peel the skin from the body of the tube. The two fins and the base of the tube may be removed (they are slightly rubbery), but we usually just keep them on. Your squid is now ready to cook.

CLEANING SHRIMP

When faced with the choice between shell-on shrimp tails and peeled and deveined shrimp tails, we always choose the former. Remember that, in general, the more processed a shrimp is, the poorer the quality. Buy your shrimp with the shells on, and be assured of a better product.

While most shrimp recipes (in this book and elsewhere) call for peeled and deveined shrimp, remember that shell-on shrimp usually work just as well (as long as you don't mind peeling the cooked shrimp and pulling out the vein)—though not always.

Starting with a whole shrimp, grasp the tail in one hand and the head in the other. Pull the two apart, discard the head (or save for another use), and you have a shrimp tail.

To peel the tail, take hold of the underside of the shell, where the legs are, and peel up, loosening the shell. Repeat the process along the tail, then remove the shell (top and bottom) more or less in one piece. You now have a peeled shrimp. You may also leave the very last segment of the shell (the telson) on, in which case you have a peeled, tail-on shrimp.

To devein the shrimp, first fill a mixing bowl with salted water (measurements are not necessary here, the water just needs to taste salty—fresh water is no better for shrimp than it is for fish), then add enough ice to chill the water completely. With a small sharp knife, slice open the back of the tail. You want to cut just deep enough to free the vein, no more. After cutting the tail, place it in the ice water, then repeat until no more shrimp remain. Swish the water around a bit, then, one by one, pull the vein out of each tail. The cold salt water helps to loosen the veins, so most of them won't even be attached anymore. You now have a peeled and deveined shrimp. After cleaning the shrimp, store them in a sealed plastic bag under ice.

For butterflied shrimp, make the cut deeper, about halfway through the shrimp.

PICKING CRABS

Bring a very large pot of heavily salted water to the boil. Dump in the crabs and cook for ten minutes, or until the water comes back to a boil. Shock the crabs in ice water and let them cool completely. Pull off the back (the top of the carapace).

To remove the meat from a Blue Crab:

- **JUMBO LUMP**: Locate the hindmost leg. Take hold of the base of the leg, then pull and twist gently until the leg comes away from the body. When it does, the jumbo lump nugget should be completely exposed, though still attached to the leg. Remove the meat and repeat the process on the other side.

- **LUMP**: Do the same process as for Jumbo, gently removing every leg and getting the meat attached to it. You might have to use a toothpick to get some of the errant pieces still in the shell.

- **CLAW**: This is all the meat in the large arms and claws. Detach the arms from the body, place them on a cutting board, then gently crack them open with the broad side of a knife, and remove the meat. Don't forget to get the meat right at the knuckles as well.

- **FINGER**: If you want, keep the claws themselves intact, removing only part of the shell. This is a fancy way of doing it, and does not, we think, contribute much.

SOFTSHELL CRABS

To prepare a softshell, lift (but do not remove) the carapace on both sides and remove the gills right underneath. Then remove the skirt (the little flap of soft shell on the belly of the crab). Finally, with a pair of scissors, trim the face (well, the eyes and mouth) from the front of the carapace. Then dredge (or bread) and fry.

CLEANING CRABS

Take a cleaver, and chop the live crab in half down the middle. You will end up with two symmetrical portions. Lift off the hard top shell from each piece, then remove the gills, which are the feathery structures on the inside edge of the carapace, just above where the legs join the body. The crab is now ready for gumbo, or the fryer, or a boil.

RECIPES

The recipes that follow come from our home, or the homes or restaurant kitchens of our friends and old customers. A great many of the recipes will be somewhat familiar, though we hope we have a few that might surprise and even delight. We begin with whole fish recipes, then cut fish, then crabs and shrimp, then the mollusks, followed by a few ideas for preserving the catch. We end with some recipes utilizing the odd bits.

While the recipes are self-contained, we wish to be clear on a few things:

- We prefer Squid brand fish sauce from Thailand. Some of our friends prefer Red Boat from Vietnam. Unless otherwise specified, assume that fish sauce is always Squid brand.

- We prefer dark, almost bitter olive oil.

- We always use Thai soy sauce, never anything else. In our own recipes, assume the soy sauce is Thai soy sauce. Also assume soy sauce means "white" soy unless we specify "black." If our chef friends' recipes call for soy sauce, assume it is Japanese.

- A wok is a very handy piece of cooking equipment. A heavy, deep mortar and pestle is even handier.

- One of the best things you can own is a small, very portable charcoal grill.

- Unless otherwise specified, all salt is kosher salt.

- Assume that our friends' contributions contain exact measurements; assume that our own recipes contain at best firm suggestions.

- None of these recipes absolutely requires a specific species, so substitute one fish for another if need be (and if the substitution makes sense!). If you have no access to Gulf of Mexico fish, find the most equivalent fish you can.

- Cooking is like fishing: the point is getting something edible and tasty on the table. Trust your own tastes.

CHAPTER 21
WHOLE FISH

WHOLE SALT-CRUSTED ROCK HIND

2 SERVINGS   This technique may be applied to the vast majority of fish in this book, provided they are of suitable size (one to three pounds). Rock Hind works well simply because it is delicious and does not have very tasty skin. Two versions are given here—one for the grill, one for the oven; of course, we recommend the former.

> 1 gutted Rock Hind, approximately two pounds
>
> 1–2 pounds salt, depending on the size of the fish
>
> Herbs for stuffing into the fish (e.g., lemongrass, lemon basil, cilantro; or dill, thyme, rosemary; other combinations to taste)
>
> 1–3 tablespoons olive oil (if grilling)
>
> 2–3 egg whites (if for the oven)

Gill the fish, but do NOT scale it. Stuff the belly cavity with the herbs.

FOR THE GRILL: Rub the fish with the oil. Pour the salt into a baking pan and put the fish in the pan. Coat the entire fish with salt, making sure it sticks all over the outside (you can't really use too much salt). The grill should be hot, but not enough to flare. Place the fish on the grill and cook about 10 minutes per side, depending on size. Test for doneness and remove from the grill.

FOR THE OVEN: Mix the salt with enough egg whites to form a very thick mass, not runny at all. Place some of this mix on a baking sheet and pat into a shape roughly like that of the fish. Put the fish on top, then mound the rest of the salt mix on top, so that the fish is no longer visible. Pat the salt into a fish shape (and draw fish features if you are feeling particularly whimsical). Bake at 410°F until the fish is done, about 30–45 minutes, at which point the crust will be golden.

TO SERVE: Place the fish in the middle of the table, surrounded by appropriate vegetables and starches and some lemon wedges. Whether you grill or bake the fish, eating it is roughly the same. In the case of the grilled fish, slowly pull back the skin. It will be stiff and remain in one piece, and most of the salt will remain on the skin. In the case of the baked fish, knock a small hole in the crust and peel away. The skin will come away with the salt crust, leaving only flesh.

APPROPRIATELY COOKED WHITING

4 SERVINGS Most of our best beach memories seem to involve whole grilled whiting. The recipe is simple, though for best results we suggest you not omit any ingredients. Should you not have whiting on hand, any whole fish under one pound will work.

- 4 whitings or more (depending on both your luck at fishing and the size of your company—allow about one pound of whole fish per person)
- About 3-4 tablespoons olive oil
- About a cup of salt
- Ground black pepper to taste
- 2-3 lime or lemon wedges per fish
- Cooked sticky rice (cook it at home before you go to the beach)
- 4 yams (and foil to wrap)
- 1-2 unhusked ears of corn per person
- 1 beach, with suitable sea and a spot to set up camp

SAUCE, WHICH SHOULD BE MADE BEFOREHAND:

- 3-7 fresh Thai chilies, according to preference
- 2-3 tablespoons peeled garlic, according to preference
- 1 bunch cilantro stems
- 2 tablespoons sugar
- ½ cup fish sauce
- ⅓ cup lime juice
- Salt to taste

FOR THE SAUCE: Before you go to the beach, take five minutes to make the sauce. Blend all ingredients in a blender.

After having arranged camp, set a fire in a small grill. Oil, salt, and pepper the yams, wrap in foil, and put in the burning coals.

Put the corn to cook on the grill, close to, but not right on, the flames.

Meanwhile, prepare your freshly caught whiting. Make a slit from the anal vent all the way to the gills. Starting at the bowel end of the fish, loosen and remove the guts. Because the fish is so fresh, all of the guts will still be intact and supple and will easily come away in one mass (usually along with the gills as well). As each fish is gutted, give the mass of entrails to a nearby child to throw for the seagulls. Wash the gutted fish in the nearby sea. Dredge in salt, and grill alongside the corn. The fish will take about 10-15 minutes per side, depending on the size of the fire and the fish, and also, the intensity of beach winds.

Serve the whole fish, roasted yams, grilled corn, lemon wedges, and sticky rice together. Watch the water and eat until it's time to go to bed. Beer is a fine accompaniment to the catching, cooking, and eating.

WHOLE MANGROVE SNAPPER WITH NUOC MAM CHAM AND PEANUT PESTO

2 SERVINGS Since the first day PJ walked into Catalan restaurant in Houston, Texas, bearing fish, Chef Chris Shepherd has been an amazing customer, a strong supporter, a vocal advocate, and, most importantly, a friend. This is his recipe, which we present with his comments and directions.

"No disrespect to the fish, but the pesto is the star of this show. This recipe builds off of the green marinade we use on chicken. But with the addition of peanuts, it becomes a fully formed sauce similar to an Italian pesto in composition (a puree of herbs and nuts), but with a markedly different flavor. There's not much that this pesto wouldn't improve."

3 garlic cloves

1½ bunches cilantro, stems trimmed

½ bunch picked mint leaves

1 bunch green onions, root ends trimmed, cut into 2-inch pieces

½ cup Red Boat brand fish sauce

½ cup dark brown sugar

2 limes, juiced

1 cup roasted peanuts

Salt and pepper for seasoning the fish

One 2-pound whole Mangrove Snapper, cleaned, scaled, and fins removed

½ cup Nuoc Mam Cham (see below)

NUOC MAM CHAM:

1 cup hot water

½ cup granulated sugar

¼ cup distilled white vinegar

⅓ cup Red Boat fish sauce

1 tablespoon chopped garlic

2 teaspoons sambal

¼ cup lime juice

"In a heatproof bowl, combine the hot water, sugar, white vinegar, fish sauce, garlic, and sambal.

Stir until the sugar dissolves, then mix in the lime juice. Taste for seasoning and adjust as necessary; it should be sweet, salty, funky, and a little spicy. Transfer to a lidded container and store in the refrigerator until ready to serve (it will keep for 2 weeks). Serve cold or at room temperature.

Preheat the oven to 350°F. In a food processor, combine the garlic, cilantro, mint, green onions, fish sauce, brown sugar, and lime juice. Puree until you get a smooth consistency. Add the peanuts, and pulse until the peanuts are chopped but still chunky.

Pat the fish dry and season both inside and outside with salt and pepper. Place on a rimmed baking sheet and roast in the oven for 8 minutes. Remove from oven and smear the peanut pesto generously all over the top side of the fish. Be careful because the fish will be hot. Return to the oven and continue to roast the fish for another 12 minutes. Remove from the oven, place on a plate, and pour the nuoc mam right over the fish. Eat immediately."

LITTLE FISH SOUP OR TRASHFISH SOUP—OUR *SOUPE DE POISSON*

12 SERVINGS MORE OR LESS This dish requires little white fish, each less than an ounce or two. It requires a lot of them, many dozens anyway. They may all be of the same species or a combination of several species (including some oily fish). There might be some small invertebrates mixed among the fish, and that is fine as well. In France, a mixed catch of such fish is sold as "*soupe de poisson*" by fishmongers, for indeed that is the primary use for them at the table (the fish themselves are bycatch from trawl fisheries). We don't enjoy such a situation in Texas. If one wishes to make *une vraie soupe de poisson*, one must make friends with someone on a shrimp boat, or one must learn how to use a cast net. The easiest route is the cast net.

The soup is intended to go along with a larger meal, or as a hot treat on a cold beach. It is enriched broth and nothing else, the way such a soup should be. To soak up every drop, we advise having a chunk of crusty bread close at hand.

About 3 pounds of mixed fish, crustaceans, and shrimp, whole, guts and scales on

1 large carrot, thinly sliced

1 yellow onion, sliced

1 head of garlic, crushed

1 bulb of fennel, thinly sliced

2 sprigs fresh thyme

3 bay leaves

Water to cover everything

At least ½ cup pastis, or more according to preference

Salt and pepper to taste

Dash of MSG

Heavy cream, optional and according to preference

1–2 slices grilled or toasted crusty bread

3–4 tablespoons olive oil

Find a suitable pot, which will be big enough to hold all of the ingredients plus a few inches of water. It should be just big enough. Fill the pot around one-third full of water, then place over high heat. When the water comes to a boil, add the fish, the vegetables, and the herbs (the water should cover the ingredients by almost an inch). Add as much pastis as you consider appropriate. Add salt and pepper to taste, along with the MSG. Cook the soup at a boil for fifteen to twenty minutes, or until all the fish have basically fallen apart. While the soup is boiling, we recommend having an aperitif (and what better aperitif than pastis?). Then, if you are using it, add the cream to the soup and continue cooking for a further 5 minutes.

Strain the soup, keeping the liquid and discarding the solids. Make sure to get all of the liquid—strain in small batches and press the mass hard as it pours through the strainer. Correct the seasoning. Serve boiling hot, with chunks of crusty bread drizzled with olive oil.

BANANA LEAF SPANISH MACKEREL, WITH ROASTED SHALLOT PICO

2 SERVINGS This recipe is from our friend Gary Ly, former chef de cuisine at Underbelly in Houston. Not only is he a talented cook, he is a determined lover of seafood.

NUOC MAM:

1 cup water

2 tablespoons Red Boat fish sauce

½ cup sugar

1 clove garlic, minced

Place all ingredients in a pot and bring to a boil. Remove from heat and let cool completely.

ROASTED SHALLOT PICO:

1 teaspoon vegetable oil

3 large shallots, peeled

Salt and pepper to taste

4 grape tomatoes, cut in half

1 sprig mint

4 sprigs cilantro

1 red Thai chili (optional)

Drizzle the oil over the shallots and season with salt and pepper. Place in the oven and roast at 350°F until they start to char and the shallots get really sweet, about 10–15 minutes. Remove from the oven and let cool. Once cooled, cut the shallots in half to smaller pieces while still leaving them in good-size chunks. Mix the shallots with tomatoes, herbs, and red chili if using. Dress with salt and pepper and nuoc mam.

THE FISH:

1 whole Spanish Mackerel, about 1 pound, cleaned and scaled

1 bunch fresh dill, picked and chopped

1 teaspoon ground turmeric

1 clove garlic, minced

Salt and pepper to taste

1 teaspoon vegetable oil

2 large banana leaves

GARNISH: Mint leaves, cilantro sprigs, dill sprigs

Score the mackerel on both sides and pat dry.

Chop 3–4 sprigs of dill very fine and mix in with the turmeric and garlic to make a light paste. Rub the fish all over, both inside and out, with the dill-turmeric paste. Season with salt and pepper, and rub with the oil also.

Lightly heat the banana leaves over a grill or a stove burner to make them more pliable. Wrap the fish in the banana leaves and tie tightly using kitchen twine. Place over a cool spot on the grill and let cook for about 12–16 minutes. This can also be done in the oven at 350°F for about 20 minutes.

Once the fish is cooked through, remove from the oven and carefully cut open the banana leaves. Pour the Shallot Pico over the top with all the juices and vinaigrette. Garnish with mint leaves, cilantro sprigs, and a few more dill sprigs.

BLUEFISH ENSHROUDED IN CURED PORK, THEN SMOKED

4 SERVINGS, AS PART OF A LARGER MEAL Much to our chagrin, Bluefish has never been a popular fish in Texas. As a practical result, this meant that we always had at least one or two Bluefish left over after everything else had been sold. Somewhere along the way, we stumbled upon a French version of what is apparently an Italian preparation. The original uses Bluefish as well. Prosciutto is easiest to use, but any thinly sliced cured pork works fine—bacon has always been our standby, mostly because we don't typically have prosciutto on hand.

It's hot-smoked, so the only thing you need to worry about is the internal temperature of the fish.

1 whole scaled Bluefish, no more than 1½ pounds, gilled and gutted

Salt and coarsely ground black pepper to season the cavity of the fish

1 lemon, thinly sliced

2 sprigs fresh sage

1 sprig fresh rosemary

A few fresh basil leaves

8–10 bacon slices, depending on the length of the fish

GARNISH: Lemon wedges, crusty bread, olive oil

START YOUR SMOKER: The temperature should be less than 200°F. Lacking a smoker, just use a grill (make a small fire, and add wet wood chips as needed along the way).

Lightly salt and pepper the cavity of the fish, then line it with the slices of lemon. Fill the rest of the cavity with the herbs.

On a cutting board, arrange the bacon strips next to each other in a single layer, edges slightly overlapping. The pieces of bacon should be oriented vertically to facilitate wrapping the fish. Place the Bluefish at the "bottom" of the square, wrap the edges of the bacon around the fish, then roll up the fish in the bacon.

Place the wrapped fish in the smoker, and smoke until the internal temperature of the fish is no more than 145°F. This should take an hour or two.

Serve with lemon wedges, crusty bread, and good olive oil.

BOUILLABAISSE

6 GENEROUS SERVINGS This is not a definitive Bouillabaisse, for no such thing exists. It is simple and straightforward and uses only fish. We occasionally add some crustaceans, but absolutely *never ever* any mussels, clams, or other mollusks. American versions of Bouillabaisse almost always veer toward the ornate, the baroque, the ostentatious—the opposite direction, in other words, from the direction they should be going. Let Bouillabaisse be itself; it doesn't need to be anything else. In his *Mediterranean Seafood*, Alan Davidson wrote that "[Bouillabaisse] does not deserve or benefit from the mystique which has been built up around it or the costly ingredients which are sometimes put into it." Let that be a good starting point.

Having emphasized that the dish should be simple (and economical), we now must qualify the argument, for the single most important fish in a Bouillabaisse is scorpionfish—which is (at least in the United States) almost always costly. Yet no other creature may fill the role. If you don't have scorpionfish, you may still make a fish soup, but it will not be Bouillabaisse. The other species may vary, as long as they are all white fish. Our version uses only northwestern Gulf fish, which are, as we have seen, quite similar to those of the Mediterranean. We list substitutions where possible.

The recipe serves about six people. For logistical and aesthetic reasons, it is not advisable to make a smaller batch. In the French fashion, grilled bread and rouille always accompany the soup, and the soup and fish are served separately—*never lumped together in the same bowl*. Our version contains whole fish only, but fillets will work (Alan Davidson's version in *Mediterranean Seafood* uses several species, all boneless;

each is added to the soup at different points during the cooking).

You will need a strong fish broth. We recommend using the Little Fish Soup recipe (page 225), with the following modifications: do not use any cream; add four peeled and seeded tomatoes; add a very healthy pinch of saffron. If you want to remain true to the spirit of the dish, use whole small scorpionfish in place of the mixed little fish. We recommend against the inclusion of shrimp or lobster shells in the broth—let the fish shine.

To make the Bouillabaisse itself, you must, as noted above, have scorpionfish. Aside from that, you will need two other whole white fish. All of the whole fish, scorpionfish included, need to be at least 1 pound, and ideally no bigger. All need to be scaled, finned, gilled, gutted, and washed clean. For the other white fish, we suggest the following: any porgy, any snapper small enough, skinned triggerfish, searobin, large mullet, Creolefish, Longtail Bass, and other such fish.

A pot large enough to barely accommodate the 3 whole fish lying side by side

Enough peeled and sliced yellow potatoes to cover the bottom of the pot in a few thin layers

1 scorpionfish, 1 pound, scaled, gutted, gilled, and finned

2 other white fish, also 1 pound each, scaled, gutted, gilled, and finned

Saffron (quantity determined according to taste)

Peel from one bitter orange (optional)

4 bay leaves

3 sprigs thyme

Salt and pepper

½–1 cup pastis

Enough soup or fumet to cover all of the fish, plus 3 inches

Slices of grilled crusty bread, 2 per person

A large soup tureen

A platter big enough for all the whole fish

ROUILLE:

2 roasted red bell peppers, seeded and peeled

About 1 cup breadcrumbs

2 cloves garlic

½–⅔ cup very good olive oil (a lighter oil, ideally Provençal)

FOR THE ROUILLE: Put all ingredients except olive oil in a food processor, and blend until smooth. With the food processor running slowly, drizzle in the olive oil until you have a thick, emulsified sauce. Season well.

FOR THE BOUILLABAISSE: Place the potatoes in the bottom of the pot. Next arrange the fish, making sure they do not overlap. Next sprinkle on as much saffron as you see fit (the danger with saffron lies in using too little, never too much). Add also the orange peel, herbs, salt and pepper, and a very generous helping of pastis (do not be shy with this). Add as much soup as necessary to cover the fish by a few inches. Turn the flame as high as it will go and bring the contents of the pot to a boil. As soon as the soup boils, immediately lower the heat to a very strong simmer. Cook for 15–20 minutes, or until the fish is fully cooked. Remove from the heat, carefully lift each fish out, and arrange them on a serving platter. Scoop the potatoes out and arrange them around the fish. Bring the broth to a boil once again, season to taste, then strain immediately into the soup tureen.

The tureen, platter, grilled bread, and rouille all come to table. Everyone gets a shallow bowl, into which they place a piece of grilled bread, then some fish, then some potatoes, then rouille and broth.

A meal of Bouillabaisse is incomplete without at least a glass or two of pastis.

DEEP-FRIED PLA TUU KEM (SALTED SCAD)

1 SERVING AS A MAIN DISH; 2 SERVINGS IF FORMING PART OF A LARGER MEAL As versatile as these small salted fish are, we prefer eating them very simply. To accompany the fish, you will want a few lettuce leaves, some lime wedges, and a few sprigs of basil. To enjoy this dish without making your own salted scad, look in the frozen section of any decent Asian market for Pla Tuu Kem (marketed as "steamed Indian Mackerel").

3 tablespoons vegetable oil

2 tablespoons sliced shallot

2 tablespoons sliced garlic

1 Pla Tuu Kem (salted scad or mackerel, see the entry below, page 273 for details on making your own)

4 dried árbol chilies, slightly toasted

½ lime

GARNISH: Lettuce leaves, basil leaves, lime wedges

Heat the oil in a sauté pan; deep-fry first the shallots until they are golden and crispy. Remove the shallots and fry the garlic in the same oil. Do *not* let the garlic get too dark. It needs to be golden, but not a shade darker. Turn the heat up in the pan, add a little more oil, and pan-fry the whole fish. Fry for 3 minutes per side.

Place the fish on a small plate, on which you have arranged the lettuce leaves. Squeeze lime on the fish, then sprinkle with crispy garlic and shallots and árbol chilies. Garnish with the basil leaves and lime wedges.

SPICY AND SOUR BAKED MOONFISH (OR LOOKDOWN)

2 SERVINGS This recipe works for any fish that is small enough to cook whole, from snappers to groupers to grunts and croakers. We found, though, that thin fish work better, as the reduced cooking time leaves flavors bright.

- 3 tablespoons fish sauce
- 2 tablespoons soy sauce
- 5 tablespoons lime juice
- 1 teaspoon sugar
- 1 tablespoon crushed garlic
- 2–5 fresh Thai chilies (according to preference)
- ¼ cup water or vegetable broth
- 1 Moonfish or Lookdown, at least 10–12 inches across, gutted, finned, and gilled
- GARNISH: 2 limes, thinly sliced

Heat the oven to 425°F.

FOR THE SAUCE: In a blender, puree together the fish sauce, soy sauce, lime juice, sugar, garlic, chilies, and water (or broth). Set the sauce aside.

Score the fish well on both sides, then place in a greased baking pan, cover the pan with aluminum foil and bake for approximately 20 minutes. When the fish is done, drizzle all of the sauce over the fish, then garnish with sliced limes. Serve right away.

DEEP-FRIED ALMACO JACK WITH CASHEW SALAD

2 SERVINGS Do not be stingy with the cashew salad.

THE FISH:

- 1 whole small gilled, gutted, and well-scaled Almaco Jack, weighing about 1½ pounds
- 2–3 tablespoons soy sauce
- ½ teaspoon ground white pepper
- 1–2 cups vegetable oil, enough to cover the bottom of the pan with about ½ inch of oil

CASHEW SALAD:

- 5 tablespoons fish sauce
- 5 tablespoons lime juice
- 2 tablespoons sugar
- 1 teaspoon thin-sliced red Thai chili
- 2 tablespoons diced lime (cut the lime into wedges, skin-on, then thinly slice each edge piece into very small wedges)
- 2 tablespoons very thin-sliced lemongrass
- ⅓ cup toasted cashews
- Salt to taste
- GARNISH: Fresh lettuce, sprigs of cilantro, fresh basil

Score the fish very well in both directions on both sides, then marinate with a little soy sauce and ground white pepper for about 30 minutes. In a wok (or sauté pan), heat the oil to about 350°F. Fry the fish, turning at least once during cooking. When the fish is golden on both sides and the meat at the bone is cooked, remove from the fat and let drain for a few minutes on paper towels.

Meanwhile, prepare the salad (which is also the sauce) by stirring together all ingredients, including the diced lime. Season with salt according to your taste.

Arrange the fish on a plate, with some lettuces and sprigs of cilantro and basil. Drizzle the sauce over the entire fish and serve.

DUTCH OVEN VERMILION SNAPPER

2–4 SERVINGS Over the years, Apple has seamlessly woven together Thai (or Isaan) cookery with American cookery, every single time with at least delicious results (PJ insists the world has never tasted chicken and dumplings equal to hers). Here, a simple and stunning Thai recipe is cooked and presented in a Dutch oven. If you have a small enough fish, leave it whole. If the fish is too long to fit comfortably in the Dutch oven, either bend the fish to fit the Dutch oven or cut the fish in two (head and tail sections). As part of a larger meal, the portion below is fine for 2 people. A 2-pound fish might be enough for 4.

1 stalk celery, cut into 2-inch matchsticks

2 carrots, peeled and sliced thin

2 cloves garlic, crushed

4 leaves Napa cabbage, coarsely torn

3 green onions, white and green parts, cut into 2-inch pieces

2–3 pieces ginger, thinly sliced

1 scaled, finned, gilled, and gutted Vermilion Snapper weighing no more than 1¼ pounds

1 tablespoon soy sauce

1 teaspoon salt

1 teaspoon white pepper

2–3 tablespoons water

Start heating the Dutch oven over medium heat. Place all the vegetables in the pan; place the fish on top of the vegetables; season the whole lot with the soy sauce, salt, and pepper. Add 2 to 3 tablespoons water, raise the heat a bit, put the lid on the Dutch oven, and let cook for approximately 15 minutes, or until the fish pulls away from the bone.

Serve in the Dutch oven in the middle of the table. Provide a few side dishes, and a lot of rice.

THE JOY OF LITTLE FISH

1–2 SERVINGS Any white fish works for this, provided the fish is not much longer than your hand. The recipe itself could not be simpler, and the result is sublime. The fish is either deep-fried or fried in a pan with a lot of oil. The following fish work well, though they are certainly not the only options: Mother-in-Law, Piggy Perch, Pigfish, Pinfish, and any other small "perch-like" fish.

2–3 little fish, scaled, gutted, finned, and scored many times on both sides in a hatch pattern

2 tablespoons soy sauce

1 teaspoon salt

1 teaspoon ground white pepper

1–4 cups vegetable oil for frying (depending on whether you are panfrying or deep-frying—for the former, use approximately ½ cup, for the latter, use it all).

Combine the fish with the soy sauce, salt, and pepper and let marinate for 15–20 minutes. Fry the fish for a few minutes per side, until the fish is golden brown and crispy.

Serve immediately, along with some rice, herbs, and maybe a spicy dipping sauce.

STUFFED WHOLE GUAGUANCHE

4–6 SERVINGS Its long cylindrical shape alone makes the Guaguanche a great choice for serving whole; its slightly soft meat reinforces the choice. The stuffing here is rather arbitrary, and, honestly, lots of combinations of vegetables, grains, and other seafood could get the job done just as well, if not better. The point is the fish and the technique, not the stuffing. And even the fish isn't really the point. Any white fish significantly longer than it is tall and not overly bony will work.

2–3 tablespoons olive oil

1 big shallot, diced

2 cloves garlic, minced

At least 1 cup mixed finely diced vegetables (e.g., summer squashes, eggplant, bell pepper)

Tiny dash of pastis (optional)

Generous pinch of saffron

Some good olives, pitted and chopped (use any kind of olive you like, in quantities according to your taste)

1 teaspoon good-quality tomato paste

1 small sprig rosemary

Salt and pepper to taste

4 ounces cooked and diced shrimp (we suggest small White Shrimp, about 60/80 count)

About ¼ cup torn basil leaves

One 2–3-pound Guaguanche (or other suitable fish), scaled, gutted, gilled, finned, and boned according to the instructions for Whole Boneless, Belly Intact (see page 218 for more on this)

Olive oil for drizzling

In a sauté pan, sweat the shallot and garlic in the olive oil. Add the rest of the vegetables, and cook for a few minutes. Add the pastis at this point, if you are going to. Add the saffron, olives, tomato paste, rosemary, and salt and pepper to taste. Let cook a few more minutes, then remove the pan from the heat and let the vegetables cool completely. When the vegetables have cooled, fold in the shrimp and basil, and check seasoning one more time.

Place the Guaguanche belly down on a piece of parchment paper and stuff with the vegetable and shrimp mixture. Use all of the stuffing, even if it overflows a bit. Drizzle some olive oil over the fish.

At this point, the fish can either be steamed or roasted. Steaming takes about 10–12 minutes, and roasting takes about 15–25. Keep the fish on the parchment, and simply transfer the whole thing to the roasting pan or the steamer. Regardless of how you cook the fish, you will be using the same vessel for cooking and serving, for the fish is far too delicate to transfer after it is cooked.

TRIGGERFISH FRIED WITH LEMONGRASS AND LIME LEAF

2 SERVINGS This recipe is best prepared in a wok, Dutch oven, or frying pan large enough to comfortably accommodate the fish; a larger deep-fryer will get the job done, but it is not ideal.

> 1 whole Triggerfish, about 2 pounds, completely skinned, finned, and gutted
>
> 1 thick stalk of lemongrass, bent in two
>
> Vegetable oil to fill the wok enough to barely deep-fry the fish
>
> Cornstarch or tapioca starch, seasoned with salt and white pepper, for dredging
>
> 1 small handful of lemongrass, cut in chiffonade
>
> 1 smaller handful of whole Makrut lime leaves
>
> GARNISH: Lettuce leaves, herb sprigs

SAUCE:

> 3–7 fresh Thai chilies, according to preference
>
> 2–3 tablespoons peeled garlic, according to preference
>
> 1 bunch cilantro stems
>
> 2 tablespoons sugar
>
> ½ cup fish sauce
>
> ⅓ cup lime juice
>
> Salt to taste

FOR THE SAUCE: Place all the ingredients in a blender and process on high speed until everything is finely chopped.

FOR THE FISH: Stuff the bent stalk of lemongrass into the Triggerfish's mouth and into its abdominal cavity. Score the fish in both directions along its body, cutting down almost to the bone.

Heat the oil in the wok until it is at least 350°F. Dredge the fish in the corn or tapioca starch, and slide it into the oil and let cook for about 5 minutes on each side, basting the exposed side all the while. Right when the fish is cooked, add the chiffonade of lemongrass and the lime leaves to the oil. Stand back slightly when you add these, as there will be some popping and sizzling. Let the lemongrass and leaves cook for no more than 10 or 15 seconds, then remove everything with a slotted spoon. Let the fish, lemongrass, and lime leaves drain on a paper towel.

Place the Triggerfish on a plate, perhaps decorated with some lettuce leaves or herb sprigs. Sprinkle over the fish all of the lemongrass and lime leaves. Serve with a large ramekin of sauce on the side.

BLACKFIN TUNA, BARDED AND ROASTED

10–15 SERVINGS, DEPENDING ON THE SIZE OF THE FISH No tuna but the Blackfin can be cooked like this, at least not without access to an industrial oven, for the tuna is cooked whole, head and all. For best results, do not use a Blackfin larger than 10 pounds. This recipe calls for roasting the fish in the oven, which produces a fine result. However, spit-roasting, or even cooking the fish in front of a large fire *à la ficelle* (where the fish is tightly trussed and then hung by the tail a foot away from the flames, which will cause the fish to continuously rotate, creating a vertical rotisserie).

> 1 Blackfin Tuna, weighing less than 10 pounds, head on, tail on; gilled and gutted
>
> A handful combined of the following herbs: basil, parsley, rosemary, sage, tarragon
>
> 1–2 preserved lemons, quartered
>
> 4–10 peeled cloves of garlic, according to your taste
>
> ¼–1 cup pitted black olives, according to taste (optional)
>
> Sheets of pig fat (this can be scrap, with skin attached, as it won't be eaten), enough to wrap the fish in at least 2 layers (The scrap and fat are readily available from a butcher. You might need to do some slicing and trimming and cutting to get the required shapes; alternatively, use a few large sheets of caul fat, enough to wrap the fish 5 times over.)
>
> Salt and pepper to season

For best results, we suggest skinning the tuna, which, given the tuna's thick skin, is a rather straightforward process (see page 218 for more on skinning a fish). If you do not feel up to the task, fear not, the recipe will still work. It will not be as good, however.

After skinning the fish, wash it well inside and out with salt water, removing the last vestiges of viscera, blood, and bits. Stuff the tuna's abdominal and gill cavities with the herbs, lemon, garlic, and olives, if using. Stuff as much as you can into the cavities; you cannot use too much.

Place the sheets of pork fat on a work surface, arranged in 2 large rectangles large enough to envelope the fish completely. One rectangle needs to be a touch bigger than the other.

Season the outside of the fish very well with salt and pepper. Place the fish on the smaller arrangement of fat and commence wrapping. After the fish is wrapped in the first layer of fat, you will have a fat-covered bundle, which you will then place on the larger rectangle of fat and wrap again. When that is complete, truss the whole thing very well from end to end with kitchen twine.

Preheat the oven to 400°F. Place the fish bundle on a perforated roasting pan over a backing pan, and place the lot in the oven. After 10 minutes, reduce the heat to 350°F, and continue cooking until the internal temperature of the fish is 145°F or done to your liking. This is an old-fashioned recipe, so we prefer it cooked almost well done. It will take 30 minutes to 1 hour or more, depending on the size of the fish.

When the fish is done, remove it from the oven and allow it to rest for just a few minutes. Do not cut off the fat yet. Carve through the fat at the table to reveal the feast awaiting.

This is obviously a dish best shared with friends.

CHAPTER 22
CUT FISH

BLACKENED BLACK DRUM WITH SPICY SHRIMP, OKRA, LEMON, TOMATOES, AND SAUCE AMERICAINE

2 SERVINGS We first met Antoine Ware when he was the sous chef at Catalan under Chris Shepherd, and he has remained one of our favorite people ever since. As demonstrated with this recipe, Antoine's food is a seamless joining of Gulf Coast tradition (he is a New Orleans native) and modern technique. Of course, he loves fish also.

THE FISH:

- 1½ tablespoons paprika
- 1 tablespoon garlic powder
- 1 tablespoon onion powder
- 1 teaspoon black pepper
- 1 tablespoon dried thyme
- 1 teaspoon cayenne pepper
- 1 teaspoon salt
- ½ cup melted butter
- Two 6–8-ounce boneless, skinless Black Drum Fillets
- 3 teaspoons butter
- ½ cup grape tomatoes
- ½ cup okra, thinly sliced
- ½ cup shallots, thinly sliced
- ½ cup medium shrimp, peeled and deveined
- Juice from half a lemon

SAUCE:

- 2 tablespoons olive oil
- 1 tablespoon butter
- 1 pound shrimp shells
- 2 tablespoons minced shallots
- 1 tablespoon minced garlic
- 2 tablespoons tomato puree
- ½ cup brandy
- 1 cup shrimp or fish stock
- ½ cup white wine
- 1 tablespoon chopped parsley
- Salt and pepper to taste
- 1 cup heavy cream
- 3 tablespoons butter
- Cayenne pepper to taste

FOR THE FISH: In a small bowl, mix together the paprika, garlic powder, onion powder, black pepper, dried thyme, cayenne pepper, and salt and set aside. Heat a cast-iron pan on high heat for about 10 minutes until hot.

Pour the melted butter in a small bowl. Dip the fish in the melted butter, coating both sides. Sprinkling both sides with the blackened seasoning, gently pat the fish.

Place the fish into the hot cast-iron pan, along with 2 teaspoons of the butter, cooking until it has a charred-like appearance, about 2–3 minutes. Turn the fish over and cook for about 2–3 minutes more.

In another sauté pan on medium heat, heat the remaining butter and sauté the tomatoes, okra, shallots, and shrimp for about 3–4 minutes or until the shrimp is done, then add the lemon juice at the end.

FOR THE SAUCE: In a sauté pan, heat the olive oil and butter. When the pan is hot, add the shrimp shells. Sauté the shells for 2–3 minutes, or until bright red. Add the shallots and garlic and sauté for 1 minute. Stir in the tomato puree. Flambé the brandy. Pour in the shrimp stock and white wine. Season with parsley, salt, and pepper. Bring the liquid up to a boil. Simmer for 15 minutes. Remove from the heat and strain through a fine chinois into a sauce pot. Whisk in the cream and bring up to a boil. Reduce to a simmer. Simmer for 2–3 minutes. Add in the 3 tablespoons butter. Season with salt and cayenne to taste.

HARDHEAD CATFISH *LAAP*

4 SMALL SERVINGS We could have used literally any animal in this book for this recipe—that is the versatility of *laap*, the famous Isaan (and Lao) dish. While the meat (or sometimes vegetable) is interchangeable, the rest of the dish is set and standard. Amounts or ratios of ingredients may be altered according to taste. We always include saw-leaf (culantro) in the herb mix, but this is not crucial.

- About 2 pounds whole, gutted Hardhead Catfish
- 1–2 tablespoons lime juice
- 1 tablespoon fish sauce
- 1 tablespoon shallot, sliced
- 1 teaspoon chili powder
- ½ tablespoon rice powder (this is *not* rice starch, but rather raw sticky rice, toasted to golden brown in the oven and then ground as fine as semolina)

- 2 tablespoons mixed chopped cilantro, green onion, saw-leaf (optional), and mint
- **GARNISH:** Green cabbage leaves torn in two, mint sprigs, sliced cucumbers

Grill the Hardheads thoroughly, then pick every bit of meat you can off the bones. Discard the bones and set the meat aside. In a mixing bowl, combine the lime juice, fish sauce, and shallot. Add the grilled fish meat, chili powder, rice powder, and mixed herbs, and toss until the fish pieces are uniformly coated with the rest of the ingredients. Serve on a small plate or small bowl, with the green cabbage, mint sprigs, and sliced cucumbers. And, of course, have some steamed rice or sticky rice handy.

HAY-SMOKED MACKEREL

APPROXIMATELY 4 SMALL SERVINGS No one ever judged our fish with a more critical eye than Horiuchi Manabu, the longtime executive chef at Kata Robata Sushi and Grill. No one in Houston (with the possible exception of Frixos Chrisinis of Blue Horizon Wholesale Seafood and Retail Market) loves fish more than Hori does. He routinely passed over whole coolers of fish, looking for the few that passed his test. Normally, such pickiness by chefs was more than slightly irritating. But the look on Hori's face when he found a fish he liked made up for it all. It goes without saying that no one we have ever met can prepare fish like Hori can. His recipe, in his words, is brief.

About 12 ounces Spanish Mackerel fillet

Dry hay for smoking

MARINADE:

3 tablespoons soy sauce

1 tablespoon sake

1 tablespoon mirin

"1. Get some fresh sashimi-grade Spanish Mackerel.

2. Cut it into fillets.

3. Marinate for 15 minutes with 3 parts soy sauce, 1 part sake, 1 part mirin.

4. Put the hay on the grill.

5. Sear the mackerel on the grill, then smoke for about 1 minute.

6. Slice the fillets with a sharp knife.

7. Enjoy your hay-smoked mackerel."

FRIED FISH

Everyone eats fried fish. Even some people who don't like fish eat fried fish. The following three recipes can be used for any white fish worth frying. We have no preference as to taste. As for utility, southern-fried is best for firmer white fish like Redfish, drums, and large snapper; English-fried works for delicate white fish like hakes, porgies, and small snappers; and chicken-fried is ideal for fish on the bone.

All three styles go well with mayonnaise—or aioli-based sauces (remoulade, tartar sauce, etc.)—or cocktail sauce, or ketchup, or anything else that tastes good with fried foods.

APPLE'S SOUTHERN-FRIED REDFISH (THE KIDS' STANDBY SACK LUNCH)

ALL THREE RECIPES SERVE APPROXIMATELY 4 PEOPLE   The crust stays intact and pretty crusty for hours, so this is the perfect to-go fish.

Canola oil for frying

1 cup cornmeal

¼ cup all-purpose flour

2 teaspoons salt

1 teaspoon pepper

1 egg, beaten

1½–2 pounds Almaco Jack fillet, skinned and sliced into long pieces ¼–½ inch thick

Heat about ½ inch of oil in a cast-iron skillet on medium-high heat. Mix together the cornmeal, flour, salt, and pepper. Dip the fish in the beaten egg, then dredge in the cornmeal mix. Fry in the cast-iron skillet, about 3 minutes per side. Drain well on paper towels.

ENGLISH-FRIED BROTULA

This recipe is included courtesy of our friend Richard Knight.

1½–2 pounds Brotula fillet, skinned and sliced into long pieces about 1 inch thick

Enough vegetable oil to fill the deep-fryer

BATTER:

2 cups all-purpose flour

2 cups cornstarch

1 teaspoon baking powder

1 teaspoon salt

One 12-ounce bottle of beer

One 10-ounce bottle of soda water (or more)

Heat the oil in the deep-fryer to 350°F. Combine all of the dry mix ingredients together in a large bowl. Add the beer and soda water, whisking steadily all the while. You'll not want to see any actual fish, just the batter, so if the batter seems thin, add a very small amount of flour and cornstarch, in equal parts.

Dip the fish slices in the batter, making sure every bit of surface area is coated well. Fry in the oil for about 3–4 minutes per side, until the internal temperature reaches at least 145°F. Drain well on paper towels.

CHICKEN-FRIED RIBBONFISH

Very firm fish don't benefit from this treatment, and delicate boneless fish will fall apart. Any white fish on the bone is good, though. Ribbonfish might be the best.

One 2–2½-pound whole Ribbonfish (at least 3 feet long), gutted, fins removed, and cut into 2–3-inch chunks (discard the head)

1–2 cups buttermilk

1–2 cups flour, well seasoned with salt, lots of black pepper, some cayenne, and other dry spices if you so desire

Vegetable oil for frying

Soak the chunks of Ribbonfish in the buttermilk for 2 hours.

If you're using a deep-fryer, turn it on to 350°F. If using a cast-iron pan, heat about an inch or so of vegetable oil over high heat.

Piece by piece, remove the chunks from the buttermilk and immediately dredge in the seasoned flour, coating the fish very well.

Fry the pieces a few at a time, for about 4–5 minutes, flipping the pieces at least once. When the crust is golden, the fish is ready (the fish will actually finish cooking slightly before the crust, but this is no problem, as the flesh is rather unctuous). Remove from the oil when done, and drain well.

SALTFISH ESCOVITCH

4 SERVINGS AS AN APPETIZER OR SNACK Escabeche is originally a Mediterranean dish made by frying seafood (or meat or vegetables) and then plunging them immediately into a strong marinade composed of vinegar, olive oil, herbs, sliced carrots, and sliced onion. Versions exist all over the world now. This one is from Jamaica (where the word "escabeche" gradually evolved into "escovitch"), courtesy of our friend Milton Jones (another lover of seafood . . . but only cooked seafood!). He explains that the ubiquitous form uses salt cod (called saltfish). This dish tastes good the day it is made, but is significantly better after a day or two.

> 10 ounces salt cod (weight before soaking)
>
> 1–3 cups vegetable oil for frying

MARINADE:

> 1½ cups white vinegar
>
> 1 large carrot, peeled and julienned
>
> 1 large shallot or 1 small yellow onion, peeled and sliced
>
> 1 red bell pepper, seeded and sliced
>
> 2 mild fresh chilies (e.g., serrano), seeded and sliced
>
> 2 cloves of garlic, minced
>
> 4 sprigs fresh thyme, chopped
>
> Generous pinch of ground allspice
>
> Salt and black pepper to taste

Soak the cod overnight in cold water, changing the water three times.

Prepare the marinade by whisking together all ingredients. Taste for seasoning and be careful with the salt—even after soaking, salt cod is still a little salty.

Heat the oil in a Dutch oven. Cut the salt cod into thick slices and fry briskly until the salt cod is fully cooked, then remove the pieces from the heat, drain quickly, and place immediately into the marinade. The fish should be completely covered. Cover and refrigerate overnight at least.

Eat the next day with bread or rice or just by itself.

NEEDLEFISH OR HOUNDFISH PERSILLADE

4 SERVINGS This is originally a Bordelaise recipe for freshwater eel, but since our local waters provide more Houndfish and Needlefish than American Eel, and since the first two have the same long cylindrical body as the last, we adapted the recipe.

> ½ head of garlic, peeled
>
> 1 bunch flat-leaf parsley, picked
>
> 1 large shallot, diced
>
> 2 sprigs thyme, leaves only
>
> 2–3 pounds Houndfish or Needlefish, scaled, gutted, headed, tailed, finned, and cut into 3-inch chunks
>
> 2–3 tablespoons olive oil
>
> 1–2 tablespoons red wine vinegar
>
> Salt and coarsely milled black pepper

In a mortar and pestle, reduce the garlic, parsley, shallot, and thyme to a coarse mass. Transfer this from the mortar to a mixing bowl. Add to the bowl the fish, olive oil, and red wine vinegar. Season liberally with salt and pepper and mix well.

Grill the fish chunks on a low fire, basting with the marinade continuously, for 10 minutes a side; or cook them under a broiler, about 7 inches from the flame, about 7 minutes per side; or roast them in a hot oven; or cook them in a pan (though this is by far the most inferior way).

FLOUNDER OFF THE BONE

ABOUT 12 SERVINGS (ONLY A FEW SLICES PER PERSON) If you are catching your own fish, we hope you remember to kill and bleed it before it goes into the cooler, and we further hope that the cooler contains not just ice, but a decent amount of seawater (see page 15 for more on this). If you should catch a flounder, and you dispatch it correctly, and later at home you happen to have a friend or two about, treat yourselves to one of the Gulf's finer delicacies.

> 1 flounder, about 3 pounds, ike jime slaughtered and cooled, at least 1 but no more than 3 days out of the water
>
> 1 very sharp fish knife
>
> A few slices of lime, maybe some other citrus as well
>
> A little bit of coarse salt

Fillet the flounder, taking care to keep the feather meat intact. Skin the fletches, then, on a clean cutting board, slice one fletch into pieces less than ⅛ inch thick. Take a slice, squeeze on a tiny amount of lime juice, add a little bit of salt, and eat. Savor and enjoy. Bid your friends do the same. Eat more, slice more, and repeat. Four people thus positioned can take care of a raw flounder rather quickly.

BONNETHEAD CEVICHE

4 SERVINGS AS AN APPETIZER; 2 AS A MEAL By and large, we don't get excited about eating shark, unless the shark is prepared as a ceviche, and then we get a little more excited. If it's a Bonnethead (or to a lesser extent a Sharpnose), we get considerably more excited, for both the Bonnethead and the Sharpnose are small species of shark; the most commonly caught are around 24 inches in length. We use saw-leaf (culantro) instead of cilantro.

> 1 pound Bonnethead fillet, skinned and diced
>
> 3 tablespoons tamarind juice
>
> 3 tablespoons grapefruit juice
>
> 3 tablespoons lime juice
>
> 2 Persian cucumbers, peeled and diced
>
> 2 ripe tomatoes, seeded and diced
>
> 5 cloves garlic, peeled and minced
>
> 2 shallots, sliced
>
> 2 jalapeño peppers, diced (do not remove the seeds), or more, according to taste
>
> ½ bunch saw-leaf, leaves only, chopped
>
> 1 bunch green onions, sliced (greens and whites)
>
> Salt and pepper to taste

Place all the ingredients in a mixing bowl and combine well. You can eat it right away, but we suggest letting it sit overnight. The texture of the shark will be vastly improved.

POT ROAST

6 SERVINGS   We make this very rarely. The dish serves at least six people.

Few fish are large enough to provide the mass necessary to make a real pot roast. Moreover, the fish must not be too delicate, as it needs to withstand prolonged heat. These parameters narrow the choices somewhat. Use Mako, Alligator Gar, Swordfish, larger Wahoo, and similar fish. You will want part of the saddle or a chunk of the tail. You will need a pot big enough to sear the fish and accommodate all of the ingredients, but just barely.

> One 2–3-pound chunk of fish, skinned if need be
>
> Some olive oil
>
> 3 carrots, peeled and cut into large pieces
>
> 2 potatoes, peeled and cut into large pieces
>
> 3 stalks of celery, cut into 1-inch pieces
>
> 1 leek, white only, washed and sliced thinly
>
> 1 head of garlic, peeled and lightly crushed
>
> 4 bay leaves
>
> 2 sprigs thyme
>
> 1 sprig rosemary
>
> A little white wine
>
> Water
>
> Salt
>
> Pepper

Preheat the oven to 300°F.

Season well the chunk of fish and heat the Dutch oven or pot. Sear the fish in a good amount of oil on all sides and remove from the pot. Drain the oil and return the pot to the heat. Place the fish back in, then arrange all of the vegetables and herbs around it. Pour over the wine, bring to a boil, then add enough water to fill the pot about a quarter of the way. There needs to be a decent amount of liquid, but you don't want the vegetables swimming and floating. Bring to a boil again and season to taste. Place in the oven, cook for about an hour, turning the fish every 15 minutes or so, until the internal temperature is right over 145°F (small, delicate white fish fillets need more precise cooking time; larger chunks of steak fish benefit from a slightly higher internal temperature).

BAKED QUEEN SNAPPER WITH ARTICHOKE *BARIGOULE*, PANCETTA, AND CALABRIAN CHILIES

4 SERVINGS We think we sold fish to Mike Potowski at both Benjy's On Washington and at Benjy's in Rice Village, and maybe even another restaurant before that, and as this recipe shows, he has always been a man to appreciate a good fish. There are not as many of that type as one would hope.

> **Four 4-ounce Queen Snapper fillet portions, skin off**

MARINADE:

> **4 tablespoons soy sauce**
>
> **2 tablespoons mirin**
>
> **1 tablespoon fish sauce**
>
> **Pinch of kosher salt**
>
> **1 teaspoon ground black pepper**
>
> **2 cups dashi broth**
>
> **4 tablespoons cane sugar**
>
> **1 teaspoon minced garlic**

BARIGOULE:

> **¼ cup pancetta, diced**
>
> **¼ cup sliced sweet onions**
>
> **4 artichokes, cleaned, blanched, and quartered**
>
> **¼ cup diced yellow pepper**
>
> **2 tablespoons lemon juice**
>
> **1 tablespoon white soy sauce**
>
> **1 teaspoon Calabrian chilies**
>
> **1 tablespoon thyme, chopped**
>
> **1 bay leaf**
>
> **½ cup dashi**
>
> **3 tablespoons butter**
>
> **Salt and pepper to taste**
>
> **2 tablespoons chopped parsley**

FOR THE MARINADE: Combine all the marinade ingredients in a mixing bowl until the sugar is dissolved. Add the Queen Snapper fillets and let sit for 2 hours.

Preheat the oven to 400°F. Place all the fish and marinade in a clay pot and place in the oven for 35–45 minutes.

FOR THE *BARIGOULE*: In a large pan, sauté the pancetta until lightly browned; remove all but 1 tablespoon of the pancetta fat and add the onions and sauté. Add the remaining ingredients except the butter and parsley, then cover and place in the oven for 15 minutes. Remove from the oven and gently fold in the butter and season with salt and pepper. Add chopped parsley just before serving.

Place the Queen Snapper on a plate and top with artichoke *barigoule*.

RED SNAPPER BAKED WITH CHEDDAR CHEESE AND MAYONNAISE

4 SERVINGS This may be the oddest recipe in the book. We have heard several versions, all from salty old commercial Red Snapper fishermen. The recipe dispenses with common wisdom and accepted seafood taboos: not only is cheese used directly with white fish, but the cheese is yellow cheddar from the grocery store, not a cheesemonger; and the mayonnaise is served hot. We admit this is not how we cook fish or, for that matter, anything. Yet it is undeniably satisfying.

> **1½ pounds Red Snapper fillet, skin off (The fillets need to be thick, so try to get them from a 5–7-pound fish.)**
>
> **Mayonnaise, enough to coat one side of the fillet(s)**
>
> **Shredded cheddar cheese, enough to cover one side of the fillet(s)**

OPTIONAL TOPPINGS:

> Sliced green onion
>
> Chopped cilantro
>
> Sliced olives
>
> Bacon bits
>
> Other items to your liking

Preheat the oven to 375°F. Line a baking sheet (large enough to accommodate the snapper fillet) with a sheet of aluminum foil. Spray with nonstick spray, then place the fillets on the sheet. Smear the fillet with a layer of mayonnaise, thin or thick, according to preference. Sprinkle on top of this the cheese, the amount again determined by personal preference. If desired, add optional toppings (one may also improvise and use toppings not listed). Bake the fish for about 25 minutes, or until it is well cooked. Serve as is, on the pan.

SHEEPSHEAD AMANDINE

4 SERVINGS   Daniel Blue is a New Orleans native, and is thus familiar with the charms of the Sheepshead. He is also just about the best chef we know. Here he prepares Sheepshead in a classic French style.

> 4 boneless, skinless portions of Sheepshead, about 5 ounces each

THE DREDGE:

> 2 cups almond flour
>
> 4 cups all-purpose flour
>
> Pinch of salt
>
> A few cracks of black pepper
>
> Mix all ingredients together.

THE EGG WASH:

> 2 eggs
>
> 2 cups milk
>
> Pinch of salt
>
> Beat eggs well and add the milk and salt.

SAUCE:

> 1½ cups butter
>
> ½ cup slivered almonds
>
> Juice of 1 lemon
>
> 2 tablespoons minced parsley

Slice the butter and reserve half. In a hot pan, brown half of the butter; once browned, add almonds to toast, then allow to cool slightly. Once cooled slightly, add lemon juice and melt in the reserved butter. Add parsley to finish.

FOR THE HARICOTS VERTS:

> 8 ounces haricots verts, tops and bottoms removed

Blanch in salty water until al dente, then shock in ice water to keep the color and stop the cooking.

TO FINISH THE DISH: Place fish in egg wash, then dredge in the dry mixture. Fry in a deep pan or tabletop fryer at 350°F until golden. Serve with the blanched haricots verts and top all with the brown butter–almond sauce.

CAST-IRON-ROASTED SHORTFIN MAKO SHARK WITH RIO GRANDE GRAPEFRUIT

4 SERVINGS   A few years back, while he was the chef at Café Rabelais in Houston's Rice Village, Jason Kerr was one of those chefs who never met a fish he didn't like. He also never met a fish he couldn't sell (at least in theory). This is his recipe for Shortfin Mako shark steaks.

> **Four 1-inch-thick fresh Shortfin Mako steaks (5–8 ounces per steak)**
>
> **4 tablespoons olive oil**
>
> **Salt and freshly ground black pepper**
>
> **2 Rio Grande grapefruits**
>
> **1 shallot, chopped**
>
> **½ teaspoon local honey**
>
> **1 tablespoon sherry vinegar**
>
> **3 tablespoons Texas olive oil**
>
> **¼ teaspoon freshly chopped tarragon or a pinch of dried**
>
> **GARNISH: Picked tarragon leaves**

To pan-roast the Mako, get a charcoal or stove-top cast-iron skillet very hot. Brush the fish with olive oil, and sprinkle with salt and pepper. Grill each side for only 2–2½ minutes. The center should be pink, like a medium steak, or the shark will be tough and dry. Allow to rest for 5–10 minutes before serving.

Using a sharp knife, cut away the peel and white parts from 2 grapefruits, then cut between the membranes to remove the segments. Squeeze the membranes over a bowl to extract the juice.

Whisk together the grapefruit juice, shallot, honey, vinegar, olive oil, and finely chopped fresh tarragon. Arrange the grapefruit segments on a platter and drizzle with the dressing. Lay the steaks over the fruit and garnish with the tarragon leaves.

RAY OR SKATE WING WITH BROWN BUTTER

4 SERVINGS   This is a completely conventional, traditional recipe. Also, and perhaps not coincidentally, it is the best recipe for these kinds of fish. All you will need for this recipe is the skinned wings; there is no need to carve them off the bone (see page 134 for more on breaking down a skate or ray). Any ray or skate will do, as long as cooking times are adjusted.

> **2–3 tablespoons olive oil**
>
> **1½ pounds ray or skate wing, skinned, bone in, and cut into 4 chunks**
>
> **Flour for dredging**
>
> **3–4 tablespoons butter**
>
> **Juice from 1 or 2 lemons**
>
> **1–2 tablespoons fried capers**
>
> **1–2 tablespoons toasted slivered almonds**
>
> **2 teaspoons chopped parsley**
>
> **GARNISH: Lemon slices**

Heat olive oil in a nonstick sauté pan. Dredge the pieces of ray in the flour and shake off excess. When the oil is hot but not yet smoking, add the pieces of ray, one at a time. Cook for about 4 minutes per side, or until golden brown and you see the ropes of muscles starting to slightly pull away from the bone. When the fish has been flipped and is totally cooked, remove to drain on paper towels.

For the sauce, pour the excess fat from the sauté pan, then add the butter. Let the butter melt, sizzle, and start to brown. When the solids in the butter have browned, and a nutty aroma emerges, add the lemon juice, capers, and almonds. The mix will spit and splash. Keep the heat high and stir to amalgamate the sauce. Taste for seasoning, add the parsley, and remove from the heat.

Put the pieces of ray on a plate, spoon the sauce over them, and garnish with lemon slices. Serve with light vegetables and some good bread.

ESCOLAR ON A GRILL, WITH GREEN MANGO SALAD

4 SERVINGS In small doses, Escolar is a superior grill fish. It is already rich, so needs little more than a bright and acidic accompaniment. But eat only one Escolar steak.

4 Escolar steaks, 4 ounces each

SALAD:

¼ cup diced green mango

2 tablespoons diced mixed bell pepper

2 tablespoons diced onion

2 teaspoons chopped cilantro

1 teaspoon diced jalapeño pepper (with or without seeds, depending on heat level desired)

2 tablespoons lime juice

1 teaspoon sugar

½ teaspoon salt

FOR THE SALAD: Combine all ingredients in a mixing bowl and taste for seasoning.

FOR THE FISH: Grill the Escolar over hot coals, marking the fish for a few minutes on all sides. To serve, pour the salad over the fish.

DOG SNAPPER TOM KHA

4 SERVINGS, WITH RICE The usual meat in Tom Kha, the famous Thai coconut and galangal soup, is chicken. A large Dog Snapper tastes a lot more like chicken than fish, so it can easily substitute, not just in this dish but in most dishes calling for boneless chicken meat (especially breast meat).

2 cups coconut milk

1 cup water

Salt to taste

3 stalks lemongrass, thinly sliced

5 slices galangal

3 Makrut lime leaves

3 shallots, cut into eighths

One 12-ounce Dog Snapper fillet, skin off, cut into slices no bigger than ½ inch thick and 2 inches long

1 cup mushrooms, sliced (we suggest straw or oyster, but any kind will do)

5 red Bird's eye chilies

2 tablespoons fish sauce

2 tablespoons lime juice

1 tablespoon tamarind juice

¼ cup cilantro sprigs

¼ cup green onion, cut into ½-inch chunks

Salt to taste

Heat the coconut milk, water, and salt in a small soup pot. Add the lemongrass, galangal, lime leaves, and shallots and bring to a boil. Reduce the heat a little bit, add the snapper and mushrooms, and cook until both are cooked through. Add the Thai chilies, fish sauce, lime juice, and tamarind juice. Cook for another 5 minutes. Remove the pot from the heat and stir in the cilantro and green onion. Season to taste.

Serve with steamed jasmine rice.

SMOKED PEACHBELLY SWORDFISH (BELLY)

3–4 SMALL SERVINGS This recipe will succeed with regular Swordfish, and with sword steak instead of sword belly; and in place of Swordfish, you can use amberjack, Cobia, tuna, or other fish (making sure to adjust curing times). But Swordfish belly is by far the superior choice. And if you ever have the chance, by all means use Peachbelly Swordfish.

CURE:

2 parts salt

1 part brown sugar

Pink salt, 8 percent of the total weight of sugar and salt

Pinch of MSG

1 pound Peachbelly Swordfish belly, trimmed, skinned, and cleaned

Good olive oil

Combine all of the cure ingredients, adding, according to taste: herbs, peppercorns, and spices.

Rub the belly with the cure, making sure every bit of surface area gets covered. Place the belly in a container just barely big enough to hold it, sprinkle with a little more cure, then refrigerate for up to 48 hours, turning the belly every few hours.

When the belly is very firm all around but not too salty, remove it from the cure, wash off excess cure, and dry very well. Rub the belly with olive oil, then place, uncovered, in the refrigerator for 1 hour or 2 so the surface may dry completely.

Ideally, the smoker should be no hotter than 145°F. Hot-smoke the belly until the internal temperature of the belly is 145°F. Let cool, wrap tightly, and store in the refrigerator or freezer.

STEAMED WARSAW GROUPER WITH DRIED SHRIMP SOFRITO

4 SERVINGS We met Justin Yu a few months before Oxheart opened and spent the next couple of years delivering an astonishing amount of fish to the restaurant. He was one of our more demanding customers, but also the most loyal. This is his recipe for Warsaw Grouper, a difficult fish to sell to high-end restaurants.

Enough grapeseed oil to cover the bottom of the pan by about ⅛ inch

2½ cups white onion, diced

1¾ cups dried shrimp, ground to a powder

¼ cup garlic, microplaned

¼ teaspoon ground black pepper

⅛ teaspoon ground red pepper flakes

¼ teaspoon ground coriander

⅛ teaspoon thyme leaves

1 teaspoon sherry vinegar

1 cup water

2 teaspoons salt

2½ teaspoons sugar

Four 6-ounce portions Warsaw Grouper fillet, skin off

FOR THE SOFRITO: In a heavy-bottomed pan, add about ⅛ inch of grapeseed oil. Heat to right before smoking temperature. The oil should have a shimmery, wavy look.

Add the diced onions and immediately stir to coat with oil. Turn the heat down to low and cover with a lid. Add half of the dried, ground shrimp. Cook on low, stirring often, until the onions are lightly golden and the shrimp is fragrant, about 30 minutes.

Add the garlic, ground black and red pepper, and ground coriander. Cook with the lid off until aromatic, about 10 minutes.

Take the sofrito off the heat and add the thyme, the other half of the dried shrimp powder and the sherry vinegar. Let this mixture sit for at least 30 minutes off the heat. Strain the oil and the solids out. Keep both at room temperature while cooking the fish.

FOR THE BRINE: Mix the water, salt, and sugar together. Warm until the salt and sugars are melted. Let this liquid cool to room temperature.

BRINE THE FISH: After the fish is cut into portions, pour the brine onto the portions and leave on for 12 minutes. Strain and cool the portions.

Set up a steamer. Steam the portions of the fish for about 9–12 minutes each, or until a toothpick can smoothly go through the fillet.

To plate, transfer the fish from the steamer to a bowl. Coat with a generous coating of the oil saved from making the sofrito. Season with flaky salt. Spoon a dollop of the shrimp sofrito over top. Serve with a small, crunchy salad or a bowl of warm white rice.

TAWD MAN PLA (THAI LADYFISH FRITTERS)

ABOUT 8 FRITTERS The original Thai dish uses a Southeast Asian fish called the Featherback (*Chitala ornata*), a bony freshwater fish with meat every bit as mushy as that of the Ladyfish. The meat is typically scraped off the bones with a spoon, then sometimes passed through a screen to eliminate awkward bones (of which there are many). Ladyfish is slightly easier to fillet, but you will still have to pass it through a food mill or sieve to get rid of the bones. In all, Ladyfish is a perfect substitute for the Featherback.

1 pound Ladyfish meat, boneless and skinless, and passed through a food mill, tamis, or sieve

1 teaspoon salt

4 tablespoons ice water

5 tablespoons Thai red curry paste

1 egg

1 teaspoon sugar

½ tablespoon fish sauce

⅓ cup fresh, uncooked green beans, thinly sliced

2 tablespoons Makrut lime leaf, cut in chiffonade

Canola oil for frying

GARNISH: Lime wedges

Put the Ladyfish meat in the freezer for 30 minutes (it is mushy under the best conditions, so freezing makes it easier to handle). Place the fish in the food processor, along with the salt and ice water. Blend the fish until it is completely pureed and very starchy. Add the curry paste, egg, sugar, and fish sauce. Process again until the mass is homogeneous, then place it in a mixing bowl. Add the green beans and Makrut lime leaves and mix well.

Form into thin patties about 3 inches across and ⅓ inch thick. Deep-fry or panfry until the fritters are golden brown and cooked throughout. Drain well on paper towels and serve with lime wedges.

PHAT PRIEW WAN (SWEET-AND-SOUR POMPANO DOLPHINFISH)

4 SERVINGS, AS PART OF A MEAL WITH RICE Most likely, it is the addition of ketchup and pineapple that makes this ostensibly Thai dish so familiar to Americans. There is nothing dramatic or even particularly interesting about the recipe. It just tastes good. In Thailand, it may be found wherever tourists congregate. Pompano Dolphinfish is not the obvious choice of fish. It is more commonly made with catfish, tilapia, or marine fish like snappers.

- One 1-pound Pompano Dolphinfish fillet, cut into approximately 1×1-inch pieces
- 1 cup tempura flour or all-purpose flour
- 2 tablespoons vegetable oil
- 1 teaspoon crushed garlic
- ¼ cup sweet onion, sliced
- ½ cup bell pepper, cut into thick slices
- ½ cup cucumber, cut into ½-inch chunks
- 2–4 tablespoons water
- ½ cup pineapple, cut into about 1×1-inch pieces
- ½ cup tomato, cut in wedges
- 4 tablespoons ketchup
- 2 tablespoons vinegar
- 1 tablespoon fish sauce
- 2 tablespoons sugar
- Cornstarch slurry (1 tablespoon cornstarch to ¼ cup water)
- ¼ cup green onion, green and white parts, cut into 2-inch pieces

Dredge the fish in the flour then deep-fry. Drain the pieces well on paper towels and set aside.

Heat the vegetable oil in a wok or sauté pan over medium-high heat. When the oil is hot, add the garlic then onion (it's okay if the garlic browns just a little bit). Next add the bell pepper and cucumber, and stir-fry for a few minutes until the vegetables have just barely softened. Add the water to moisten everything (you might not need it all), then add the pineapple and tomato, and season with the ketchup, vinegar, fish sauce, and sugar. Quickly stir the slurry into the pan and let the sauce thicken for a few seconds. Turn the heat off, then add the fish meat and green onion. Stir well and serve.

BOHN PLA (BLUE RUNNER CHILI DIP)

4–6 SERVINGS AS A SIDE DISH OR APPE-TIZER This dip is a splendid way to use almost any kind of fish—white, red, or anything in between. Of course, the darker the fish, the fuller the flavor, so we usually go for something like the Blue Runner.

- 2 Hatch chilies, grilled
- 1 shallot, grilled
- 3 cloves garlic, peeled and grilled
- 10 ounces cooked Blue Runner meat (grilled or baked), picked free of all bones
- 2 tablespoons water
- 1 teaspoon salt
- 1 teaspoon fish sauce
- 1 tablespoon chopped cilantro
- 1 tablespoon sliced green onion, green and white parts
- Garnish: Halved boiled eggs, steamed pumpkin, lettuce, raw herbs of your choice

In a stone or textured ceramic mortar, pound the chilies, shallot, and garlic, then add the fish meat. Add the water, then pound once again to thoroughly break down the fish and mix it with the vegetables. Season with salt and fish sauce. Transfer the dip to a bowl, and sprinkle with cilantro and green onion. While not absolutely essential, we recommend the additional garnishes of halved boiled eggs, steamed pumpkin, lettuces, and some raw herbs. Serve with sticky rice.

CHAPTER 23

CRUSTACEANS

SPICY BLUE CRAB, ACCORDING TO APPLE

2 SERVINGS   You will need the biggest live Blue Crabs you can find, and they will need to be cleaned for frying. Of course, smaller Blue Crabs will suffice, as will other kinds of crabs.

> About 2 pounds Blue Crabs, split, cleaned, and cracked
>
> Up to 1 cup of holy basil leaves, according to your preference

SAUCE:

> 1 cup shallots
>
> ¼ cup garlic, peeled and crushed
>
> 5–6 tablespoons oyster sauce
>
> 4 tablespoons white soy sauce
>
> 2 tablespoons water
>
> 2 tablespoons sugar
>
> 6–10 dry árbol chilies, according to preference
>
> Salt and ground white pepper to taste

FOR THE SAUCE: Process all the ingredients in a blender until everything is finely chopped and homogenized. Transfer to a saucepan and cook for 15 minutes at a simmer. Cool the sauce and set aside.

FOR THE CRABS: After the crabs have been cleaned, cook them by either steaming or deep-frying them (we prefer the latter). They need to be completely cooked, as they will only warm up in the last step.

Put some vegetable oil in a wok and place over high heat. When the oil is smoking, add the crabs and toss well. Add the sauce. Toss all of this very well over the heat, making sure the crabs get completely coated. Add the holy basil leaves, toss again a few more times over the heat, then immediately transfer to a platter and serve.

GOONG CHAE NAM PLA (MARINATED ROCK SHRIMP)

ABOUT 4 SERVINGS AS AN APPETIZER The shrimp in this recipe is eaten raw, having been marinated for just a few minutes. For raw dishes, we always prefer White Shrimp. The recipe works well with raw fish, other crustaceans, and mollusks as well. We had it once in Thailand with raw swimming crab, which was not an overly pleasant experience, and one we cannot really recommend.

10 ounces butterflied White Shrimp

SAUCE:

> **2–3 fresh Thai chilies**
> **2 cloves garlic, minced**
> **2 tablespoons fish sauce**
> **3 tablespoons lime juice**
> **2 tablespoons sugar**
> **GARNISH: 1 teaspoon chopped mint**

Combine all of the ingredients for the sauce in a blender and process until everything is finely chopped, but the whole is not yet smooth.

Arrange the shrimp on a plate or small platter. Spoon the sauce liberally over all of the shrimp, making sure to equally distribute the sauce. Garnish and serve immediately.

PICKLED CRAWFISH

MORE THAN 2 DOZEN SERVINGS (THESE TASTE PUNGENT, AND NO ONE EVER EATS A LOT AT ONE SITTING) Across Southeast Asia, wherever some kind of fish sauce exists, people are using it to pickle things, especially crustaceans. Shrimp, Mantis Shrimp, crabs (marine and patty)—all of it gets pickled in fish sauce. In Texas and Louisiana, Lao and Khmer immigrants discovered that crawfish served just as well. If you catch a bunch of small crabs at the beach (like ghost or fiddler crabs), for example, consider pickling them. Any crustacean will work, as long as it is alive.

> **1–2 pounds live crawfish**
> **A bucket (with a tight-fitting lid!) big enough to easily hold the crawfish**
> **One 1-gallon bottle of fish sauce**

Wash the crawfish well, picking out any dead ones. Place them all in the bucket, cover them with at least 1 inch of fish sauce, cover tightly, and let them drown. They will not take long to die. Refrigerate the bucket for at least 3 days and as long as a month or more. They will never spoil, but they will eventually become so salty that they can't be eaten on their own (but they can still substitute for pickled patty crabs in *som tam*). Refrigeration is not strictly necessary, but it prevents the worst of what some might consider strong, even unpleasant smells.

After a few days, take out one crawfish and peel the tail. If it is opaque white and contracted and looks cooked, it is ready to eat. Pickled crawfish are eaten out of hand or used in salads, sauces, dips, and even soups.

HAW MOK BUU (STEAMED CURRIED CRAB)

6–8 SERVINGS We hesitate to call this a custard, as it has very little egg. The end result does look similar, however. Any boneless seafood works here, as do meats and vegetables. The traditional recipe uses folded banana leaves as cups for the custard. Here, we use aluminum cups, the same kind used for muffins and nut breads. The number of servings is determined by the size of the aluminum cups.

½ cup coconut milk

2 tablespoons fish sauce

1 egg

3 tablespoons red curry paste
   (recipe below)

20 ounces jumbo lump or lump crab
   meat, plus 5 ounces more for
   garnish

1 cup Napa cabbage leaves, torn

1 tablespoon red jalapeño pepper,
   sliced (but not seeded)

1 tablespoon cilantro leaves

RED CURRY PASTE:

30–60 dried árbol chilies (according
   to your preference)

5–8 dried guajillo chilies

1 tablespoon coriander seeds

1 tablespoon cumin seeds

3 tablespoons galangal, sliced

2 tablespoons salt

4 tablespoons cilantro stem/root

4 tablespoons lemongrass, sliced

3 heads garlic, cleaned and peeled

10 shallots, peeled and quartered

2 tablespoons shrimp paste

FOR THE CURRY PASTE: Soak the chilies in almost boiling water for ten minutes, then drain them and combine with the other curry ingredients in either a stout mortar or a strong blender and process until smooth. *This makes far more curry paste than you will need for this recipe; it stays good for weeks in the refrigerator and months in the freezer, so save leftover curry paste for future uses.*

FOR THE CRAB: Mix together the coconut milk, fish sauce, egg, and curry paste, then carefully fold in the crab meat. Place some Napa cabbage at the bottom of the aluminum cups, add the crab mix, and steam the cups for 20 minutes. Garnish with the remaining crab meat, jalapeño, and cilantro. Serve immediately.

MANTIS SHRIMP BANGPU STYLE

2 SERVINGS   A few years ago, we ate a gigantic Mantis Shrimp at an always busy and crowded seafood restaurant near Bangkok. The shrimp was taken from the live tank (one of many tanks, all containing an impressive number of shellfish, crustaceans, and a lesser number of fish), and prepared within minutes. The species in Thailand is larger than our Gulf specimens.

If you have access to Mantis Shrimp, by all means use them in this recipe (your best bet for finding them, as with a great many animals in this book, is at a large and bustling Asian market); chances are you will not, so substitute instead big head-on shrimp (10/15 or larger, no matter the origin of the shrimp) or the smallest lobster you can get (the only Gulf lobsters you might find are the Rock Lobster and the Slipper Lobster, neither of which is easily available in Texas). Instructions are given below for cleaning the Mantis Shrimp. Obviously, these steps are not necessary for shrimp or lobster (though it might be a good idea to split the lobster lengthwise).

This recipe uses a good amount of fried garlic, even by the standards of Thai cookery. The amount given is correct, we assure you.

> 2 cups vegetable oil (for frying)
>
> 1½ pounds of Mantis Shrimp, dead but whole (Make sure they are dead—see the Mantis Shrimp description for more on this.)
>
> ½ cup plus 2 tablespoons vegetable oil
>
> At least 5 tablespoons garlic, peeled and coarsely minced
>
> 1 teaspoon soy sauce
>
> 1 teaspoon fish sauce
>
> 1 teaspoon ground white pepper
>
> 1 tablespoon oyster sauce
>
> 1 teaspoon sugar
>
> GARNISH: Cilantro sprigs

TO CLEAN THE MANTIS SHRIMP: Just as in a shrimp, the meat of the Mantis is in the tail. Unlike the shrimp, the Mantis has a hard, spiked shell, and some trimming is necessary to get at the cooked meat later. With a pair of kitchen shears, trim either side of the tail from the head all the way down to where the top of the shell meets the bottom. Make sure you trim enough off to basically separate the upper and lower sections of the carapace.

Heat about ½ cup of the oil in a wok until the oil is quite hot but not smoking, then add the Mantis Shrimp one by one. They will sputter a lot, so beware. After the Mantis Shrimp have turned purple orange, have contracted, and are barely cooked, remove from the heat and drain well. Discard the used oil.

To finish, heat 2 more tablespoons of oil in the wok and add the garlic when the oil is hot. Stir the garlic briskly, then add back in the Mantis Shrimp. Carefully stir a bit. Add the rest of the ingredients, stirring to thoroughly mix, and let cook for about 30–45 seconds. Stir more, then remove from the heat.

Pour everything on a plate, arranging the shrimp in an attractive fashion. Garnish with the cilantro. Ideally, this dish would be part of a larger shared meal. Or, just eat it all yourself with a lot of rice.

CRISPY WHITE SHRIMP AND A RATHER SPICY SAUCE

SERVES 4 GLUTTONOUSLY The sauce is meant to be chunky. The tempura flour makes a bit more than you will need. Never fear, it will keep a long time.

> Vegetable oil, enough to cover the bottom of a Dutch oven by 4 inches or to fill a deep-fryer
>
> 2 pounds White Shrimp, peeled, deveined, and butterflied

TEMPURA FLOUR:

> 2½ cups all-purpose flour
>
> ¾ cup tapioca flour
>
> ¾ cup rice flour
>
> 3 tablespoons baking powder
>
> 2 tablespoons baking soda
>
> 3½ tablespoons salt
>
> 3½ tablespoons ground white pepper
>
> One 10-ounce bottle Topo Chico (or other sparkling mineral water)

RATHER SPICY SAUCE:

> 2–8 fresh red Bird's eye chilies (according to preference)
>
> 8 cloves garlic, peeled
>
> 1 bunch cilantro, stems only (reserve leaves for another use)
>
> 1½ tablespoons salt
>
> Generous ¾ cup lime juice
>
> ¾ cup fish sauce
>
> 1¼ cup white sugar
>
> 4 tablespoons ginger, chopped
>
> 3–5 tablespoons toasted peanuts

TO MAKE THE SAUCE: Place all ingredients in a blender and process on high until everything is finely chopped. Check seasoning and set aside.

FOR THE SHRIMP: Heat the oil in a deep-fryer or Dutch oven to 350°F. Prepare the batter by mixing approximately one-quarter of the tempura flour with enough Topo Chico to make a mass with a consistency between pancake and crepe batters.

Dip the shrimp in the tempura batter, then deep-fry on both sides until the shrimp is golden, crispy, and cooked (less than 5 minutes total). Fry the shrimp in batches, draining them well afterward.

Put the shrimp on a platter in a single layer or pile, and very liberally pour over the sauce. You will have more sauce than necessary, but you will discover that it goes well with almost everything.

CHAPTER 24

BIVALVES, GASTROPODS, AND CEPHALOPODS

TAIWANESE-STYLE SALT-AND-PEPPER OYSTERS WITH CRISPY BASIL

2–4 SERVINGS AS AN APPETIZER; 1 SERVING AS AN INDULGENCE Sam Chang spent time at the best restaurants in Houston and well beyond. We could say a lot of wonderful things about him, but his recipe says it better.

"You can find sweet potato starch at most Asian grocery stores, but there seem to be two general types: one that is superfine (think cornstarch) and another that has large, irregular granules that is sort of like the texture of coarse sand. You'll want to use the coarse one for this recipe, as coarseness equals crispiness."

FRIED OYSTERS:

2 cups sweet potato flour
½ cup panko
1 tablespoon salt
2 eggs
2 tablespoons water
12 medium Eastern oysters, shucked
2 quarts frying oil
8 Thai basil leaves

SEASONING SALT:

1 teaspoon white pepper
1 teaspoon salt
¼ teaspoon five spice powder
¼ teaspoon chicken bouillon powder (Knorr, etc.)
Combine all the ingredients in a mixing bowl, stir, and set aside.

SWEET-AND-SOUR SEAFOOD SAUCE:

¼ cup ketchup
½ cup soy sauce
2 tablespoons rice vinegar
½ cup cold water
1½ tablespoons brown sugar
½ tablespoon miso
½ tablespoon cornstarch
½ tablespoon cold water
Salt to taste

FOR THE OYSTERS: "Thoroughly combine the sweet potato flour, panko, and salt in a bowl that's large enough to fit all of the oysters. Crack the eggs into a separate bowl, add 2 tablespoons of water, and whisk until thoroughly beaten. Bread the oysters by first dipping into the egg wash and then placing them into the sweet potato starch mixture.

There should be enough sweet potato starch mixture to completely bury each of your oysters, but this will likely depend on the size of your container. If you need to, make more sweet potato starch mix to cover the oysters.

"Cover the bowl with plastic wrap and place in the fridge for 2 hours or even overnight. This will allow the breading to stick to the oysters better. When you are ready to fry your oysters, heat the oil in a heavy-bottom pot to 375°F.

"Fry your basil leaves until crispy—about 1 minute. Be careful, as they tend to pop. Give your oysters a final toss in the sweet potato starch mixture to make sure that they are well coated. Gently place the breaded oysters into the hot oil one at a time, making sure not to overcrowd the pot. Fry the oysters until they are crispy, turning occasionally. This should take about 2–3 minutes. Once the oysters are crispy and golden brown, remove from the oil and place on a large plate lined with paper towels.

"While the oysters are still piping hot, season well with the seasoning salt mixture. Toss the fried oysters with the crispy basil, serve hot with the Sweet-and-Sour Seafood Sauce and additional seasoning salt."

FOR THE SAUCE: "Combine all of the ingredients in a small pot or saucepan except for the cornstarch and water. Bring the ingredients in the pot to a simmer. Stir the cornstarch and the reserved water together to form a slurry. Pour the cornstarch slurry into the pot with the boiling ketchup mixture and give it a good whisk to thoroughly combine. Bring the mixture back up to a boil.

"Transfer the mixture to a bowl, cover, and chill."

MOON SNAIL ESCARGOTS

2 SERVINGS OF 6 SNAILS EACH Marine snails replace vineyard snails, but aside from that, it's the same classic French dish.

SNAIL BUTTER:

- 1½ cups butter, softened somewhat
- 2 shallots, finely diced
- 3 cloves garlic, peeled and finely chopped
- 2 tablespoons parsley, chopped
- 3 tablespoons watercress, washed well and chopped
- 1 tablespoon tarragon
- Juice and grated zest of 2 small lemons
- Salt and pepper to taste

TO POACH THE SNAILS:

- Enough chicken stock to completely cover the snails in a small pot
- 3 bay leaves
- 1 teaspoon black peppercorns
- Half a head of garlic
- A few parsley and thyme stems
- A smidgen of MSG

TO MAKE THE SNAIL BUTTER: Blend all of the ingredients in a food processor until everything is finely chopped and completely mixed with the butter. Transfer the butter to a bowl and set aside.

FOR THE SNAILS: Bring the chicken stock, bay leaves, black peppercorns, garlic, herb stems, and MSG to a boil in a pot just big enough to accommodate the snails. Add the snails, reduce the heat to a medium simmer, and let cook for about 45 minutes to 1 hour, or until the meats pull easily out of the shell and have a toothy but not crunchy texture. Remove the snails when they are thus cooked. Dispose of the poaching liquid.

After the snails have cooled completely, winkle out all of the meats, then remove the viscera and preoperculum from the feet. Wash the feet and shells completely afterward and discard the rest. Dry the shells completely, then place one snail meat in each shell. Plug up the snail shell with the herb butter, using a liberal amount and making sure to fill the shell completely (much of this butter will unfortunately run out of the shell during cooking). Refrigerate the snails until the butter has hardened completely.

TO COOK: Heat the broiler in your oven to high. If your oven does not have a broiler, then set the oven as high as it will go. Place a layer of salt, about 1/2 inch thick, on the bottom of a small sheet pan. Arrange the snails on the salt with the apertures pointing directly up. Press the snails into the salt to fix their positions. When the broiler (or oven) is as hot as it is going to get, place the snails directly under the flame, and broil for about 3–6 minutes, or until all of the butter is bubbling.

Serve immediately, with grilled or toasted bread.

THE ROLE OF CALAMARI WILL THIS EVENING BE PLAYED BY THE LIGHTNING WHELK

2 LARGE APPETIZER PORTIONS Not everyone enjoys eating snails. Some find the taste musty and overpowering; others just cannot bring themselves to eat such an animal. This preparation addresses both issues, as the snails in this recipe neither look nor taste like snails. The sauce is more or less a common red sauce, with the addition of Thai sriracha sauce and a touch of sugar.

You will need live Whelks (or Oyster Drills), which are commonly available at the retail level, for this recipe. Smash the shells, pick out the soft part, then separate the meat (the foot) from the viscera (which may be

discarded). Wash the feet very well, getting rid of all traces of slime, guts, and grit. With a meat mallet, pound each foot to about ⅛-inch thickness. Cut each foot into 2–4 pieces, depending on size, before pounding.

We use ground toasted rice to dredge the snails in before frying. Semolina and cornmeal work just as well.

THE DREDGE:

> 2 cups all-purpose flour
> 2 cups finely ground, well-toasted rice, with salt and pepper to taste
> 4 eggs, beaten, with a little water added

THE SNAILS:

> 1–2 quarts vegetable oil
> 1 pound pounded snail meats

SAUCE:

> 2 tablespoons olive oil
> ½ small yellow onion, chopped
> 3 tablespoons chopped fennel
> 3 cloves garlic
> One 20-ounce can diced tomatoes, blended
> 2 tablespoons chopped parsley
> 1 tablespoon sugar
> 1 teaspoon cayenne pepper
> 4 tablespoons Thai sriracha sauce
> Juice from 1 lemon

TO MAKE THE SAUCE: Heat a little olive oil in a saucepan, then sweat the onion, fennel, and garlic. Add the rest of the ingredients (except for the sriracha and lemon juice) and cook over medium-high heat until enough water has cooked out to thicken the sauce a bit. Add the lemon juice and sriracha and check the seasoning. Remove the sauce from the heat and let cool completely.

Mix together the flour and toasted ground rice, then dredge the whelk pieces by dipping them in the egg then completely coating them in the flour/rice mix. As you finish each snail, set it aside on a large sheet pan. Ideally, allow the dredged pieces to set up in the refrigerator for a few hours.

To cook, heat the frying oil in a Dutch oven (or fryer) to 350°F, then fry the snails in small batches, turning them several times during cooking. Cooking time is approximately 3 minutes. Drain the snails on paper towels.

Serve the snails in a big bowl, with a ramekin of the sauce on the side. The sauce is good hot, cold, or at room temperature.

SOUTHERN CLAMS IN A YANKEE CHOWDER

APPROXIMATELY 4–6 SERVINGS We reproduce this recipe almost exactly as it appears on the old, stained index card upon which it was written many decades ago by PJ's maternal grandfather. The recipe itself came from PJ's great-grandfather Rupert Austin, a Rhode Island Yankee in New Jersey, and from all accounts, an exceptional cook and an even better human being. The instructions are verbatim, we have added some modern translations in parentheses.

> One 2-inch square of salt pork
> 2 tablespoons butter
> 1 large (white) onion
> 2–3 stalks celery
> 1 tablespoon flour
> 2 cups shucked clams, in their liqueur
> 1 cup russet potatoes, peeled and diced fine
> 4 cups milk
> 1 tablespoon chopped parsley
> 1/2 teaspoon paprika

"Try out [render] the salt pork, cut in tiny cubes, over low flame. Drain off fat and put crisp bits on paper toweling. Do not wash the pan.

"Slice onion very fine and dice celery very fine. Drain clam juice through cheesecloth and save.

"Wash clams in ½ cup cold water, save water, and strain. Chop clams.

"Put butter, onion, and celery into pork pan and cook gently until soft—*don't* brown. Sprinkle with flour and cook, stirring, another minute or two.

"Cook potatoes in clam juice—simmer until almost done. Add celery, onion, and clams and simmer gently for 3 minutes. *DO NOT BOIL.*

"Scald milk in a double boiler—add clams and vegetables. Serve sprinkled with parsley, paprika, and hot pork bits."

LIMPETS OR SLIPPER SHELLS OVER COALS

SERVES 2 COMFORTABLY, 4 AS AN APPETIZER Neither of these snails requires much preparation before or after cooking. Just wash them off with clean seawater, and they are ready to go. Grilling can be done anywhere, but it seems to work better on the beach.

> 2 pounds limpets or Slipper Shells
> Approximately 2–3 tablespoons salt
> 2–3 tablespoons good olive oil
> 1 lemon per person, cut into wedges
> A thin, short-bladed knife for scraping out the meats

Get a hot fire going, and place the grill very close to the flame, no more than an inch or two away (if the grill can sit directly on the coals, all the better). Place the limpets or Slipper Shells shell down on the grill (you will recall that these two species have only partial shells), with the soft bodies pointing skyward. If the fire is hot enough, the snails will cook in just a few minutes. When you see the foot meat tightening and curling around the edges, and wisps of steam come out of the shells, the snails are ready.

Detach the meat with the knife, sprinkle with salt, lemon juice, or olive oil (or all three), and enjoy.

OYSTER DRILLS AND GRUEL

4 SERVINGS We've been friends with Richard Knight since we started selling fish to Feast, the groundbreaking restaurant he and James Silk owned and operated in Houston years ago. Richard is not only a lover of seafood but a charming raconteur .

THE SNAILS:

> **2–3 dozen Oyster Drills, according to your generosity**
> **6 bay leaves**
> **A handful of parsley stalks**

Wash the snails thoroughly, place in a pot of water, and bring slowly to a boil. Cook for 5 minutes, then drain the snails and discard the water. Replace the water, return the Drills to the pot, and bring the water to a boil. After the water boils, turn down the heat to a simmer and add the bay leaves. Simmer for an hour and a half, then drain and rinse the snails under cold water. Winkle the snail out of the shell, and pull or cut off the foot.

SAUCE:

> **2 tablespoons olive oil**
> **1 yellow onion, peeled and diced fine**
> **4 garlic cloves, peeled**
> **1 can crushed tomatoes**
> **2 tablespoons tomato paste**
> **1 teaspoon white sugar**
> **GARNISH: 1 tablespoon chopped rosemary leaves and 8–10 flat-leaf parsley leaves**

Heat the oil in a pan on medium heat, and sweat the onions for 5–8 minutes until they have softened and taken on some color. Using a zester, grate in the garlic. Add the crushed tomatoes, lower the heat to a simmer, and cook down for 30 minutes. Add the sugar and taste for seasoning.

GRUEL:

> **Just under 2 cups old-fashioned oats**
> **¾ cup chicken stock**
> **¾ cup cream**
> **1 vanilla pod**
> **1 tablespoon unsalted butter**

Take half of the oats and toast them in a pan on the stove (or in the oven), stirring frequently until golden. Cool and set aside. Bring the chicken stock and the cream to a boil, and stir in all of the oats. Reduce to medium heat for 5 minutes, then remove from heat. Slice open the vanilla pod lengthwise, then scrape the contents into the oat mix; stir and taste for seasoning.

TO SERVE: Warm the tomato sauce gently and add the snails. Warm the oats over gentle heat, adding a little water if necessary to adjust consistency. Finish the oats by folding in the butter. Place the oats in a warm bowl, making a small well in the middle, into which spoon in the snail-tomato mix. Sprinkle the snails with fresh, finely chopped rosemary and a few parsley leaves. Enjoy.

OYSTERS WITH NO ADORNMENT

ASSUME YOU AND YOUR COMPANION WILL EAT AT LEAST A DOZEN OYSTERS EACH. You will need three components for this dish. All three are equally important; do not attempt this recipe unless you can procure everything. Optional ingredients are listed below the recipe.

> A lot of fresh live oysters from a dependable supplier (or from your own hunts)
>
> One dependable and comfortable oyster shucker
>
> One companion who loves oysters as much as you

Find a comfortable place to sit (outside is best). Make a pile of oysters between you and your companion. Start shucking. Eat oysters until you need to take a nap.

For best results, do not add anything to the oysters.

However, if you insist on gilding the lily, you may add a few drops of lemon juice, tabasco sauce, horseradish, cocktail sauce, or other condiments.

PHAT CHAA (SPICY ANGELWING CLAM STIR-FRY)

4 SERVINGS This dish works with any kind of clam. Some can be used whole (e.g., littlenecks, steamers, etc.); others, like the Angelwing or larger clams, need a bit of preparation.

> 1 tablespoon vegetable oil
>
> 1 teaspoon minced garlic
>
> 1 pound shucked Angelwing Clam meat (you can use whole Angelwings, but we don't recommend this—the shells are so delicate that they sometimes shatter during the stir-frying)
>
> 1–2 teaspoons sliced red jalapeño pepper or Thai chili
>
> 1 tablespoon sliced *krachai* (a rhizome from Southeast Asia that is never found fresh in the United States but is always available frozen; it is usually marketed in the United States under the generic market name "rhizome")
>
> 3 kaffir lime leaves
>
> 2 sprigs of green peppercorn, fresh or brined
>
> 2 tablespoons oyster sauce
>
> 1 tablespoon soy sauce
>
> 1 teaspoon salt
>
> 1 teaspoon ground white pepper
>
> 1 teaspoon sugar
>
> Dash of MSG

Heat the oil in a pan or wok, add the garlic, stir once or twice, then add clam meat. Cook for about 5 minutes, or until the clams are cooked according to your preference (in this dish, we prefer to err on the side of over-cooked). Add the chilies, *krachai*, lime leaves, and the peppercorns. Cook for another 3–5 minutes, then season with oyster sauce, soy sauce, salt, white pepper, sugar, and MSG. Remove from the heat. Serve hot with steamed rice.

COQUINA NECTAR

1 POUND OF COQUINAS YIELDS ABOUT 1 CUP OF NECTAR   To procure Coquina nectar, one just needs a pot large enough to hold the clams with about two inches of clearance at the top. One also needs fire, upon which to place the pot filled with the clams. A small amount of water should be added to the pot, maybe a few inches at the bottom. After that, one simply steams the clams until they all open up, a process that should take about 10 minutes. Strain the resulting liquid, first through a coarse strainer, then through a coffee filter. Drink this broth warm, perhaps with a squeeze of lemon juice. Or use it as a base for other dishes.

After you've drained off the nectar, keep the shells in the pot, and add water enough to cover them by several inches. Have ready an equally large pot, with a fine-meshed sieve placed on top. With a large spoon, stir the lot vigorously. The cooked meats fall out of their shells easily, and stirring the water helps expedite the process. After stirring for 1–2 minutes, quickly drain the water into the waiting pot, but do not let any shells fall out. The sieve will catch some of the meats. Place those meats aside and repeat the process until the water runs through the sieve without leaving any meat. It will take maybe 5 repetitions.

The meats, after they are extracted, may be used in any way you would chopped clams. We use them for fritters.

GRILLED SQUID

2 SERVINGS   The shape, taste, and texture of squid make it easy to use in a lot of ways. However, for pure squid-eating pleasure, grilling is the way to go. It is simple, quick, and satisfying.

> 1 pound whole squid
> 2–3 tablespoons olive oil
> 2–3 tablespoons red wine vinegar
> 2 sprigs fresh thyme, chopped
> 2 cloves garlic, peeled and chopped
> 2 tablespoons fresh parsley, chopped
> Salt and black pepper for seasoning
> GARNISH: Lime wedges

Combine all ingredients except the squid and whisk well. Pour this marinade over the squid and let marinate for at least 2 hours. Skewer the tubes and tentacles lengthwise.

Get a good fire going (coals should still be actively burning, not just glowing). Season the squid with a little more salt and black pepper. When the fire and grill are both very hot, add the squid, making sure that the tubes lie straight and nothing is crowded. Let cook for 2 minutes, then turn and cook for 2 more minutes. Turn again, cook for a few seconds, turn a final time, then remove from the grill. If the fire flares up and licks the squid during cooking, do not fear, for this will only improve the taste.

Slice the tubes and arrange them and the heads on a plate with lime wedges.

PERIWINKLE CURRY

4 SERVINGS Making a meal out of peri-winkles alone is a chore, for it's a lot of work for not much meat. As part of a larger dish, though, the effort is much more reward-ing. This is a curry from southern Thailand called Gaeng Khua Bai Chapuu. As always, the recipe makes more paste than the dish needs; refrigerate or freeze the remainder for future use.

CURRY PASTE:

- 25–40 dried árbol chilies (according to your preference)
- 5–8 dried guajillo chilies
- 4 tablespoons fresh turmeric, chopped
- 3 tablespoons galangal, sliced
- 2 tablespoons salt
- 3 heads garlic, cleaned and peeled
- 10 shallots, peeled and quartered
- 1 teaspoon black pepper
- 10 Makrut lime leaves

PERIWINKLES:

- One 13.5-ounce can of coconut milk, plus ½ can of water
- 2 tablespoons tamarind juice
- 1 tablespoon sugar (palm sugar preferably)
- 2 tablespoons fish sauce
- 1 teaspoon salt
- 2 pounds periwinkles, washed off
- 1 bunch of heart leaf, julienned (Heart leaf, a common vegetable in Southeast Asian markets, gets its name from its shape. If need be, substitute spinach.)

In a blender, combine curry paste ingre-dients and process until smooth. (A stone mortar and pestle make a paste with a better texture, but such a method is not practical for everyone.)

Bring the coconut milk to a boil in a large soup pot. Let it boil for a few minutes, then add the curry paste, stirring well. Let cook for a few minutes more, until the broth has become an attractive shade of orange and an appetizing aroma wafts through the kitchen.

Add the water and the rest of the soup ingredients except the snails and the heart leaf, lower the heat to a simmer, and cook for 10 minutes.

Raise the heat to boiling and add the snails; cook for about 15 minutes. Remove from heat, stir in the heart leaf (or spinach, if using).

Correct seasoning and serve in a large bowl, with lots of jasmine rice on the side.

CHAPTER 25

PRESERVING THE CATCH

RAINBOW RUNNER GRAVLAX

APPROXIMATELY 60–80 THIN SLICES We have no Gulf of Mexico fish equivalent to salmon. The closest would be the Rio Grande Cutthroat Trout, but that is a far West Texas freshwater species, and one not suitable for gravlax at any rate. Almaco Jack, amberjack, Swordfish—these would all be acceptable substitutions were they more consistently fatty and more manageably sized. The Rainbow Runner, of all Gulf fish, might be the best suited for curing in such a fashion, provided it weighs at least 8 pounds.

Along with the fish, you will need a long, wide, and shallow plastic pan (big enough for a single layer of fillets, along with slightly less than an inch of salt on top).

1 Rainbow Runner, weighing as close to 8 pounds as possible, filleted with the (scaled) skin on (The thinnest part of the belly needs to be trimmed away to achieve more uniform thickness. Remove all the pin bones with pliers.)

CURE:

1 pound salt

¾ pound brown sugar

4 tablespoons cracked black pepper

4–6 tablespoons aromatics (e.g., thyme, fennel, citrus, spices, even pelletized hops)

Mix the cure and aromatics. Sprinkle a thin layer of the cure in the pan, enough to just barely cover the bottom. Place the fillets in the pan skin-down. Then cover the fillets entirely with the cure. You don't want to be able to see the fish at all. Cover the pan and place it in the refrigerator, where it will stay for 36–48 hours, or until the flesh is firm throughout.

Wash the cure off completely, rubbing it with your (gloved) hand where necessary. Dry the fish well, then wrap in paper towels and place on a tray in the fridge for a few hours to allow it to dry completely.

Remove the paper towels, then wrap the fillets in plastic wrap, and store flat in the refrigerator.

Slice thinly and serve as you would any gravlax.

SLOWLY AGED AND CAREFULLY DECOMPOSED BONITO

YIELD: UNKNOWN   One day, we had a lone unsold Atlantic Bonito. So PJ salted it. Then he forgot about it for a few days too many. Upon finally checking it, he discovered that while it had not gone bad, it had started to ferment in an unusual fashion. So he hung it from the rafters of the backyard patio and waited to see what would happen. Flies came near, but they didn't really want to land on the Bonito, which was good news. Over the next three months, the fish just kept aging, getting more and more yellow, but never stinking or smelling off. Eventually, it smelled of aged cheese. When we cut it open, the meat was beautiful.

It tasted very strong, like a Gorgonzola made with anchovies—which was surprisingly better than it sounds.

It was a serendipitous accident. We have tried since and have never come close to performing the same magic.

SMOKED SOUTHERN HAKE

ENOUGH MEAT FOR 2–4 SERVINGS, DEPENDING ON THE SIZE OF THE FISH   Our poor little Southern Hake gets very little respect. It is small, it is as far from glamorous as a ball of mud, and the meat is watery and soft. Never mind, of course, that the flesh is also sweet and mild, and that it goes well with just about anything.

Smoking the fish whole is probably the best treatment. The curing firms the flesh, and using the whole provides a much higher yield than filleting beforehand. Any white fish can be smoked this way, the leaner the better.

You will need a smoker big enough to hang the hake while it smokes, or you will need to be clever enough to devise a suitable alternative. The fish is smoked hot, and only takes a few hours.

1 (or more) Southern Hake, between 1 and 3 pounds, scaled and spatchcocked

Salt, a generous amount

First, make sure that all traces of blood, scales, and viscera have been completely removed, then rub both the skin and cut sides very well with salt (you can't use too much salt). Place the fish skin side down on a plate or small sheet pan, sprinkle more salt on the cut side, and refrigerate. Salting time will depend on the thickness of the fish—figure on 30 minutes per half inch of thickness.

After the appropriate amount of salting time, the flesh of the fish should have firmed somewhat, but it will still feel pliable. Rinse off any salt and debris, then dry the fish well. Rub with a little olive oil or lard, then place in the refrigerator for several hours to dry completely.

Prepare the smoker. The ideal temperature in the smoker should be around 150°F. You want the fish hot-smoked, but if the smoker temperature exceeds 200°F, the fish will be completely cooked before it has taken on all the smoke it could. Smoke the fish until it is a nice bronze color and the meat easily teases from the bone.

The fish, thus smoked, is great on its own with a bit of rice or bread and some butter. It can also be used for dips, fish salad, and as a base in vegetable dishes.

MOJAMA

**YIELD FROM RAW TO CURED: APPROXI-
MATELY 65 PERCENT** This Spanish version
of air-dried meat (in this case, tuna) has
ancient roots, going back several thousand
years. The process is simple and straightforward, and the drying process may be done
in the refrigerator or outdoors. We suggest
the latter, if at all possible. However, if
you are going to dry the tuna outdoors, we
recommend doing it when the average daily
temperature doesn't exceed around 70°F,
the nightly temperature doesn't drop much
below 40°F, and there's not a lot of rain or
humidity. And it needs to stay like this for
at least two weeks. In Houston, that means
we can go a whole year or more without the
appropriate weather.

Mojama is typically sliced thinly and
eaten as is, with only the slightest of garnishes (e.g., very good olive oil). In other
words, it's used like a fine ham or prosciutto
(or the air-dried beef from Switzerland
called Viande des Grisons or just Grisons).
You can also use it as a substitute for bacon
or ham in cooked recipes. It is excellent, for
example, with beans.

You will need a chunk of Yellowfin Tuna
loin, skin off. Use a piece from the front of
the loin. You will also need salt. Those are the
only two ingredients, but you will also need
a glass or plastic container just barely big
enough to hold all the slabs in a single layer.

Sprinkle a bit of salt in the bottom of the
container. You do not need to completely coat
the bottom, you just need some coverage. Cut
the loin into rectangular slabs measuring
about 6×2×2 inches. Rub each slab very thoroughly with salt, then place in the container.
When everything is salted, cover the container and place it in the refrigerator (you
can also leave at room temperature). The fish
needs to be in salt for about 1–2 days, and the
slabs need to be turned every 12 hours or so.
When the color has darkened to a deep car-
mine red wine color, and the slab is as firm as
the very tip of your nose, it is ready.

At this point, wash the slabs and dry them
completely. They will need to be hung for a
few weeks, so, using twine or hooks, prepare
the slabs. Keep checking the slabs every few
days. They are ready when they have stopped
exuding any moisture; the outside surfaces
are slightly crusted and pleasingly discolored
(slight tan tinge to red brown); and they are
as firm as a good cured ham.

To store the slabs, wrap them in plastic
wrap and keep in the refrigerator (they will
keep in the refrigerator for more than a
month). They may also be frozen, but bear
in mind that the texture will be somewhat
affected.

BOTTARGA, THOUGH NOT WITH MULLET ROE

8–9 OUNCES OF FINISHED PRODUCT Bottarga is salted and dried roe sacs from, most commonly, members of the Mugilidae family (i.e., the mullets, like the Striped Mullet [*Mugil cephalus*]). It is usually served sliced thinly, as one would a ham; or the sacs are broken and the eggs are crumbled in sauce or used as a garnish or to finish a dish. Like mojama, bottarga has an ancient lineage, going back at least several thousand years to either New Kingdom Egypt or Phoenicia, or both, or some other as-yet-unknown people. One finds it around the Mediterranean today, everywhere there is a legacy of ancient peoples.

Texas fishing regulations prohibit the retention and possession of large Striped Mullet during the spawn, so we are not able in Texas to get the ideal (and ideally sized) roe sacs directly. (This is not the case in Florida, where at least a few companies make Striped Mullet bottarga.) However, most fish produce roe sacs suitable for bottarga. We suggest using sacs that weigh at least 3–4 ounces, for anything smaller tends to become excessively salty. There is no maximum size limit, we suppose—we once made bottarga from one single lobe of Bluefin Tuna roe that weighed 13 pounds. Just make sure you adjust the salting time accordingly.

The following fish provide at least suitable roes for bottarga: Black Drum, Redfish, all large mackerels and tunas. As always, this is an easily scalable recipe.

1 pound roe sacs, membranes completely intact

About 1 gallon of 6 percent saltwater brine

1–2 cups salt

A pan big enough to hold all of the roe sacs in a single layer

Paper towels

2 wooden cutting boards, about an inch thick, and each big enough to hold the roe sacs in a single layer

Clean the roes of extraneous material, then soak them in the brine overnight. The next morning, rinse them off and discard the brine, which will at this point be brownish red. Dry the roes completely.

Line the pan with two layers of paper towels, then sprinkle a thin broken layer of salt on the paper towels. Arrange the roes, then sprinkle them with salt. About 6 hours later, change the paper towels and resalt the roes. Keep doing this until the moisture stops leaking out and the towels remain dry. This will take up to 3 days for roes weighing under a pound.

When the roes have stopped sweating moisture, remove excess salt and sandwich them between the cutting boards, then place the cutting boards on a sheet pan. Put a table knife under one edge of the bottom cutting board so that moisture will drip off. Place the whole in the refrigerator. Let the roes stay like this for 1 to 3 weeks. Or, you may hang the roes and dry them that way—a method we do not recommend you attempt unless storage conditions are absolutely perfect (less than 60°F and dry).

ISAAN-STYLE FERMENTED FISH SAUSAGE (MADE HERE WITH BLUEFIN TUNA BELLY SCRAPS)

3 SAUSAGES, APPROXIMATELY 3/4 POUND PER SAUSAGE Isaan cookery relies heavily on pickled and soured foods, almost all of which involve rice-based lactofermentation. In this recipe, the sausage is not cased, but rather wrapped tightly in several layers of banana leaves, where it ferments for several days. Fermentation will occur in the refrigerator, but we suggest room temperature storage if possible (even hotter, around 85°F, is optimal).

If you do not have access to Bluefin Tuna belly scraps (and you more than likely will not), use the fattiest fish you can find. In this case, you will need to reduce the amount of fish by about 4 ounces and add 4 ounces of pork fat (which you will mince along with the fish).

And for whatever it might be worth, this recipe is an amalgam of two Isaan sausage techniques. It is Sai Grok, but instead of being cased, it is fermented in banana leaves like Naem. And, of course, we use saltwater fish rather than pork.

- 1¼ pound well-minced Bluefin Tuna belly scraps
- 1¼ cups cooked and cooled jasmine rice
- 3½ heads garlic, cleaned and chopped
- 1½ tablespoons salt
- 1½ tablespoons ground white pepper
- ½ teaspoon MSG
- ⅛ teaspoon Instacure #2 (a dry cure mix, commonly used in aged and fermented sausages to maintain quality and help ensure a safe product; it may be bought online quite easily)

FOR WRAPPING:

- 12 pieces of banana leaf, each about 15×12 inches, singed over a flame until softened

Mince the tuna meat well. Add all of the other ingredients and mix everything together until the mass is homogeneous. Set aside.

On a work surface, divide the banana leaves into three piles, with all of the pieces oriented the same direction. Divide the mix among the three piles of leaves. Roll each bundle into a tube (like you would roll a burrito), tucking in the sides so the mix cannot leak out. Make the wrap as tight as possible, and do your best to ensure that the mass inside doesn't have air pockets or a weird shape. Then wrap each bundle in several layers of plastic wrap.

Set the bundles somewhere out of the way and let them ferment. At room temperature, this will take 3–6 days. In the refrigerator, it will take 5–8 days. You will know it is ready when you unwrap the plastic and get slapped in the face with an incredibly sour smell. If it smells sour, then all is well. Sour is the key. If it smells rotten, it is.

The last step is steaming the bundles until the internal temperature reaches 160°F (this is a high temperature for fish, but it is necessary to make sure that it's safe to eat). You can eat the sausage now, or let it cool and use it later. We recommend grilling the bundles before serving them.

"RED FISH" CONFIT

**TWELVE TO FIFTEEN 4-OUNCE POR-
TIONS**   Any red (pelagic) fish will work
here, but Albacore and Crevalle Jack are our
favorites. This is an actual confit, so it will
keep for quite a long time in the refrigerator
(as long as the fish remains buried in the fat).
And because it is a true confit, it is a bit salty,
but less so than, say, a confit of duck leg. As
for the fat, we recommend melted lard or
inexpensive olive oil.

> **1 loin, or a piece of a loin, weighing
> about 5 pounds**
>
> **Salt, enough to bury all of the meat**
>
> **Enough fat (see above) to cover
> completely all of the fish in a
> suitable vessel**
>
> **6 bay leaves**
>
> **5 sprigs of thyme**
>
> **2 tablespoons black pepper**
>
> **A plastic lidded container and a pot
> large enough to accommodate all
> the fish**

Cut the loin into steaks about 1½ inches
wide. Cover the bottom of the container
with a layer of salt. Arrange the steaks in
flat layers, with lots of salt in between the
layers. When you have finished with all the
steaks, pour over enough salt to cover the
fish completely. Replace the lid, and store in
a refrigerated spot.

Let the meat sit in the salt for 6–24 hours,
checking frequently after the first 12 hours.
You will know the pieces are ready when
they have turned a dark blood color, are
visibly shrunken, and, most importantly, are
as salty as a dry ham (this you will know by
tasting a bit).

When they are appropriately cured,
remove the pieces, wash them off, and
dry them completely. Preheat the oven to
its lowest setting, which will be around
170°F–180°F. Arrange the fish in a deep-sided
ovenproof pot, layer upon layer. Pour in
enough fat to cover the fish pieces entirely,
and add the bay leaves, thyme sprigs, and
black pepper.

Heat the pot on the stove until the fat is
hot to the touch. Cover the pot with a lid or
aluminum foil, and place in the oven. Allow
the fish to cook unmolested for several
hours, until the internal temperature of the
fish is 150°F. Remove the pot from the heat
and allow it and its contents to cool completely. When the oil and fish are at room
temperature, very carefully transfer the
steaks to a clean plastic container. Move all
of the steaks thusly, then pour in enough of
the oil to cover the fish entirely. Cover the
container and refrigerate.

Use this confit in any way you might use
duck confit. Or use it to make "tuna" salad or
a real Salade Niçoise.

PLA SOM (ISAAN SOUR MULLET)

2–3 SERVINGS This is an incredibly ancient way of preserving fish, in which whole fish (or large bone-in chunks) are packed in cooked rice, some salt, and some garlic and allowed to ferment. The end product is bitingly sour and pungent. The soured fish is cooked whole, and then served as a whole fish, or the meat is cooked for another dish. Chunks are used in the same way, and also for soups. Only use mullet you have caught yourself, and only catch them from the beach (at least if you're in Texas). Any other white fish will do, as long as it is not too big or too thick.

> About 1 pound small whole mullet
>
> 1 cup cooked jasmine rice
>
> 2 tablespoons minced garlic
>
> 2 tablespoons salt
>
> Pinch of Instacure #2
>
> Scale the fish very well. Gut and gill it just as carefully, making sure to remove all the innards, including the kidneys.

Make a series of slashes on each side of the fish—start at the head and make about five cuts, each cut almost to the bone, going from the top of the fish to the bottom. The cuts should be made diagonally, and you should make about 5–7 cuts before you get to the tail. Make another series of slashes going from the tail to the head, resulting in a lattice pattern of cuts. Repeat on the other side.

Mix together the rice, garlic, and salt. Rub the fish all over with the rice mix, making sure to work the rice into the abdominal cavity and the scores in the skin. Put the fish in a large Ziploc bag, and put the bag on a small sheet pan. Cover the fish with the rest of the rice mix. Seal the bag, refrigerate, and allow to ferment for at least 5–7 days, turning the bag every day. You'll know when it has soured.

FISH SAUCE

ABOUT 2½ POUNDS OF WHOLE, UNGUT-TED FISH YIELDS APPROXIMATELY 1 CUP OF FISH SAUCE. A very strong word of warning: although making fish sauce can be a rewarding experience, it can also be slightly unpleasant, especially for those not involved in the making (i.e., neighbors, loved ones, and roommates).

Another note: This is only one style of fish sauce and is certainly not definitive.

Any species of anchovy, sardine, menhaden, or herring—small oily fish in other words—is ideal for fish sauce, but most all small fish will get the job done. Squid and shrimp could be used, but we advise against that, on the grounds of taste and decorum (the smell is rather cloying during production, and the end result always tastes slightly off). The process takes many months, and you don't want to be moving the container after it starts. A few drops on your clothes, and people will be walking away from you all day.

The ratio of fish to salt is 5:1.

Unless the fish are larger than your hand, do not gut them (you really shouldn't be using fish that large for fish sauce anyway). The fish do not have to be at the peak of freshness, though they should still be edible. We recommend keeping them in the fridge for a day or two before salting, to allow the guts and bellies to soften enough to break apart easily.

You will need a lidded container big enough to hold all of the fish with several inches to spare. The lid needs to be secure enough to keep out flies, but it does not need to be, and indeed should not be, airtight. We highly recommend something made of clear plastic.

Sprinkle some of the salt on the bottom of the container. Dump in an inch of fish, then add more salt. Repeat this process until you have used up all the fish and salt. Then mix the lot a bit to distribute everything evenly. Put the lid on the container and place somewhere warm to hot, but not directly in the sun. Bearing in mind that this process was born in tropical regions, don't worry about the container getting too hot. It *needs* to be hot. Aside from a periodic peek, forget about the container for a few months. Then move the container into the direct sunlight and leave for two days (here is where the clear container comes in handy—you won't have to take the lid off at all). Then put the container back in its original location, and, once again, forget about it for a few months. Repeat the process twice. After 7–12 months (more if you want), decant the liquid slowly and strain through a fine strainer, then through a coffee filter. Though you can use the sauce at this point, we highly recommend boiling it first, which eliminates any foodborne dangers, as well as the slightly raw flavor common to small-batch fish sauce.

The fish sauce is now shelf stable and can be used in any recipe calling for fish sauce. It may be stored in the cupboard, and it will never go bad.

SALTFISH (WITH BROTULA BECAUSE WE DO NOT HAVE COD IN THE GULF)

1 POUND OF RAW BROTULA YIELDS ABOUT 5 OUNCES OF FINISHED PRODUCT. We never sold all the brotula that was unloaded. We would always sell some, but it's not exciting, so we always had a few fish left over. We made quite a bit of saltfish over a few years.

As we described earlier, the brotula is only distantly related to the cod. The fillets of both, however, are rather similar in appearance (though the brotula tends to be pinker and more translucent), and neither has any fat to speak of—a crucial requirement for this kind of preservation. Traditionally, whole spatchcocked fish were used for salt cod. We've done it both ways with brotula. Fillets are easier unless you have room to let whole fish dry.

> **Brotula fillets, boneless and skinless; or spatchcocked brotulas**
>
> **Lots of salt (about ½ pound of salt per pound of fish)**
>
> **A container big enough for the fish, with enough space to allow the salt to cover the fish completely**
>
> **A place for the fish to dry (usually this has to be in the refrigerator)**

Make sure the fillet (or whole fish) is clean and free from scales, viscera, and debris. Put a thin layer of salt on the bottom of the container, then put the fish in a single layer, not overlapping at all. Pour in enough salt to half cover the fish. If there's more fish than space, simply make additional layers as needed, making sure that every piece of fish is adequately covered by salt.

Put the container in the refrigerator, and let it sit for a day or two, depending on the thickness of the fillet. You will know the fish has sat in the salt long enough when it is as firm as a ripe eggplant. Do not worry overly about exact salting times, for a few hours too many will result in, at worst, discoloration of the final product and a slight damage to texture (neither of which prevents you from eating and enjoying said oversalted fish).

Wash all the salt off the fish, then dry completely with paper towels.

TO DRY THE FISH: Place the fish on a rack and place the rack on a baking sheet. Place the baking sheet, uncovered, in the refrigerator (preferably near the fan). Let the fish dry for 2 weeks or more. The refrigerator is not the ideal environment, but it does work well enough, although saltfish made this way is not shelf stable and needs to be kept refrigerated or frozen.

Alternatively, dry the fish outside. It's best to do this during the colder months of the year if you live anywhere near the Gulf Coast (the process works during even hot months, but the end product is inferior, and the flies and smell might bother your neighbors). Tie the fish securely with twine (if you're working with fillets, trussing is the easiest way; whole fish may be tied at the tail or head), then hang the fish somewhere with a good breeze. The fish is done when it is completely dry and brittle. This kind of saltfish is shelf stable.

To use saltfish, soak it in cold water overnight or up to 24 hours, changing the water at least 3 times. It will then be ready for any saltfish recipe (see Saltfish Escovitch).

KING MACKEREL DAED DIAEW

TEN 3-OUNCE PORTIONS   Daed Diaew is an old-fashioned Thai way to preserve fish (or really any meat at all) for a few days. The fish is only half dried (hence the Thai name, which means "one day" [literally "one sun"]), so the end product has a week or less of shelf life at room temperature, though it will keep in the refrigerator for up to a few weeks. It's not for everyone, but if you like fish, you will probably love this. Typically, small whole fish are used, but larger fish, cut into appropriate pieces, also work well.

Note: The final dried product is not ready to eat. It must be cooked first (almost always by frying).

> 2 pounds King Mackerel, cut into roughly ½-inch steaks
>
> 3 tablespoons white soy sauce
>
> 1 tablespoon crushed garlic
>
> 1 teaspoon ground white pepper
>
> 1 teaspoon toasted coriander seed (optional)
>
> 1 teaspoon salt

Combine the ingredients for the marinade. Pour this marinade over the steaks, rubbing everything into all the nooks and crannies. Let them marinate for about 30 minutes.

Remove the steaks from the marinade and place in a suitable drying apparatus (either a machine or between screens outdoors). Allow to dry about halfway (the fish should still feel slightly soft at the thick part of the fillet). This will take a few hours in a food dryer and most of the day outside.

If drying outside, choose a place that gets full exposure to the sun all day. The fish will rot rather than dry if it is not in a sunny place all day. A bit of breeze is good also, as it helps dry the fish and disperses the fish aroma. Crucially, make sure the fish is completely protected from marauding flies.

Few things in life are more heartbreaking than walking outside to check on your fish, almost salivating from the visions of fried dried fish dancing in your head, only to find your dinner ruined by maggots. We recommend buying a length of window screen and cutting it to the required size.

Cooking is simple: fry in a pan or deep-fry. We eat it with rice and vegetable dishes, but that's not gospel.

MENHADEN CHIPS

ABOUT 4 OUNCES OF DRIED CHIPS   When they were a bit younger, our children might have eaten their weight in these chips. They taste rather like fish, if we are being honest, but they are as addictive as a potato chip.

> 1 pound small menhaden (less than 4 inches long) fillets

BRINE:

> 1 quart water
>
> At least 1 cup salt

MARINADE:

> 2 tablespoons soy sauce
>
> 1 teaspoon salt
>
> 1 tablespoon sugar
>
> 1 teaspoon ground white pepper

You cannot buy whole menhaden, much less fillets, so you will first need to catch some with a cast net, then fillet enough of them to get 1 pound of meat. You will need to scale and fillet up to several dozen fish to get that much weight. This will take a while, but at the end you will have not only the meat but also the knowledge that you can take apart little fish. The operation is more efficient with a partner.

Make the brine by stirring as much salt as you can into the water. Add a cup of ice, then the fillets. Let them soak in salt water for no more than 5 minutes, swishing them around to clean off stray debris. Drain the water off.

Mix the marinade ingredients together, and then add the marinade to the fish. Combine well and place in the refrigerator for 1 hour. Then arrange the fish in single layers, not overlapping, on the dryer racks, and dry at 145°F until they are hard and desiccated enough to be shelf stable.

To cook, heat some oil in a pot to about 350°F. When the oil is hot, cook the menhaden fillets in small batches. They will cook very quickly and will go from perfect to burned in a few seconds, so be careful. As soon as the chips are a dark golden color, remove them immediately, and drain well.

Uncooked, the chips will last for years on the cupboard shelf. Once fried, they stay crispy, in a wrapped container, for several days.

PLA TUU KEM (SALTED INDIAN MACKEREL, MADE, IN THIS CASE, WITH SCAD)

4 PORTIONS (1 FISH PER PERSON) Pla Tuu Kem are ubiquitous in Thailand, sold in little baskets or in plastic trays (always packed 2 to a tray). Most commonly, they are fried and served whole, and the meat is picked off the bone and eaten with rice, some spicy sauce, and steamed vegetables. After cooking and picking, the meat is also used in an array of dishes as a primary or secondary component.

"Kem" is the Thai word for "salty" (or, in this case, "salted"). "Pla Tuu" is the Thai word for the Indian Mackerel (*Rastrelliger kanagurta*). This species is so closely associated with these type of salted fish that Pla Tuu is always taken to mean the salted, rather than the fresh, form. In fact, the salted form is widely available throughout the country in cities and towns alike, whereas outside of coastal areas, one hardly ever sees the fresh form.

We do not have a mackerel like that in the Gulf. But we do have other small mackerels, as well as scads—all of which work nicely.

Note: This method is only used to preserve the fish for a relatively short period of time. At room temperature, it will keep for up to a week; in the refrigerator, maybe 3 or 4 weeks. If you make a large batch, we suggest freezing the bulk.

4 whole, gutted, and gilled mackerels (make sure the abdominal cavities are completely free of kidneys and viscera)

2 cups salt (approximately ½ cup of salt per fish)

You will need a tray with a perforated bottom, big enough to hold all the fish in one layer. The resulting brine should be allowed to drain off; you do not want the fish swimming in it.

Rub each fish liberally all over with salt, making sure that the gills and abdominal cavities are well covered in salt. Place the fish in the pan belly side down, packing them all into a single layer. Sprinkle the rest of the salt over the fish. Don't worry about oversalting, because the fish will not be curing for long. Let the fish rest in the refrigerator for 24–48 hours. You will know they are done when they are firm and the skins are slightly shriveled.

Wash off the salt with fresh water, dry the fish well inside and out, and leave them uncovered in the refrigerator for a few hours so as to allow them to dry completely.

CHAPTER 26
BITS AND PIECES

BARBEQUE MOCK DUCK NECKS

1 TAIL PER PERSON AS A SNACK; 2 TAILS PER PERSON AS PART OF A LARGER MEAL The caudal peduncle is the bit of the fish where the tail attaches to the body. On most white fish, there's not a lot of meat there, but if it's a pelagic fish that weighs more than about 40 pounds, there's more than enough to work with. Wahoo and Greater Amberjack have the best tails, followed by any of the larger tunas. After the tails are cleaned (more on that below), the resemblance to duck necks is obvious enough. And like duck necks, the meat is clustered around large central bones. Seafood companies and larger fishmongers should be able to help you with procuring tails.

- 8 Greater Amberjack caudal peduncles (the tail chunks)
- 1 bottle of your favorite barbecue sauce (we hope and assume you do have a favorite, whether you make your own or buy it off a shelf)
- 2 lemons, juiced
- 2 tablespoons sugar

TO CLEAN A CAUDAL PEDUNCLE FROM A LARGISH FISH: With a cleaver or a good serrated knife, hack or saw through the tail fins themselves, cutting at the junction of fin and tail, parallel to the tail. Basically, you want the body bit (which has the meat), not the fin bits (which do not). Using a thin-bladed knife, skin the tail. Starting at the thick end, make a shallow slit lengthwise, taking care to cut only through the skin, not the meat. Use that entrance to get under the skin, then tease the skin off with the knife. This is not a difficult procedure as long as you pay attention to the task at hand.

Marinate the necks in the barbeque sauce, lemon juice, and sugar, letting them sit at least a few hours or even overnight.

Smoke the pieces at a low temperature (150°F) or slowly grill, turning them often. They are done when they almost want to fall apart. Grilling will take about 30–45 minutes, whereas smoking will take 2 hours or more.

FRIED BLACK DRUM BLADDERS

1 BLADDER FROM A LARGE COMMERCIAL DRUM YIELDS ABOUT 1½ CUPS OF CRACKLINGS. We learned of the delights of drum bladders from drum fishers in South Texas. We fry them and use them like cracklings or crispy pig ears.

> 1 or more bladders (as many as you want and can wrangle)
>
> Enough vegetable oil to fill a deep-fryer or a deep pot with a few inches
>
> Salt and black pepper to taste

TO CLEAN THE BLADDERS: Run the back of a knife over the bladder, scraping off the translucent membrane. Peel off all of this membrane. Split the bladder down the middle, turn it inside out, and repeat the scraping process. This is not difficult and should not take more than a couple of minutes per bladder. Slice the cleaned bladder into strips about 1/2–1 inch wide.

Heat the oil to 300°F. Blanch the pieces of bladder until they have shriveled, hardened up a bit, and bubbled a bit. Remove from the heat, and increase the temperature of the oil to 350°F. When the oil is hot enough, fry the pieces again until they are slightly puffy and very crispy. Remove from the oil and drain very well. Season well and put on a paper towel to drain further. These are best when still hot but very good at room temperature. If they get a bit stale, a few minutes back in hot oil will correct the situation.

EGGS AND BACON

2 SERVINGS If you should find yourself with a surfeit of fish roe, use some of it for breakfast. We don't really give measurements here because it's all pretty flexible. You may use more or less of any ingredients with no adverse effects.

> 4 chicken eggs, beaten
>
> Half that amount in weight of fish roe
>
> Dash of cream
>
> Salt and black pepper to taste
>
> Small dash of nutmeg (optional)
>
> 1 tablespoon butter, plus ½ tablespoon olive oil
>
> 3 tablespoons Gruyère cheese, grated
>
> As much crisp bacon as you care to eat
>
> Toasted bread, preferably thick and buttered

First, the individual fish eggs must be freed from the lobe membrane. Slit the lobe and peel. Scrape the eggs off the membrane with the back of a knife if necessary.

Add the fish eggs to the beaten chicken eggs, along with the cream and salt and pepper. Also add the nutmeg if you are using it.

In a sauté pan, heat the butter and olive oil until the butter is sizzling. You will need enough to coat the bottom of the pan, but you don't want the eggs swimming in fat. Add the egg-roe mixture and cook over medium-low heat, stirring all the time. When the eggs are cooked to your liking, remove the pan from the heat, add the cheese, and fold in well. Adjust the seasoning and serve with the bacon and toast.

GRILLED CREVALLE JACK OR LITTLE TUNNY DARK MEAT

4 SMALL SERVINGS AS AN APPETIZER OR SNACK   All members of the mackerel and jack families have relatively well-developed dark meat muscles. Usually, this dark meat (regardless of species) ends up in the trash can—which is nothing but a shame. Just as in a chicken, dark and light meat on a fish have different tastes and textures. If you like dark meat from the one, you will like it from the other. The taste and texture of the final product is reminiscent of something like grilled pork neck or beef flank. This recipe is pretty Thai influenced, but the result is just as good with other marinades, so experiment. You can use this piece of the fish as you would a piece of grilled beef flank.

> 1 pound of cleaned dark meat from a Crevalle Jack or Little Tunny (it is usually quite thin, though if necessary, trim big pieces to no more than around ½ inch thick)
>
> 3 tablespoons white soy sauce
>
> ½ teaspoon sugar
>
> 1–2 teaspoons coarsely crushed coriander seed (or cumin seeds, or a combination of the two)
>
> At least 2 garlic cloves, finely crushed
>
> Pinch of salt
>
> Smaller pinch of MSG

Combine all ingredients together and pour over the meat. Let the meat marinate for at least 1 hour but no more than 4.

In the meantime, get the grill hot. A few pieces of wood added to the charcoal works well here. When the initial flames have died down but the coals are still bright orange, grill the dark meat. Regardless of the species, the meat will cook quickly. Grill each side for about 2–4 minutes, depending on the heat of the grill.

BIG EEL STOCK

2–4 QUARTS OF STOCK, DEPENDING ON COOK TIMES   As discussed in their brief entry (see page 130), the marine eels commonly encountered by humans in the northwestern Gulf have limited culinary uses. They do, however, add considerable body and flavor to broths and soups. With that in mind, we use large eels for stock. Not fumet, the delicate fish broth, but *stock*, like a meat stock. Most fish flakes as it cooks, and dissolves as it overcooks, which means that one can only cook a fish fumet for so long before it ends up a gooey mess. Not so with the large marine eels. You can cook eel for a considerable amount of time before it breaks apart. This stock is modeled on a meat stock and as such, will be tan to brown, depending on your preferences.

> 1 medium gutted marine eel, such as conger or snake eel, cut into 3-inch chunks; or about 10 pounds of smaller gutted eels, such as Shrimp Eel, cut into 5-inch chunks
>
> 3–4 tablespoons vegetable oil
>
> 2 yellow onions, skin on, quartered
>
> 3 carrots, cut into large chunks
>
> 3 stalks celery, cut into large chunks
>
> 1 head garlic
>
> A few sprigs of fresh thyme
>
> Some parsley stems
>
> Some black peppercorns
>
> Pinch or two of MSG

Toss the eel chunks with the oil and roast in a hot oven until the pieces are well browned all over, almost an hour; add the vegetables up to and including the garlic about halfway through cooking. Transfer the eels and vegetables to a pot big enough to cover them with a couple of inches of water. Add the water to cover, along with the rest of the ingredients. Bring to a boil, then reduce to a simmer. Cook for at least 2 hours, and up to 4. Strain out the liquid into a clean pot, then put back on the stove to reduce. After the stock has reduced by at least one-third, remove from the heat, chill rapidly, and store in the freezer. The meat can be picked afterward, though there will be a mountain of bones to wade through. The meat can be used anywhere you might use shredded chicken or pork.

TOM YUM HUA PLA (GROUPER HEAD TOM YUM)

4 SERVINGS   Apple can't remember how many times she made this over our years of fishmongering, or how many different kinds of fish heads made their way into the pot over the years. Which is to say, just about any fish head works for this. We use grouper here, partially because the head tends to be big, and also because it is easily available. All reputable fishmongers, seafood markets, and grocery store seafood departments along the Gulf coast will have whole grouper (and thus grouper heads). This recipe is easily scaled up if you have lots of fish heads, or a few, or one giant head.

1 good-sized fish head (about 1 pound and change)

1¾ cups water

1 tablespoon sliced lemongrass

1 tablespoon sliced galangal

2 shallots, quartered

2–3 Makrut lime leaves

½ cup mushrooms (we use oyster or straw mushrooms, but any kind will do)

Three 13.5-ounce cans coconut milk

2–3 tablespoons lime juice

2 tablespoons fish sauce

1 tablespoon chili paste

1 tablespoon salt

¼ cup total of cilantro and green onion, cut into 1-inch chunks

2–3 whole Thai chilies

TO PREPARE THE HEAD: Gill the head, remove all remaining viscera, and make sure all scales have been removed. You can cook the head like this; or split it in two; or cut it into 4 pieces by separating the collars from the head, then splitting the head itself. Wash the pieces well.

Bring the water to a boil with the lemongrass, galangal, shallots, and lime leaves. Lower the heat a little, add the fish head, and cook for 10 minutes, or until the fish is done. You really don't want to stir the pot much, or the fish will start breaking up. Add the mushrooms and coconut milk, then season with lime juice, fish sauce, and chili paste. Cook for 5 minutes or until mushrooms are cooked. Season to taste. Remove from the heat and add the herbs and whole Thai chilies.

Serve with steamed rice.

STUFFED COBIA HEAD

6 SERVINGS   Not every fish has a head made for stuffing. But Cobia heads, long, bullet shaped, and with a large gill cavity, are perfect. Monkfish (though not available from the Gulf) would also work . . . but you would need a lot more stuffing, and dining companions who are not easily frightened.

This recipe had two inspirations. The first was a recipe for stuffed conger, found in the *River Cottage Fish Book* (which we shamelessly adapted); the second was a lone Cobia head in a cooler at the end of a very long day of fishmongering. We have conger in the Gulf, of course, but it was a Cobia head in the cooler, not an eel.

This is a rather ornate recipe. It is also a little messy—and time consuming. It might also require some fortitude. And bear in mind you might have some leftover stuffing, depending on the size of the head.

1 Cobia head, gilled, collar attached (should weigh at least 10 pounds)

5 slices bacon, diced

1 small onion, chopped

Half a head of garlic, cleaned and chopped

1 stalk celery, diced

1 small carrot, diced

½ Granny Smith apple, diced

1–2 tablespoons of calvados (or cider or apple juice)

1 sprig of sage, leaves only

1 sprig of thyme, leaves only

Some chopped parsley

Pinch each of ground mace, black pepper, ground allspice

12 ounces ground pork

1 egg, beaten

1½ tablespoons salt (The head will be braised, so a little overseasoning is helpful, but salt according to your taste.)

3 carrots, peeled and cut into large chunks

2 potatoes, peeled and cut into large chunks

1 head garlic, whole

4 shallots, halved

2 sprigs fresh thyme

Chicken broth (or water), enough to almost cover the head

1 cup water

3 tablespoons cornstarch

FIRST, THE HEAD: Wash the whole head outside and inside. You will need to remove the gills. For this a sharp, serrated knife is recommended (we do not generally advocate serrated knives for anything; this is a rare exception). The gills are attached at the top and bottom of the fish head. Saw through where they connect and remove the gills. This is easier said than done. Wash the head again. There will be a surprising amount of slime and blood left. At the end of the process, you should have a head ready for stuffing.

THE STUFFING: Render the bacon in a large sauce pan, then add everything down to and including the carrots. Let cook until tender, then add the apples. Add the calvados and herbs and spices and cook at a brisk pace until the liquid is mostly cooked out and the apples are mushy. Remove from the heat and cool completely.

When the mix is cold, add it to the ground pork, along with the egg and salt. Mix very well.

THE REST: Stuff all the mix into the head of the Cobia, taking care to keep the gill slits closed so as to ensure that the stuffing stays inside the head. After stuffing, you may stick an apple wedge in the fish mouth. Carefully wrap the head in a large square of cheesecloth, folded over itself 3 times. Wrap the head completely in the cheesecloth (the square should be large enough to wrap the head twice). Truss the wrapped head securely with kitchen twine. The trussing should be sturdy; it need not look pretty.

Place the trussed head in a roasting pan. Add the rest of the ingredients, bring to a boil, then cover, place in the oven, and cook at 300°F until a thermometer inserted into the heart of the stuffing reads 160°F.

Remove the head from the pan and allow to rest for about 10 minutes. Remove the vegetables and arrange on a platter. Reduce the cooking liquid by about one-third and thicken very slightly with a slurry made by mixing together the water and cornstarch. Correct the seasoning.

Carefully cut the twine and remove the cheesecloth. Place the head on the platter with the vegetables arranged around it. Pour some of the sauce over the head; the rest of the sauce may be served alongside.

Eat with rice or bread or both.

ACKNOWLEDGMENTS

We would like to thank the University of Texas Press for giving us the opportunity to write about the fish we love. And of course, Casey Kittrell, our initial editor at UT Press—more than five years elapsed between our initial conversations and actually signing a contract, but Casey's enthusiasm and belief never wavered.

A chance meeting on the curb outside a hotel in San Francisco led to all the illustrations in this book—thanks to our talented illustrator Javier Gutiérrez for all of his incredible work.

Thanks to Jim Gossen for showing PJ that the Gulf of Mexico is a large and wonderful universe indeed.

And thanks to Frixos Chrisinis, whose frenetic generosity knows no limits.

COMMON SEAFOOD HAZARDS

A FEW PRECAUTIONS AND WORDS ABOUT SEAFOOD-BORNE ILLNESSES AND AILMENTS

Eating any animal, or even any plant, carries risks. Those risks increase sharply when the animal or plant is wild. And when that wild plant or animal is harvested from waters influenced by humans, the risks increase even more.

Unfortunately, few areas anywhere on Earth have been left unspoiled by humans—there might not be any—but the Gulf of Mexico is neither better nor worse off than any other sea or ocean. Perhaps rather than seeking the mirage of the pristine elsewhere, we should accept the present situation and seek to make it better for those in the future.

What follows are some common hazards relating to fish and seafood. The first, "Pathogen Growth," is the only hazard over which you will always have at least some control. The rest of the hazards are managed (and quite effectively) by harvesters, processors, and relevant governmental authorities. We describe them all briefly here *only* for the purpose of general information. We have never had any problems related to any of these hazards, and incidents are infrequent. But it is better to be forewarned and forearmed.

PATHOGEN GROWTH: Bacteria, including pathogens, are going to try to grow on any piece of dead flesh. These pathogens are the same no matter if the flesh is from sea or land, and the only method of control is to maintain the meat in a way that creates an inhospitable environment for pathogens. With few exceptions, pathogenic bacteria need oxygen, some moisture, and the right temperature to grow and reproduce. Deprive them of one, and they slow down; deprive them of all three, and they don't grow at all.

If you are going to cook your piece of fish, the growth of pathogens is less of a concern, as *all pathogenic bacteria are rendered inactive at 140°F.* Keep your fish cold anyway, because even if they do not make you sick, pathogens can shorten the shelf life of your fish.

METHYLMERCURY: This is a form of mercury that is particularly harmful to humans. While it is naturally occurring, humans have introduced most of the methylmercury now present in the environment, via coal power plants and other industrial practices. The methylmercury, initially airborne, falls to the ocean or into waterways from where it eventually ends up in the ocean as well. Small fish absorb the mercury through their food, then larger fish eat those fish, and so on. Large pelagic fish are most notorious for mercury, though Golden Tilefish are considered just as prone to high levels. On one hand, one would have to eat dizzying amounts of mercury-laden fish to develop mercury poisoning; on the other, mercury is inordinately dangerous for developing brains. To further muddy the waters, the issue is less of one in the European Union, where consumption of fatty pelagic fish is encouraged in a healthy diet. We suggest moderation for adults. We don't feed our kids meat from big Swordfish, tilefish, or tunas.

VIBRIOSIS: This illness is caused by one of several species of *Vibrio* bacteria (in the Gulf, *Vibrio vulnificus* is responsible for most such poisonings). Humans get *Vibrio* infections either by eating contaminated raw or undercooked seafood or by exposing open wounds to salt water. Oysters are most associated with vibriosis, and most humans who contract vibriosis do so from eating oysters. Shellfish authorities routinely monitor waters year-round and shut down areas if and as needed.

NOROVIRUS: Norovirus is another shellfish-related ailment. This time, the virus is not at all a product of the marine environment, but rather of humans alone, as it is transmitted to coastal waters via human waste. As with *Vibrio*, shellfish authorities continuously monitor the situation and close waters to harvesting if needed.

PARALYTIC SHELLFISH POISONING: This shellfish illness is caused by microalgae toxins. The side effects can be severe. As with the other illnesses, shellfish authorities are continuously monitoring for this, and will close areas if needed.

CIGUATOXIN: Small fish graze on tropical coral reefs (and only tropical coral reefs) and eat all the algae they can find, including *Gambierdiscus toxicus*, a microalgae that produces a toxin that builds up in the little fish. Larger predatory fish (like snappers, groupers, barracudas, etc.) eat a lot of these little fish, and the toxin thus builds up in the larger fish as well. Humans then eat these larger fish, and feel side effects like dizziness, tingling extremities, nausea, vomiting, and so on, which can last for a few days or for years, depending on how much of the affected fish one eats. This is not such a concern in the northwestern Gulf, mostly because of our lack of coral reefs, but also because commercial boats may not fish in areas that may harbor such fish. For recreational fishers on offshore trips, we recommend not keeping or eating very big groupers, snappers, or even amberjacks caught right over one of our few coral reefs.

SULFITES: Sulfites are compounds used, in the context of seafood, in the processing of shrimp to preserve the appearance and marketability of the end product. Most people have no reaction to this, but a small percentage of the population (around 1 percent) is allergic. Overuse of sulfites can severely affect texture and taste. Also, and perhaps most importantly, the application of sulfites is fraught with dangers to workers (in terms of exposure and toxic reactions).

SCOMBROTOXIN: All mackerels, all jacks, all herrings, and also Dorado and Escolar (as well as very few other species) have just the right body chemistry to allow the growth of certain bacteria that can cause an allergic reaction in some people. To be clear, this is not the same thing as an allergy to fish. The bacteria grows with particular abandon after the fish has died and is warmed up over 40°F. Happily, this is easily controlled with an adequate cold chain across processing and distribution. Keep the fish cooler than 40°F at all times, and there will be no scombrotoxin problems for anyone. You should be keeping your fish that cold anyway. About 1 percent of the population has this allergy.

GEMPYLOTOXIN: Associated only with Escolar and Oilfish, this is the wax ester that has such explosively purgative qualities. Some people are more sensitive to it than others. We recommend caution.

TETRODOTOXIN: This is the toxin that can build up in the bodies of pufferfish, making them so potentially deadly.

BOTULISM: The lowly bacteria *Clostridium botulinum* produces a toxin that is responsible for the deadliest foodborne illness known to science. Mortality rates, even for healthy adults, are shockingly high. Fortunately, this bacteria is anaerobic, meaning it can only thrive in the *absence* of oxygen, when all other (and usually stronger) foodborne pathogens have been rendered inactive. Practically speaking, you need only be concerned with botulism if you are canning, vacuum-sealing, or drying whole fish. Food processors and distributors have manufacturing and storage protocols in place on their end that control any risk of botulism in their canned, vacuum-sealed, and dried products.

PARASITES: Wild animals tend to have parasites, and fish are no exceptions. Some fish parasites can be nasty inside humans, but those are mostly limited to freshwater fish. A very few species live inside saltwater fish, just waiting to get inside a mammal. Luckily, those types of parasites don't exist in Gulf salt waters. The fish parasites here only want to be in fish bodies and cannot live in humans. Our bodies kill them either outright or within a day or two. Those killed outright produce no side effects; those that take a little longer to die can provoke food poisoning–like symptoms. The most obvious Gulf worms are those that sometimes infest the bodies of drums, amberjacks, and croakers. These parasites, like those that bore into Swordfish, might look unappetizing, but they are utterly harmless to humans.

SPECIES NOT DESCRIBED BUT OF INTEREST

EDIBLE FISH NOT DESCRIBED IN THIS BOOK, BUT PRESENT AND ACCOUNTED FOR IN THE GULF (AND FISHED IN OTHER WATERS)

Only edible finfish are listed here. Species names are given when practical; *most genera include at least six to more than twenty species.*

We did not include invertebrates.

COMMON NAME	SCIENTIFIC NAME
Silver Dory and Rosy Dory	*Zenopsis conchifera* and *Cyttopsis rosea*
Soles, various species	*Achiridae* spp.
Yellowfin Aulopus	*Aulopus filamentosus*
Atlantic Trumpetfish	*Aulostomus maculatus*
Offshore flounders, various species	Bothidae; Paralichthyidae
Codlets	Bregmacerotidae
Lesser brotulas	Bythitidae
Dragonets	Callionymidae
Boarfish	Caproidae
Gulper Shark and Little Gulper Shark	*Centrophorus granulosus* and *Centrophorus uyato*
Basking Shark	*Cetorhinus maximus*
Silver Spinyfin	*Diretmus argenteus*
Cornetfish and Red Cornetfish	*Fistularia tabacaria* and *Fistularia petimba*
Mojarras	Gerreidae
Gobies	Gobiidae
Halfbeaks	Hemiramphidae
Blennies	Labrisomidae
Blackfin Goosefish	*Lophius gastrophysus*
Rattails and grenadiers	Macrouridae
Goatfish	Mullidae
Frogfish and batfish	Ogcocephalidae
Cusk-Eels	Ophidiidae
Offshore searobins	Peristediidae
Threadfins	*Polydactylus* spp.
Offshore skates and rays	Rajidae
Atlantic Saury	*Scomberesox saurus*
Deepwater scorpionfish	Scorpaenidae
Deepwater thornyheads and rockfish	Sebastidae and Setarchidae
Snaggletooths	Stomiidae
Eelpout	*Lycenchelys bullisi*

FURTHER READING

Arenas Fuentes, Virgilio, and Lourdes Jiménez Badillo. *Fishing in the Gulf of Mexico: Towards Greater Biomass in Exploitation.* Corpus Christi: Harte Research Institute for Gulf of Mexico Studies, Texas A&M University, n.d.: 468–477. harteresearchinstitute.org /sites/default/files/inline-files/25.pdf.

Blackford, Mansel G. *Making Seafood Sustainable: American Experiences in Global Perspective.* Philadelphia: University of Pennsylvania Press, 2012.

Bowling, Brenda. *Identification Guide to Marine Organisms of Texas: Fishes and Invertebrates.* Austin: Texas Parks and Wildlife Department, 2012–2018; College Station: Texas A&M University. txmarspecies.tamug .edu.

Branstetter, Steve. *Bycatch and Its Reduction in the Gulf of Mexico and South Atlantic Shrimp Fisheries.* Tampa, FL: Gulf and South Atlantic Fisheries Development Foundation, July 1997. gulfsouthfoundation.org/uploads/60 _FINAL_REPORT.pdf.

Britton, Joseph C., and Brian Morton. *Shore Ecology of the Gulf of Mexico.* Austin: University of Texas Press, 1989.

Cancelmo, Jesse. *Texas Coral Reefs.* College Station: Texas A&M University Press, 2008.

Clover, Charles. *The End of the Line: How Overfishing Is Changing the World and What We Eat.* New York: The New Press, 2006.

Clucas, Ivor. "A Study of the Options for Utilization of Bycatch and Discards from Marine Capture Fisheries." FAO Fisheries Circular No. 928 FIIU/C928. Rome: Food and Agriculture Organization of the United Nations, October 1997. fao.org/docrep/W6602E /w6602E00.htm.

Darnell, Rezneat M. *The American Sea: A Natural History of the Gulf of Mexico.* College Station: Texas A&M University Press, 2015.

Davidson, Alan. *Mediterranean Seafood: A Comprehensive Guide with Recipes.* Berkeley, CA: Ten Speed Press, 2002.

———. *North Atlantic Seafood: A Comprehensive Guide with Recipes.* Berkeley, CA: Ten Speed Press, 2003.

———. *Seafood of South-East Asia: A Comprehensive Guide with Recipes.* Berkeley, CA: Ten Speed Press, 1976, 2004.

Davidson, Alan, and Charlotte Knox. *Seafood: A Connoisseur's Guide and Cookbook.* London: Mitchell Beazley, 1989.

Fearnley-Whittingstall, Hugh, and Nick Fisher. *The River Cottage Fish Book: The Definitive Guide to Sourcing and Cooking Sustainable Fish and Shellfish.* London: Bloomsbury, 2012.

FishBase. We recommend this site for all general invertebrate research. The site was developed and is maintained by working scientists. fishbase.org.

Gibbons, Euell. *Stalking the Blue-Eyed Scallop.* Putney, VT: Alan C. Hood, 1964, 1988.

Goodson, Gar, and Phillip J. Weisgerber. *Fishes of the Atlantic Coast: Canada to Brazil, Including the Gulf of Mexico, Florida, Bermuda, the Bahamas, and the Caribbean.* Stanford, CA: Stanford University Press, 1985.

Gore, Robert H. *The Gulf of Mexico: A Treasury of Resources in the American Mediterranean.* Sarasota, FL: Pineapple Press, 1992.

Harrington, Jennie M., Ransom A. Myers, and Andrew A. Rosenberg. "Wasted Fishery Resources: Discarded By-Catch in the USA." *Fish and Fisheries* 6, no. 4 (December 2005): 350–361. Wiley Online Library: onlinelibrary .wiley.com/doi/abs/10.1111/j.1467-2979.2005 .00201.x.

Helies, Frank C., and Judy L. Jamison. "Reduction Rates, Species Composition, and Effort: Assessing Bycatch within the Gulf of Mexico Shrimp Trawl Fishery." NOAA/ NMFS Cooperative Agreement Number NA07NMF4330125 (#101). Tampa, FL: Gulf and South Atlantic Fisheries Foundation, October 2009. gulfsouthfoundation.org /uploads/reports/101_final4.pdf.

Hilborn, Ray, and Ulrike Hilborn. *Overfishing: What Everyone Needs to Know.* New York: Oxford University Press, 2012.

Hoese, H. Dickson, and Richard H. Moore. *Fishes of the Gulf of Mexico: Texas, Louisiana, and Adjacent Waters.* 2nd ed. College Station: Texas A&M University Press, 1998.

Jackson, Jeremy B., Karen E. Alexander, and Enric Sala, eds. *Shifting Baselines: The Past and the Future of Ocean Fisheries.* Washington, DC: Island Press, 2011.

Kells, Val, and Kent Carpenter. *A Field Guide to Coastal Fishes: From Maine to Texas.* Baltimore, MD: Johns Hopkins University Press, 2011.

Lehman, Roy L. *Marine Plants of the Texas Coast.* College Station: Texas A&M University Press, 2013.

Levesque, Juan C. "Commercial Fisheries in the Northwestern Gulf of Mexico: Possible Implications for Conservation Management at the Flower Garden Banks National Marine Sanctuary." *ICES Journal of Marine Science* 68, no. 10 (November 1, 2011): 2175–2190. academic.oup.com/icesjms/article/68 /10/2175/614895.

McEachran, John D., and Janice D. Fechhelm. *Fishes of the Gulf of Mexico: Volume 1—Myxiniformes to Gasterosteiformes.* Austin: University of Texas Press, 1998.

———. *Fishes of the Gulf of Mexico: Volume 2— Scorpaeniformes to Tetraodontiformes.* Austin: University of Texas Press, 2005.

Monterey Bay Aquarium Seafood Watch, seafoodwatch.org

Pauly, Daniel, and Jay L. Maclean. *In a Perfect Ocean: The State of Fisheries and Ecosystems in the North Atlantic Ocean.* Washington, DC: Island Press, 2012.

Richardson, Alfred. *Wildflowers and Other Plants of Texas Beaches and Islands.* Austin: University of Texas Press, 2002.

Roberts, Callum. *The Unnatural History of the Sea.* Washington, DC: Island Press, 2009.

Rothschild, Susan B., and Nick Fotheringham. *Beachcomber's Guide to Gulf Coast Marine Life: Texas, Louisiana, Mississippi, Alabama, and Florida.* 3rd ed. Lanham, MD: Taylor Trade, 2004.

SeaLifeBase. We recommend this site for all general invertebrate research. The site was developed and is maintained by working scientists. sealifebase.org.

Stoops, PJ. *Professor Fish Heads* blog, 2010–2012, professorfishheads.blogspot.com.

Tull, Delena, Michael Earney, and George Oxford Miller. *Edible and Useful Plants of Texas and the Southwest: A Practical Guide, Including Recipes, Natural Dyes, Harmful Plants, and Textile Fibers*. Austin: University of Texas Press, 2008.

Tunnell, John W., Jr., Jean Andrews, Noe C. Barrera, and Fabio Moretzsohn. *Encyclopedia of Texas Seashells: Identification, Ecology, Distribution, and History*. College Station: Texas A&M University Press, 2010.

RECIPE INDEX

GENERAL INDEX

Note: *Italic* page numbers refer to illustrations.

engawa, flounder feather meat as, 197

Escolar, 123–124, *123*, 195, 205

Exclusive Economic Zone, of West African
countries, 117

exotic species, 3

eyes, and buying fish, 204, 207

False Moon Snail, 159, *159*

farmed fish and seafood
and Almaco Jack, 52
and oysters, 148, 149
and Redfish, 41
and shrimp, 6, 172, 179
sold as whole fish, 194
and wild fish, 6–7

feather meat, 197

fillets and filleting
and buying fish, 205–206, 207
and gaping, 206
and killing your catch, 16
methods of filleting, 216–217
number of fillets, 195
skin on or off, 195–196
storage of, 212

finfish
and bycatch, 5, 13
and fish trade, 7, 112, 118
rough catch and sashimi grade, 194
species of, 9, 284–285

fingers, as market form of crab, 200, 221

Firefly Squid, 168

fisheries
federal fisheries, 10
rational management of, 4–6, 112
regulation of, 24, 26–27, 73, 81, 146, 193
rough catch designation, 194
state fisheries, 10, 146

fishing pressure, 5, 132

fish maw, swim bladder as, 198

fishmongers
filleting process, 195–196
finding, 187, 188–193
on freshness, 191–192
and frozen shrimp, 210

on harvest date, 207
honesty of, 189
sanitation practices, 189–190
and smelling fish, 204–205

fish species
common names in Texas, 8
exotic species, 3
finfish, 9, 284–285
in Gulf Coast region, 7–8
inshore fish species, 20–38
kinds of, 19
multispecies fisheries, 4–5

"fish story" flounder, 23

fish tongue, 197

fish trade, 3, 4–6, 7, 73

flatfish
feather meat of, 197
filleting of, 216
flounders as, 23
gutting of, 214
little flatfish, 36–37, *36*
as shrimp bycatch, 5
sold in loins rather than fillets, 196

fletches, 196, 205–206

Florida
Black Grouper from, 84
Gray Triggerfish from, 107
Red Grouper from, 193
scallops from, 156
scorpionfish from, 97
squid from, 167
Stone Crab from, 177
White Shrimp from, 175
and Yucatán Current, 9

Florida Horse Conch, 7, 166, *166*

Florida Pompano, 49, 55, *55*

flounders
cut into loins, 196
feather meat, 197
and gigs, 12
Gulf Flounder and Southern Flounder,
23–24
sold as round fish, 194
and sports fishers, 20

and longline fishing, 11, 53, 97
Longtail Bass, 88–89
Red Grouper, 81, 82
Rock Hind, Red Hind, and Graysby, 87–88
Sand Perch and Spanish Flag, 90–91
Scamp and Yellowmouth Grouper, 81, 82–83, 203
shallow-water groupers, 10
sold as gutted on boat, 194
Speckled Hind and Marbled Grouper, 86–87
and Texas City dike, 2
tongues of, 197
Warsaw, Snowy, and Misty Grouper, 81, 85–86
whole peeled fish, 218
Yellowedge Grouper, 81, 82
Yellowfin Grouper, 81, 84–85
grunts. *See* croakers and grunts
Guaguanche, 92, 105, *105*
Gulf Butterfish, 37, *37*
Gulf Coast region
fish trade in, 3, 4–6, 7
Karankawa's use of, 2
Gulf Flounder, 23–24, *23*
Gulf Hake, 118–119, *119*, 205
Gulf Kingfish, 45–46, *45*
Gulf Longtail Bass, 88
Gulf Loop Current, 9
Gulf Menhaden
as pelagic fish, 68, *68*, 69
and purse seines, 12
Gulf of Mexico
commercial fishing in, 10–14
as estuary for migratory species, 53
federal waters of, 7, 10, 13, 14, 112
general information on, 9–10
groupers of, 81, 192, 193
recreational fishing in, 14–17
recreational shellfishing in, 17
reef areas of, 92
snappers of, 71, 192, 193
species represented in, 7–8, 9, 145
state waters of, 14

Gulf Toadfish, 31, *31*, 32
gutted fish
G&G fish, 195
gutting at home, 17, 214
offshore fish sold as, 194–195
gutting fish, 17, 214

H&G (headed, gutted, and tailed) fish, 195
hagfish, as jawless fish, 19
half-shell bivalves, 199
handlining, 11–12
Hardhead Catfish, 24–26, *25*
Harvestfish, 37, *37*
heading fish, 215
head-on shrimp, 200
Hermit Crab, 180, *180*
herrings
Atlantic Thread, Scaled, and Red-Eye Round Herring, 69
eating of, 58
in Gulf of Mexico, 9
rows of pin bones, 195
Skipjack Herring, 59
Threadfin Herring, 68
4-Hexylresorcinol, 201, 202
high-grading, 4
Highly Migratory Pelagic Species (HMPS), 195
Hogfish, 102
hook-and-line fisheries, 5, 10–11, 112
Hooked Mussel, 157–158
Houndfish, 34–35, *34*
Humboldt Squid, 199

Icelandic Hákarl, 133
Icelandic regulations, 5
iconic fish, as bycatch, 4
ike jime method, 16–17, 28, 57
Individual Fishing Quota (IFQ) system, 82
Individually Quick Frozen (IQF), 210
industrial toxins, 25
Inshore Lizardfish, 33–34, *34*
inshore waters
Atlantic Midshipmen, 31–32

Cownose, Spotted Eagle, and Bullnose
  Rays, 135–136
description of, 132–133
fillets of, 195
Southern, Atlantic, and Bluntnose Stingrays, 133–135
Spiny and Smooth Butterfly Rays, 137
recreational fishing
  catch-and-release, 58, 85
  killing your catch, 15–17
  and Red Snapper, 72
  regulation of, 14–15, 16, 24, 27, 151
recreational shellfishing, regulation of, 17,
  151, 152, 157, 158
Red Crawfish, 180–181
Red-Eye Round Herring, 69, 69
Redfish, 39, 40–41, 40, 44, 45
red fish
  loin of, 195
  and meat color, 205–206
  organs of, 198
Red Grouper, 9, 193
Red Hind, 87–88, 87
Red Sea Urchin, 162
Red Snapper
  from American waters of Gulf, 193
  and bandit rig, 10
  Cardinal Snapper compared to, 78
  description of, 71–73, 72
  Dog Snapper as substitution for, 75
  and federal fisheries, 10
  and fish trade, 3, 73
  Lane Snapper sold as, 76
  Mangrove Snapper compared to, 74
  Mutton Snapper sold as, 76
  population of, 106
  postharvest handling of, 72
  prices for, 82
  Silk and Blackfin Snapper sold as, 78
  size of, 2, 72
Redtail Scad, 51–52, 52
reefs. *See also* offshore reef, rubble, and rock
  fish
  of Gulf of Mexico, 92

oyster reefs, 13–14, 153–154, 157
remoras, 125
Ribbonfish, 27–28, 27
Rock Hind, 87–88, 87
Rock Shrimp, 173–175
rod-and-reel fishing, 12
roe
  of Atlantic Croakers, 43
  of Black Drum, 42
  of Bluefin Tuna, 60
  description of, 197, 198
  of Gulf Menhaden, 68
  of Striped Mullet, 26–27
Roudi Escolar, 123
Rouget, 110, 111
Rough Triggerfish, 107–108, 108
Roundel Skate, 138–139, 139
round fish, whole, ungutted fish as, 194, 195
Round Scad, 51–52, 52
Royal Red Schrimp, 173–175

Sailfish, 120
salmon
  farmed salmon, 6
  floating pin bones of, 196
Saltwort, 183
Sand Perch, 90–91
Sand Seatrout, 39, 43–45, 44
Sand Tilefish, 98–99, 98
sardines, 58, 204
Sargassum, 183
sashimi, 60, 94, 105, 194, 199, 206
sawfish, 133
Sawtooth Pen Shells, 159–160, 160
Scaled Herring, 69, 69
scales, and buying fish, 204
scaling fish, 214
scallops
  appearance and smell of, 208
  Atlantic Bay Scallop, 155–156
  shucked dry scallops, 208
Scamp Grouper, 81, 82–83, 83, 203
scombrotoxin, 283
Scrawled Filefish, 108–109, 109

Striped False Limpet, 153–155
Striped Mullet, 26–27, *26*, 102, 216
Sucgang, Ricky, 198
sulfites, 199, 201–202, 208, 282–283
Surfside Beach, 75
sushi, 30, 60, 94, 105, 194
sustainability, 4, 81
swim bladders, 39, 42, 195, 198, 214
Swordfish
    bellies of, 196
    and bycatch, 124, 142
    description of, 120, 127–128, *127*
    and federal fisheries, 10
    as H&G fish, 195
    and longline fishing, 11, 121
    Peachbelly Swordfish, 127, 197
    and rod-and-reel fishing, 12
    soft bones of, 19, 128
    and trolling, 11

tail-off, as market form of shrimp, 201
tail-on, as market form of shrimp, 201
tails
    as market form of shrimp, 201, 219
    of pelagic fish, 198
tai pla, 198
Tarpon, 58–59
TEDs (turtle-excluding devices), 13
tetrodotoxin, 110, 283
Texas coast
    changes in, 2
    and continental shelf, 10
    and Gulf Loop Current, 9
    midden mounds on, 2, 165
Texas Department of State Health Services
    (TDSHS), 10, 17, 146–147, 149
Texas Hill Country, 2
Texas Parks and Wildlife Department
    (TPWD), 10, 17, 25, 40–41, 162
Texas Quahog Clams, 164–165, *165*, 208
Texas Rangers, 1
Thailand, 3
thawing of seafood, 212
Threadfin Herring, 68

thrown-back fish
    mortality of, 11, 20, 72, 132
    and recreational fishing, 14, 72
    use of fish, 15, 46, 111
Tiger Shark, 133
tilapia, 6
tilefish. *See also* Golden Tilefish
    Blueline Tilefish, 97–98, 113
    and federal fisheries, 10
    gills of, 203
    Goldface Tilefish, 97–98, 113
    and longline fishing, 97
    sold as gutted on boat, 194
    US Gulf fisheries for, 193
    whole peeled fish, 218
Tomtate, 47–48, *48*
top loin, 196
toxins. *See* pathogens and toxins
traps, 13, 177–178
trawls
    and bycatch, 5, 13, 20, 28
    for finfish, 112, 118
    and shrimp, 4, 13
triggerfish
    Black Durgon, 107–108, *108*
    and fish trade, 7
    Gray Triggerfish, 106–107, *106*
    livers of, 198
    Ocean Triggerfish, 107–108, *108*
    Queen Triggerfish, 107–108, *108*
    Rough Triggerfish, 107–108, *108*
tripletails, 20
trolling, 11
Tropical Pomfret, 121
trotlines, 12, 42
Tulip Mussel, 157–158
tunas. *See also* pelagic fish
    bellies of, 196–197
    and bycatch, 121, 142
    and federal fisheries, 10
    feel of fish, 205
    filleting of, 217
    in Gulf of Mexico, 9
    as H&G fish, 195

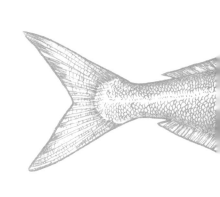

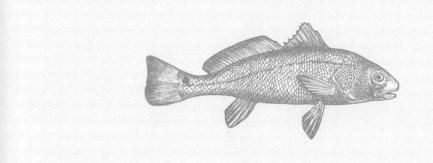
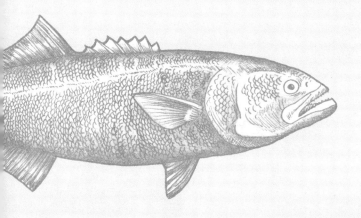
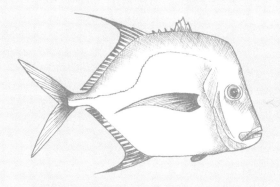